Solar Thermal Systems

Successful Planning and Construction

Dr. Felix A. Peuser
Karl-Heinz Remmers
Martin Schnauss

Solarpraxis • Berlin • 2002

Impressum

Publisher: in association with	Solarpraxis AG, Germany James & James (Science Publishers) Ltd, UK
Authors:	Dr. Felix. A. Peuser, Karl-Heinz Remmers, Martin Schnauss
Graphics Layout, Typesetting:	Solarpraxis AG
Translation:	Office H. Seigneurgens, Roland Krohn, Tina Barroso Guerra
Copy Editors:	Eveline Goodman, Prof. John Twidell
Printing:	MEDIALIS Offsetdruck GmbH, Berlin phone + 49 30 5332740
Published by:	Solarpraxis AG • Torstraße 177, D-10115 Berlin Tel + 49 30 726 296 - 300, Fax - 309 www.solarpraxis.de; info@solarpraxis.de
Solarpraxis-ISBN	3 - 934595 - 24 - 3
in association with:	James & James (Science Publishers) Ltd. 35-37 William Road, London NW1 3ER, UK phone + 44 20 -7387 - 85 58, fax - 8998 www.jxj.com; jxj@jxj.com
James & James-ISBN:	1 - 902916 - 39 - 5
Copyright © 2002	Solarpraxis AG

The texts and illustrations in »Solar Thermal Systems« have been prepared to the best knowledge of the authors. All photos and diagrams without citation have been created by Solarpraxis AG. Neither the authors nor Solarpraxis AG accept any responsibility or liability for loss or damage to any person or property through using the material, instructions, methods, or ideas contained herein, or acting or refraining to act as a result of such use.

Expression of thanks

This book is a recapitulation of the substantial results from numerous research projects on solar thermal installations that have been performed in Germany within the last 30 years. These projects were subsidised by several ministries of the Federal Republic of Germany.

For the revision and translation of the German version of the book »Langzeiterfahrungen Solarthermie«, additional funds were made available by the Project Management Organisation Jülich (Projektträger Jülich, PTJ) in the Forschungszentrum Jülich GmbH. This funding was provided by the

- German Bundesministerium für Wirtschaft und Technologie (BMWi)

and the

- European Commission, DGTREN: within the framework of PTJ's contract as an Organisation for the Promotion of Energy Technologies (OPET)

We would like to express our thanks to the advisory personnel of the BMWi and the Projektträger Jülich for their interest in this work and their continuous support as well as for the administrative and financial supervision of the project.

In addition, the book has been enriched by the experiences of international institutions and companies. In particular, we would like to thank Dott. Marcello Antinucci, Agencia per l'energia e lo sviluppo sostenibile, Italy; Joseph Jenni, Jenni Energietechnik, Switzerland; Dr. Iordanis Paradissiadis, Intersolar, Greece; Rob Meesters, Solarhart, Belgium; Werner Weiss, Arbeitsgemeinschaft erneuerbare Energien, Austria; and many others for their technical support.

We acknowledge the contribution of Professor John Twidell of the AMSET Centre, UK, for his help in editing the English version of this book.

Last but not least, our special thanks go to the following companies, which have enthusiastically supported the production of this unique edition with their professional and financial assistance:

INTERPANE Solar Beschichtungs GmbH & Co, Lauenförde, Germany

Steca Präzisionselektronik GmbH, Memmingen, Germany

TYFOROP Chemie GmbH, Hamburg, Germany

VIESSMANN Werke GmbH & Co, Allendorf, Germany

Preface

The sun is the origin of all life on earth. For millions of years it has been delivering all the energy to keep our planet and our atmosphere in the small temperature range necessary for the biological stability.

During various natural climate catastrophes in earth history, the equilibrium of earth's energy balance has suffered significant interferences. They have often led to serious interferences in evolution, death and cultural collapse. Today, we have the power to alter our climate, largely by the so-called greenhouse effect that has resulted from industrialisation. The long-term impact of this is not measurable yet, but unfortunately life-threatening climate change cannot be excluded.

In such a situation it is vital to use all the possibilities in our energy scope to decrease noxious emissions in order to reduce the greenhouse effect and in this way avert this danger from our lives.

One of many possibilities is the use of solar energy for production of heat and electricity. The sun is – using our time scale – an inexhaustible energy source with a contribution of radiation topping by far our energy demand. The task of technology is to transform with high efficiency at low costs this energy supply that reaches our earth with a small and, unfortunately, strongly varying power density so that mankind might use it.

The thermal use of solar energy for the production of heat from sunlight is one of these transformation methods. This technology has been known and – sometimes even unconsciously – used for ages. It has been rediscovered and used again over the last 30 years. Today it is ready for application, but after this short growth time there is a large potential for development and application in the sector, some times passive as well as active utilisation.

Since 1977, in Germany various research projects have been realised on the active thermal utilisation of solar energy. A lot of demonstration systems for domestic water heating as well as heating the water in public swimming pools have been subsidised.

The aims of the programmes subsidised by the European Union (EU) and the Federal Ministries were to get experiences, to obtain information on the aging behaviour of the systems and its components materials, to analyse the performance and to obtain guidelines for optimal system design and configuration (including connection to the conventional system) as well as for the optimal dimensioning and integration of the single components into the solar system.

First results were published in 1997 by F. A. Peuser, R. Croy, J. Schumacher and R. Weiß with the title »Langzeiterfahrungen mit thermischen Solaranlagen« /1/ which was supplemented by F. A. Peuser, R. Croy, U. Rehrmann, H. P. Wirth with an information package of »Solare Trinkwassererwärmung mit Großanlagen« /2/ in 1999.

The experiences and cognition from more than 25 years planning, installation and operation of solar thermal systems in Germany were compiled in 2001 by F. A. Peuser, K.-H. Remmers and M. Schnauss in the book »Langzeiterfahungen Solarthermie« Solarpraxis Berlin 2001.

Due to the topic's worldwide importance and large interest, this book was enhanced to cover international system technology and experiences and so an English translation has been completed for the international use.

The revision, incorporation of international experiences, translation and print of this book was subsidised by EU funds and the Federal Ministry: Deutsches Bundesministerium für Wirtschaft und Technologie (BMWi).

In this way the new technical book pools the experience of 25 years production and supervision of solar systems and the newest cognition for technical and economic successful implementation of this knowledge in planning, installation and operation of solar thermal systems.

Thus, it is a comprehensive tool for craftsmen and planners for:

• Proof of durability and efficiency of solar systems

• Accurate planning and installation of solar thermal systems

• Showing and debugging of possible defects

This book enables technical planners and installation companies to show customers clearly the worth of their investments, enabling them to value and asess implementations according to today's state-of-the-art.

We hope that our collected experiences, the descriptions, research results and our critical remarks will encourage further developments, so that solar systems in the future might work more efficiently, be more reliable and more cost-effective, on condition they are produced at high quality and low costs, planned precisely, installed accurately and operated correctly.

Felix A. Peuser

Karl-Heinz Remmers

Martin Schnauss

Contents

1. Introduction and Basic Knowledge

1.1 Market Development of Solar Thermal Systems

Fossil energy sources are limited; crude oil and natural gas will be significantly depleted within the next 40 years due to the worldwide increasing demand. The continuous use of fossil fuel is leading to grave damag of our environment and to far-reaching climate changes.

In many arid countries, the use of firewood for cooking and water heating leads to deforestation, creation of steppes and erosion.

The 1972 Club of Rome report »Limits to Growth« and the first oil-price crisis of 1973 both attracted worldwide the attention to these problems. Consequently, they initiated the development of solar technology in many countries.

Solar power is an inexhaustible source for the permanent maintenance of our energy supply and wealth. During the next decades, solar technology will transform today's structures of energy supply, especially since modern worldwide markets change rapidly.

1.2 Market Development in Europe

From 2002, many European countries have been intensifying their activities in the solar technology field. For instance, numerous countries have introduced environmental taxes and corresponding subsidy programmes for renewable energy technologies. Within the energy sector, the EU White Paper envisages an increase of renewable energy supplies to 12% throughout the EU by 2010.

The estimated related investment costs for this period are about 165,000 million Euros, the associated creation of 500,000 jobs predicted. Additionally, by 2010, an annual export market of 17 000 million Euro is estimated, with the opportunity of 350,000 additional jobs. /3/

These ambitious aims are being met by different EU states with market stimulating programmes.

1.2.1 Germany

Regarding the technology of solar thermal systems, Germany is a worldwide market leader. The USA and Japan are progressive in the field of solar electricity generation. All three countries are striving to obtain the leading position.

In Germany, a stable governmental subsidy for solar thermal installation was first established in 2000. Also that year, a stable and sensible subsidy for solar photovoltaic production was introduced with the

»Act on Granting Priority to Renewable Energy Sources«. This new law led to increased market activity. The Act was advantageous for German solar technology to become well known and to top the league in worldwide turnover.

Recent market estimations are for 30% annual growth in association with reducing prices.

Therefore, almost all significant suppliers in the fields of heating technology, of roof and façade building (e.g. VIESSMANN, BUDERUS, Braas Dachsysteme, SCHÜCO), and various oil companies (e.g. BP, Shell, Total) invested in the development of solar technology.

All trade professions (e.g. sanitary, heating, roofing, joinery, repairs, façade building, electrical) recognized the growth of the market in utilising renewable energy sources and are starting to invest in the market. Planners and architects subsequently followed the trend.

The past market development of solar thermal installations in Germany can be seen in Figure 1.1.

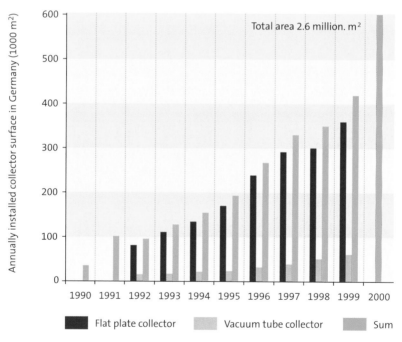

Figure 1.1 Collector area annually installed in Germany (source: DFS e.V. /3)

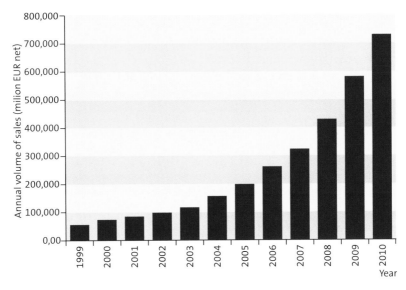

Figure 1.2 Turnover forecast in the solar thermal field according to different surveys made by DFS e.V. /3/; own calculations

1.2.2 **Austria**

Recently, Austria met about 25% of the whole energy demand with renewable energy sources.

Besides the use of hydropower, traditional wood-heating stoves are very common.

High environmental awareness, highly developed technology (also in and due to combination with wood-heating stoves) and governmental subsidy programmes prepared conditions for an early market development.

At the beginning of the 1990's the strong market growth may be ascribed to self-construction initiatives. Such local programmes of mutual assistance installed and helped thousands of systems by means of a »pyramid« structure. Thus, the initiatives saved installation expenses and obtained favourable material prices due to collective volume orders. This also benefited the installations of relatively large systems with an average solar collector surface of 20–30 m², these also gained support for heating. Numerous wood-heating boilers in combination with large buffer storage allow a sensible supplementation by solar technology. Therefore, the percentage of solar systems giving space heating support is about 50%, which is very high. /4/

In 1994, almost 40% of all installed area of collectors was built by self-construction initiatives.

Meanwhile, the market became more professional and so four manufacturers now supply glazed collectors to 50% of the domestic and

20% of the European market. With the production of nearly 20 m^2 plane collectors per 1,000 inhabitants, Austria topped the league in the world.

In the year 2000, about 2,000,000 m^2 solar collector surface were installed. This area supplies annually 3.22 PJ of final energy for hot water and space heating.

1.2.3 Switzerland

At the end of 2000 approx. 270,000 m^2 of glazed collector surface have been installed. An area in similar dimension is used in the form of absorbers for the swimming pool heating and approx. 780,000 m^2 are in use for solar hay drying (special roofs or unglazed collectors).

The volume of the unglazed collector surface installed per year increased significantly due to a regulatory ordinance. This regulation requires owners of new or rebuilt swimming pools to assure that at least 50% of the heat required by a swimming pool is provided by solar systems. This is an example of the influence of the governmental controlling mechanisms into the market.

The market growth is 15% – 30% per year.

1.2.4 Greece

Of all European countries, solar technology has reached the highest market penetration in Greece. There is in total 2,800,000 m^2 of collector surface installed; this is equivalent to a surface of approx. 268 m^2 per 1,000 inhabitants.

In the 1970's, very simple compact natural flow systems were developed and made ready for the market. So far these systems have a market share of 95%. They are completely pre-assembled, not susceptible to failures, low-maintenance and easy to install. Almost all are for domestic hot water supply. Large irradiance and the flat roofs of buildings allowing common construction, favour the market. For some time, collector production has been constant at 150,000 m^2 per year, which is equivalent to 1/18 of the totally installed surface. It is apparent that the market is saturated, so mainly existing installations are being replaced with new ones, since the life-time of the installations is estimated to be approx. 15 years.

1.2.5 Cyprus

Cyprus has an exceptional position, with 800 m^2 of installed collector per 1,000 habitants, i.e. 0.8 m^2 per person. Therefore virtually every person is equipped with sufficient solar surface in order to provide ca. 80% of the annual heat demand for hot water supply from solar energy /5/.

1.2.6 **Italy**

In Italy, the solar technology boomed after the oil-price increases in the 1970's. However the number of collectors sold declined strongly in the 1980's and the market was stimulated only for a short time by the 1983–85 subsidy campaign »Acqua calda dal sole« (hot water from the sun).

The development of annually installed collector surface in Italy is described in Figure 1.3. Sales in the year 2000 were approximately 45,000 m².

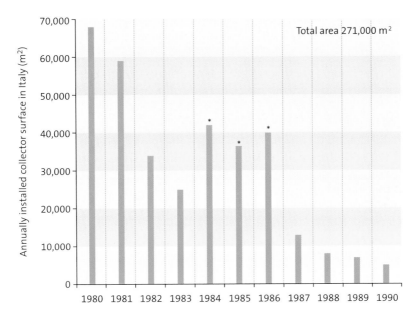

*) Campaign: "Acqua calda dal sole"

Figure 1.3 Collector surface installed in Italy in the 1980s

The systems are used so 80% are for heating domestic hot water and 15% for swimming pool water heating. The remaining 5% are used to assist space heating. Approx. 1/3 of the systems work by the principal of natural flow, the remaining larger share have forced circulation.

»ENEL« (Ente Nationale per l'Energia Elettrica – the national energy provider) reported that during the 1983–85 campaign about 12,000 solar thermal systems (with approx. 100,000 m² of collector surface) were dispatched. Nevertheless, the campaign was only a short-term success. The reason was reported as the lack of quality of the products. Also, there was an absence of technical knowledge and experience for the design and installation of the systems by planners and trade companies. This led to failure of many systems /6/.

An analysis of 150 systems in 1989 had the following results:

- 41 systems had problems with the heat transfer circulation
- 25 systems had wrong installed temperature sensors inside the warm water storage tank
- 17 systems showed a wrong located security valve.

The short period of subsidy was obviously not effective enough to stabilise the market. The manufacturers could not be motivated to develop new, sophisticated products and the maintenance groups could not accumulate the necessary experience. This intensely damaged the image of solar technology in Italy (similarly in some other countries).

Even today, solar systems are often considered to be expensive, unreliable, not aesthetic and difficult to install.

Many plumbers are sceptical of the technology (partly due to negative experiences) and discourage customers from use of solar energy /7/.

1.2.7 Spain
In the late 1970's and early 1980's, Spain experienced the first growth of the solar thermal market. After a few years the market dropped again and stagnated at a very low level for over 10 years (all Figures: IDAE). The reason for this progression can only partially be attributed to declining energy prices, but rather to insufficient performance and reliability of the systems installed.

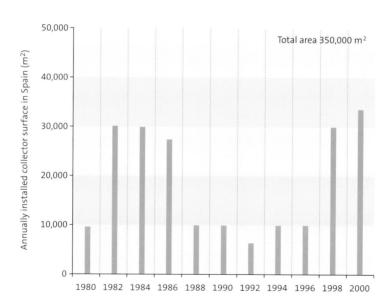

Figure 1.4 Annually installed solar collector area in Spain

According to experts interviewed, the reason for the poor quality of systems of the »first generation« was mainly due to lack of know-how, rather than insufficient component quality. Today counter-examples of »good« systems still in operation underline this conclusion. These negative experiences have had a lasting effect on the reputation of solar thermal from which Spain is only now beginning to recover. Therefore several experts interviewed recommended avoiding a similar effect in the current market upturn, and allocating resources for better information and training. Thereby there should be sustained growth in the coming years.

At the beginning of the new century, the boundary conditions have changed for two main aspects of solar technology. There is (a) increasing awareness of environmental issues, which has increased political pressure to support renewable energy technologies, and (b), professionalism within the solar thermal market at a European level has increased production volumes, so giving cost reductions, technical improvements and a stronger »solar lobby«.

Contrary to other countries, ecological motivation of consumers is not a driving force in Spain. Progress is mainly supported by government programs and manufacturers' marketing initiatives.

The national government has evaluated a potential of $26.5\,M\,m^2$ of collector area for Spain and has set ambitious goals for 2010 ($4.5\,M\,m^2$ installed by 2010, as outlined in the »Plan de Fomento«, assuming an annual increase of approx. 40%). Manufacturers also anticipate annual growth rates from 20% to 100% for the next years.

With an annual insolation from 1,300 to 1,700 kWh/(m^2year), Spain has very favourable conditions and already solar thermal systems are economically competitive for several applications. Mass production, technological progress and market professionalism will re-enforce the trend in the long run, making more and more applications become state of the art (i.e. cooling, process heat) .

The main focus in the market for solar thermal systems in Spain is medium and large (collective) systems.

The market is divided approximately into the following segments (as a percentage of total collector area):

- small compact systems of a few m^2 (thermo siphon): 25%
- small compact systems of a few m^2 (forced circulation): 5%
- medium and large systems with forced circulation up to several hundreds or thousands of m^2: 55%
- swimming pool heating and others: 15%

Future trends and frameworks, such as communal legislation, are supposed to increase the share for medium and large collective systems /8/.

1.2.8 **Denmark**

Denmark is considered to be one of the main protagonists of renewable energy technology. Denmark has made overwhelming development efforts in the field of wind power technology and active solar energy since the 1970's.

From the beginning of the 1980's, experience has accumulated with the integration of large collector surfaces, of several $1,000\,m^2$, into district heating networks. The collector area is located at ground level over farm and pasture land to avoid additional costs.

One of the largest solar thermal systems today is situated on the Danish island of Aerø in the Baltic Sea. The collector surface, with an area of $9,000\,m^2$, was completed in 1999 and gives its heat to the district heating network of the small town of Marstal. In this way it produces approximately 16% of the annual heat demand.

The Danish Heat Production Law of 13th June 1990 anticipates that, if possible, existing district heating plants change their production to use natural gas, and other environmental friendly energy sources. The Marstal district heating plant was based on oil-fired boilers. As Marstal is not connected to the national natural gas supply network; possibilities for using renewable energy sources were investigated. The Danish target is to reduce carbon dioxide emissions by 20% from 1988 levels by 2005, and it was seen as important to assist meeting this target.

Figure 1.5 A collector surface of 9,000 m² provides a small town Marstal on the Island Aerø with solar energy

In Denmark there are approx. $300,000\,m^2$ of collector surface installed; this is equivalent to $55\,m^2$ per 1,000 inhabitants.

40% of the systems are also for heating support. The collector surface installed is approx. $15,000\,m^2$ per year.

1.2.9 **Sweden**

The early development of solar thermal systems in Sweden was focused on large collector installations, and therefore 25% of the installed collector surface is related to large systems (each of more than 500 m^2). To date the largest plant in Europe is situated in Kungälv, 20 km north of Göteborg, with 10,000 m^2 of collector surface installed. Sweden pioneered work in the field of large solar thermal systems, with very large seasonal storage. This led to the installation of similar systems, e.g. in Germany. In Sweden, there is approx. 200,000 m^2 of installed glazed collector surface, i.e. 22 m^2 per 1,000 inhabitants of the country's population. 15 % of this surface is used for district heating systems. Generally, the percentage of the systems giving space heating support is reaching 20 %, which is very high.

The most common system in detached houses is a so-called »combi-system«. This has 10−15 m^2 of flat plate collectors in combination with a buffer storage tank of 500−1,500 litres. The system may be used in combination with a wood stove. The large collective systems comprise fifty to 1,000 m^2 roof-integrated collectors for pre-heating domestic hot water and which may be connected to a district-heating network for both domestic hot water and space heating. The district-heating systems comprise 500−10,000 m^2 of ground-mounted collector arrays connected to small district heating plants.

The per unit system costs can be noticeably reduced by the installation of large systems. The costs for Swedish installations are indicated below. These are exceeded in Germany by approx. 50 %.

Solar Systems Costs for Typically Sized Systems EURO/m^2		
	Individual	Project (large scale)
Cost excl. VAT	400 EURO/m^2	200 EURO/m^2
VAT	100 EURO/m^2	50 EURO/m^2
Total cost incl. VAT	500 EURO/m^2	250 EURO/m^2
Typical size of system	10 m^2	5,000 m^2

Table 1.1 System costs of small and large solar installations in Sweden

The annually installed collector surface comprises approx. 12,000 m^2 flat collectors and 400 m^2 vacuum-tube collectors/9/.

1.3 Development in Asia

1.3.1 China
Considering collector surface installations and the annual production of flat plate and vacuum-tube collectors, China has the worldwide leading position.

In the year 2000, approx. 20 million m^2 solar hot water systems were installed in the whole country . This is equivalent to a collector surface of 20 m^2 per 1,000 inhabitants.

The development of the installed collector surface during the last 10 years is to be seen in Figure 1.6.

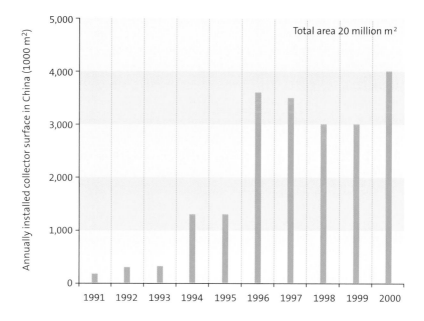

Figure 1.6 Installed collector area of solar hot water systems in China during the last decade

In 2000 the production from approx. 2,000 national manufacturers reached 4 million m² collector surface per year. Therefore, China alone produces 50% of the worldwide market of flat plate- and evacuated tube collectors, with an output value of 400 million US$ / year /10/.

1.3.2 India

Due to the average insolation being 4.5−6 kWh/m² per day, and with an average of 280 clear days in a year, solar thermal technologies have a natural advantage in India. Out of a number of solar applications for consumers, solar water heating systems have reached the stage of commercialisation in India.

Technology

Flat plate collectors are mainly used for water heating systems. Though different materials, e.g. stainless steel, aluminium and galvanized iron, can be effectively used for the production of absorbers for the flat plate collectors, almost all manufacturers in India use copper tubes (risers) and copper plates for the absorbers. In addition, the absorber is selectively coated with metal oxides. Non-selective coatings (such as black paint) are not used currently. The collector has a standard 2 m² absorber area and a single glazing of hardened glass.

In order to guarantee the quality of the collectors, they are tested following the standards set by the BIS (Bureau of Indian Standards). The standards are reviewed periodically. As a result of various promotional efforts by the MNES (Ministry of Non-conventional Energy Sources), the manufacturing base has improved substantially with 44 manufacturers having secured BIS certification for their products. Evacuated tube collector technologty has recently been introduced into India.

Market

There are two different market sectors for solar water heating systems in India:

- domestic and

- commercial and industrial.

Therefore, the majority of installations in India are in the commercial and industrial sector, with 80% of the collector surface installation. Whereas in Europe, the focus is mainly on the domestic sector. However the domestic market is increasing in India, due to the improved economics of solar systems and to the increased electricity prices. According to the reports of MNES, the potential for solar water heating systems in India is approx. 30 million m^2 of collector surface. The MNES policy (draft) has set a target of installing 5 million m^2 collector surface from 2000 to 2012, with equal distribution of collector area in both the domestic and the commercial/industrial sectors. The ministry suggested various subsidies to achieve this target.

As a result of promotional efforts, a steady growth in the cumulative installed collector area has been recorded. The total collector area installation has increased from 119,000 m^2 in 1989 to 500,000 m^2 in December 2001. This is equivalent to a surface of 0.5 m^2 per 1,000 habitants. The annual production of collector surface increased by 2001 to almost 500,000 m^2 /11/.

1.3.3 Nepal

A very interesting example of the development of solar technology can be seen in Nepal. The main source of income of the small kingdom in the Himalaya is tourism. Therefore, solar systems are very common for providing hot water in hotels and guesthouses. The »Solar hot shower« is almost standard, even in very solitary mountain lodges along tourists' trekking trails.

Moreover, solar technology is also used increasingly in commerce and industry, due to very high prices for kerosene and energy.

Almost always, natural flow systems are used. The absorbers are welded from zinc-galvanized steel tube, with domestic water directly as the flow. Black painted aluminium plate is fixed with wire onto the tubes.

The cases are made from zinc-galvanized plate and covered with window glass. Such a construction of collectors has been manufactured for 30 years without further improvements. Practically, every small hand-craft company can produce the collectors from the materials available locally. However there is often a lack of expertise for the design, so known systems are simply copied repeatedly. Users state that some installations have been working for 30 years and are still adequate. A system of this type of construction can be seen in Figure 1.7.

Figure 1.7 Typical natural flow system (Patan hospital, Kathmandu, Nepal)

The productive efficiency of the systems is limited not only by the simple type of construction but mainly by inadequate or no thermal insulation of the piping.

Meanwhile the market is enlarging with imported systems from India and China.

Total collector surface installed is now estimated as approximately 100,000 m^2. This is equivalent to a collector surface of 5−7 m^2 per 1,000 inhabitants. The current annual increase is presently approx. 50,000 m^2 per year.

1.4 **Development in Africa**

The solar insolation in Africa is particularly favourable for the use of solar energy. 47% of the continent has annual insolation values of more than $2,100\,kWh/(m^2a)$, 27% between 1,900 and $2,100\,kWh/(m^2a)$ and 26% between 1,500 and 1,900 $kWh/(m^2a)$ /12/.

The regions south of the Sahara are the poorest in the world. Up to 90% of the energy demands are satisfied by firewood, charcoal, livestock dung and agricultural trash. This often goes together with associated decline of forests and the creation of arid steppes over whole districts.

The potential for the use of solar energy is enormous, but the market launch of solar technology fails due to the political situation (which is often unstable) and small purchasing power. Significant installations can only be named in some countries. For instance, in cooperation with the Consortium Renewable Energies (CRE) from Austria, a thermo-syphon system has been developed in Zimbabwe that can be produced with local available resources and is simple to manufacture. Application is mainly in rural districts without central water supply. So far, approx. 200 of these small systems have been installed. Since December 2000, larger systems with about $20\,m^2$ surface area have been produced mainly for schools, hotels, etc.

1.5 **Development in USA**

With the foreseeable depletion of their own crude oil resources, during the last 10 years, after a long pause, the USA is increasing its commitment again in the solar market. The Americans anticipate an annual increase of 25% of the world market for solar technology /13/. The declared target of the USA is to become the worldwide market leader.

The »100,000-roofs-programme«, passed in 1998, will probably begin implementation in the current year.

1.6 Survey of the Solar Market

The following presentation shows the glazed collector surfaces installed per 1,000 inhabitants of the different countries/14/.

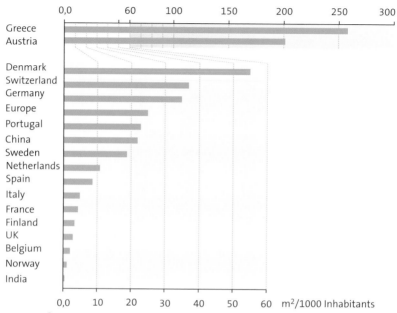

Figure 1.8 Survey Collector surface installed per 1,000 inhabitants of different countries

1.7 Arguments for the Installation of Solar Systems

Below is a list of important arguments for the installation of solar systems.

- As solar systems are energy supplies completely free of exhaust gases, their owners contribute actively to climate protection.

- Solar systems, with their average lifetime of 20 years, demonstrate a sophisticated and reliable technology.

- Operators of solar systems avoid additional expenses due to increases of energy prices and green taxes; thereby they gain some economic independence.

- The largest cost item of solar thermal systems is the capital commitment. The cost may be calculated accurately and in advance over many years. In contrast, fuel costs for conventional heating plants vary strongly and are not calculable in advance, say 20 years ahead. Therefore, a solar system is a safe investment providing a cost advantage.

- Solar systems have low maintenance requirements and need, – if at all, little electrical auxiliary power.
- Operators of solar systems often benefit from tax advantages and governmental subsidies.
- Solar systems enhance the value and image of a property. »Solar houses« are easier to lease.
- In buildings with solar systems, the rent, inclusive of heating, may be increased a little.
- Solar systems use a permanently available energy source. The application of solar systems conserves conventional energy sources (oil, gas, etc.). They provide countries with a greater economic and political independence.
- The purchase and application of solar systems ensures and enhances expert knowledge in the country. This establishes a stable basis for positive economic development and opens new domestic and international markets.
- Having a solar systems is demonstrating responsibility.
- Due to the continued extension of the use of solar thermal energy, new jobs are added in industry and trade skills.

1.8 Solar Radiation on the Earth

Inside the Sun, atomic nuclei of hydrogen are fused under immense pressure to atomic nuclei of helium. During this process, immense energy fluxes are released at temperatures of millions of degrees. The surface temperature of the Sun is therefore about 5,500°C.

Thus, the Sun is a nuclear reactor that has been working reliably for 5 billion years by nuclear fusion. Astronomers estimate the Sun's lifetime is about another 5 billion years.

The radiative power of the Sun arriving at the top of the Earth's atmosphere, at a distance of approx. 150 million km, is about 1,360 W/m^2. This value is called the Extraterrestrial Solar Constant.

The Earth's atmosphere absorbs part of the radiation, so that reaching the Earth's surface has a maximum value of approx. 1,000 W/m^2. This solar radiation flux (called insolation) is obviously reduced even more by clouds. The resulting radiation may be called »global radiation« and is composed of both diffuse and direct components. Both components can be utilized in solar technology.

The solar energy annually radiating onto the whole Earth's surface has an immense potential. It exceeds the annual energy demand of the world population ten thousand-fold. The solar resource is far larger than all available fossil and nuclear energy reserves.

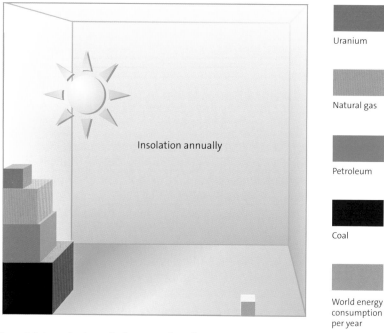

Uranium

Natural gas

Petroleum

Coal

World energy consumption per year

Figure 1.9 Annual solar radiation to earth surface, energy resources available in form of coal, oil, gas and uranium as well as annual world energy demand by comparison

The solar energy availability is geographically unequally spread and subject to seasonal variations. In desert regions near the Equator, the annual radiation flux may total 2,300 kWh/(m²a). This is twice the average solar radiation flux of Canada, Middle Europe, Middle Asia, South Argentina or New Zealand.

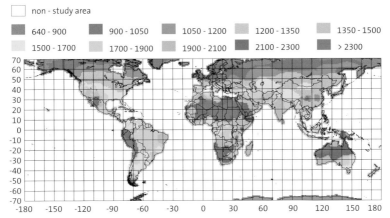

Figure 1.10 Radiation values worldwide/METEOTEST, Bern, Switzerland; www.meteonorm.com/

Both the absolute value and the distribution of solar radiation over a year, depend strongly on latitude. In regions near the Equator, the average monthly insolation is evenly distributed through the year, but at higher latitudes, it is greater in summer. However the weather and the slope and orientation of the collecting surface greatly effects these generalities. Solar radiation for locations on the northern and southern hemisphere with different latitudes is shown clearly in the following pictures.

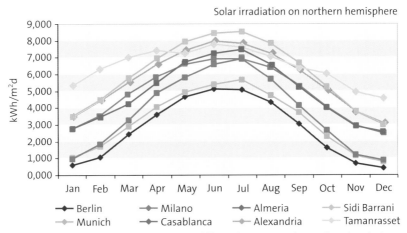

Figure 1.11 Average daily solar radiation for different locations in the northern hemisphere in kWh/d

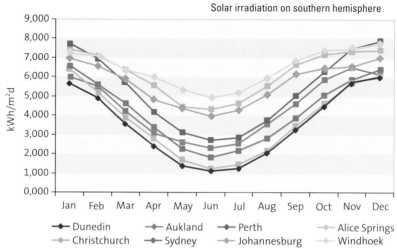

Figure 1.12 Average daily solar radiation for different locations in the southern hemisphere in kWh/d

The energy provided annually and gratis by the Sun per m² is equivalent to 100 litres oil in the middle latitudes and up to 230 litres of oil in desert districts.

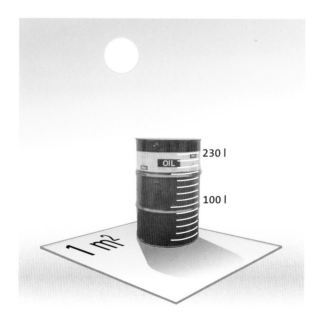

Figure 1.13 The annual solar radiation per m² is equivalent to an energy content of 100 l to 230 l of heating oil.

Today's solar thermal systems can utilise from 30% to 60% of the solar radiation incident on the collector.

2. Survey of Long-term Experiences with Solar Thermal Systems

Solar thermal technology has been used as a modern development in various countries for more than 20 years. During this time, researchers and manufacturers gained valuable experience on materials, design, production and utilisation.

Very detailed studies have been carried out in Germany.

2.1 Long-term Experiences in Germany

Between 1978 and 1983, there have been 141 solar systems installed in Germany for the thermal use of solar energy in buildings owned by the Federal Government. Examples are in military barracks and dwellings, and public service buildings. These systems were installed in order to prove their serviceability and, at the same time, stimulate public authorities, commerce and private interested parties to increase utilisation of this environmental friendly energy source.

Most systems were for domestic hot water supply. As is usual in Germany, they are provided with circulation pumps for a closed solar circuit, which is filled with anti-freeze mixture.

In 1980, the central office for solar technology (Zentralstelle für Solartechnik−ZfS) within the organisation for the promotion of heating and climate technology (Gesellschaft zur Förderung der Heizungs- und Klimatechnik mbH−GFHK) was asked by the Federal Ministry for Education, Science, Research and Technology to carry out a monitoring programme for certain projects.

During support of these installations by the ZfS, optimising measures significantly increased both, efficiency and safety at many of the solar systems. This led to an increase of profitability, as well as higher consumer acceptance.

Within the scope of another programme for solar thermal systems (»Solarthermie 2000«) further research has been carried out from 1993. Studies of aging, stability and long-term reliability were made for a representative sample of systems installed at the end of the 70's and beginning of the 80's. Most results can be transferred to today's systems, which are similar concerning their method, structure and components.

Studies of materials were also carried out within the scope of the research programme. For this, components of 18 systems were removed, taken apart and intensively examined.

In order to evaluate the performance of old collectors, the operational efficiency of 21 such collectors (13 different manufactures) were measured. After the collector efficiency tests, measurements were made on some of the optical features of absorbers and covers, and on the thermal conductivity of the insulation materials.

2.2 Stock Data of the Future Invest Programme (»Zukunftsinvestitionsprogramm« – ZIP)

Beginning in 1994, an inventory of the systems installed between 1978 and 1983 has been taken in order to see the percentage of the installations still working.

The results can be seen in Figure 2.1.

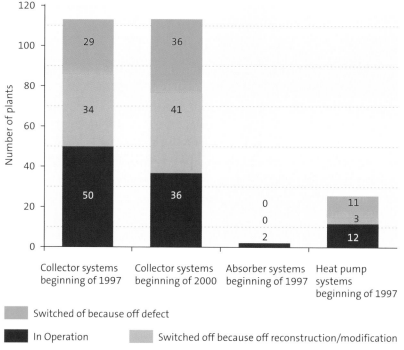

Figure 2.1 Results of the inventory of the current status of the solar systems within the Future Invest Programme (ZIP)

Out of 113 solar systems installed within the scope of the Future Invest Programme (ZIP) 50 were still working by the end of 1997 (i.e. approx. 44%). At the beginning of 2000, 36 systems were still working.

At the beginning of the 1980's, many initial systems had to be shut down due to defects. However these systems were experimental collectors and production has ceased for such designs and use of materials. From the beginning of the 1990's, the number of annual shut-downs or removals increased due to different utilisation of the buildings or restoration of the roofs. By the end of 1999 there had been only 36 (i.e. 32%) removals due to system defects, but 41 (i.e. 36%) were due to non-solar technical circumstances (see Chapter 2.1).

If the 41 dismantled systems are neglected of the original 113, than 72 (more than 50%) of installed systems were still working 20 years later in 2000. This percentage proves the durability of the early solar systems regarding design and system technology. Probably individual components were not optimally constructed.

Until 1999, the 36 system shut-downs due to major system defects included 21 systems whose design cannot be compared with today's technology. These were, for example, systems with prototype collectors of the first generation (do-it-yourself-construction collectors, heat pipe flat collectors, non evacuated glass tube collectors, flat roof collectors with specula reflector and high acrylic hood, collectors with cushion-steel absorber) or prototype system variations (collector circuits filled with water/nitrogen).

Of the systems partly or completely meeting today's construction standards (i.e. about 90%), only 15, (i.e. approx.7%) were shut down due to serious system defects. After about 20 years of operation, this is an outstanding result.

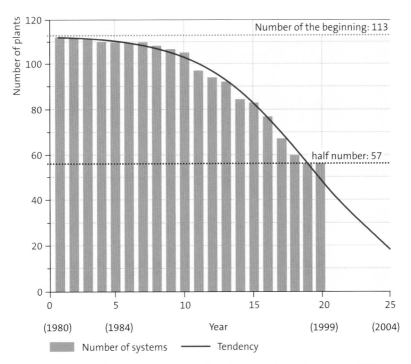

Figure 2.2 Inventory line of collector systems from the Future Invest Programme (ZIP) (state: end of 1999)

In Figure 2.2 the reasons for system shut-downs have been incorporated into a mathematical model in order to predict future development. The curve was normalised for a primary stock of 100% (equivalent to 113 systems).

The following considerations have to be taken into account for interpreting Figure 2.2:

- Between 1977 and 1979, 81 of the 113 systems were installed (more than 70%), but later only a few systems were installed (1983/1984). Therefore 1980 was considered as the first year of operation for all installations. Some of them were already 2–3 years old at that time and some were installed up to three years later.

- Certain installations in this experiment show similarities to the earlier solar technology (systems of the »first generation«). They were left in the defect analysis, although most of these systems or their components failed tests; they soon showed serious defects and were therefore shut down. Such systems with »experimental technology« disappeared from the market. Today's system components are almost all sophisticated, so overcoming early design faults. Therefore the defect analysis presents far too poor a picture of today's systems with their improved technology. System failures of the early designs are no longer being seen (see Chapter 2.3) .

- As stated above, solar system shut downs due to non-solar technical measures should not be included in defect statistics. Nevertheless, if these systems had been still working, probably some of them would have been shutdown due to defects. This probability was taken into account by assuming that among the system shut downs due to non-solar reasons (such as renovation, different building utilisation), the same percentage of defects would have occurred as happened to the other systems. In this way, non solar system shut downs were treated as if they would have continued working.

Technical devices often have a characteristic that early defects in a small number of systems is followed by a long period with low failure rates. Statistical analysis might then imply that some devices seem to be indestructible. However, any device will fail in a realistic period of time, except if it is repaired repeatedly without considering expense. The solar systems of the ZIP-programme clearly show this characteristic. A Boltzmann curve fits the data quite exactly, so it can be used for the mathematic model in Figure 2.2. As the Boltzmann curve approximates asymptotically to the zero line, the unrealistic implication is that, even after 100 years some systems could still be working.

Therefore, a new »sensible« zero point was fixed for this curve (mathematically with an asymptotic approach to the value of approx. −4). It is noteworthy that the last ZIP system was shutdown about 30 years after its installation.

For the analysis, it is more important that 20 years after the installation (at the end of 1999) approx. 50% of all systems were still working (however the adapted Boltzmann curve cuts the 50% line sooner). This half-life period can be defined as the life-time of the solar systems. The implication is, after this time, shut down of the remaining systems is likely to happen relatively soon (in the mathematic model, within the following approx. 10 years).

The causes for removals carried out for reasons other than system defects (i.e. not related to solar technology) are mentioned below:

- Changes in ownership structures or in the current utilisation of the buildings (after the German reunification, these were often buildings of the Federal Armed Forces or the Frontier-Defence) or:
- Necessity of renovation of some flat roofs on which collector area was installed.

If renovation of a flat roof is necessary after the installation of a solar system, often removal of the collector area (including the rig) is required. Although in many cases the disassembled collectors were still functioning, they were not installed again. This was probably because the costs of re-assembling the old collectors were not justifiable, since the remaining life-time of collectors werere estimated to be short. Reinstallation with new collectors was only realised in few individual cases.

The experiences of this study prove that, it is important to pay attention to the durability of the building cover, as later renovations lead to either higher system life costs or premature shut downs of the solar system. This is due to the necessary removal and re-installation of the collector area.

For future building projects, it should be stipulated that the roof is either relatively new, recently renovated or will be renovated as a precaution at the owner's expenses before installation. In addition, it is important to make sure that the rig and the collectors are easy to remove and to re-install, or that there is enough space under the construction in case of unforeseeable minor damage to the roof (or the collectors). In the later case, the higher rig construction should not lead to significant additional expense or to careless roof renovations.

2.3 **Frequent Defects**

The following information on frequent defects and failures of collector systems result from an additional questionnaire campaign in 1997, with a very extensive choice of questions. Later further subsidiary questions were received at the end of 1999. Despite the very detailed questionnaire, the 83% rate of return from the owners of the 113 installed collector systems was good. The failure statistic for these systems is therefore well attested.

In Figure 2.3 the most important results are summarised. In some cases, we included information on defects obtained from subsidary questions, in order to obtain the full picture. The percentile specifications in Figure 2.3 refer correctly to the number of questionnaires received in 1997 (98) and not to the complete number of collector systems installed (113 systems). However, supplementary information on defects (by the end of 1999) has been taken into consideration. The defects are arranged to show the frequency of their appearance. The coloured marking makes the classification of the stated components easier. The total sum of all percentages is higher than 100%, because multiple defects on the same systems are included.

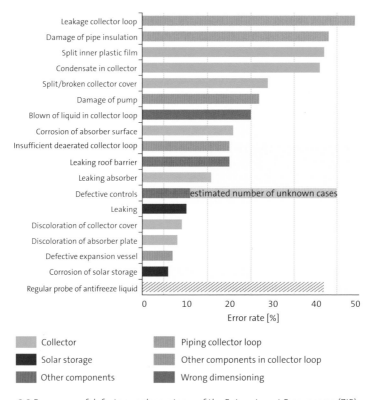

Figure 2.3 Frequency of defects on solar systems of the Future Invest Programme (ZIP) (as at the beginning of 2000)

As may be seen in Figure 2.3, leakage of the collector circuit takes first place in the list of defects. These leaks often appeared in unsuitable flexible hose connections between collectors and valves, at pumps or at control sensor connecting nozzles. This is directly related to »cringe-capacity« of the glycol in the heat transfer liquid. A system that appears to be impervious to water is not necessarily also impervious to a water-glycol-mix. The high percentage of leaks indicates, that many systems might not maintain the necessary overpressure, so often air was absorbed as the systems cooled down after high liquid temperatures in the circuit. If subsequently the system is not regularly filled with heat transfer liquid (not pure water) and also vented, then air accumulates in the upper parts of the system. Normally, these are the upper collector edges, especially at the upper collector tube connection. Corrosion may appear in steel or aluminium collectors, but rarely in absorbers with copper piping (see Chapter 5.3). This metal corrosion may lead to corrosion damage and leaks. If the absorbers are corroded completely, then the system cannot work. Because of such faults, 20 % of the systems were found faulty by the operators due to defects in venting function or the installed venting valves.

Therefore, it is necessary that the collector circuit is leak-proof to water-glycol mixtures. Leaks should be immediately sealed. The installation of suitable vents (e.g. with manual valves) and a very effective air separator within the collector circuit, should be operated most carefully. Air in the collector circuit not only stimulates corrosion, but also reduces the rate of flow of the heat transfer liquid (possibly causing shut down) and therefore reduces the efficiency of the system.

Today, the previously frequent leakages of the tube connections at collectors have become less likely as better connection technologies have been used.

Older collectors incorporated inner, secondary, transparent foils to reduce heat loss. These were frequently recorded as cracked and inoperative. However today's technology does not need secondary foils, using selective surfaces, so the difficulty is eliminated.

Condensate in flat-plate collectors in cold temperatures is relatively unimportant, provided that this does not cause corrosion on the absorber surface and the liquid infiltrated passes out at higher collector temperatures as heated water vapour.

Defects of external pipes or other metal tubing are mainly caused by corrosion and possibly rusting through failure of zinc-galvanized iron coatings, including joints at installation (e.g. joints between pipes and at outlets; see Chapter 7.5). Often humidity penetration was noted into the insulation of outer tubing, due to corroded or carelessly installed covers that certainly were not leak-proof. In addition, there was sometimes damage by birds to non-sheathed insulation materials (e.g. Armaflex and others); the birds often pecked such materials for nest building. Therefore, such unprotected plastic sheathing should not be used in external parts of the system.

Breakage and cracks of the transparent front covers were almost always due to the acrylic covers being unsuitable for large forces (e.g. caused by high temperatures inside the collector, gusty wind forces on unsuitable construction etc.). Nowadays, acrylic covers are seldom used, because modern glass with reduced iron has much better transparency and is resistant to mechanical forces for a longer period. Most of such recorded damages is only an outdated difficulty of solar systems. Breakages of the glass cover were infrequent, (apart from one system at Davos, Austria, with very long heat-pipe absorbers that had high temperature gradients at some points of the glass, due to collector construction and therefore large temperature expansion forces). Some other systems had glass breakages due to using poor quality glass.

Collector circuit »steam venting« was recorded in 30% of the systems. This is because systems within the investigation program (ZIP) were often designed with oversized collectors. Therefore, the storage tank reached maximum temperature about noon and consquently the collector circuit stagnated. Due to the expansion vessels being dimensioned too small, the heat transfer liquid vaporised in the absorber and water vapour (steam) was vented. Moreover, air probably entered the collector circuit when the system cooled. If these experiences are considered when solar systems are designed, such failures should not occur.

Noticeably, roof cover leakages occured on (a) flat roofs , and (b) inclined roofs with collectors integrated within the roof cover. Such leaks produced significant damages in the rooms below. However such faults could also appear with other installations, such as dormer windows, antenna and aerial ducts etc. Nevertheless, solar technology is blamed for such defects, because they would not have appeared without the solar installation.

We will consider detail in later Chapters about other defects with the different components, as mentioned in Figure 2.3. Some of these defects are due to the system (e.g. corrosion of the absorber surface, discolouration of the cover; mainly with glass fibre reinforced plastic, others are due to lack of maintenance (e.g. corrosion of the storage tank due to a depleted sacrificial anode), and others have to be seen as normal deterioration of systems operating for about 20 years.

Defects with controls (e.g. sensors and electronics) were infrequently recorded in the questionnaire responses (only 11%). However the experience of the Central Office for Solar Technology (ZfS) during the support of now approx. 100 solar systems, shows that this low number is not realistic. Owners do indeed register control defects when systems obviously fail (e.g. incorrectly installed control sensors, aging sensors with incorrect control signals, defective electronic). However defects that only decrease system efficiency are often not recognised. This is because the conventional heating system takes over the complete heating supply in the case of solar system defects and the energy yield of the solar system is seldom monitored. Even if the energy supply is recorded or metered, the owner often does not know how to interpret the measured results. The experience during the investigations led to estimates that about 40 to 50% of controls are incorrectly adjusted or faulty.

In conclusion, a further very important result from the questionnaires was that the heat transfer medium in the collector circuit was only regularly checked in 40% of the systems. Moreover it was not mentioned if »regularly« means that the check was made annually or otherwise. In Chapter 7.3 you can see that this check is very important, especially if inappropriate material is used.

To summarise we can state that a large number of systems were dismantled due to non-solar reasons (e.g. change in use of the building, flat roof renovation etc.). Such removals cannot be blamed on the solar technology. Also, many technical defects leading to system shutdown occured in systems with collectors that are not produced anymore (e.g. changed choice of material due to adverse experience). If such systems are removed from consideration, the defect rate is about 30% after about 20 years of opration (i.e. about 70% remain successful). If the lack of experience concerning sophistication of components, dimensioning and long periods out of use is considered, then the defect rate would have been less with improved system design.

Even the first generation of the solar systems proved that they could have a long life-time. For today's solar systems, with significantly improved components and a carefully chosen design, the defect rate in 20 years will certainly be less than 30%.

2.4 **Life-Time of Solar Thermal Systems**

Solar system life-time is often asked in sales and marketing. This can be estimated now from the experiences and explanations of the previous defect analysis of this Chapter. With today's sophisticated technology, solar system life-time is certainly expected to be 20 years (with good components, 25 years). Therefore, solar systems are not only valuable but also an extremely long-lasting asset. It is essential to take this into consideration for a solar installation before decision making.

Pre-Conditions for a solar system life-time of 20 to 25 years are:

- Correct design of the solar system according to the measured consumption. Avoidance of over-dimensioning, and of too long and too frequent standstill periods
- Careful and detailed system planning and choice of devices
- Use of high-quality components (cost-value ratio is to be taken under consideration)
- Careful installation of all system components
- Intensive installation supervision by the planner
- Careful checking at inspection, certification and during the test operation
- Dedicated checking of the system behaviour during operation and careful maintenance

However these are valid requirements for all technical installations. A solar system does not require any extra care more than other systems.

In our considered opinion, today's solar systems have a life-time of 20 to 25 years. For longer service of today's collectors to more than 25 years, some parts of the system technology should be improved.

For example, the insulation sheathing of the external tubing should be considered. It is surely more beneficial to use more expensive outer material (e.g. aluminium) from the beginning, rather than making an expensive replacement in the middle of the life span of a system. Moreover, if the costs for the sheathing depend primarily on labour hours, and not on the material, it would surely be interesting to develop pre-fabricated tubes complete with thermal insulation. This is similar to district heating pipes laid under-ground. This would significantly reduce installation effort for the outside tubing. However, higher temperatures inside the collector circuit would have to be taken into consideration. For further faults of the old systems, and developments carried out, please see the later Chapters concerning individual system components and further development opportunities.

3. **Basic Information on the Construction of Thermal Solar Installations**

The basic principles of solar heating systems are described in the following sections. The fundamentals of their construction are shown in examples, which cover many, but not all, possibilities. The number of system variants is so wide that not all related variants can be dealt with. System dimensioning, the function and design of the individual system components and the experience in long-term operation are all considered in detail in subsequent sections.

It is recommended that the system assembly be kept very simple with regard to the lowest possible costs for the available solar heat. Unfortunately the »gadgets« frequently installed to increase system efficiency usually have a poor cost/benefit ratio and increase susceptibility to failure in the system.

3.1 **Development of Technology for Thermal Solar Installations**

The demand for hot water in most situations (e.g. in households) remains virtually constant throughout the year, which is why increased solar availability in Summer can be used efficiently to heat water without loss of convenience.

This is why the vast majority of installations in all countries are used to heat potable water.

The water quality and requirements for tap water vary between individual countries. Tap water is regarded as a foodstuff in some countries, where it is subject to corresponding hygiene provisions and is thus designated potable water. If similar provisions also apply to heated water, then this is described as »potable hot water«. The requirements on water hygiene affect the system configuration (also see 3.2).

Solar heat can also be used for heating buildings. The increasing efficiency of solar systems, optimised connection and storage technology, as well as matched heating systems for relatively low temperatures (e.g. wall and underfloor heating), all enable solar energy to back up space heating.

Obviously due to climatic conditions, less solar insolation is available when space heating is most demanded. In cold regions with little winter solar insolation, a major or complete contribution by solar energy to heating demand is only possible with large inter-seasonal storage tanks. In contrast, in warmer climatic zones with low heating demands and short heating periods, frequently only temporary, dispersed (often electric) sources of heat are used. The installation of central, solar heating systems requires additional expense in this case. Figure 3.1 shows: (i) a diagram of the annual solar energy availability standardised to the maximum, (ii) the energy demand for potable water heating and space heating in Central Europe. The demand for potable water heating remains practically the same throughout the year (only slightly decreasing in summer), whereas energy for heating is mainly required in winter since the insolation is less during this period and then only at a lower intensity.

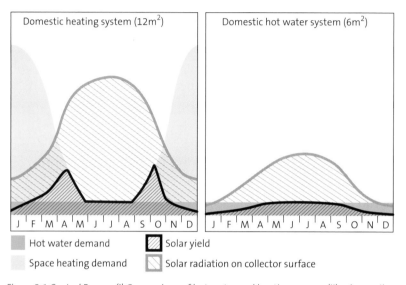

Figure 3.1 Central Europe (i) Comparison of hot water and heating energy, (ii) solar availability (iii) possible yield for installations to heat potable water or to back up space heating

The vast majority of new thermal solar installations set up today are used for potable water heating due to the context shown in Fig. 3.1. In Germany however, the proportion of installations combined for both potable water heating and for space heating demand in the so-called transitional periods (Spring and Autumn) has increased to approx. 15 %. In Denmark, the proportion of systems including space heating back-up is 40 %; in Sweden 20 %.

In countries at low latitudes and with high insolation, systems including heating back-up are less common, although there may be similar high heating demand to that in Central Europe due to the reduced insulation standards for buildings.

3.2 **Characteristic Values of Solar Energy Systems**

Characteristic values serve to assess the dimensioning, operation and economy of a solar energy system. All the characteristic values defined below are important for assessing a thermal solar installation. If only one of these quantities is missing, then a solar installation is not described sufficiently. Equally, only one good characteristic value (e.g. high solar fraction) does not state anything about the quality of the solar energy system itself.

In addition, the interfaces in the system, where the respective energy flows occur and can be measured, have to be clearly defined. In the following Figure, this is shown in outline on an installation with a buffer storage tank.

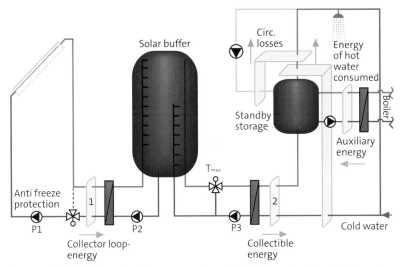

Figure 3.2 Basic structure of a solar energy system with interfaces to determine the system characteristic values in a system with buffer storage tank and forced circulation

3.2.1 **Specific Load**

Hot water consumption per person varies greatly, e.g. in comparison of homes and hospitals. Therefore stating a single value for solar collector area per person, living unit or hospital bed is insufficient to describe the design of a solar energy system. Thus it is useful to define a quantity which sets the collector area in proportion to hot water consumption.

The specific load states how many litres of cold water are passed through the solar installation to be heated per day (d) and per square metre collector area (m^2). This value here is only relevant for systems purely for domestic water heating. It is a valuable characteristic for such installations for dimensioning the solar energy system. Note that for a given hot water demand, specific load decreases with increase in area of collector.

In Central Europe and comparable climatic zones reasonably designed large-scale installations purely for heating potable water have a high specific load, approx. $60-70 l/(d \cdot m^2)$ or more. Generally, it is satisfactory to have a specific load of approx. $50-60 \, l/(d \cdot m^2)$, however below $50 \, l/(d \cdot m^2)$ usually indicates over-dimensioning.

A lower specific load (e.g. $30 l/(d \cdot m^2)$) may only be justifiable with small-scale installations if there is favourable specific costs (costs per m^2 collector area).

See Chapter 4.2 for the correct determination of the cold water flowing through the solar energy system.

The dimensioning depends, of course, on the solar insolation at the location. However lower levels of insotion can, to a certain extent, be countered out by more efficient technology. In such countries it is common to use, high-quality collectors with selective surfacces, solar glass and more complex systems with controlled pumps; stratifying storage systems and better heat insulation. Thus the design criteria shown can be applied in various climatic zones when using correspondingly adapted systems.

For installations to back up space heating, stating the relation of collector area to specific heating energy demand is appropriate (kWh per m^2 living area, per year). This is in addition to the specific load defined above for water heating.

3.2.2 Degree of Utilisation

The solar energy incident on a collector (as inclined and aligned) serves as the reference for determining all aspects of utilisation in a solar energy system. For this, the collector field area (either gross, aperture or absorber area) must be given (see Chapter 5.1.). This value is measured using a radiation sensor. For guaranteed solar results, a high quality instrument is needed. For checking operation, a medium quality instrument is adequate. Recent solar radiation (insolation) maps and publications by weather services may also be used for approximate determinations.

Since there are various definitions of degrees of utilisation, the particular definition used must always be stated (or asked) when a value is given.

Collector Circulation Degree of Utilisation

The 'collector circulation degree of utilisation' is the ratio of (a) the heat passing from the collector loop to the heat-exchanger or solar storage tank (interface 1 in Fig. 3.2) to, (b) the solar energy which arrived on the collector field in the same period. This ratio does not take into account the losses in the piping outside the collector loop interface and from the storage tank etc. It is thus always higher than the 'system degree of utilisation'.

System Degree of Utilisation

The system degree of utilisation is the ratio of (a) captured solar heat given passed to the conventional system by the complete solar energy system (including all solar storage tanks and heat-exchangers) (interface 2 in Fig. 3.2), to (b) the solar energy which arrived at the collector field within the same period.

Note that interface 2 in systems with combi-storage tanks (feeding solar heat and conventional heat into the same storage tank) may not be clearly defined. If so, the last interface, where clearly only solar energy flows through, must be used for measurement. Then the assessed losses in downstream solar components should be deducted from this measurement (e.g. solar section of combi-storage tank) (see. Fig. 3.3). In the case of natural flow systems, the collector circulation degree of utilisation is virtually impossible to determine, since the flow volume cannot be measured mechanically without influencing the circulation. In this case, it can only be determined from the energy balance sheet of hot water consumption, less the additional energy and storage losses.

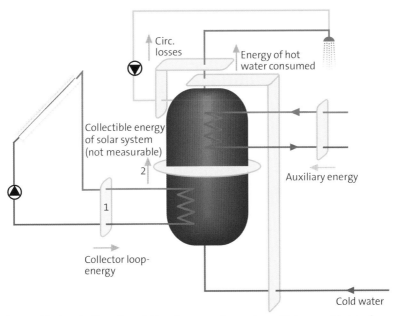

Circ. losses

Energy of hot water consumed

Collectible energy of solar system (not measurable)

2

Auxiliary energy

1

Collector loop-energy

Cold water

Figure 3.3 Determination of available solar energy in a system with inaccessible interface between the solar and conventional system

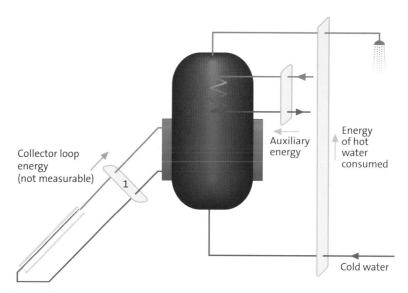

Figure 3.4 Principle structure of a solar energy system with interfaces for determining the system characteristic values in a gravity system

3.2.3 Solar Fraction

The basic value for determining the solar fraction is the amount of available solar heat supplied by the solar installation to the consumer (see system degree of utilisation). It is measured with a heat quantity meter at interface 2 (in Fig. 3.2) or determined as described for the system degree of utilisation.

This value can be related to various consumption values resulting in different definitions for the solar fraction. Thus the definition used must always be stated (or asked) when determining a solar fraction.

Solar Fraction of Consumption

The 'solar fraction of consumption' is the proportion of available solar heat in the total energy needed to heat the hot water consumed. Not included is the energy required (a) to cover losses in conventional storage tanks, (b) for the hot water circulation, (c) for space heating .

Stating the solar fraction assesses a solar installation purely for potable water heating. This is appropriate if the system is not capable of contributing to covering circulation losses etc. and when it is not connected to the space heating system for constructional and design reasons.

Solar Fraction of Consumption and Delivery Losses

This may also be called 'solar fraction of consumption and circulation losses', since the hot water may be delivered in a circulation system in the building. It is the ratio of (a) available solar heat to (b) the energy demand in consumption and delivery for the hot water. The energy covering the losses in the conventional storage tank and the demand for the space heating itself are not included here.

This definition is relevant, if the solar installation has been designed for solar energy to for solar energy to cover both the domestic water heating and the delivery/circulation losses. It is useful if the conventional heat quantity used for the consumption system is not measured. It presumes the measurement of two heat quantities in the conventional system (energy of hot water consumed and the delivery/circulation losses).

Total Solar Fraction of Demand of a Hot Water System

The solar fraction of total energy consumption by the hot water system is the ratio of (a) available solar heat, to (b) the energy demand for the entire hot water system (consumption, losses in delivery/circulation, and conventional storage tanks). Since the losses in the conventional standby storage tank are generally proportionally low (good heat insulation presumed), the total proportion covered is usually only slightly lower than the solar fraction of consumption and circulation. Both values can normally be equated to one another in initial approximations.

The determination of this solar fraction presumes, in addition to the measurement point of available solar heat, only one additional heat measurement for the heat generated conventionally, which is fed into the hot water system. However, in this case, the determination of the energy content of the hot water taken off and of the circulation losses is dispensed with. Moreover, no check is carried out whether the system was correctly designed for the energy demand. We have also omitted the determination of the often enormous circulation losses and the need for reducing energy losses.

Solar Fraction of Total Heat Demand of the Building

The solar fraction of the total heat demand is the ratio of (a) available solar heat, to (b) the energy demand for both hot water and space heating, including all losses. It is stated when there is a combi-system to provide heat for both potable water and back-up space heating.

The determination of this fraction requires only one further heat quantity measurement to determine the entire energy conventionally generated; this is the heat fed into the heating system of the building for hot water and space heating. In this case, the determination of the energy demand per individual is dispensed with, so no check can be carried out for a comparison with any expected solar fraction per individual consumer. This only becomes possible with more complex measurements.

3.2.4 System Performance Figure

The performance Figure describes the ratio of (a) available heat supplied from the solar heating system, to (b) auxiliary energy for electricity used for the control system, pumps, control valves etc. Measurement technology for special monitoring is excluded. It states how many kWh of solar available heat have been supplied per kWh electricity used.

3.2.5 Cost of Available Solar Heat

The costs for available solar heat may be used to derive the price per kWh of solar-thermal energy. These costs are calculated from the ratio of (a) absolute debt servicing (annuity), (e.g. in € defined by the complete construction costs for the solar installation, the service life of the system and the interest rate for the capital to be used) and (b) the yield of solar heat throughout one year in kWh. In the case of a system service life of 20 years, and an interest rate of 6%, a debt servicing factor (annuity factor) of 8.72% results. If conventional components are replaced by the solar heating system (e.g. conventional hot water storage tank in small solar installations with bivalent potable water storage tank or tiles (in the case of in-roof integration of the collectors), then the costs thus saved have to be deducted from the cost of the solar heating system.

The costs above do not include operating costs (e.g. costs of auxiliary energy, maintenance) which may increase the costs above by approx. 15 to 25%.

On the other hand, the cost saved by the replacement of conventional fuels must be considered. However this cost depends largely on the price trend in conventional energy supplies and on the quality of the conventional heating system that no general and permanently valid statements can be made. To give an example using heating oil in a boiler of 80% 'degree of utilisation' at a price of approx. 0.5 EUR per litre, the delivered heat could be at a price of approx. 0.06EUR per kWh .

3.3 Requirements for Potable Water Hygiene

(prevention of legionella growth)

The thermal solar installations heat potable water using the solar energy. Since the sun does not shine continually, these solar installations require a storage tank, to bridge the time and power differences between solar radiation and energy demand. These differences generally require greater hot water storage volumes than with conventional systems. This necessity contradicts the requirements for increased potable water hygiene, which are best fulfilled if as little potable water as possible is stored and if long retention times are avoided. Thus, from a hygiene point of view, potable water storage tanks with a volume which is close to, or even more than, the daily consumption of hot potable water should be regarded critically.

Temperatures of between 30 and 50°C frequently occur in solar storage tanks. If potable water is stored at such temperatures for longer periods than a day, then particular attention must be paid to water hygiene because the highest reproductive rates for bacteria are observed in this temperature range (e.g. for legionella).

However, bacterial growth in potable water is not a problem specific to solar installations. Any potable water circulation systems can be affected, e.g. installations with instantaneous water heaters (that is no storage tank), cold water networks, and in particular hot water installations in which cold, potable water is pre-heated in conventional stages (e.g. waste heat utilisation). Due to the extreme hazard, particular attention must be given to preventing the reproduction of **legionella** in potable water.

Legionella (lat.: legionella pneumophilla) are bacteria which are present in trace quantities everywhere in water and which can reproduce rapidly in hot water at favourable temperatures (around 35°C).

These legionella bacteria present no danger to humans in the gastrointestinal system, however they can be inhaled in minute water droplets (as an aerosol) into the lungs, for example under the shower, and cause clinical pictures similar to pneumonia which may lead to death. Ill and elderly people are particularly at risk, thus special attention must be paid to water hygiene in old people's homes and hospitals.

The term »Legionella« arose because this disease was first observed in 1976 among American legionnaires. They had met in a hotel where the air conditioning system was contaminated.

The bacteria were distributed in the rooms via the ventilation system and 220 of the 4,000 participants contracted the disease, of which 30 died. Appropriate guidelines were set up after this incident.

There are different guidelines in the various countries to ensure water hygiene and to reduce legionella growth. Very detailed guidelines have been devised in Germany and are presented below as an example:

The work sheets of the »Deutsche Vereinigung des Gas- und Wasserfaches e. V« (DVGW) W551 and W552 /15/ list requirements for technology in potable water heating installations to prevent legionella reproduction. The most important are stated here briefly:

- The guideline distinguishes between small and large-scale installations. No particular measures to prevent legionella growth are deemed necessary in small-scale installations. If, however, the volume of the hot water storage tank filled with potable water is more than 400 litres, or if the volume in the hot water piping from the storage tank to the furthest draw-off point is greater than three litres, then it is defined as a large-scale installation.

- The temperature in the standby storage tank of such a large-scale installation is to be kept constantly at a temperature of at least 60°C for thermal disinfection. A temporary reduction by 5°C is permitted. The lowest temperature in the entire network (also in the circulation drainback) may only be 5 K (Kelvin) below the storage tank temperature.

- Pre-heating stages upstream of the standby storage tanks must be heated to a minimum of 60°C once a day. Pre-heating stages are systems in which cold water is only pre-heated before it is heated in the standby storage tanks to the 60°C required. These include installations to utilise waste heat etc. and also the storage tanks of thermal solar installations if they are filled with potable water.

The afternoon hours (approx. 2:00 to 4:00 p.m.) have proved to be the most favourable time for this thermal disinfection of solar storage tanks. This is to use less conventional energy, since at this time, it is highly probable that the storage tanks would have been at least partly pre-heated by solar energy. Normally there is less hot water consumption at this period, which might otherwise prevent the required 60°C being reached. At other times, expected consumption peaks (e.g. late afternoon) would lead to rapid discharge and less opportunity to reach 60°C if the storage tanks were not sufficiently dimensioned.

3.4 Solar Installations Purely for Heating Potable Water

Similar demands occur in summer and winter for hot water for showers, baths and the household. Since there is greater availability of solar energy in summer, it is reasonable to use this energy to heat potable water. Thus the majority of solar installations in Germany serve to provide solar heat for these consumers.

The following examples deal briefly with the principle structure of selected system circuits.

3.4.1 Small-scale Installations to Heat Potable Water with Natural Flow

Thermosyphon installations make use of the density differences between hot and cold heat fluid. The fluid in the collector circuit rises, as heated by the sun. This is due to the lower specific density of the heated fluid compared to the cold. The heated fluid moves into the storage tank above the collector, where it transfers heat – directly or indirectly – and then sinks back to the collector in the drainback piping. This is the 'thermosiphon principle'. Such the natural flow installations work without a pump or controls. Thus they operate without any electrical auxiliary energy for pumping and may be used where no mains electricity is available.

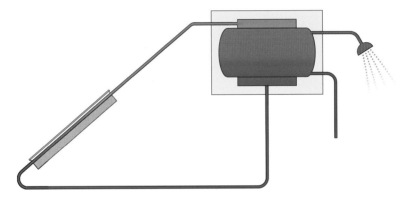

Figure 3.5 Diagram of a natural flow installation with a storage tank arranged above the collector

This very simple principle is used preferably in countries within the hotter climatic zones. Since there is no or only slight danger of frost, the storage tank can be located above the collector on the roof without any difficulty, so long as the roof can support the additional weight from the collectors and mostly from the heavy, filled storage tank.

These systems are usually pre-fabricated and supplied as a complete unit with collector and storage tank combined. The easy assembly and low susceptibility to malfunction are the reasons for the great success of these systems. Installation is particularly easy with traditional houses haveing flat roofs, especially since water installations and tanks are already located on the roofs.

Thermosyphon lifting forces are small. Therefore relatively large pipe cross-sections, with short and straight piping paths are needed to keep flow losses also small. A sufficient inclination between collector and storage tank is necessary. The base of the storage tank should be above the top edge of the collector. The systems generally work more sluggishly than installations with pumps. In addition, it is only possible to limit the temperature in the solar storage tank with the help of thermally controlled valves, if no electrical auxiliary energy is to be used. Of course pressure release valves are always present.

This principle is mostly only used for small solar heating systems. If several collectors are connected in parallel, then these must be connected with exactly the same respective flow resistances to ensure even flow throughout. This is easiest to achieve with equal path lengths of advance and return piping for all collectors. The hydraulic connection becomes more difficult the greater the number of collectors and subsequent pipe lengths, because the lifting forces are possibly no longer sufficient to ensure the flow required. The construction of the collectors should thus be matched to the application (vertical tubes with large cross-section), nevertheless the number of modules which can be used is restricted.

Very simple systems without heat-exchangers can be used in frost-free regions. In these systems hot water for domestic or industrial use flows directly through the collectors. However, this principle requires high standards for water quality and collector corrosion protection. Pollution, or high lime content in the water, can lead to deposits in the absorber tubes and hinder both heat transfer and natural circulation.

Therefore systems are usually fitted with heat-exchangers and operated with antifreeze in the collector loop. 'Tube serpentines' or 'jacket-heat' exchangers are used and these are characterised by low flow resistance and are thus particularly suitable for thermosyphon installations.

3.4.2 Small Installations for Heating Potable Water with Forced Circulation

In this case, small-scale installations are solar heating systems for single family and double family homes (up to approx. $10\,m^2$ collector area) which have a maximum storage tank volume of 400 litres. This limitation (regarding storage tank volume and thus indirectly also collector area) is made in consideration of the DVGW instructions on the legionella problem /15/.

The majority of solar installations have been set up in detached or semi-detached houses, whereby many of the installations correspond to Fig. 3.5. This is a single-storage tank system with potable water filled bivalent storage tanks (solar storage and conventionally heated standby section in one storage tank).

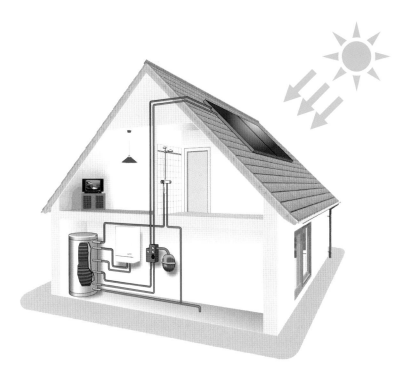

Figure 3.6 Typical construction of small-scale single-storage tank systems for heating potable water

In the case of a single-storage tank system, Fig. 3.6, the collector circulation pump is generally switched on when then temperature in the collector exceeds the temperature in the lower section of the solar storage tank by a pre-set value (e.g. $\Delta T=7\,K$). The pump switches off when this ΔT is less than, say, $3\,K$. A bypass circuit parallel to the collector circulation heat-exchanger which can be installed depending on requirements, can prevent temporary storage tank discharges when the system is switched on in the mornings. The solar heat is transferred directly to the potable water in the bivalent storage tank via the collector circulation heat-exchanger. If the potable water storage tank in the upper section does not reach the target temperature required, then the conventional auxiliary heating kicks in. The temperature in the storage tank is restricted to 65 °C for water with a high lime content to prevent furring. If higher temperatures are permitted, then an admixture valve (cold water mixing) is to be installed as a scale protection device.

Such small-scale installations are available in great variety on the market. Their technology has been perfected and they are, presuming a good track history, easy to install and integrate into existing systems by specialists and also by well-trained laypersons. The maintenance required is slight.

3.4.3 Medium and Large-scale Installations for Heating Potable Water

Installations with a collector field size of more than 10 to approx. 50 m² are defined here as medium-scale solar installations. They are installed in multiple dwellings or also in small hospitals, hostels, commercial buildings etc. in which the daily hot water consumption exceeds 500 litres. Large-scale installations are systems with more than 50 m² collector area.

The technical construction of medium-scale installations may in principle follow that for small-scale systems (solar storage tank carrying potable water). If potable water is to serve as the storage medium, then these systems, in contrast to smaller-scale installations, are double-storage tank systems with potable water solar storage tanks, in which the solar and auxiliary heating storage tanks are separated (see Fig. 3.7). In addition, the internal heat-exchangers are often replaced by external plate heat-exchangers because these can better be adapted to the particular flows in the system and generally have more favourable heat transfer behaviour than internal exchangers. Existing auxiliary heating storage tanks are located downstream of the solar storage tank and can thus continue to be used without modification. Such systems have a simple construction, are easy to upgrade and operate reliably.

Systems with Solar Storage for Potable Water

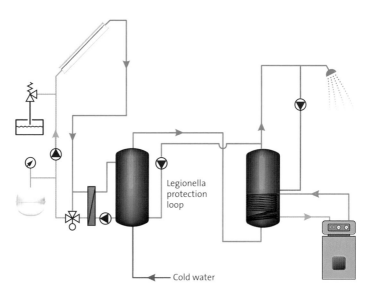

Figure 3.7 Double-storage tank installation with potable water solar storage tank and legionella protection circuit

In the installation diagram of 3.7, as insolation is absorbed, the collectors first heat the closed circuit circulation fluid. The potable water storage tank is then heated via the external collector circulation heat-exchanger,but only after a useful temperature difference has been reached enabling the charge pump to be automatically switched on. The bypass, parallel to the collector circulation heat-exchanger, is only opened if, for example, circulation fluid with a temperature of below +4°C reaches the heat-exchanger from the external piping after a cold winter night, since then there is otherwise the danger of the water freezing on the tank side. This precautionary measure is useful in all installations with long, air-exposed outside piping and only short piping paths in the warm inside of the building. Any auxiliary heating necessary is arranged as in the small-scale installation, however in this case in the separate auxiliary heating storage tank.

However, in the case of such system constructions, legionella protection must be considered. For instance of the German regulations to prevent legionella growth, the entire potable water storage tank (which also includes the relatively large lower solar section of the storage tank) has to be heated to at least 60°C once a day for thermal disinfection. This is required if the storage tank volume exceeds 400 litres and if no other precautionary measures to prevent legionella growth are carried out. Since the storage tank volume is very large, the fraction of solar energy into it can be negatively influenced on average. The energy yield of the solar heating system can thus fall by approx. 15 % as compared with otherwise identical conditions .

This daily heating of the entire storage tank volume can be made with forced mixing of the entire storage tank contents in connection with conventional auxiliary heating (see »Legionella circuit« in Fig. 3.7). Thermal disinfection should be carried out in the later afternoon before the major evening take-off, in order to reduce the solar yield as little as possible. The solar storage tank should be mostly discharged by the morning consumption peak and so the system will switch on at an early stage with commencement of solar radiation. The circulation return in the lower storage tank section should not be used for this heating, since the return temperature for a stand-by storage tank heated to 60°C is always less than 60°C. Thus heating of the lower storage tank section to 60°C would be impossible!

Since large additional potable water volumes are required to store the solar heat, which must be heated to 60 °C once a day using conventional energy, the energy demand of the auxiliary heating may increase, since greater storage tank losses have to be covered conventionally.

Solar storage tanks filled with potable water with a volume of more than 400 litres may be installed without thermal disinfection, if monitoring of the potable water is assured by the operator or if other effective legionella disinfection measures (e.g. UV radiation) are used. Theoretically, installations without any anti-legionella measures can be set up in countries outside the area of application of the DVGW guideline W551. Since, however there is also a legionella risk in these countries, we cannot recommend this.

Since the introduction of the recommendations of DVGW W551, the use of system configurations of Fig. 3.7 in medium-scale installations in Germany has decreased greatly, and they are avoided completely in large-scale installations.

Summary of the advantages and disadvantages of double-storage tank systems with solar potable water storage tanks of Fig. 3.7:

Advantages:

- Lowest possible collector temperatures since there is only one heat-exchanger between collector and cold water
- Simple installation technology
- Omission of discharge control and discharge heat-exchanger
- Lower auxiliary energy consumption compared to buffer system (see below; Fig. 3.8), since there are only two solar pumps

Disadvantages:

- Higher storage tank costs than with buffer systems due to pressure-resistant solar storage tank complying with requirement for potable water hygiene (see below)
- Reduced solar yields when carrying out thermal disinfection (legionella circuit)
- Increased costs and greater control required due to legionella circuit compared to buffer systems

Solar System with Buffer storage

If the potable water volume is to be limited and if the energy use for thermal disinfection is to be reduced, then buffer storage tanks are used to store the solar energy. These may be filled with building-circuit space-heating water instead of potable water (since there is no contact to potable water).

Such a buffer-storage tank system is shown in Fig. 3.8 (without the conventional auxiliary heating system and without the hot water installation).

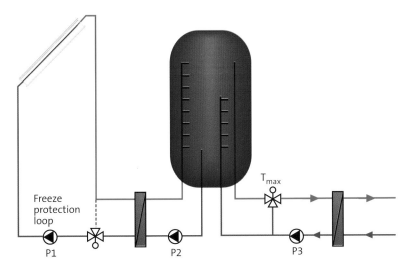

Figure 3.8 Diagram of a solar installation with buffer storage tanks (shown without conventional system)

In buffer-storage tank systems, the heat gained in the collector circulation (where antifreeze is required) is first fed to the solar buffer storage tank via the collector circulation heat-exchanger. Then the energy is transferred via a second heat-exchanger (not necessary if the solar storage tank has potable water) to heat potable water (not shown in Fig. 3.8; see Figs. 3.9 to 3.11). When an adjustable minimum solar radiation level or a useful (adjustable) temperature difference between collector field and buffer storage tank has been reached, then the collector circulation pump switches on and heats the collector circulation. If there is then a useful temperature difference at the input to the collector circulation heat-exchanger, then the buffer charge pump is switched on and the buffer storage tanks are charged. The charge pump and the collector circulation pump switch off simultaneously when the temperature difference between input in the heat-exchanger in the collector circulation and the lower section of the solar buffer falls below a pre-set value. Minimum operating times protect the pumps from intermittent operation (see Chapter 10).

There are differences in the detail of charging of the solar buffer (one feed-in point, two or more feed-in points with temperature-dependent drive or stratifying charging lance; also see Chapter 10.2).

There are several variants for joining of the solar buffer to the hot water system; three of these are shown in Figs. 3.9 to 3.11.

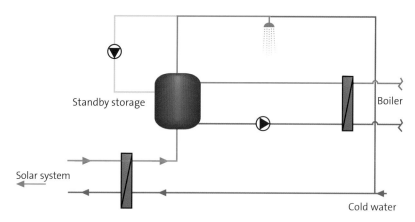

Figure 3.9 Buffer storage tank discharge with instantaneous heating

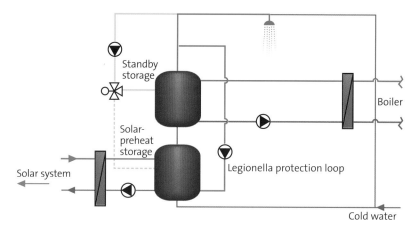

Figure 3.10 Buffer storage tank discharge with storage tank charging principle, with an additional solar pre-heating storage tank

Construction of Fig. 3.9 is easy and inexpensive. The solar installation can be added without modifying the conventional auxiliary heating system. Losses to be covered by conventional energy only occur in the auxiliary heating storage tank, as is the case without solar heating system. This circuit has proved to be the most suitable in comparison to various concepts for auxiliary heating of potable water to the temperature required for consumption. The design considers the maximum degree of utilisation of the solar installation and as little use as possible of conventional energy /16/. These investigations were however carried out using simulation programs which could not take into account the frequent, slight (yet critical) discrepancies which can be expected to occur in practice.

Potable water to be heated, only flows through the discharge heat-exchanger, when hot water is drawn off in the building (instantaneous heater principle). The buffer discharge pump should only operate when a useful temperature level between the upper section of the solar buffer and the cold potable water exists. In addition, it should only be in operation when hot water is drawn off. At the same time, the potable water is to be optimally heated, yet the return in the solar buffer should be cooled to the greatest possible extent. Various control principles for this have been put into use in installations in the research program »Solarthermie−2000«. None of them hase worked completely satisfactorily up to now, even if initially there was optimism (see Chapter 10.3). There is urgent need for further development of such systems.

Large-scale installations (daily hot water consumption $>3\,m^3$) with a great range of short term variations in draw-off rate have operated uncertainly. In particular, there is difficulty concerning the dimensioning of the discharge heat-exchanger (see Chapter 9).

Furthermore, with this circuit, solar energy can only be transferred to the conventional auxiliary heating storage tank when hot water is taken-off. Overcoming of circulation losses outside draw-off times is practically impossible without additional measures even with sufficiently high temperatures in the solar buffer.

Due to still unsolved problems, we can only at present recommend such system circuits for large-scale installations, with restrictions, despite their simple and inexpensive construction with simultaneous high solar fraction (only with careful preliminary investigation and subsequent check of discharge circulation). However, we assume that solutions can be found to the problems mentioned above.

For the system variant of Fig. 3.10, the discharge heat-exchanger is directly linked to (a) the cold water which flows during consumption, and (b) also, at the same time, to a small potable water-filled pre-heating storage tank. The latter can be heated with solar energy regardless of hot water consumption. The discharge of the buffer is controlled by two temperature sensors between the upper temperature in the solar buffer and the lower temperature in the pre-heating storage tank. In this case, water passes across the heat-exchanger both during consumption, and when there is no consumption, Energy can be transferred to the potable water storage via the pump between discharge heat-exchanger and solar pre-heating storage tank. The additional pump also ensures that clear flow relationships exist on the potable water side of the discharge heat-exchanger. This greatly simplifies the design of the heat-exchanger.

The pre-heating storage tank is to be heated to 60°C once a day to reduce the risk of legionella, of regulations applicable in Germany (see »Legionella circuit« in Fig. 3.10).

The return of the hot water circulation should never be used to heat up the lower section of the storage tank, since the return temperature (at 60°C target temperature in the auxiliary heating storage tank) is always below 60°C and thus the storage tank could never be completely heated to 60°C. Thermal disinfection of the pre-heating storage tank may also be carried out directly from the auxiliary heating circulation in the case of an external heat-exchanger for the auxiliary heating.

Since the volume of the pre-heating storage tank is quite small in relation to the solar buffer (10−20% of the buffer), skillful selection of the heating period (e.g. between 4:00 and 6:00 p.m.) assures maximum of solar energy because the hot water consumption that usually occurs in the early evening rapidly empties the pre-heating storage tank. In addition, at this time, it is highly probable that the pre-heating storage tank is still partially charged by solar energy so that little conventional energy is required for this heating to 60°C. The use of conventional energy is only slightly higher due to the temporarily increased storage losses in the pre-heating storage tank shortly after thermal disinfection.

If a somewhat higher temperature is permitted in the solar pre-heating storage tank than in the auxiliary heating storage tank, then part of the circulation losses of the hot water system can be covered by solar energy without any further measures. This is because, on draw-off (but only then!), this temperature reaches the auxiliary heating storage tank. If a higher solar fraction of energy consumption for the hot water circulation is to be achieved, then the circulation return must be fed, temperature-controlled, to the solar pre-heating storage tank (shown in Fig. 3.10 as broken lines). This occurs when the pre-heating storage tank temperature is higher than the temperature in the circulation return. Since, however, the pre-heated volume is relatively small, input of the circulation return can considerably disturb the temperature stratification in this storage tank which may have a negative effect on system efficiency. In addition, systems which were dimensioned just sufficiently for cost / benefit reasons only seldom reach the high temperatures required of approx. 5 K above the level of the hot water circulation return. Therefore such measures are mostly not particularly promising.

In addition, connecting of Fig. 3.10 does not cause any modifications on the conventional auxiliary heating system. However, an additional component is used compared to the system variant of Fig. 3.9. This is the solar pre-heating storage tank with a further pump and a »Legionella circuit«. Although the buffer discharge heat-exchanger now no longer has to be designed for the highest draw-off peaks and is therefore, as is the simpler discharge control, cheaper, there are slightly higher costs for the total system. The increased consumption of conventional energy due to the legionella circuit (heating an additional storage tank with losses) is slight, due to the restricted volume of the solar pre-heating storage tank and its rapid discharge (if heated at a favourable time) (see above).

Despite the slight cost disadvantages of the variant of Fig. 3.9, compared to the variant of Fig. 3.10, we now prefer this circuit, with solar pre-heating storage tank, at present for the normal market. This is because the components are designed straightforwardly and the discharge of the buffer is easier to control (and thus less monitoring is required).

The system variant of Fig. 3.10 can be modified by combining the solar pre-heating storage tank and the conventional auxiliary heating storage tank in one tank (auxiliary heating storage section at the top, pre-heating section with »Legionella circuit« below; see Fig. 3.11). In this case, a slightly greater proportion of the solar energy can be used to cover circulation losses since the solar temperature level also reaches the auxiliary heating section when there is no hot water consumption.

However, the use of such a storage tank presumes that neither the circulation not the conventional auxiliary heating disturbs the temperature stratification in the storage tank. In this case, a particularly high storage form is of advantage. In addition the flows of circulation and auxiliary heating are to be kept as low as possible. Circulation networks are thus to be operated with the maximum permitted temperature difference between the flow (advance) and return and they must be well matched hydraulically. The integration of circulation with too high-flow rate can lead to deterioration in the solar energy yield. Attention must still be paid that these flows are only passed through the upper storage section. If they are fed through the lower storage section (through the solar pre-heating volume) (see negative example in Fig. 3.12), then conventional energy is displaced in this pre-heating section. This prevents the energy transfer from the solar buffer and causes deterioration in the degree of utilisation of the solar heating system. Internal heat-exchangers for the auxiliary heating are of advantage in this case of the storage tank due to the lower mixing.

Since conventional auxiliary heating generally discharges from the bottom of the storage tank, this variant with bivalent pre-heating and auxiliary heating storage is hardly suitable for upgrading so a completely new installation is required.

The circuit with the combined solar pre-heating and auxiliary heating storage tank of Fig. 3.11 only offers slight advantages as compared to the circuit with separate solar pre-heating storage. This is the possibility of slightly higher solar fraction regarding circulation losses (Fig. 3.10). However it has the possible disadvantage of reducing solar heating system efficiency, if installed carelessly. Therefore at present, it can only be recommended with restriction. Investigations of this system variant have not yet been completed and thus no definite statement concerning operating behaviour is possible.

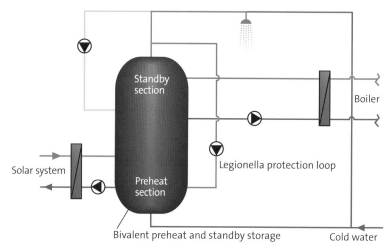

Figure 3.11 Buffer storage tank discharge using the storage tank charging principle and storage tank with combined solar pre-heating and auxiliary heating section

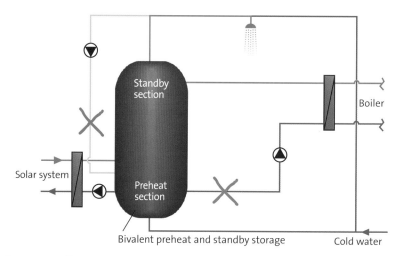

Figure 3.12 Buffer storage tank discharge using the storage tank charging principle Faulty connection of combi-storage tank (thus heating of entire volume using conventional energy)

In both variants, auxiliary heating is already carried out in the hot section of the buffer storage tank or in the discharge circulation of the solar buffer storage tank.

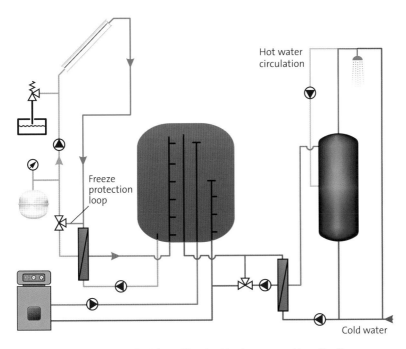

Figure 3.13 Buffer storage tank with auxiliary heating in upper section of buffer

In the installation concept of Fig. 3.13, the auxiliary heating is placed in the upper section of the solar buffer storage tank (or in the hottest buffer storage tank if the buffer volume is distributed over several tanks) and from there the standby storage tank is charged. In this case solar and conventional energy are combined in the buffer storage tank. The auxiliary heating section of the buffer storage tank is heated with conventional auxiliary heating to 70°C, in order to generate a temperature of, say 60°C in the standby storage tank. The discharge heat-exchanger is dimensioned according to the requirements of supply safety for the potable water system. The standby storage tank and auxiliary heating section in the buffer storage tank are also designed with a view to supply safety.

Consider these and similar system circuits, with auxiliary heating in the buffer storage or also in the buffer discharge circulation (only one of the various possibilities is shown in Fig. 3.13). There is an increased danger that conventional energy is displaced in the cold section of the solar buffer. This causes a decline in the solar heating system efficiency /16/. The expense of the control system required (to achieve return temperatures in the solar buffer as low as possible), may be great. Whether such increased control, the poorer system efficiency and the compactness outdo the cost saved by the system construction should be debated.

As part of the research program »Solarthermie−2000«, two installations were set up with conventional auxiliary heating via a heat-exchanger in the buffer discharge circulation. Neither of the installations achieved the guaranteed values for solar yield.

Summary of the advantages and disadvantages of systems with buffer storage tanks of Figs. 3.9 (instantaneous heater principle), 3.10 (separate solar pre-heating storage tank) and 3.11 (combi-storage tank):

Advantages for all buffer storage tank systems:
Lower costs for buffer storage tank compared to potable water storage tank due to the lower pressure and hygiene requirements.

Disadvantages for all buffer storage tank systems:
Two heat-exchangers between cold water and collectors; thus somewhat higher collector temperatures and costs. At least one additional pump at discharge heat-exchanger; thus somewhat higher auxiliary energy consumption.

Instantaneous heater principle (Fig. 3.9)

Advantages:

- No modification of existing conventional system necessary

- Existing conventional stand-by storage tank can continue to be operated unmodified after integration of the solar installation; purely instantaneous systems can be supplemented by the solar installation.

- The solar installation is very easily integrated into the existing potable water network by integrating the discharge circulation heat-exchanger.

- Cold water flows directly over the discharge heat-exchanger. Correct control of the buffer discharge flow can mean that well cooled return reaches the buffer storage tank so that a high solar yield is achieved.

- No legionella circuit necessary for solar heating system

- Very inexpensive system variant

Disadvantages:

- The discharge circulation heat-exchanger must be designed for high peaks of hot water consumption and so it becomes large and expensive particularly for large-scale solar installations. The extent of the draw-off peaks is also unknown (standard values for conventional systems do not provide sufficiently good values), thus they must be determined by measurement with high time resolution.

- In large-scale installations with great short-term fluctuations of consumption rates, the heat-exchanger must ensure optimum energy transfer over a very wide range. This is only possible to a limited extent and with great sluggishness in the case of brief draw-offs.

- Control of the discharge must work very precisely with regard to recognition of a draw-off and an optimum flow on the buffer storage side of the heat-exchanger. Most products do not fulfil these conditions in practice.

- Even at increased temperatures in the potable water outlet of the heat-exchanger, cover of the circulation losses is hardly possible without special measures.

Separate Solar Potable Water Pre-heating Storage Tank (Fig. 3.10):

Advantages:

- No modification of existing conventional system necessary

- Existing conventional stand-by storage tank can continue to be operated unmodified after integration of the solar installation; purely instantaneous heating systems can be supplemented by the solar installation.

- The discharge of the buffer storage tank is possible to a certain extent, independent of the current hot water consumption.

- The buffer discharge heat-exchanger can be kept relatively small and inexpensive, it is also very easy to design.

- The discharge control for the buffer is very simple and inexpensive

Disadvantages:

- The system requires an additional solar pre-heating storage tank, a further pump (charging pump for pre-heating storage tank) and a circuit for legionella disinfection; it is therefore somewhat more expensive
- There are slightly greater storage tank losses to be covered by conventional energy (due to legionella circuit for pre-heating storage tank)
- Temperature mixing may occur in the pre-heating storage tank, such that at times slightly higher temperatures than that of the cold water reach the discharge heat-exchanger even when hot water is consumed. However the difference in efficiency compared with the instantaneous heating system is slight.

Combined solar pre-heating and auxiliary heating storage tanks (Fig. 3.11)

Advantages:

- The same advantages as with separate solar pre-heating storage, however generally cannot be integrated into conventional systems without difficulties
- Cover of circulation losses without any special measures, most likely of all three variants

Disadvantages:

- Generally not easy to integrate into existing conventional systems
- High potential hazard of defects in integrating the various energy flows to the combi-storage tank
- Danger of storage tank mixing with high-flow rates for auxiliary heating and circulation – even with correct connection

3.5 Solar Installations to Heat Domestic Water and for Space Heating

Only basic statements are made in the following on the systems for combined heating of domestic water and space heating and some examples of system circuits are explained in principle. Information on the dimensioning of such installations and their main components as well as operating results of installed systems follows in Chapters 4, 8, 11 and 12.

3.5.1 Basic Information for Systems for Combined Heating of Domestic Water and Space Heating

The heat demand of a building depends to a great extent on the local climate and the building regulations for thermal comfort and insulation.

As already explained in 3.1, better insulation standards are demanded in colder regions. Thus the expected heating demand per m² living area in Scandinavia is slightly less than in Germany and the same as regions of Northern Italy.

In principle there are two different approaches to using solar technology for space heating:

- High solar fraction (50 – 100 %) of total heat consumption (potable water and heating)
  Such a solar fraction can only be achieved with collector areas located on the house roof, if the building is constructed as a low-energy or passive-solar house. In this case, the volume of the large solar storage tank required (to be thermal buffer volume for some weeks) remains in a range which makes integration of the storage tank into the heated inside of the building possible. The relatively high storage losses are therefore used for heating the building.
  However, increasing insulation of the building and possible passive use of solar energy using large window areas facing south, leads to a longer non-heating period during the year. In this case, the heating demand mainly occurs during periods of weak solar insolation and not in periods of strong solar radiation. Without very large solar storage tanks (in relation to heat demand), so having intermediate storage of energy over several weeks, very long stagnation periods occur for the solar heating system and these have a negative effect on installation efficiency and can reduce the system service life.

- Low solar fraction (20 – 50 %) of total heating consumption
  Such systems can also be set up on »normally« insulated buildings (e.g. insulation of 'Heat Insulation Regulations 95'). Collector field areas and solar storage tank sizes only have to be increased moderately, as compared with a system purely for heating domestic water. The standstill periods of the solar heating system during periods of high solar radiation are limited; system efficiency drops relatively slightly compared to potable water systems.

Both variants presume a low-temperature space heating (underfloor heating or large surface area radiators) if good system efficiency is to be achieved. The higher the degree of system utilisation and the solar fraction is to be, the lower the return-temperature from the space heating system must be.

The following arguments favour an enlarged solar heating installation for combined use to heat potable water and for space heating, with the restrictions explained:

- The additional costs of a solar heating installation for combined use for hot water and space heating back-up (low efficiency) are relatively low, particularly for small-scale installations, as compared with a system purely for heating potable water. The specific costs (costs per m^2 collector area) of combined systems are lower than with domestic water installations due to the strong specific cost reduction with increasing system size for small-scale installations. However, at the same time, the specific system yield drops due to the unavoidable standstill periods in summer. If the combined system is designed not to bee too large (i.e. with relatively low solar fraction), these two effects can compensate for one another. Therefore the costs for available solar heat of the combi-system are roughly the same as those of the purely potable water system or only slightly higher.
  However this statement does not apply to large-scale installations in which reduction of system efficiency is not compared to a corresponding decline in specific costs (due to the weaker specific cost reduction with increasing size).

- A large-scale solar heating installation can save considerably more CO_2 than a small-scale solar installation, but may possibly lead to higher costs per unit of CO_2 saved. If the funding available for solar installations is limited, then only one section of several buildings can be fitted with solar technology. Thus it is more favourable, from a potential savings point of view to install small-scale installations of high efficiency on a great number of buildings than to install larger-scale systems on a few buildings at the same cost.

- The systems have been perfected and are mostly easy to integrate.

3.5.2 **Construction in Principle of Solar Installations for Heating Domestic Water and to Back-up Space Heating Systems**

Double Storage System

At the beginning of the development of solar installations to heat domestic water and back-up space heating in the range of lower solar fractions, there was enlargement of the collector area and supplementation of the solar storage tank to heat potable water by a solar buffer storage tank for the heating (see Fig. 3.14).

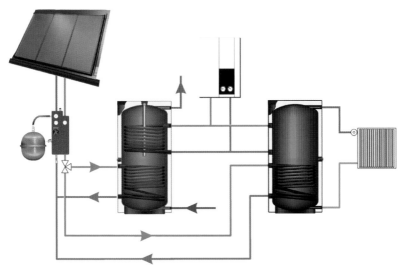

Figure 3.14 Solar installation for potable water heating and back-up of space heating with a potable water tank and a buffer storage tank

As for heating domestic water, in this system the solar potable water storage tank is charged first. When this storage tank has reached the temperature required, a three-way valve in the circulation switches to charging the second (buffer) storage tank. Depending on the availability of solar energy, the buffer storage tank is also charged to a temperature required or a maximum temperature of 95°C. The potable water storage tank is discharged by the consumption of hot water e.g. in the shower or bath. Depending on the control system, charging via the collector circulation switches to charging of the potable water storage tank when this temperature falls.

The buffer storage tank is discharged using the heating control. In simple systems it serves to increase the return of the space heating circulation (also see description of increased return in combi-storage tank system). In addition, it should be possible to transfer the energy collected in the buffer storage tank into the potable water storage tank if needed in non-heating periods (on days with low solar radiation), since otherwise this energy cannot be used during this period. In order to make perfect functioning of the complicated total system possible, a control system should be included in this variant which »recognises« all the components in the system and makes overall control possible. These controls are, however, only available as standard from a few manufacturers.

Combi-Storage System

The combi-storage tank was developed to simplify the construction and control of such installations, as well as reducing the set up space required and costs. Fig. 3.15 shows the diagram of such an installation.

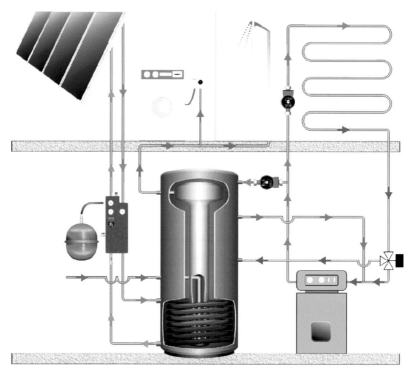

Figure 3.15 Solar installation for heating potable water and to back-up space heating with a combi-storage tank

In these systems, the combi-storage tank is charged as with the »small« solar installation to heat potable water via the collector circulation using a simple temperature difference control mechanism. The maximum temperature in the combi-storage tank is usually set at 95°C. Thus a thermal mixing valve (admixture valve) must be fitted in the potable water network on the hot water side to avoid temperatures over 60°C at the tap (scalding protection).

On the heating side, the combi-storage tank is included in the return of the space heating circulation. The switching of the return of the space heating system into the combi-storage tank return is effected via a simple temperature difference control and a three-way valve as can be seen in Fig. 3.15. If the temperature in the storage tank is e.g. 8 K higher than that in the heating circulation return, then the return is passed through the corresponding section in the combi-storage tank. The temperature of the space heating return is thus increased using solar energy. The heating boiler does not kick in depending on the temperature of the pre-heated return or it only works at a low power level or very briefly. If the return is only e.g. 2 K colder than the combi-storage tank, then the three-way valve in the heating circulation return switches past the solar buffer directly to the heating boiler. Thus undesired heating of the storage tank by the heating boiler is prevented. Heating of the potable water standby section in the combi-storage tank is independent of the use of solar energy for the space heating, by a storage tank charging pump which is controlled by the heating control mechanism as can be seen in Fig. 3.15.

In addition to the storage-within-storage systems of Fig. 3.15, buffer storage tanks with devices for stratified charging and external heat-exchangers to heat potable water as shown in Fig. 3.16 were developed. This stratifying charging means that the upper section of these storage tanks can be rapidly heated to a useful temperature (specific charging to a certain temperature level). The conventional auxiliary heating and the space heating circulation are connected so that they can also discharge the storage tank while maintaining this stratification.

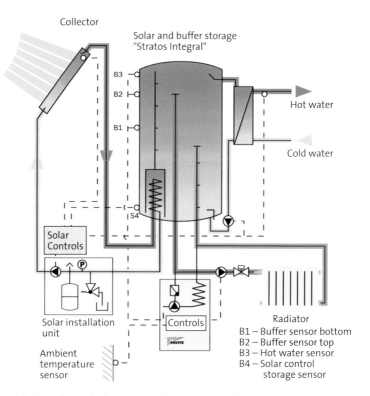

Figure 3.16 Solar installation for heating potable water and to back-up space heating with stratifying charge storage tank /SOLVIS, Germany/

If the buffer or combi-storage tanks are also to serve as buffer storage tanks for the heating boiler and circulation to reduce the number of boiler starts, then the control of the heating boiler or the heating circulation must have a corresponding charging and discharging function. If this function is not present, as with the vast majority of conventional heating control systems, then the buffer storage tank is not recognised as such by the heating system. The buffer volume can in this case only be used by the solar installation; as far as the heating system is concerned, the buffer storage tank is only an extension of the contents of the heating system.

A further step towards integration of solar installations, boilers and storage tanks is taken in systems of Fig. 3.17. The product SOLVIS MAX from SOLVIS Energy Systems represents a pre-fabricated unit for very small spaces with a condensing boiler with an integrated solar installation to back-up the space heating. This and similar products provide compact and easy-to-install systems to utilise solar energy also to back up space heating.

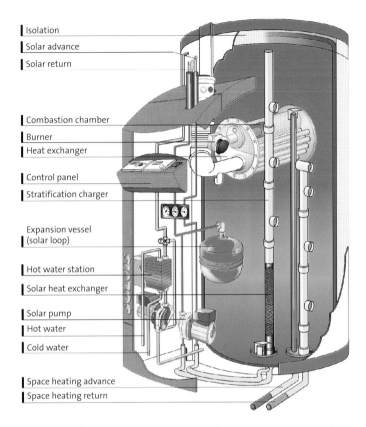

Isolation

Solar advance

Solar return

Combastion chamber

Burner

Heat exchanger

Control panel

Stratification charger

Expansion vessel
(solar loop)

Hot water station

Solar heat exchanger

Solar pump

Hot water

Cold water

Space heating advance

Space heating return

Figure 3.17 Solar installation for potable water heating and back-up for space heating with a buffer storage tank integrated condensing boiler /SOLVIS, Germany/

Solar System with High Solar Fraction

The construction in principle of a solar installation of high solar fraction for potable water heating and space heating is shown in Fig. 3.18.

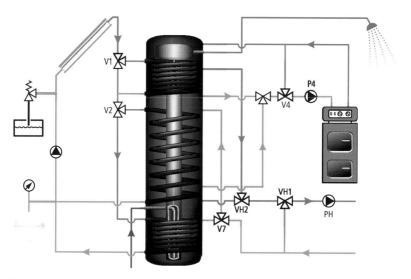

Figure 3.18 Solar installation with high solar fraction for potable water heating and space heating (up to 100% solar fraction)

The collector circulation pump switches on as soon as the collector field is approx. 5 K hotter than the lower storage tank temperature. The three-way valve V1 and optional V2 open to charge the storage tank. This occurs via the internal heat-exchanger, when the temperature in the collector circulation is higher than the corresponding temperatures in the respective storage tank section. Thus the solar storage tank is heated to a temperature of approx. 90°C. The heating pump PH and the two three-way valves/mixer VH 1 and VH2 are driven by the space heating circulation control mechanism (generally ambient-temperature controlled). The two valves are intended to regulate the temperature of the heating advance. The storage tank section is discharged first, which has just sufficient temperature for the consumer's requirements (that is, always the lowest possible section). The return valve V7 passes the space heating return to the lower storage tank section if it can take up solar heat there. If the heating return is hotter than the lower storage tank section, then it is passed to a higher storage tank layer. The valve V7 is not required for a heating return which is always at low temperature e.g. with a radiant heating system.

If the storage tank is discharged during the winter, then the upper storage section can be recharged by the heating boiler. This is effected using pump P4. The three-way valve V4 in this case serves to maintain the boiler return temperature to prevent corrosion damage to the boiler.

The control mechanism of this installation occurs as either an individual or an overall control device.

3.6 Solar District Heating

The term »solar district heating« means the inclusion of solar heating systems in district heating networks. An extensive collection and explanation of the advantages are included in books listed in the Literature: /17, 2/. This also includes the planning stages necessary for the integration of very large-scale solar installations with seasonal storage tanks of various construction types in the heating network.

Some of the following explanations of important aspects of solar district heating originate from these works among others. The descriptions of such solar installations have been kept very brief, since both books contain detailed descriptions of these systems.

3.6.1 Technology for the Integration of Solar Installations in Heating Networks

Solar installations included in district heating networks can achieve solar fractions of up to 50% for the entire energy demand of the heating network (potable water heating and space heating) in connection with extensive heat insulation of the buildings. Such a solar fraction, however, involves very high expenditure. In addition to large collector fields which mostly have to be distributed over several buildings, very large solar buffers are required for the sufficient seasonal storage from summer to winter. These seasonal storage tanks are very costly and often represent difficult tasks for engineers, architects and specialist trades, in both conception and in detail.

In the case of solar district heating networks with low solar fraction (10−25%), the solar buffer volume can be relatively small (depending on the solar fraction required for daily or weekly storage). Since the storage volume can be compiled at a central point and the collector areas are mostly very large, the specific costs of such a large-scale system (with low solar fraction) can be very low; a very favourable price for the solar heat is the pleasing result.

The potential for solar district heating is generally regarded as very good. However, the pre-requisite is the success in producing seasonal storage tanks which are creep resistant and inexpensive. One focus of the research, development and demonstration in the Solarthermie − 2000 program is this area (subprogram 3).

3.6.2 **Examples of the Integration of Solar Installations in Heating Networks**

The integration of solar installations in district heating networks is only dealt with very briefly at this point. Further information can be taken from the literature already mentioned in Chapter 3.6

In the case of conventional heating networks, there is a differentiation into two principles:

- The 4-pipe network (two separate networks for hot water and space heating energy; previously often used in small-scale networks), and

- The 2-pipe network which is customary today with transfer stations for district heating to the space heating and potable water network system in individual buildings or groups of buildings

In the case of conventional 4-pipe networks, a decision can be made as to whether the solar installation is only to heat potable water, as shown in Fig. 3.19, or whether the space heating network is to be backed up. The support for the heating network can be similar to the system described in Chapter 3.5.

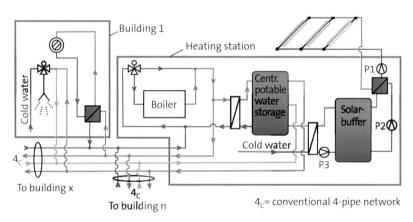

Figure 3.19 Integration of a solar installation purely for potable water heating in a conventional 4-pipe heating network

In the installation of Fig. 3.19, the collector field is installed on the roof of the main heating station. It may also be distributed over the roofs of several buildings. In the latter case, two solar pipes have to be laid in the ground in addition to the four conventional district heating pipes; the collector fields are connected to these.

The collector fields transfer their energy to the buffer storage tank which subsequently pre-heats the potable water (purely potable water heating as in Fig. 3.19) or also additionally raises the temperature of the space heating network return (installation with heating back-up). The pre-condition for good system efficiency with connection to the heating network is a low return temperature in this network, below 40°C if possible.

Control of the system is effected as described above in the corresponding Chapters.

In the case of heating networks with only two pipes from the main heating to the buildings which are customary today, the solar installation can only be connected to the single network return. Otherwise smaller decentralised installations for potable water heating have to be installed in the individual buildings. The installation then automatically covers part of the energy demand for potable water heating and also backs up the space heating.

Since very large collector fields are usually required with these systems, the collectors are distributed over several roofs. Thus two additional district heating pipes for the connection of the collector fields to the central buffer storage tank are required (with the exception of the so-called three-pipe systems). Such a system construction is shown in diagram form in Fig. 3.20.

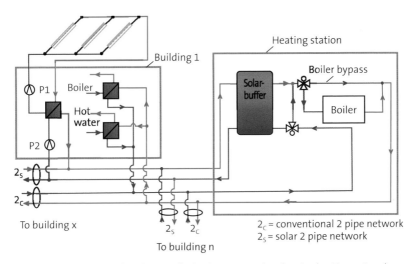

Figure 3.20 Integration of a solar installation in a conventional 2-pipe heating network

Charge control for the buffer storage tank is similar to the manner described in previous Chapters. If the collector fields are similarly inclined and orientated, a central main control device is sufficient for all fields. If the fields are orientated differently, then individual control devices are necessary.

Discharge is effected by the network return being passed through the solar buffer when, and only when, its temperature is a few degrees lower than that in the buffer. If necessary, the required advance temperature is achieved by heating from the conventional boiler. In this process, care must be taken that the auxiliary heating boiler is not cycled too frequently or heated unnecessarily high (for example if there is a preset of a minimum runtime for the boiler). This presumes a well-stepped boiler capacity, and possibly also a return admixture between the solar buffer and boiler. This ensures minimum difference in the temperature of the water flowing into the boiler from the target pre-flow temperature, if auxiliary heating is required at all.

The collector area and buffer volume have to be dimensioned, depending on the required total solar fraction of the complete energy demand of the heating network. In the case of low solar efficiencies between 10 and 20%, daily or weekly storage tanks are sufficient (related to the summer energy demand). These are filled with water as is the case with customary buffer storage tanks. If a higher solar fraction is to be achieved (up to approx. 50%), then seasonal storage tanks have to be used (in connection with correspondingly large collector fields). These store solar heat from summer to winter.

Various storage concepts can be used for seasonal heat storage. The most important aspects are listed briefly in the following. Further information can be taken from the literature /17; 18/.

- Ground-sunk concrete storage tanks, filled with water
- Ground-sunk sealed »troughs« with a gravel-water mixture
- Use of naturally-occurring water layers in the ground (aquifer storage)
- Subterranean caverns blasted into rock
- Embedding subterranean heat exchange probes

The decision in favour of a particular storage system type depends, above all, on the local conditions at the site. This is so with aquifer and subterranean probe storage concerning the geological and hydro-geological subterranean conditions.

For the integration of solar installations in district heating networks with a high degree of utilisation, it is usually necessary that the solar heating system operates with the network return temperature as lowas possible, i.e. less than 40°C. Without space heating in summer, the network return temperature is only determined by the quality of the building heat-transfer stations for hot potable water generation. Therefore it is not sufficient for only the building space heating and the space heating transfer stations to be designed for low return temperatures, since this only affects the total return during the space heating period. Unfortunately in many heating networks, the potable hot water supply replaces the otherwise low temperatures from the space heating system, so the return temperature is too hot (see Chapter 11.4).

If solar heating systems, which are also to partly supply space heating energy demand, are to be integrated into conventional heating networks (2 or 4-pipe networks), then integrated planning is essential. It is essential that the planners of the conventional network, of the solar heating systems and of the building technology work closely together so that the different system requirements and the interactions of the systems can be sufficiently taken into account. Without such co-ordination, it is impossible to achieve high efficiency for the integrated solar heating system.

3.7 Special System Variants

3.7.1 Drain-back Installations

These systems are normally constructed in the same manner as the usual thermal solar installations described in the preceding chapters. The main difference is in the method of operation. In the drain-back installations, the collector is emptied when the pump is switched off. The heat transfer fluid is located in an enclosed subsidiary collecting tank. If the collector is heated by the sun, then the pump switches on, forces the fluid into the collector and the air into the catcher. If the pump switches off, then the collector empties again.

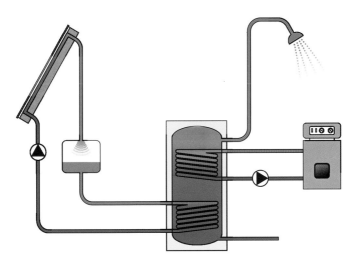

Figure 3.21 Drain-back system in operation

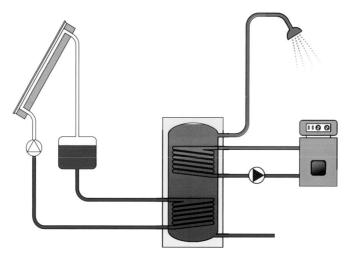

Figure 3.22 Drain-back system during stand still: the collector empties when the pump is switched off

Since in such systems, the collector is only filled with heat-transfer fluid when it is warm, there is no danger of frost if water is used for the heat-transfer fluid. So water can be used in the collector circulation without hesitation; water has more favourable chacteristics for the collector circulation as compared to a water-glycol mixture. In addition, boiling of the heat medium is avoided when the installation is at standstill (e.g. when the maximum storage tank temperature has been reached), since then the collectors are emptied. A further advantage is that when the pump is switched off, no gravity circulation can take place.

If the collector circulation has to be refilled after standstill, then large lifting heights have to be overcome. This presumes the use of particularly efficient pumps. Gear pumps are mostly used; these generally cause more noise during operation than the otherwise customary centrifugal pumps.

Collectors, and the input and output piping, must be very carefully laid out with the necessary inclinations (or necessary descending slopes), so that all air is forced out of the collectors when they are filled and so no pockets of water remain on emptying. If assembly of the piping to the collectors is not carried out with extreme care, then the collector cannot drain completely due to the construction or can only be de-aerated with difficulty. Consequently, there is the danger that the installation will not work properly or that frost damage occurs due to air inclusions.

If several collectors are used, then reliable filling or complete emptying is sometimes difficult to implement. This depends on the collector construction and connections.

4. Basic Principles of Dimensioning Thermal Solar Installations

The dimensioning of solar thermal installations depends on (i) local climatic conditions, especially insolation (solar radiation) and ambient temperature, (ii) heating demand (consumption), (iii) the solar fraction required and (iv) the effectiveness (thermal efficiency) of the system used. Generally rules for system dimensioning cannot be made because of the wide variation in climatic conditions, the great variation in requirement and the major differences in system efficiency.

The procedures associated with dimensioning solar installations and with tackling difficulties can therefore be explained only by using examples and actual experience. However, the statements made can be extended by analogy to differing conditions.

Dimensioning Smaller-scale Solar Installations

The most frequently installed systems world-wide are small-scale installations with less than $10\,m^2$ collector area. They are mainly used to heat water in small residential buildings and detached houses.

Small-scale solar installations are usually dimensioned in various countries and climatic zones by manufacturers and fitters according to location-related rules of thumb and values gained from experience. Detailed dimensioning and consumption measurements are not generally carried out. The installations are often designed for high solar fractions and they are less orientated towards profitability than installations in commerce and public buildings.

Dimensioning Large-scale Solar Installations

Large-scale installations are almost always installed in — literally — »commercial« buildings. They are thus subject to strict requirements regarding profitability and monetary value is placed on these installations on their providing solar heat at favourable costs.

An investigation of over one hundred large-scale installations set up around 1980 in Germany (Future Investment Program, ZIP), has shown that solar installations were, almost without exception, dimensioned too large. Dimensioning was typically based on the following assumed values:

- Hot water consumption of 50 litres per day and per person at 60°C

- Annual mean daily insolation on the array of only approx. $3\,kWh/(m^2{\cdot}d)$

The result of this dimensioning was that the solar installations were much too large for summer operation, since (a) the assumed consumption was never reached and (b) the solar insolation is much more than 3 kWh/(m2 d) in the summer. The thermal efficiency of these installations was usually poor. Overall, the very high costs of the available solar heat were mainly caused by the incorrect dimensioning and the frequent unfavourable integration of the solar installation into the existing conventional system, rather than poor components.

4.1 Differences in Dimensioning Conventional Installations and Solar Installations

Conventional water heaters can be switched on whenever required and their output may be regulated, whereas a solar heating system always and only captures energy in daylight and according to the strength of the insolation. Even when no energy is required by the thermal storage, the array captures heat when the sun shines; this heat is then, at high collector temperature, given off to the surroundings without being used. Thus there are different rules for dimensioning a solar installation as compared to a conventional system. This is not often considered in the planning of a solar installation.

Supply reliability is central to the dimensioning of conventional energy systems. That means that a conventional system must also be capable of covering every demand even during high rates of consumption, since otherwise users complain.

These demands on the conventional system are taken into consideration by:

- fixing the energy consumption relatively high (in the upper range of the assumed spread)
- calculating the dimensioning energy demand for the period with the highest value (generally winter)
- including additional factors for secure supply (although not usually specified) in the dimensioning of the energy system
- considering a possible expected extra consumption (e.g. due to possible expansion plans)

In contrast, the requirement in solar technology is that the system should not provide any more energy than is required in periods of low demand so that high temperature stagnation of the collector array is avoided. The exception is with systems having very large storage tank capacities designed to supply through long periods with weak solar radiation or installations to back up space heating, (see below). Solar installations which have been dimensioned too large and have frequent periods of stagnation (i) are unnecessarily expensive, (ii) have a poor annual efficiency, (iii) lead to high costs for the available solar heat and (iv) are subject to considerably greater thermal loading, particularly during periods of stagnation (with possible reduction in service life). They also react more sensitively to reduced consumption, minor system defects or deficiencies in regulation.

In a conventional energy system complete cover of the energy demand is aimed for. However, with solar installations there are different target values for dimensioning. The system can be dimensioned for:

- a required solar fraction or
- as high a yield per m^2 collector area as possible, which, especially for large-scale systems, is synonymous with low costs for the available solar heat generated

The available roof area itself is never a variable parameter in the dimensioning of a solar installation. The available roof area may only represent a maximum limiting value.

It is relatively easy to plan technically a solar installation with a high solar fraction: the system design is enlarged until the solar fraction required is obtained (e.g. according to simulation program). Therefore the following Chapters mainly deal with the requirements for »high specific yield« and »low costs for available solar heat«. These targets require considerably more design and care than obtaining higher solar fraction.

4.2 Use of Conventional Standard Demand Data for Solar Technology

The use of consumption values from the standards, guidelines of literature of conventional heating technology is discussed here, using the example of potable water heating.

There are several instructions in regulatory publications for estimating hot water consumption:

In Germany:
(e.g. in VDI 2067 Sheet 12 and DIN) in more recent literature sources, a hot water consumption (referring to 60°C) is given as approx. 50–60 litres per person and per day with a spread from 20 to 80 l/(p·d).

This range only approximately corresponds to our experience if detached and semi-detached houses are included. However, this does not infer a mean value of ((80+20)/2) = 50 l/pd. Instead this mean value should have been determined for the various types of houses with a weighted mean of all individual values. If a straightforward average is taken, then all values go into the mean consumption Figure with the same weighting. This includes a few extremely high values without specification of building size, which is completely misleading for practical applications in solar technology. Since, according to measurements in Germany (see Chapter 4.3.4), daily consumption per person in large multiple residential houses is only 20–33 litres per person on an annual average, it can be presumed that the weighted mean is considerably less than 50l/(p·d).

The mean values in the German guideline VDI 2067 Sheet 12 are set substantially lower than 50 l/(p d) and are a good representation of reality. Depending on the facilities in the apartment approx. 30–60l/(p·d) at only 40°C is the region of the weighted mean! This corresponds to approx. 18–36l/(p·d) at 60°C). These values coincide well with our experience and others from Austria and Germany /19, 20/.

Yet even more recent »standard values« for conventional installation technology cannot replace careful measurement; even if the spread is stated correctly since, as also shown by VDI 2067, the range of the scatter is very great. In addition, the summer periods of weak loading, which are important for solar technology, are not taken into consideration in these values. Older »standard values« should not be used any more under any circumstances.

Only in the case of new building plans, in which measurement is not possible, can the mean values (30–60l/(p·d) at 40°C) be used for residential buildings, after deduction of approx. 20% for the reduced loading in summer and after, if necessary, conversion to a storage temperature of, say, 60°C. Even so, in such cases, we recommend using our tighter set of dimensioning figures (see Fig. 4.4 in Ch. 4.3.4 and Table 4.4 in Ch.4.3.3). This statement only applies to large multiple residential buildings. In single family homes, double family homes or small multiple residential buildings, individual adaptation is recommended if economic aspects are to be considered.

4.3 Solar Installations Purely for Heating Potable Water

4.3.1 Basic Principles to avoid Over-dimensioning

Over-dimensioning of a solar installation to heat potable water can only be avoided if the hot water consumption in existing buildings is measured. This should be done either (a) in periods of low consumption in summer (best), or (b) at other times. If the latter, then the data should be converted to the expected values in the summer period of weak loading (see Ch. 4.3.2); but such conversion, rather than direct measurement, is only warranted due to pressure of time. The system should be dimensioned to these weak-loading values, if a high degree of utilisation is to be achieved (i.e. high yield per square metre of collector area for maximum substitution of conventional fuel and thus higher value per square metre of collector area in preventing emission of pollutants). The fluctuations in specific consumption (per person) for buildings are so great in our experience (up to a factor of 2; see Fig. 4.4 in Ch. 4.3.4), that measurements should not be dispensed with in the case of existing buildings. If consumption cannot be measured for a planned building, the following must be taken into account in planning a solar installation:

- dimension the system for consumption in the lower proportion of the consumption distribution for buildings having similar use
- use the energy demand in summer periods of weak loading for dimensioning (least loading because insolation is a maximum and cold-feed water is warmest at this time)
- make safety of load also, so that collector stagnation is unlikely during the summer periods of weak loading
- consider the possibility of both extra and also reduced consumption (e.g. due to planned installation of energy-saving fittings)
- take into account pre-heating stages or other changes in temperature level of the cold and hot water (particularly in summer, see Chapter 4.3.3)

4.3.2 **Relevant hot Water Consumption**

The hot water consumption in summer is generally decisive for dimensioning for solar installations, since the greatest danger of over-heating is posed during this time. Beware of the significant fluctuations in seasonal consumption. Thus the measurement period for consumption should be selected so that the period of weak loading in summer, which is so important for dimensioning, is registered. However, this is not always possible if considerable delays of several months are to be avoided under certain circumstances. In many cases, therefore consumption in summer must be concluded from measurement data from some other periods.

Note that the output of the hot water storage tank is normally the measurement point for hot water consumption; see Ch. 4.3.3.

Some factors must be taken into account in converting consumption values to the summer period of weak loading:

- In winter the cold water temperature is generally lower than in summer. In Germany a difference of approx. $7-8\,K$ between summer and winter was measured. At a constant target temperature in the hot water storage tank (e.g. $60\,°C$), less cold water has to be added in winter to achieve a temperature of approx. $40\,°C$ at the draw-off point. Thus, with constant draw-off volume, the energy throughput of the storage tank automatically increases in winter by approx. 10 to 12 %.

- In winter, showers are generally taken at a somewhat higher temperature and baths are taken more often than in summer, so this may result in a further winter increase of approx. 5−10% in buildings in which the shower water consumption accounts for the principle part of hot water consumption. Yet in some patterns of use, baths or showers may be taken more often on warm summer days.

In total an increase in daily hot water throughput through the standby storage tank results due to the above mentioned factors alone of approx. 15−20% from Summer to Winter.

Overall the daily energy consumption for potable water heating increases in winter, as compared with summer, by approx. 30−35% (approx. 15−20% due to the change in quantity, a further approx. 15% due to the greater temperature span).

Fig. 4.1 shows the standardised water throughput through the conventional hot water storage tank for a large residential building. The mean value of the approx. 6-week period of weak loading was set to 100%. The determination of the summer consumption for dimensioning by taking the mean of approx. 6 summer weeks may lead to some short periods of stagnation for the collector array. Dimensioning for the absolute consumption minimum would prevent this, however the solar installation would then be under-dimensioned too much for the remaining periods and the solar fraction would fall to a very low level. The method selected in this case represents a reasonable compromise between preventing stagnation and increasing the solar fraction.

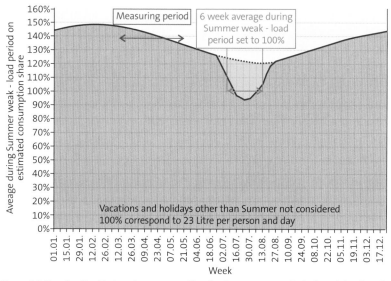

Figure 4.1 Standardised hot water consumption for the summer period of weak loading for a large residential building

If measurements cannot be carried out in the summer period of weak loading, then Fig. 4.1 offers the possibility of converting measurement data from any other period to the values to be expected in the summer holiday period.

Example for the measurement period illustrated in Fig. 4.1 are from dates of approx. 9.4. to 21.5.:

Mean measured consumption in these 6 weeks: 6 m^3/d
Relative consumption in the measurement week
related to consumption in the summer period
of weak loading: 138%
                                                (read from Fig. 4.1)

Probable consumption in the summer period
of weak loading: 6 m^3/d/1.38 = 4.3 m^3/d

Since summer holidays vary in individual countries, a mean holiday period had to be selected in Fig. 4.1. A period from approx. 10.7. to 20.8. was defined. The theoretical regime in this 6-week period (excluding the reduction due to holidays) has been drawn as a broken line. If holidays were, say, in August/September and measurements were made in, say, July, then the % value for the measurement data correction would be read at the broken line.

This graph can also be applied analogously for countries in the Southern hemisphere or countries with different holiday periods, for example by shifting the time axis by 6 months.

The measurements (regardless of which period) should be carried out over a period of approx. 4 weeks if possible and not, of course, in periods with particular consumption conditions such as other holiday periods or public holidays not considered in Fig. 4.1. The registration of daily totals suffices for the time selectivity of the measurement values, unless the particular design of the solar installation presumes different selectivity or completely atypical daily patterns. However, generally it can be assumed that a daily pattern as shown in Fig. 4.2 (which only applies for a very large residential building) reflects the daily regime of the draw-off with sufficient accuracy, even though there are considerable deviations in the daily pattern even with similarly used buildings. Actual deviations from this standardized regime for a particular residental building, usually have only a slight effect on the yield of the solar installation or the yield calculations with simulation programs, unless they are extremely and unusually large.

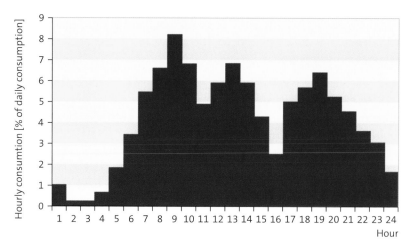

Figure 4.2 Typical daily regime of the half-hourly hot water consumption quantities, standardised to the total daily consumption in the case of very large residential buildings in Germany (data in % of daily consumption)

Similar annual regimes, for the hot water volume flowing through the storage tank shown in Fig. 4.1 were determined for many other types of buildings, e.g. old peoples' homes, hospitals etc. In individual cases, and above all for special types of buildings (e.g. student hostels, sports centres, hotels etc.), these relatively constant curves may however be superimposed by greatly varying user behaviour and greatly fluctuating numbers of users in the annual regime (e.g. very great decline in occupancy in semester holidays; use of outdoor sports facilities instead of indoor facilities in the summer, increase in occupancy in hotels in holiday periods and many others).

It has been shown, that hot water consumption may fluctuate both in quantity and regime, over a wide range at otherwise similar facilities in a country. Even greater differences are to be expected in different countries and climatic zones. Thus it is impossible to make generally applicable statements at this point; this requires many more detailed investigations. At this stage, we will explain the significance of an accurate consumption registration and set out a general procedure.

4.3.3 Measurement of Relevant Consumption
At least the following parameters should be measured in determining consumption:

- Volume flow through the water heater
- Temperature at the outlet of the water heater (usually at the storage tank)
- Temperature of the water flowing into the water heater (usually cold water)

- If possible: the number of residents
- Circulation losses, in systems which are specially designed for solar partial coverage of circulation losses

Since the solar installation is generally integrated in the consumption network upstream of the conventional auxiliary heating system, it can only heat the quantity of water which flows to this integration point. Thus it is important that only the volume which flows through the conventional water heater is measured, since this value determines the consumption for dimensioning the solar installation (see principle Figures in Ch. 3.4). The volume at the draw-off point itself is not relevant, since at this point small or great quantities of cold water are added – depending on storage tank temperature – and this cold water would not flow through the solar installation.

Storage tank throughput, with the same draw-off volume, is smaller, the higher the storage tank temperature is above the draw-off temperature (generally approx. 40°C). The storage tank temperature together with the volume and the input temperature of the water to be heated, determine the energy consumption for which the system is dimensioned. These values must also be registered in the preparatory measurements. Subsequent changes to the storage tank target temperature affect the capacity of the solar installation.

Table 4.1 states the water quantities for the three different storage tank temperatures if 1,000 l hot water at 40°C is drawn off at the draw-off point.

Temperature in storage tank [°C]	[40] theoretical	45	50	55	60
Storage tank throughput at cold water temperatures of: 14°C in summer / 6°C in winter [l]	1,000 / 1,000	839 / 872	722 / 773	634 / 694	565 / 630

Table 4.1 Storage tank throughput for a storage tank at 1,000 l draw-off volume (40°C) and different temperatures in the storage tank (cold water in summer: 14°C; in winter: 6°C)

It can be seen that an increased storage tank temperature reduces throughput through the storage tank and that the storage tank throughput rises with decreasing cold water temperature (see Ch. 4.3.2). In order to minimise energy losses in the hot water system it would be useful to keep the storage tank temperature as low as possible. However due to water hygiene reasons, maintaining an outlet temperature of 60°C is recommended. Thus this value is usually set in larger buildings.

Hot water consumption is frequently derived from other indirect measurements, e.g. the energy measured for the entire hot water system or from the total water consumption (cold and hot water) in a building.

These methods are useless since, (a) the measurements include the proportion of circulation losses which vary greatly between buildings and (b) the calculation must be made using so-called »standard values«. The latter are taken from the literature, for the proportion of hot water consumption in the total water consumption, which is only sometimes applicable. Such estimates can thus under no circumstances replace a direct measurement.

The correct positioning of the volume meter and temperature sensor is decisive for the accuracy of the measurement (see Fig. 4.3). The correct position for the hot water meter is at the cold water input to the stand-by storage tank. There should not be any unblocked branches between the flow meter and the input of the cold water pipe into the stand-by storage tank, and, of course, there should not be any additional flow with the following exception. If the circulation return does not lead directly into the hot water storage tank, but upstream of the storage tank into the cold water pipe instead, then the measurement point has to be set so that the circulation volume is not included in the registration. The flow meter should not be installed in the hot water outlet of the storage tank since it would also measure the circulation flow at this point. This position is only permitted (but not intended) if the circulation volume is measured separately with a second meter in the circulation return. A volume meter installed at the correct point can be used subsequently for measurement in the solar installation.

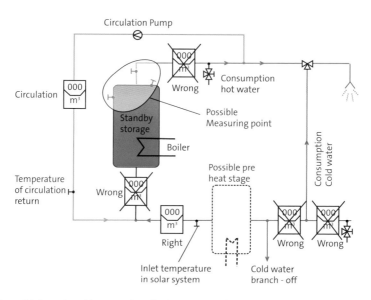

Figure 4.3 Correct and incorrect installation positions for the measurement sensor for consumption measurement

In the case of larger buildings, we also recommend registering the circulation losses (volume, advance and return temperatures) since they provide interesting information on the condition of the hot water network and allow great savings potentials to be recognised.

The manufacturer's specifications are to be observed when installing the volume meter. It is particularly important to carefully estimate the nominal flow of the meter. Since the piping is mostly over-dimensioned, a nominal width one stage lower suffices for the meter. If the meter is selected clearly on too large a scale, then there is the danger that small flows are not registered and the measurement is inaccurate.

In order to determine the hot water consumption in the measurement period, the total quantity during this period is divided by the number of measurement days to obtain a mean value. Thus in principle, it is sufficient if the meter reading is registered at the beginning and at the end of the measurement period. However, we recommend daily readings since, firstly, exceptional days can then be recognised and eliminated from the calculation and secondly differences between working days, Saturdays, Sundays and public holidays become apparent. Some simulation programs can take such differences into account in the yield calculation.

For the temperature measurement in the hot water storage tank, it is usually sufficient if several water samples are taken at the outlet of the storage tank (draw-off point without cold water addition) and a mean value from the measurements taken. Such measurement is then sufficiently accurate if the storage tank temperature is kept nearly constant over the day. The cold water temperature can also be determined by taking several draw-off samples in the course of a day. Water should be drawn off at different times during the day, at a draw-off point near the storage tank input, to record the variation of the cold water temperature. The scatter provides information on the cold water pre-heating due to the absorption of energy in the ambient air.

In particular cases (e.g. if pre-heating stages are present) more accurate selectivity may be necessary.

4.3.4 Recommended Consumption Values for Dimensioning

This Chapter only deals very briefly with the recommended consumption values for dimensioning systems for potable hot water only. Considerably more detailed information concerning hot water consumption can be found in the literature.

In the previous Chapters it was pointed out several times that the range of daily hot water consumption per person is rather large even in buildings used similarly. The range for the consumption in some types of buildings in Germany determined within the framework of the research program »Solarthermie 2000« is shown in Fig. 4.4.

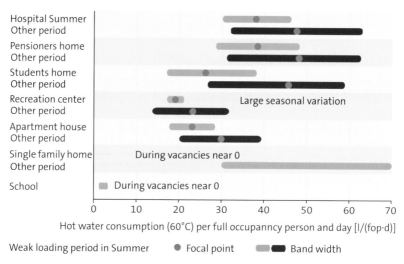

Figure 4.4 Daily hot water consumption per full occupancy persons (fop) in various buildings during the summer period of weak loading

The daily consumption figures in Fig. 4.4 were related to the number of planned full occupancy persons (fop) and not to the number of persons actually living in the building in the individual weeks. The number of full occupancy persons corresponds, for example to the number of beds in a hospital, or to the planned occupancy figure in a residential building (see below). We selected this reference figure, since this is generally the only figure the planners receive from the operator for the dimensioning of the solar installation. In the case of a planned new building, there are no other figures. In the case of existing buildings, the number of actual occupants is frequently available, however this is often not notified to outsiders. In the case of large residential buildings, the number of persons who actually live in the individual flats is mostly unknown. In this case, usually only the planned full occupancy number (number of residential units multiplied with planned persons per residential unit) is available as a planning value. In Germany the figures for the number of persons per residential unit in the VDI Guideline 2067 Sheet 12 can be used. The values from DIN 4708-2 (10/79) are obsolete and set much too high.

Thus for a planner, it is usually only possible to calculate using the number of full occupancy persons (as a fixed planning figure) and using a consumption during the period of weak loading related to this full occupancy number. This consumption value per full occupancy person does not correspond with varying occupancy to the actual consumption per resident present. However this is completely irrelevant for the dimensioning of the solar installation since in this case, only the absolute daily total of energy consumption (for hot water supply) is important.

Figure 4.4 Demonstrates clearly how important it is to carry out measurements in the case of existing buildings, since the great spread in experience hardly permits a matched dimensioning in individual cases.

The consumption range is relatively small in large residential buildings. The relatively large scatter in the case of, say, hospitals depends greatly on the considerable differences in the facilities in these buildings (bathing departments, therapy pools, hospital-own laundry etc.). The relatively low value in student hostels is caused by the reference to the full occupancy persons. In the period of weak loading used as a basis here (summer semester holidays) the full occupancy number is of course considerably higher (by approx. the factor 2; the factor greatly depends on the type of university and on the attractiveness of the location) than the number of students actually present. Values approximately twice as high would result per resident present.

Based on the results from the research program »Solarthermie 2000«, the values for hot water consumption in the summer period of weak loading listed in Tab. 4.2 are recommended for dimensioning a solar installation (reference temperature: 60°C). However, these values should only be used if, no measurements are possible, e.g. for a planned new building.

Only if it is certain that consumption will be higher than normal due to special facilities connected to the hot water supply system (e.g. therapy pools in hospitals), should upward deviations be made from the values in Tab. 4.2, without however overestimating the additional consumption.

	Hospital	Old peoples' home	Student hostel	Holiday hostel	Residential building
Specific consumtion l/(fop·d)	30−35	30−35	20−25	20−30	20−25

Table 4.2 Recommended daily hot water consumption for the dimensioning of a solar installation per full occupancy person (l/(vp·d); 60°C); determined from summer period of weak loading in Germany

In order to obtain the absolute daily consumption (l/d), the Figures in Table 4.2 only have to be multiplied with the plan full occupancy figure (not with expected actual occupancy figures, which are mostly unreliable anyway!). The advantage of our reference to the full occupancy figure for planning tasks becomes clear in this simple calculation. It makes speculation about the expected actual occupancy superfluous.

4.3.5 **Dimensioning of Collector Array and Solar Storage Tank**

The following text only deals briefly with the dimensioning of the most important components (collector array and solar storage tank). More detailed information on dimensioning these and also other system components (also the components not mentioned above) can be found in the literature /2/.

Collector Array

The size of the array decisively influences the dimensioning of the other system components. The stipulation of the array should thus be carried out very carefully. In the case of large installations, the general aim is to keep the costs for available solar heat as low as possible. The following dimensioning proposals have been devised with this in mind. However there is nothing against setting up a larger dimensioned system (within limits) if money or economy play an unimportant role and if one is prepared to bear the increased risk of a possible reduced system service life due to more frequent collector stagnation in the system.

The dimensioning proposals devised here apply to large-scale installations with more than $50\,m^2$ collector; they are only for potable water heating in Germany and regions with similar solar radiation conditions. Medium-scale installations are always dimensioned more generously in consideration of more favourable solar heat costs with decreasing size, until finally the maximum factor of 2 is achieved for detached and semi-detached houses compared to large-scale installations.

The reason for this change in dimensioning can be seen in the (decreasing) graphs for the specific system costs (costs per m^2 collector area). Fig. 4.5 shows specific costs depending on the system size. Since the values greatly depend on the components selected, on the system structure, on the connection to the conventional system, on the installation conditions and also on the labour cost level at the location, a range was drawn in Fig. 4.5 which should apply to most systems.

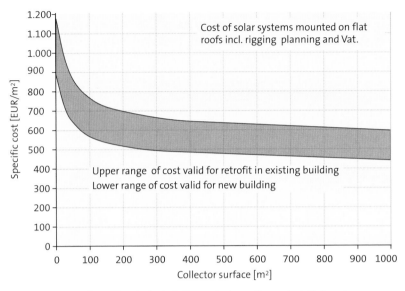

Figure 4.5 Range of specific solar installation costs depending on installation size (costs incl. planning and incl. VAT)

In principle, the specific costs of a solar installation decrease with increasing installation size, since some components are not more expensive in a linear relationship to installation size. This decrease is steeper in small-scale installations as compared to large-scale installations. However, the energy yield per unit area also decreases if an installation is dimensioned more generously since the working temperature of the system increases and collector stagnation occurs more frequently. These two tendencies, one specific cost-reducing and one specific yield-reducing, with increasing size should finally lead to an optimum for specific installation dimensioning.

If economic aspects are also to be considered, as is mostly the case for large-scale installations (mainly installed in »commercial« areas), then it is a question of finding an installation for a given dimensioning consumption in which an optimum cost/benefit relationship results. In other words: the minimum cost for available solar heat is sought.

It can be assumed in principle that a large-scale solar installation, in which the specific cost decrease with increasing size is only small, will be most economical when the system always produces useful energy, when useful radiation is available.

This leads to the following estimate:

- On a high-radiation summer day, approx. 7−9 kWh solar radiation fall on each square metre collector area depending on location.

- A system purely for heating potable water with sufficient dimensioning (without periods of stagnation) has a degree of utilisation of approx. 50 % on such a day, that is it supplies roughly 3.5−4.5 kWh useful heat per m^2.

- This energy must be taken up completely (or at least excluding a slight surplus quantity to be stored) by the user on such a day, if too large (expensive) storage tank volumes are not to be installed.

- In summer, the cold water is, for example, heated from approx. 12−14 °C to mostly 60 °C in the conventional storage tank (temperature increase by approx. 46 to 48 K). This requires approx. 55 Wh per litre of water.

- With 3.5 to 4.5 kWh, approx. 64 to 83 l hot water can be supplied at 60°C (starting from approx. 13 °C).

- If there is no over-dimensioning, then it must be ensured that there is a hot water consumption of approx. 60−80 l per square metre of collector area at a temperature increase of approx. 13 °C to approx. 60 °C (heating span approx. 47 K). The specific load of the solar installation (see Ch. 3.2) should be around 70 l(d·m^2) under these assumptions.

It becomes clear from the above estimate, that the heating span must be considered in the determination of the specific load (litre of cold water to be heated per square metre collector area). The dimensioning load of approx. 70 l/(d·m^2) must be adapted if deviations from the summer »normal value« of approx. 47 K occur (e.g. if water is only heated to, say, 50°C in the conventional storage tank) or if the cold water flowing in is considerably above 14°C (e.g. at 24 °C) due to location or upstream pre-heating stages.

Example:

Normal values: heating in storage tank to 60 °C;
        heating span: 47 K
        specific load: 70 l/(d·m^2)

New values: heating in storage tank to 50 °C
        or cold water temperature 24 °C
        new heating span: 37 K
        new specific load: 70 l/(d·m^2)·47 K/37 K=89 l/(d·m^2)

In order to be able to check this logical starting point, calculations for solar installations of various sizes with a fixed specified consumption of 11 m^3/d at 60°C in the summer period of weak loading were carried out using simulation programs. To determine the system costs, the costs of various components were determined from some installations of suitable size. The individual component costs were adapted to the changed system scale on a linear or non-linear basis depending on their dependency on the system scale. These calculations were carried out for two solar hot water networks one with and one without circulation.

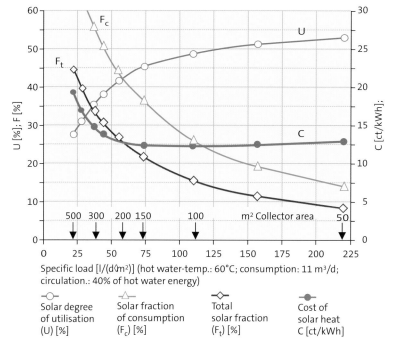

Figure 4.6 Degree of utilisation, solar fractions and costs of available solar heat in solar installations of different sizes and constant consumption (average component quality)

Fig. 4.6 shows – with the exception of solar fraction – the results only for the system without circulation losses. The solar fraction of the energy consumption of the hot water system changes when the circulation losses are taken into account. This is mainly because then the energy demand, to which the available solar energy is related, increases (see Ch. 3.2). If circulation is included for collector areas of less than approx. $250\,m^2$ the other parameters shown in Fig. 4.6 are only slightly effected. Even at $500\,m^2$ collector area, and specific load only $22\,l/(d{\cdot}m^2)$, the relative deviations are only approx. 5%.

Only a very weakly defined minimum for the costs of available solar heat results from the calculations carried out. This minimum is at $120-130\,m^2$ collector area for the daily consumption of $11\,m^3$ hot water specified in this case. Since, however, this minimum is very flat, slight changes to the system or to the operating conditions may shift its position very easily. However it is certain that the minimum will hardly be lower than at $50\,m^2$, and not at higher values than $200\,m^2$. At $11\,m^3/d$ hot water consumption this also means that in the case of installations of this size, at least a consumption of approx. 50 and at the most roughly 200 litres hot water with a heating span of approx. 47 K, must be available per square metre collector area.

The following dimensioning can be defined as a compromise between economic optimum and suitably high solar fraction under the conditions stated:
70 l daily hot water consumption in the period of weak loading (with $\Delta\vartheta=47\,K$) per $1\,m^2$ flat collector area

This value of $70\,l/(d\cdot m^2)$ (designated as specific load) is not far from the lowest value in the above mentioned range, however offers sufficient scope to the lowest limit so that any decline in consumption due to falling occupancy, optimisation of fittings etc. does not yet lead to over-dimensioning of the solar installation. This has been justified without doubt in practice.

In the case of different values of $\Delta\vartheta$, a measured volume must be converted correspondingly or the dimensioning load must be re-defined according to the example stated above.

If this dimensioning proposal is related to the energy of the hot water instead of to the hot water volume, then the following relation results: depending on region, approx. 3.5 to 4.5 kWh daily draw-off energy consumption for hot water per $1\,m^2$ collector area.

This corresponds approximately to the useful energy which such a dimensioned solar installation can provide on a high-radiation summer day (approx. $7-9\,kWh/(m^2\cdot d)$ insolation on the collector area). Since this energy value includes the temperature difference, a measured energy (in contrast to measured volume) does not have to be converted to any different temperature conditions.

In the case of this installation load (correspond to some $150\,m^2$ collector area for the installation according to Figure 4.6) an annual degree of utilisation of the solar installation of approx. $45\%-55\%$ (depending on component quality and location) and a solar fraction (referring to the energy for the hot water drawn off) of $30-40\%$ can generally be expected. Depending on the local insolation, this means that an installation thus dimensioned can supply approx. 450 to 650 kWh useful energy per square metre collector area per year.

At this point it is again expressly pointed out that this dimensioning recommendation only applies to large-scale solar installations (collector area $>100\,m^2$ or hot water consumption $>7\,m^3/d$). In the case of small-scale installations, the cost minimum shifts somewhat towards lower specific load.

If part of the circulation losses in the hot water network are to be covered by solar energy, then particular action is required for systems with buffer storage tanks (e.g. additional heat exchanger to heat the circulation return from the buffer, reversing valve to drive this heat exchanger, temperature difference controller etc.). Even if the system is enlarged correspondingly, it will only be possible to cover part of the circulation losses on sunny days, since there must be temperatures of at least over 60°C in the buffer if the circulation return is to be heated to e.g. 55°C using solar energy. The benefit of such measures will thus remain relatively slight, however the system costs increase and the system becomes more complicated and has more components to go wrong. However in principle – excluding economic aspects – there is nothing against the active integration of the circulation return in the solar installation.

However, planners or operators (sometimes also subsidy guidelines) frequently specify a total solar fraction of 60% of the annual energy consumption for hot water generation, usually due to ignorance of the factors mentioned above. It must be remembered that the total solar fraction does not only refer to the available solar heat generated and to the consumption of energy for hot water drawn off, but also to the sum of draw-off and circulation energy losses, including losses from the conventional hot water storage tank. Figure 4.7 shows that the frequently stated solar fraction of 60% (even if only referring to the draw-off energy) is only achieved with a system which is larger, by a factor of more than 2 (350 m^2) than recommended by us and is far from the cost minimum.

If circulation losses etc. are also taken into consideration, then completely over-dimensioned installations are designed. The annual average circulation losses are (a) approx. 30% of the total energy demand for the hot water system in residential buildings with well insulated hot water piping; and (b) often over 50% of the total energy demand in older buildings with widely branching hot water networks. Thus these losses are sometimes higher than the energy demand for the hot water drawn off. Fig. 4.6 also shows the solar fraction of the total energy (F_T) for a hot water network with circulation losses of approx. 40% of the total energy. It can be seen that the system size for the solar fraction target of 60% would be way outside the range shown in Fig. 4.6. Active integration of the circulation return in the solar installation would allow a certain reduction in the collector area required, yet such an installation would have to be enormous and would operate beyond any economical justification.

For heating potable water, we see no necessity for the use of vacuum-tube collectors. Since these are also mostly considerably more expensive than the flat collectors, the system costs would greatly increase. These additional costs are not compensated for by a correspondingly higher gain in available solar heat. Simulation calculations and practical experience have demonstrated this frequently enough. Generally the costs for available solar heat increase with the use of vacuum tubes by approx. 20–30%, thus the economy of such systems is poorer than with flat collectors. Even if the vacuum-tube collector had a much longer service life than the flat collectors (20–25 years), this would not change anything in the basis for economic results, since the annuity for such long service lives is practically only determined by the interest rate and no longer by the service life. The correct application for these highly efficient collectors is in process heat at a temperature of around 100 °C. Their efficiency advantage is at its best in this case.

The use of vacuum tubes to heat potable water may be appropriate in individual cases for technical reasons, e.g. if only a limited roof area is available and this is to be partially balanced out by higher specific collector performance, or if the roof only permits a limited load. The tubes may therefore be mounted with a less expensive rigging above a flat roof. However, these advantages may only offset the cost disadvantages in special cases. We recommend a specific load of approx. 80–90l hot water per day and per square metre of collector area for the dimensioning of solar installations with vacuum tubes for heating potable water.

Solar Storage Tank
The size of the solar storage tank depends, of course, on the size of the collector array, and also on the daily hot water consumption during the week (e.g. approximately constant consumption on all week days, or only consumption on work days, e.g. in factories, workshops etc.). The aim is for the solar storage tank to store, on an intermediate basis and until needed, the solar heat collected during the day and not directly passed to the consumer.

Simulation calculations with variation of the solar storage tank volume were carried out for location in Cologne, Germany, for a solar installation with a hot water consumption in the building of $7\,m^3/d$. The calculations were carried out for two types of building, for a residential building with approximately constant consumption on all week days and for a workshop with no consumption on Saturdays, Sundays and public holidays. In addition, the system load for both buildings was changed ($70l/(d \cdot m^2)$ and $40l(d \cdot m^2)$) by increasing the collector area from $100\,m^2$ to $170\,m^2$. The calculations presumed that the storage tank volume can be accommodated in one single container. In practice it is often necessary to install two or three storage tanks. This would lead to a slight increase in storage losses, so that the degree of utilisation of the system would be slightly less than the values calculated. The results of these simulation calculations are shown in Figure 4.7.

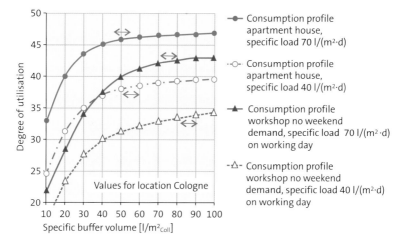

Figure 4.7 Degree of utilisation of the solar installation as a function of specific storage tank volume (volume per square metre of collector area), for two buildings used differently and for two specific loads respectively (medium quality solar installation components)

In the case of buildings with approximately constant consumption over all the week days, (residential buildings, hospitals, old peoples' homes etc.), there is hardly any noticeable increase in the degree of utilisation of the system with a specific load of $70 l/(d \cdot m^2)$ from a specific storage tank size of 40 to $50 l/m^2$ collector area for a location in Germany. The additional costs of the increased storage volume would not be balanced by a correspondingly higher yield. A value of 40 to $50 l/m^2$ (storage/collector) with the specific load of $70 l/(d \cdot m^2)$ corresponds to a storage volume of approx. 60–70% of the daily hot water consumption. Since, however, a buffer storage tank can heat up to about 80–90°C, this fully charged volume contains about one whole day's energy consumption. A solar storage tank filled with potable water with its temperature limited to 65°C (e.g. due to the danger of furring) would have to have a specific volume of $60–70 l/m^2$ (approx. 90–100% of a day's consumption) in order to be able to absorb the same energy.

For installations with low specific load (approx. $40 l/(m^2 \cdot d)$; $170 m^2$ collector area) the situation is basically the same. The curve only flattens out somewhat more gradually. In this case, a specific volume of approx. $40–50 l/m^2$ would be suitable for buildings with constant consumption, as a compromise between solar yield and storage tank size. Seen absolutely, this is approx. 7 to a generous $8 m^3$, which is approx. 100–120% of the daily consumption. A system dimensioned in this way has an annual degree of utilisation of approx. 10% (absolutely) or almost 20% (relatively) less than a sufficiently dimensioned pre-heating system. This reduction in efficiency is only be slightly influenced by a considerable increase in the storage volume. In addition, for a large-scale installation, it cannot, be compensated for by lower specific system costs (costs per m^2 collector area) and thus leads to higher costs for available solar heat.

Fig. 4.7 also shows that when weekend and public holiday consumption is missing (e.g. for a workshop), the degree of utilisation of a solar installation with the same dimensioning is approx. 8% (absolutely) or relatively about 15% below that of an installation with constant consumption. This decrease in efficiency can be moderated if (a) the solar installation in the workshop is scaled down by spreading the weekly consumption (5·7 m^3/d) over all 7 weekdays as a calculation (i.e. in this case in 5 m^3/d) and (b) by dimensioning the collector array to the mean value of consumption. In which case (at a specific load of 70 l/d·m^2) approx. 70 m^2 collector area would then be installed. In doing so, the degree of utilisation would increase on work days (due to the then higher specific load of the solar installation), however the solar fraction would fall.

Incidentally the relationships in the comparison between the two dimensioning variants are similar for the workshop and the residential building. In this case the degree of utilisation compared to a pre-heating installation decreases by approx. 10% absolutely (approx. 25% relatively) in the case of a large dimensioned system. The optimum storage size is some 70 l/m^2 with the specific load variants. Due to the necessity of storing energy over consumption-free days, this value is more than that for an installation at constant load on all days. Regarded absolutely, this corresponds to approx. 7 m^3 in the case of sufficiently dimensioned systems and approx. 11−12 m^3 for large-scale dimensioned systems.

In summary, the following can be emphasised concerning the dimensioning of the solar buffer storage tank:

- A specific storage volume of approx. 50 l/m^2 (±10%) offers an optimum cost/benefit ratio in large-scale solar installations for heating potable water, if the hot water consumption is roughly constant on every week day. This value is roughly the same for different dimensioning of arrays if the dimensioning is kept within a useful range.

- If a solar installation is installed in a building in which there are consumption-free week days, then it is recommended that the weekly consumption be obtained over all 7 days. This is then used to optain the theoretical average daily consumption, that is as the dimensioning value. In this manner, the decease in efficiency as compared to a constant load system is partially compensated for. The specific volume of the buffer storage tank should be set at approx. 70 l/m^2.

- If it is not necessary to supply solar energy to various consumers with greatly deviating temperature levels, then attempts should be made to combine the solar buffer volume in one tank. Distribution over a maximum of four tanks may be tolerated if the special features of the storage switching possibilities are taken into consideration (see Ch. 8.4). If there is a larger number of individual tanks, then the heat losses increase due to the unfavourable ratio of surface to volume. In addition, the costs for the storage tanks themselves greatly increase and also for piping to one another.

4.4 Solar Installations for Combined Potable Water Heating and Space Heating Back-up

If a solar installation is planned for partial coverage of the energy consumption for space heating in addition to potable water heating, then the systems must be dimensioned on a larger scale than for purely potable water heating. Since however, in summer, there are many days of intense radiation when no heating is required, there is collector stagnation in these installations in such periods, which reduces the annual degree of utilisation. Very large solar storage tanks could prevent these periods of stagnation, however they would make the system considerably more expensive.

On the other hand, systems are also used which dispense with additional buffer storage tanks. These give off superfluous heat directly, e.g. via wall or under-floor heating, and thus store the heat in the building.

Reducing the annual degree of utilisation or increasing costs with enlarged storage tanks can only be compared in small-scale installation with equally reduced specific system costs (costs per m^2 collector area) with increasing system size. This cost reduction is only slight in the case of large-scale installations. Thus the comparative costs of available solar heat from (a) installations for both potable water heating and space heating back-up, and (b) for purely potable water systems, are roughly the same only in the case of small-scale systems. For large-scale installations, having the heating back-up generally leads to higher costs for available solar heat.

This purely commercial argument is opposed by the fact that the consumption of conventional fuels in installations to back up space heating is reduced much more considerably than in purely potable water systems. The same applies for the quantity of air pollutants given off.

The same applies for installations purely for potable water heating. A large solar fraction is desirable from the point of view of saving energy and avoiding pollutant emission, however correspondingly dimensioned systems supply solar heat at costs which are far beyond any competitiveness as compared to the costs of heat generated conventionally. Thus it is necessary to find reasonable compromises and not exaggerate.

4.4.1 Energy Consumption for Hot Water and Space Heating

In the case of large residential buildings insulated according to the current valid regulations in Germany, the energy consumption for the hot water (draw-off quantity + circulation losses) accounts for approx. 20% of the total heat consumption for the building in the annual total. In the case of buildings constructed earlier and poorly insulated, this value is sometimes only 10%. In the case of so-called »low-energy« or »lowest-energy« houses it may reach 30–40% or even more.

The greater the heat insulation of a building and the better the passive use of solar energy, e.g. by large window areas facing South, the longer the non-heating period. This is bacause the passive use of solar energy and the internal loads (internal heat sources e.g. from the residents themselves, electrical appliances, lighting etc.) are often sufficient on only slightly colder days to cover the heating demand.

Fig. 4.8 shows the relationships described above for the three cases stated (poorly insulated old building, building according to German Insulation Regulations of 1995 and low-energy house). The scale of the freely dimensioned X-axis was maintained for all three sections so that the above mentioned relationship becomes apparent.

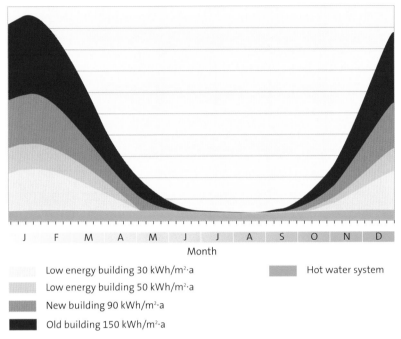

J F M A M J J A S O N D

Month

Low energy building 30 kWh/m²·a   Hot water system

Low energy building 50 kWh/m²·a

New building 90 kWh/m²·a

Old building 150 kWh/m²·a

Figure 4.8 Energy consumption for hot water and space heating in Germany with different insulation standards
Top: Old residential building with poor insulation (heating energy: approx. 150 kWh/(m²·a)
Centre: residential building with insulation according to German insulation standard 95 (approx. 80 kWh/(m²·a)
Bottom: low-energy house (approx. 30 kWh/(m²·a)

The relative demand for heating energy can be very different, by up to a factor of 2, between two houses of identical structure or between two identical flats in the same building. This is because the demand is greatly influenced by user behaviour (temperature of rooms, number of rooms in which no heating is used, use of roller shutters, decreased room temperature periods etc.).

All the reasons above mentioned make it difficult to determine the heating energy demand in a building, including the considerable difficulty of determining the energy demand for heating water.

The rule of thumb for dimensioning a solar installation for partial coverage of the energy demand both for heating potable water and for space heating, as explained in the following Chapter, must thus remain very generalised. It is essential to consider actual conditions when planning the installation, especially for a large solar fraction.

There are several case studies in the literature which should not be generalised. Two books with interesting information and tips for the implementation of such installations are given below. Some of the recommendations given in the following Chapter were taken from these publications /21; 22/.

4.4.2 Rules of Thumb for Dimensioning

For all solar installations which back up space heating, it is recommended that any existing hot water circulation (return) be connected to the solar installation so that, in the non-heating period, as much energy as possible can be passed to the hot water system.

It is recommended for all solar installations for space heating, that a steeper collector angle is used than for installations purely for heating potable water. This is is because (a) exess heat in summer (when the sun is high) is thereby lessened and (b) the collector is more favourable orientated to the low sun in the transitional periods and in winter. The greater the solar fraction required, the steeper the array position.

The specific volume of the solar storage tank (volume per square metre of collector area) must be dimensioned much larger than for potable water installations due to the necessity of storing solar energy from high insolation periods, with low heating demand, into periods with less insolation and higher heating demands. The specific volume increases to a great extent with the solar fraction required for heating demand. If large solar fractions are to be achieved, particular attention must be paid to having good temperature stratification in the solar storage tank (slim, high construction), well-adapted stratification charging and discharging which takes account of the temperature required and available at various storage tank levels. This also includes a potable water storage tank in the combi-storage tank, which must reach down to the lower cold area of the buffer so that this disturbs the stratification as little as possible.

If high system efficiency is to be achieved, then the heating system must have advance and return temperatures which are as low as possible (advance under 40°C as far as possible, return less than 30°C on the dimensioning day). The larger the solar fraction selected for the space heating, the greater the effect of excessive temperatures on the heating system is on the efficiency reduction of the solar installation. In extreme cases of a 100% fraction, a temperature increased by 10K reduces the annual degree of utilisation of the system by approx. 5−7%. In the case of installations with low solar fractions, the degree of utilisation decreases by approx. 2% in the conditions.

Installations with a Low Solar Fraction

In Central Europe and comparable climatic zones (or comparable heating demands) the dimensioning of combi-installations is generally as stated below:

For installations with a low solar fraction of the heating demand for space heating (max. 25% with very good insulation), the solar installation is not enlarged excessively compared to potable water heating installations. A collector area increase of roughly a factor 2 to 4 is selected. This results in a specific load related to hot water consumption of approx. $20-35 l/(d \cdot m^2)$.

The specific volume of the solar buffer is set at approx. 60–100 litres per square metre collector area (the greater the system is dimensioned, the greater the specific storage volume has to be selected). The resulting large storage volume with a heating span of approx. 70–80 K presumes careful calculation of the major expansion vessels.

Installations thus dimensioned achieve a solar fraction of the heating energy demand of approx. 5–25 % (higher solar fraction with better insulation and greater collector area) and a solar fraction for the energy to heat potable water (incl. circulation losses) of approx. 30 %. The solar fraction of the total heating demand for the building is some 10–25 % depending on insulation standard. The annual degree of utilisation of the system is approx. 30–40 % and thus, depending on dimensioning, is below the value for potable water systems.

There will be collector stagnation in these systems in summer when there is strong solar radiation on several consecutive days, since there is then no heating demand. These stagnation periods decrease in the transition periods – and this occurs to a greater extent the earlier the heating period begins.Sufficiently dimensioned systems work particularly well if the building is not excessively well insulated, and/or if it is in a region where heating is used almost the entire year due to weather conditions (high altitudes etc.). If the non-heating period is very long due to very good insulation, then it becomes difficult to provide large solar fractions of the space heating energy demand. Also, with a sufficiently dimensioned installation additional to the solar fraction of hot water, the solar heat generated in the winter months could also be almost completely taken up by the consumer without connection to the space heating (hot water system).

The statements above however only apply to regions with climates similar to Germany (low-radiation, cold winter). They do not apply to regions with high insolation in winter. The dimensioning of a solar combi-system is always much more dependent on the installation location than is the case with potable water installations.

Fig. 4.9 shows this connection for the German climate in the two extreme cases from Fig. 4.8. The low time selectivity and the rough curve smoothing in Fig. 4.9 almost completely blur the actual conditions with great daily differences so that an exaggeratedly unfavourable impression occurs. Nevertheless, the statements above are demonstrated in the trend.

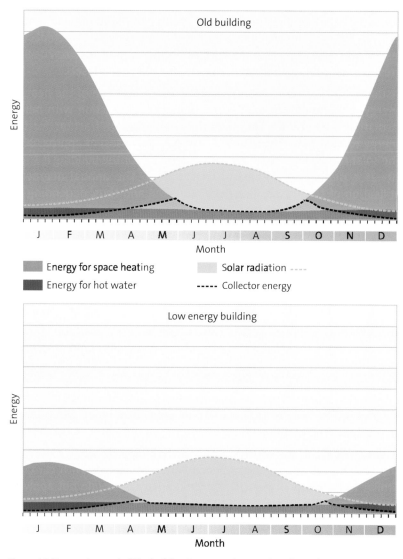

Figure 4.9 Energy demand of the building in comparison to the solar radiation and the delayed supply of useful energy, caused by the storage tank of a solar installation having a low solar fraction for hot water and space heating (German or similar climate)
Top: For poorly insulated old building (heating energy for floor area: approx. 150kWh/(m²·a)
Bottom: for low-energy house (approx. 30 kWh/(m²·a)

Installations with a High Solar Fraction

If a high solar fraction (50% or more) of the total heat demand for the building is to be achieved, then a basic prerequisite is that the building should be particularly well insulated, i.e. the energy consumption has to be a minimum. Otherwise the collector array would have a larger area than generally available for it on the building. In order to achieve a solar fraction of approx. 50%, without seasonal storage, about $3\,m^2$ of collector area would have to be installed per MWh annual energy consumption for hot water and space heating.

Such installations presume however that at least a major part of the solar heat produced in high-radiation periods can be »saved« for periods requiring heating, e.g. at low insolation winter conditions. This requires very large storage tanks able to store solar energy for several weeks, but not necessarily seasonaly. The storage tanks should either be as low-loss as possible or pass their losses to the building itself when installed in parts of the building requiring heat. In the latter case, remember that such storage tanks will release energy when this may not be desirable, e.g. on hot summer days. If over-heating of the building is to be avoided, then heat lost from the storage tank must be »ventilated away« during periods of warm weather. As a specific storage size, 120 to 150 litres per square metre of collector area is recommended /22/.

The annual degree of utilisation of such dimensioned systems, with a solar fraction of approx. 50% of the total heat demand, is only about 20−30%. This is approximately half that of potable water installations, but greatly dependent on climate.

Fig. 4.10 shows the relationships between energy demand and energy supply for the two extreme cases already used in Fig. 4.9 (German or similar climate; solar fraction in both cases approx. 50%). The comments regarding accuracy of trends apply as mentioned previously for Fig. 4.9. However it can be seen that systems with high solar fractions are also well suited for low-energy houses with large thermal mass, due to the considerably larger quantity of energy stored. Their theoretical suitability for poorly insulated buildings is contentious; however implementation may fail due to the lack of space for the necessary very large collector array.

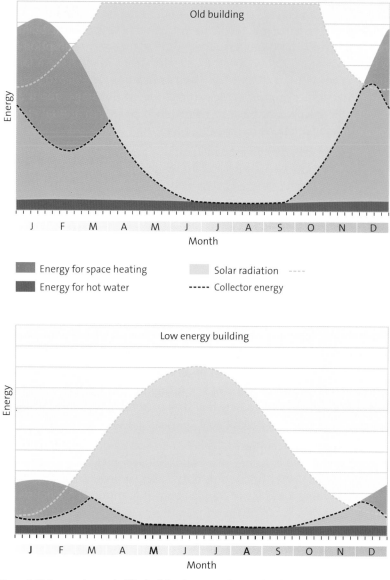

Figure 4.10 Energy demand of the building in comparison with solar radiation and the delayed supply of useful energy caused by the storage tank of a solar installation with high solar fraction for hot water and space heating (approx. 50%) (German or similar climate) Top: For poorly insulated old building (heating energy: approx. 150 kWh/(m²·a) Bottom: for low-energy house (approx. 30 kWh/(m²·a)

Installations with a solar fraction of nearly 100 % can only be installed on low-energy houses (due to the collector area limitation). In addition, they presume the use of a very large seasonal storage tank.

At this point, we do not discuss wheather or not large-scale solar installations with low degrees of utilisation represent the optimum technical, ecological and economical solution for the small energy demand of low(est)-energy houses, or whether there are, or may be, other more suitable possibilities (e.g. heat recovery, heat pumps, fuel cells etc.). However, an examination of such alternatives or extension would certainly be appropriate.

Installations with Medium Solar Fraction

Installations with medium solar fraction of the entire heat demand (20 to 50%), have requirements between the dimensioning for low and high solar fractions described above. The components should be dimensioned correspondingly.

4.5 **Solar District Heating**

Detaileds of the dimensioning of solar installations which are integrated into the heating networks are not presented here. However conclusions can be taken from the literature: / 17/.

These state the following standard values for a solar fraction of 40−70% of the total heat demand of the building connected to the network:

Array size: approx. $1.4-2.4\,m^2/MWh\cdot a$
Storage tank volume: approx. $1.4-2.1\,m^3/m^2$ collector area
Heat exchange fluid: water (or water-equivalent in the case
                             of other storage media)

The network return temperature is particularly important in district heating, since in the conventional 2-line networks, which are customary today for potable water heating, the network return temperature is considerably higher than otherwise the cold water temperature. A network return which is unnecessarily high by 10 K (e.g. 55 instead of 45°C) reduces the degree of utilisation of the system by approx. 6%. In this case, the network return temperature in summer has a particularly large influence.

5. **Solar Collectors**

5.1 **Task, Function and Characteristic Values**

The collector is the driving force behind the solar installation. It is here that the energy in sunlight, the insolation, heats the heat transfer fluid. The heat generated is fed through the collector circulation and mostly stored in an intermediate solar storage tank. From there it is fed to the consumers connected to the system depending on requirements.

All constructions aim to convert the insolation into heat with high efficiency and to supply this heat to consumers as efficiently as possible. The collector constructions differ considerably in quality, performance, construction and costs. In the following Chapters, the properties of collectors are described using characteristic curves and values.

A complete listing of all characteristic values is part of the correct definition of the collector properties. No analysis or comparison between collectors is possible if some key characteristic values are missing.

5.1.1 **Collector Efficiency**

The collector efficiency η, describes the relationship of output energy (heat) discharged from the collector, to input (irradiation). As such, it has no units and is stated as non-dimensional or in %. However other quantities having units may be involved, as below:

$$\eta = \eta_0 - \frac{a_1(\vartheta_m - \vartheta_L)}{E_e} - \frac{a_2(\vartheta_m - \vartheta_L)^2}{E_e} \quad \text{with } \eta_0 = \alpha \tau F'$$

abbreviation	unit	description	value
η	[-]; [%]	Collector efficiency	
η_0	[-]; [%]	Zero loss collector efficiency $\Phi = 0°$ »optical efficiency« $= \alpha \cdot \tau \cdot F'$	
a_1	W/(m^2·K)	Linear heat transfer coefficient	1.2−4
a_2	W/(m^2·K^2)	Quadratic heat transfer coefficient	0.005−0.015
ϑ_e	°C	Heat transfer fluid inlet temperature into collector	
ϑ_a	°C	Heat transfer fluid outlet temperature from collector	
ϑ_m (or T_{col})	°C	Mean temperature of heat transfer fluid in absorber	
ϑ_L (or T_a)	°C	Ambient air temperature	
E_e (or E_g)	W/m^2	solar irradiance	1,000
F	-; %	Absorber efficiency factor	0.92−0.97
τ	-; %	Transmission factor of cover	0.88−0.91
α	-; %	Absorption factor of absorber	0.90−0.96
additional values: K (Φ)	-; %	Incident angle modifier dependent on incident angle (see Chapter 5.1.2)	
$a_{eff} = a_1 + a_2 \cdot \Delta\vartheta$		Effective, temperature-independent heat transfer coefficient	
c	kJ/(m^2·K)	Thermal capacity of collector	

Table 5.1 Signs and symbols used in the collector efficiency formula

η_0 is the efficiency of the collector at zero temperature difference between mean absorber temperature and ambient temperature. If therefore collector is at ambient temperature then it has no thermal losses and the associated term in the formula becomes zero. In this case, only optical losses would occur. The factor η_0 is therefore also named the »optical efficiency« or »zero loss efficiency«.

The »optical efficiency« $\eta_0 = \alpha\cdot\tau\cdot F'$ (the straightforward multiplication of the absorption of the absorber with the cover transmission coefficient and efficiency factor) is frequently incorrectly stated as »efficiency of the collector«.

The thermal losses of the collector are described by the two heat transfer coefficients a_1 and a_2 . In this case, a_1 stands for the linear, and a_2 the quadratic heat loss increasing with the temperature difference between collector and surroundings. It is a mathematical approximation of the physical model. The higher the a values of the collector, the lower its efficiency with increasing temperatures.

a_1 and a_2 are not physical quantities but are only intended as factors to represent the measurement points within the performance curve. A direct comparison of these as a sole description of various collectors is thus mostly misleading. In the past, both coefficients were combined to form a_{eff}. However this description is insufficient.

The collector characteristic values and characteristic curves are determined by recognised test institutes using standardised methods. These stipulate the test procedure (see Figure 5.10) and assure the comparability of the collectors. Unfortunately several national and international standards are or have been in use. Thus it is imperative that the particular standard used is also stated when giving collector characteristic values, since such values determined according to different standards are **not** necessarily compatible (despite apperances). This fact sometimes receives insufficient attention in company brochures. Thus there is a danger that collectors are compared using characteristic values or solar yields determined using simulation programs, despite such characteristic values **not** being mutually comparable.

The efficiencies measured during the testing at the collector are entered in efficiency/temperature difference diagrams. The measurement data are entered in a computational model which calculates the characteristic values η_0, a_1 and a_2 from the measurement data and draws the complete characteristic curve.

The collector test reports show the efficiency via a quotient from the temperature difference and the irradiation, because this then results in one single characteristic curve for all irradiations (see Fig. 5.1). This representation has the advantage of being able to describe the collector with one single characteristic curve, however it is less useful for practitioners.

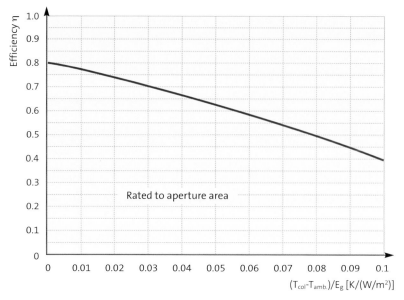

Figure 5.1 Collector efficiency diagram with representation of efficiency via a coefficient from temperature differences and radiation (characteristic curves representation from test institutes)

If the efficiency is plotted directly against the temperature difference between collector and surroundings, and if irradiation used as a parameter, a different characteristic curve is obtained for every radiation. Such a family of characteristic curves is shown in Fig. 5.2. Using these, the practitioner can very easily read off which radiation conditions and which operating temperatures result in a particular efficiency .

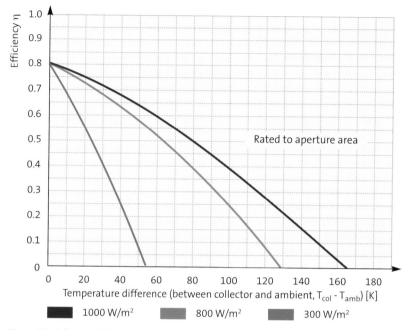

Figure 5.2 Collector efficiency dependent on the temperature difference between collector and surroundings with differing radiation as parameter

The diagrams clearly show that collector efficiency decreases with (a) decreasing solar radiation and (b) increasing difference between mean collector and ambient temperature.

A characteristic curve is part of the description of every collector. However it cannot replace the complete list of all collector characteristic values.

5.1.2 Reflection at the Glass Cover

The efficiency curves shown in Chapter 5.1.1 for solar collectors apply for the vertical incidence of sunlight on the front of the glass cover of the collector.

The maximum light transmission (transmission coefficient τ) of the collector cover is specified by the properties of the glass. It depends on the absorption of the radiation in the glass and on the reflection at the surface of the glass. If a beam of sunlight hits the surface of the glass vertically, then only a slight proportion of the energy is reflected by the glass.

The shallower the incident angle to the pane, the greater the reflection. With an incidence parallel to the glass, the transmission moves towards zero, the glass acts as a mirror. These relationships are made clear in Figure 5.3.

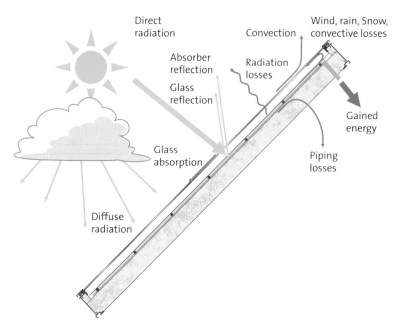

Figure 5.3 Reflection of light beams at a pane of glass and heat losses of a collector

This fact is taken into account in the collector test according to EN 12975-2 /23/ from the determination of the incident angle modifier K(ϕ) at 50°. It is determined for direct and for diffuse radiation. This value is required in simulation programs to calculate the operating behaviour of solar installations.

Further information on determining the incident angle modifier in /23/.

5.1.3 Other Characteristic Values of the Collector

Thermal Capacity of the Collectors
The thermal capacity c of the collector is determined in tests according to EN 12975-4.

The thermal capacity is a measure of the thermal inertia and thus the response behaviour of the collector on heating and cooling. A low thermal capacity is of advantage for the use of collectors with changing weather conditions in central Europe.

Loss of Pressure in Collector
The pressure drop in the collector for different flows is determined within the framework of tests according to EN 12975. This test is generally carried out with water which means that an adjustment must be made for the water/glycol mixture usually in use in the collector circulation.

Stagnation Temperature

If the collector is exposed to steady insolation of $1,000\,W/m^2$ (ambient temperature approx. $20-25\,°C$) without heat being drawn off, then an equilibrium between energy uptake and heat loss is reached. The maximum temperature which occurs in this case is described as the stagnation temperature.

In the characteristic curve of Figure 5.2, the temperature difference between collector and surroundings at stagnation can be found at the intersection of the characteristic curve for radiation of $1,000\,W/m^2$ with the X-axis. In Figure 5.1, this value must be multiplied by $1,000\,[W/m^2]$ to obtain this temperature difference. If the value of the ambient temperature (e.g. $25\,°C$), is added to the temperature difference, then the stagnation temperature is obtained.

5.1.4 Information on Collector Area

In order to calculate the energy yield from the collector, it is important to define which of the collector areas stated below provides the basis for the radiation exposed area. The exact definitions of these areas are in the Appendix to EN 12975-2/23/. According to EN 12975-2, the collector characteristic values relate to the aperture area; however according to ISO 9806-1 (1994) /ISO9806/ they relate to the absorber area.

Gross collector area (total area) A_G: this is the area between the outer boundaries of the collector, generally the outer boundaries of the collector casing.

Aperture area A_a: this is the transmission aperture of the collector for vertical or angular solar radiation incidence, generally the visible glass area within the pane seal. In the case of vacuum tube collectors without reflectors, it is the product of the inner diameter, the unshaded cylindrical inner length and the number of tubes. In the case of reflectors attached to the reverse side or in the collector, it is determined using the projection of the area formed by the absorber and reflector in the collector level. (Used in: EN 12975-2 (01.1998) /23/)

Absorber area A_A: the absorber area equals the absorber vanes in flat plate, as well as in tube collectors, together with the projection of the connection pieces and the header which may receive radiation. (used in: ISO 9606-1 (1994))/24/.

Active absorber area: generally corresponds to the absorber area A_a. Some collectors however are constructed so that the absorber area below the collector frame is larger than the aperture area. The active absorber area is then the absorber area not affected by shading from the frame (in this case it is equal to the aperture area).

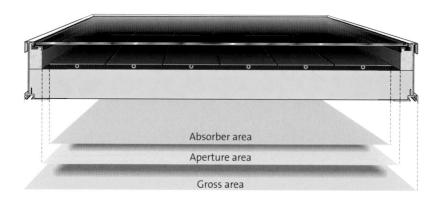

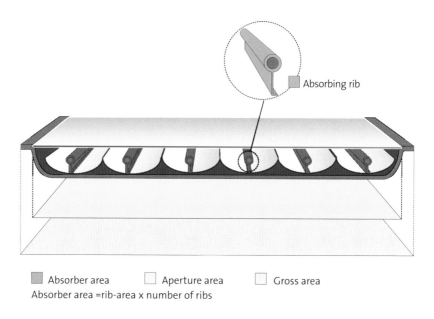

Figure 5.4 Areas at a flat plate collector

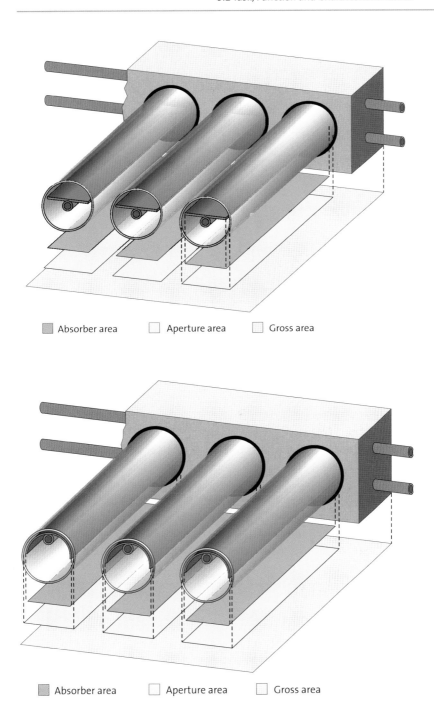

Figure 5.5 Areas at a vacuum tube collector without reflectors

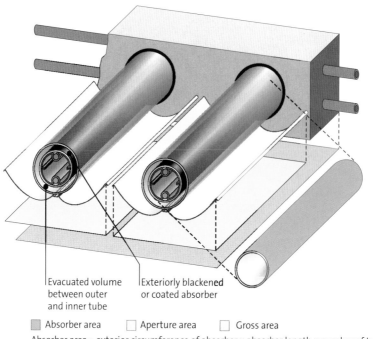

Evacuated volume between outer and inner tube

Exteriorly blackened or coated absorber

☐ Absorber area   ☐ Aperture area   ☐ Gross area

Absorber area = exterior circumference of absorber x absorber length x number of tubes

Figure 5.6 Areas at vacuum tube collector with reflectors

The collector characteristic quantities are partly related to different areas at the various test institutes. This results in parameters which are not directly comparable. Thus it is important to know which reference values were selected for the respective characteristic values. In addition, in the past and depending on the standard used, different test procedures were used which led to considerable differences in the characteristic values. Thus the characteristic curves and characteristic value tables should always include information about which test procedure was used for measurement and which area was used as the basis.

The test results from the Solar Technology Test Institute (SPF) in Rapperswil, Switzerland are represented in an exemplary manner, however only recently. Here a differentiation is made between test procedures and areas to which values may refer (see Table 5.2). Previously measurements were only carried out by SPF according to their own test procedure, which led to (apparently) better results than a test according to DIN / EN or ISO. This Table clearly shows the differences between the test procedures and also between different area selections in the same test procedure.

Test procedure	ISO 9606-1, DIN V 4757-4, EN 12975-2 with air movement			Rapperswil measurement specifications (old) without air movement		
Definition reference area	Absorber	Aper- ture	Gross	Absorber	Aper- ture	Gross
Collector area [m^2]	4.871	5.099	5.686	4.871	5.099	5.686
η_0	0.798	0.762	0.684	0.801	0.765	0.686
$a_1 (=k_1)$ [W/(m$^2\cdot$K)]	4.12	3.94	3.53	3.77	3.60	3.23
$a_2 (=k_2)$ [W/(m$^2\cdot$K^2)]	0.0095	0.0091	0.0081	0.0091	0.0087	0.0078

Table 5.2 Exerpt from a collector test of Solar Technology Test Institut (SPF) in Rapperswill, Switzerland

There should not be any uncertainty about correct reference area. If collectors without reflectors or concentrators are compared with one another, then the absorber area presented to the radiation (= active) is certainly the most useful physical value. The area which is always clearly defined for all collectors (even those with reflectors) is, however, the aperture area. Thus the latter has been selected as the reference area in the standards. If the solar yield of a solar installation is calculated using a simulation program and if the corresponding collector characteristic values are used for the correct collector area, then the results (within the same measuring specification) are the same for all cases. Despite this, a standard reference area should be selected in all tendering documents. In the German demonstration program, Solarthermie 2000, all information refers to the active absorber area (optically presented to solar radiation) (see above).

5.2 Collector Types

Often in early times of collector construction, old heating »radiators« were painted black, protected by a pane of glass and attached to the roof more or less professionally. In addition to these purely home-made collectors a number of different, sometimes highly experimental, collector structural forms arose. Some design and constructions proved to be unsuitable and rapidly disappeared from the market. However they left the public with the impression of poorly functioning technology. Some of these old designs are described in Chapters 5.4 and 5.5. Fig. 5.7 shows a typical example from 1980.

Figure 5.7 Flat plate collector from 1980 with acrylic cover

The flat plate collector shown in Fig. 5.7 corresponds, with the exception of the acrylic cover and a second film cover underneath it, to today's standard flat plate collectors regarding principles of construction and design.

Today there are again and again collectors on the market with designs and constructions which are clearly very different to the customary standard products.

5.2.1 **Standard Flat Plate Collectors**

Figure 5.8 »Small« in-roof collector from Roto Frank Bauelemente

Figure 5.9 »Large« in-roof collector from Solvis Energiesysteme

In flat plate collectors, the solar absorber is protected against heat loss by insulation material, mostly rock wool and a flat pane of glass. Hardened, highly transparent (poor in iron) solar glass specially designed for low reflection is used today for the cover in high-quality collectors.

Aluminium or zinc sheet is mostly used for the side frame; aluminium laminated insulation, roofing felt, aluminium, zinc or stainless steel sheet is used for the backing. Aluminium, plastic or stainless steel troughs are also possible for the casing.

In the structural form, there is a differece between (a) small, completely prefabricated collectors (approx. $2m^2$) and (b) large collectors ($5m^2$–$12m^2$) which are glassed-in on the roof or lifted into place by crane.

The flat plate collectors have a market share of approx. 85 % to 90 % in solar potable water heating. The advantages of flat plate collectors are:

- simple, robust structure
- technically perfected
- favourable price performance ratio
- more optically appealing due to flat surface areas

There are a number of features, which differentiate the collectors from one another in detail. These are: structure and coating of the absorbers, hydraulic circuitry and loss of pressure, design of connections, thickness and quality of insulation, quality of collector casing, the transparent cover, the seals and processing up to assembly systems, roofing frames, transport devices, optical design and service life.

Some of these criteria are dealt with in the following Chapters.

5.2.2 Special Structural Forms of Flat Plate Collectors

Transparent Heat Insulation Collectors
This type of collector has a cover of Transparent Insulation instead of a pane of glass. (»Transparent Insulation« is manufactured thick material designed to allow transmission of solar radiation, yet prevent returning heat loss by conduction and convection). The collectors generally achieve very high yields and very high stagnation temperatures. Therefore there are high physical demands on the thermal characteristics of transparent insulation collectors which are difficult to fulfil. Transparent heat insulation collectors are more expensive in total and heavier than standard collectors, due to the larger amount of material included in the whole construction.

Other Structural Forms
The »exotics« on the market are, for example, collectors in which the angle of absorber fins can be adjusted, e.g. using a chain. Enlarged absorber areas, semi-spherical constructions or blinds to cover the collector are among other rarities.

Great importance should be placed on the testing of the properties, which is necessary particularly for unusual constructions. In cases of doubt, the advice of a test institute (addresses in Appendix) should be sought, in addition to the test certificates described in Chapter 5.9.

5.2.3 **Vacuum Tube Collectors**

Vacuum tubes are evacuated similarly to thermos flasks, in order to reduce heat losses from convection and thermal conduction. The extent of the vacuum is of decisive importance for the interruption of the heat transport mechanism, of convection (and thermal conduction). Figure 5.10 shows that the pressure must be reduced to considerably below atmospheric pressure in order to achieve a reduction of the »a« factors in the collector. As with flat plate collectors filled with inert gas, one variant of the Schott tubes is filled with xenon in order to achieve a significant reduction in the »a« factor with even a slight partial vacuum. Lower partial vacuums make considerable savings in material and production possible.

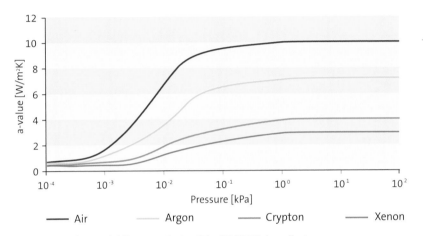

Figure 5.10 a-factor of different variants of the SCHOTT tube collector

Since vacuum tube collectors can reach substantially higher temperatures than flat plate collectors, the thermal load on the insulation of pipes, the control sensor and the heat transfer fluid can be very high. The insulation near the tube collectors must resist permanent temperatures of over 150 °C. Only heat transfer fluid expressly approved for operation with tube collectors may be used in installations with direct-heat vacuum tubes. Check that this is so with the manufacturer.

The connection technology for the piping must be adapted to the temperatures in the collector circulation (up to 160 °C). Thus copper pipes should not be soft soldered. In addition, ensure that a large-volume evaporation of the heat transfer fluid can occur in the piping of the collector circulation, particularly at low pressure and high temperature.

Advantages of vacuum tubes:

- Higher operating temperatures can be achieved than with flat plate collectors. The higher temperatures can be of benefit for process heat (e.g. for industry and solar cooling).

- Reduced thermal losses than with flat plate collectors due to excellent heat insulation.

- Higher energy yield than flat plate collectors with the same effective absorber area. This can be of advantage with installations in small set-up areas. However the energy yield of the vacuum tubes is only considerably more than from flat plate collectors at high working temperatures.

- Close compact construction of the collector which requires no interior insulation material, and thus no penetration of moisture or dirt into the collector, and no deposits due to dispersal of interior insulation etc.

Disadvantages of vacuum tubes:

- High stagnation temperatures with corresponding demands on all materials used near the array and on the heat transfer fluid.

- Considerably higher specific costs (costs per m² absorber area) than with flat plate collectors. The increase in cost is not compensated if only low to medium working temperatures are required (e.g. with solar potable water heating), despite higher efficiency and resulting possibility of reduced array area.

- Higher costs for available solar heat at medium operating temperatures range, since cost advantages only at higher operating temperatures.

Direct-flow vacuum tubes
In this structural form, the heat transfer fluid flows directly through the absorber in the vacuum tubes. A high performance is achieved due to the direct heat transmission. If needed (e.g. with facade mounting) the absorber can be turned at installation for better alignment to the sun.

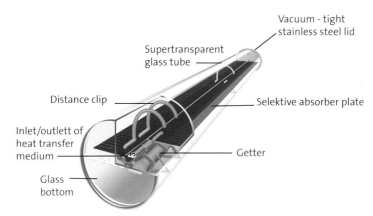

Figure 5.11 Cross-section through a direct-flow vacuum tube

Vacuum tubes with direct flow have an additional advantage to the general advantages of vacuum tubes, since they can be directly mounted on flat roofs (but only in low-snow regions). This means that the costs for the sub-construction can be minimised. They are not as conspicuous with this type of mounting (also applies for collectors according to the Sydney principle; see below).

Vacuum Tubes using the Heat Pipe Principle

In vacuum tubes incorporating the heat pipe principle, the absorber tube contains a very slight amount of water (or a different fluid depending on temperature requirements). This fluid is vaporised at partial vacuum, rises upwards as a vapour in the absorber duct, condenses in the condenser and flows in liquid form back into the absorber. The condenser transfers heat to the heat transfer medium of the collector circulation.

The principle requires a minimum incline of the absorber tube in contrast to tubes with direct flow through, this incline is given as 20° to 30° by the manufacturers.

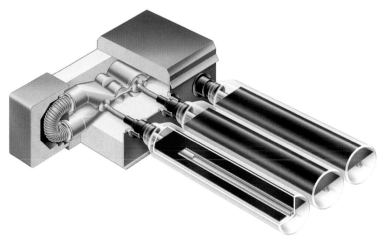

Figure 5.12 Cross-section through a heat pipe vacuum tube

If the condenser has a temperature more than the evaporation temperature of the fluid in the absorber, complete vaporisation takes place.
For instance this may happen at »stagnation« when insufficient heat
is used. In this case, no heat is transported to the condenser by the
absorber medium. This »inherent temperature restriction« can have a
positive effect in systems that are exposed to frequent, but short,
stagnation phases. If the absorber is at stagnation for a substantial
period then a very high stagnation temperature will occur in the
condenser, and thus also in the heat transfer fluid in the collector
circulation. This is because there will be some heat transmission from
the absorber to condenser despite this theoretical »inherent temperature restriction«.

The possible working temperature of these collectors is in principle
somewhat lower than with tubes with direct flow due to the additional
heat transmission between the condenser and collector circulation
heat transfer fluid.

Vacuum Tubes »Sydney« / CPC
The »Sydney« tube was developed as a purely double-walled glass
tube to avoid possible vacuum loss through the metal/glass connection
of other tube collector constructions. In contrast to other vacuum tubes,
the absorbing surface is directly on the inner glass tube in »Sydney«
tubes. A reflector is necessary to make use of the absorber area away
from the sun due to the rounded absorber. These reflectors are
frequently used as concentrators and the entire collector unit is marketed
as a so-called CPC (Compound Parabolic Concentrator). The effect of
the reflectors outside the cover may decline with time due to weathering influences. The reflectors should therefore be checked and cleaned
during maintenance , which is necessary in any case.

This tube type has achieved a good position on the market due to its low price, despite the lower performance compared with other tube technologies for smaller installations.

Note that when making comparisons between different types of system the differing information regarding »areas« must be taken into account. CPC collectors generally offer a larger aperture area due to the reflector, but a relatively small, rounded absorber area.

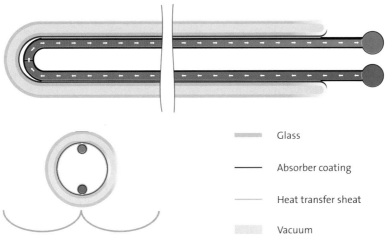

Glass

Absorber coating

Heat transfer sheat

Vacuum

Figure 5.13 Cross-section through a »Sydney« tube with round absorber

A new development by Schott-Rohrglas combines the »Sydney« tube with a reflector within the tube. The reflector is protected against the effects of weathering in this tube.

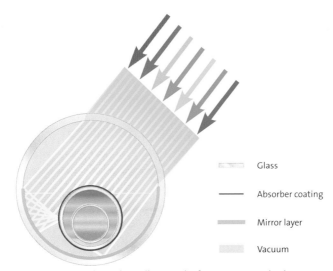

Glass

Absorber coating

Mirror layer

Vacuum

Figure 5.14 Cross-section through a collector tube from SCHOTT Rohrglas

5.3 **Absorber**

5.3.1 **Function and Constructional Features of the Absorber**

The light energy in sunlight is converted into heat in the absorber, also called the »solar absorber«. A heat transfer fluid flows through channels in the absorber; this fluid transports the heat generated to the storage tank or consumer. The absorber efficiency F', already mentioned in Chapter 5.1 describes the deviation of the actual absorber efficiency from the ideal value (=1) on the basis of the heat transmission from the absorber to the heat transfer fluid flowing through it. This transmission is never uninterrupted in practice.

The channels containing the heat transfer fluid should not be too far apart so the emission of heat from the absorber to the heat transfer fluid is effected with a high and uniform efficiency over the entire area. In practice, a tube interval of 100–120mm is usually selected. This represents a compromise between optimum heat elimination, low heat capacity, reduced material use and low processing costs.

In addition, the absorber must be made of a material with good thermal conductivity, yet this material should not be too thin. In practice, copper or aluminium sheet with a thickness of 0.2mm is mostly used, within a range of 0.15mm and 0.3mm. The heat conductivity of copper is clearly better than that of aluminium, which is in turn considerably better than that of steel or stainless steel.

Good contact between the absorber sheets and the heat transfer fluid channels as well as between channel tube wall and heat transfer fluid are additional pre-requisites. Heat transmission between tube and fluid is decisively influenced by the properties of the fluids (water-glycol mixtures are used in many countries due to the climatic conditions; these have a lower heat capacity than pure water) as well as the flow through the tube. When the flow through the tube goes from the turbulent to the laminar range, then the heat transmission falls drastically. In the case of low-flows, e.g. in installations according to the low-flow principle, an absorber designed for a high-flow rate can lose considerably in performance.

A constant flow through the absorber must be ensured. If parts of the absorber receive no or insufficient flow through, then the collector performance falls proportionally to the size of the area without sufficient constant flow.

The flow distribution in the absorber depends on the relationship between pressure loss in the collecting and distributing pipes, and that in the absorber channels. Pressure loss in the collecting and distributing pipes should always be a maximum of 20–30% of pressure loss in the absorber channels. If this rule is observed, then a virtually constant flow through the individual absorber channels can be guaranteed.

Figure 5.15 and Figure 5.16 show two infrared images of an aluminium rollbond absorber with grid-arranged flow channels. The absorber rear side is shown in Figure 5.17. The absorber which is stored at approx. 20°C, was connected to a hot water pipe (60–62°C) (input lower right, output upper left). The water throughput was set at 22 l/(h•m^2) in the first trial, at 65 l/(h•m^2) in the second trial. The infrared images were taken after approx. 20 minutes respectively (that is after equilibrium conditions had been reached).

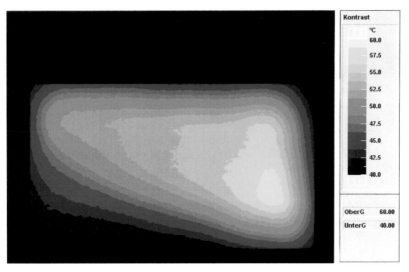

Figure 5.15 Surface temperature of a roll-bond absorber at a flow rate of 22 l/(h•m^2)

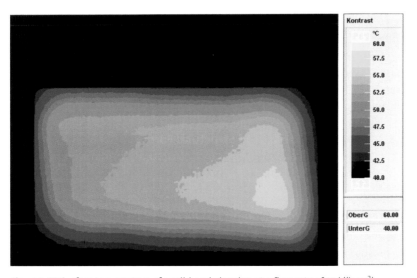

Figure 5.16 Surface temperature of a roll-bond absorber at a flow rate of 65 l/(h•m^2)

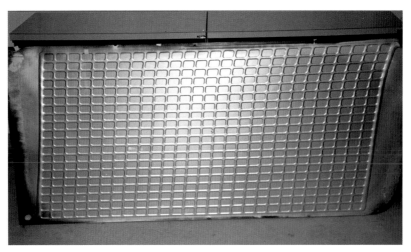

Figure 5.17 Rear side of a roll bond absorber with grid-arranged channels

It can be clearly seen that with the low volume throughput (Figure 5.15) the absorber flow through is not constant. The lower left corner has a low temperature of approx. 40 °C. It must be taken into consideration that this temperature level was generated by heat conduction in the aluminium instead of by flow through with warm water. This absorber is not suitable for such through flows. Constant flow through is only reached at throughputs above 60l/(h•m²) (Figure 5.16).

The absorber must have a high absorption coefficient for the entire spectral range of solar radiation, so that it can convert as much radiation into heat as possible. Special absorber coatings or selective coatings ensure this. In order to keep heat loss from the absorber as low as possible, it is fitted in a well insulated casing (i.e. a box for flat plate collector, a vacuum tube for vacuum tube collectors). The casing must of course be radiation-transparent on the side facing to the sun (transparent front cover for flat plate collector). The losses due to heat radiation from the absorber can be minimised by applying selective coating to the absorber.

5.3.2 Absorber Materials and Structural Forms
Very many absorber materials and structural forms were used in installations from the 80s

Steel:
- Steel meander type absorbers produced by pressing two meanders into two steel plates which are subsequently welded together
- Steel cushion type absorbers shaped from steel sheets welded point-wise and subsequently »blown up«

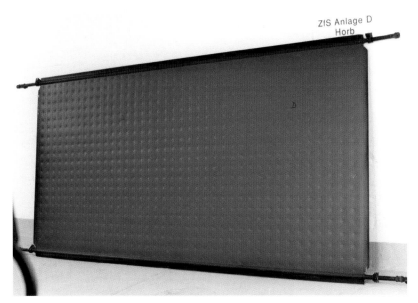

Figure 5.18 Rear side of a steel cushion absorber

The steel cushion absorbers proved to be very susceptible to corrosion. In the case of some absorbers, the corrosion was so great that wall breakthrough even occurred (see Figure 5.19). This corrosion damage occurred especially in installations in which either (a) the inhibitors in the heat transfer fluid were effectively used up or (b) when the absorbers were not constantly filled with heat transfer fluid because they had run empty after stagnation (drain-back systems); this occured despite the nitrogen filling in drain back cases. Such cushion absorbers are always sensitive to corrosion since very narrow clearances are formed at the welded points and these are not sufficiently filled with heat transfer fluid with inhibitors.

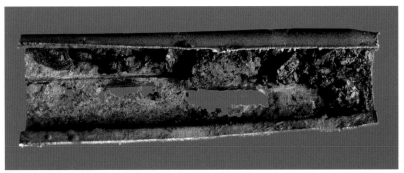

Figure 5.19 Corrosion damage (wall breakthrough) at a steel absorber

Steel absorbers have not proved usually successful and are seldom offered on the market today.

Stainless steel:

• Stainless steel meander tube inserted between two aluminium sheets with corresponding half-rounds. The sheets and tubes are subsequently bonded.

The absorbers with stainless steel tubes bonded between two pre-stamped aluminium sheets did not show any corrosion. However some loss of contact between the sheets and the tubes occurred since the adhesive was not stable. This led to considerable loss of efficiency.

Large-scale adhesive bonding of this type is no longer used today so that such defects should no longer occur.

Figure 5.20 Rear side of an absorber made of aluminium with enclosed, sunk-in stainless steel meander tubes.

Aluminium:

- **Aluminium roll-bond absorber** in which two aluminium plates are firstly coated linearly in the structure of the planned flow channel network and then pressed together so that they are joined over the entire surface (except at the coated areas). The flow channels (parallel or grid-arranged) are then formed at the non-joined parts of the sheets through »blow-up«

- **Aluminium heat pipe absorber** with stainless steel heat-exchanger

- **Absorber sheets made of aluminium** which are glued, clamped or bonded at high pressure with heat transfer fluid tubes made of other materials (copper, stainless steel; see sections on these materials) (tube arrangement as harp or meander)

If the heat transfer fluid flows directly through aluminium e.g. as with roll-bond absorbers, then particular attention must be paid (a) to the content of suitable corrosion inhibitors in the heat transfer fluid in mixed installations (i.e. various materials in collector circulation) and (b) to the avoidance of narrow clearances between the aluminium and other materials. Aluminium absorbers proved to be non-critical regarding corrosion with suitable heat transfer fluids containing good corrosion inhibitors. Slight local attack inside the absorbers was acceptable due to the relatively large wall thickness.

Figure 5.21 Rear side of an aluminium roll-bond absorber with parallel flow channels

Damage to purely aluminium absorbers occurred however if the absorber was already treated incorrectly before installation e.g. due to storage outdoors without the inlet and outlet being sealed. Thus moisture and air contaminants could penetrate into the absorber and start the corrosion process. If aluminium is handled correctly then it is a corrosion-resistant material.

However aluminium roll-bond absorbers are seldom used today.

Figure 5.22 Rear side of aluminium absorber with clamped-on copper tubes in meander shape.

These absorbers only used aluminium as the absorber sheet and had flow channels for the heat transfer fluid made of stainless steel or copper. These correspond to the most common constructions customarily used today. No damage preventing successful functioning occurred in absorbers of this construction, apart from local attack on the surface of non-flow through aluminium sheets.

Copper:

• **Copper-plated flow channels** in aluminium sheets

• **Copper tube absorbers** joined with copper or aluminium absorber sheets (see under »Aluminium«)

In summary it must be said that corrosion damage to absorbers was relatively rare. Moreover, corrosion generally affected absorber materials or structural forms which are no longer in use. Absorbers which were constructed according to the principles customary today, did not show any corrosion attack, which could affect function, even after approx. 20 years.

5.3.3 **Current Absorber Materials and Structural Forms**

Today, copper is used in most collectors for the heat transfer fluid tubes or channels. The absorber sheets themselves are also made of copper or aluminium; steels are seldom used for this purpose. Plastic or stainless steel are only used in applications where an aggressive medium flows directly through the absorber (e.g. swimming pool water).

The most important customary structural forms today include those listed below with their special features.

Meander Absorbers (Serpentine Absorbers)

In the case of meander absorbers, a single meander-shaped tube containing the entire heat transfer fluid passes through the absorber sheet (see Chapter 5.3.2). This structural form did not assert itself for a long time due to the somewhat higher specific loss of pressure and to difficulties in absorber production. However, it has spread recently due to the advantages in circuitry (e.g. low-flow installations).

Advantages:

- Less production effort required
- Parallel switching of many collectors is possible
- Operation of individual collector units under low-flow conditions is possible (turbulent through-flow)

Harp Absorbers with Absorber Fins

Due to the wide-spread use of absorber fins, the harp absorber has achieved a greater market share up to now than the meander absorber despite the greater production effort required. Several parallel tubes with a forward and return pipe are combined to form a »harp« construction for this structural form. This type is also used for natural flow collectors due to the lower flow resistance. There are different variants of parallel and row systems of absorber fins within the collector on the market. Until 1995, most absorbers were produced using absorber fins. Until the beginning of the 90s, aluminium/copper absorbers from Sweden with the name »Sunstrip« paved the way for selective absorbers. The falling copper prices improved processing methods, and increased heat conductivity meant there was increasing conversion to copper absorbers. This resulted in an increase in performance for the collectors.

For production technical reasons in coating, in the installations for further processing and above all due to the large proportion of collectors manufactured as home-made, mainly narrow copper strips were used. Increasing professionalism in collector production means that these absorber fins are rapidly losing importance due to the greater production effort required. Their use in the future will be reduced to tube collectors and large-scale collectors in small production runs, as well as for architecturally adapted collectors.

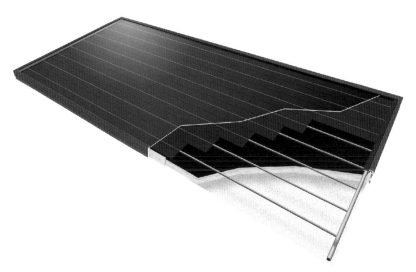

Figure 5.23 Collectors with harp absorber

Advantages:

• Low pressure losses in individual collectors possible (pressure loss dependent on switching of absorber fins in collector)

• Use in natural flow systems possible

• Universal use in vastly differing array switching

Absorbers with Flow Through over Complete Area

In this concept, tubes pass through the entire absorber. These tubes have a small distance between each other which can be selected freely. The individual tubes may have very small cross-sections due to their great numbers. Absorbers with flow through the entire area, are generally manufactured by »large-area joining« e.g. from two stainless steel plates using pressure or laser welding (cushion absorber). The so-called complete area absorbers can only be further processed using production devices, since handling and processing make greater demands than the processing of absorber fins.

Convective heat transport mechanisms, as occur between the overlapping absorber fins in a harp absorber, are avoided here so that higher degrees of efficiency can always be achieved. The pressure resistance of complete area absorbers is restricted by the strength of the connection and the sheets. It is generally 300 kPa.

The type of absorber is now only offered by a few manufacturers, however it is gaining in importance.

Figure 5.24 Absorber as absorber plate

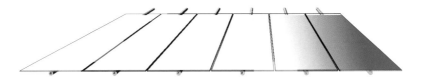

Figure 5.25 Absorber made of individual absorber fins

5.4 **Absorber Coating**

5.4.1 **Function of the Absorber Coating**

Since metal surfaces reflect light to a relatively great extent, the metal absorbers must be provided with a coating which absorbs very strongly in the solar radiation wavelength range (high absorption α). Therefore at the start of thermal solar technology, specially developed black solar paints were used (without selective properties). Later however so-called »selective« layers were used. These have the advantage over the solar paints of having greatly reduced emittance, ε, in the heat radiation wavelength range and thus decrease thermal losses.

In general, high absorption of solar irradiation, with low emission of heat radiation characterises an efficient absorber. These two radiation regions have different wavelength bands. Thus, in the case of a body at 200 °C, 99 per cent of the heat radiation from it is emitted at wavelengths more than 2.5 µm. Yet 98 % of the energy of sunlight arrives as irradiation with wavelengths less than this value. So minimising heat radiation at wavelengths above 2.5 µm does not hinder optimum absorption of the sunlight. Thus it is possible to design surfaces so that, on one hand, solar radiation can be absorbed at wavelengths below 2.5µm with a high degree of efficiency (say absorption coefficient $\alpha = 0.95$) and at the same time the undesired radiation loss of heat at wavelengths above this value can be greatly reduced (say emission coefficient $\varepsilon = 0.05$ to 0.2).

This capability of separating two functions, namely both high light radiation absorption and low heat radiation loss, has led to these surfaces being described as »selective«.

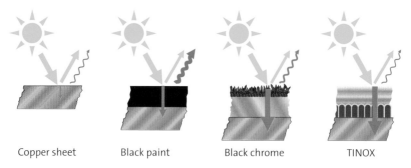

Copper sheet Black paint Black chrome TINOX

Figure 5.26 Absorption, reflection and useful heat on various surfaces

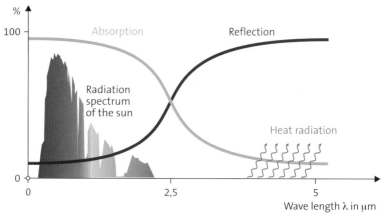

Figure 5.27 Absorption/emission spectrum

5.4.2 **Absorber Coatings in the Past**

In Germany, investigations of absorber coatings and collectors installed in the 80s within the framework of a research program (future investment program) were carried out. The following coatings were used:

- Solar paints (not selective)
- Nickel-pigmented aluminium oxide on aluminium (selective)
- Black chrome with nickel sandwich layer on copper (selective)
- Black chrome directly on copper (selective)
- Cobalt sulphide / oxide (selective) on steel sheet
- Selectively acting enamel on steel

The results of the investigations on these absorber coatings, after approx. 15–20 years use on collectors, are summarised below. More detailed information can be found in the first edition of »Langzeiterfahrungen mit thermischen Solaranlagen« /2/.

Measurements of the degree of spectral absorption and emission were carried out on selected absorbers. The results of the spectral measurements shown in the following Chapter demonstrate the regime of the absorption and emission in the wavelength range from 0.38 to 50 µm. The wavelength range up to approx. 2.5 µm is decisive for solar radiation absorption. The absorption coefficient (α) should be as large as possible below this value. The range above 2.5 µm is important for the minimum emittance (ε) of heat radiation.

The measurements were carried out with an artificial solar spectrum having the spectrum of a full radiator at a sample temperature of 100 °C (373 K). The α and ε mean values were calculated using weighted integration of the measurements over the spectrum.

Non-selective Absorber

The »α« values of absorbers coated with non-selective solar paint were in the range of 0.95 after at least 15 years in operation. This indicates that absorption capacity has not diminished. However the emission coefficients of old collectors were between approximately 0.90 and 0.95. It is not clear whether deterioration of a selective surface has occurred or whether the values were initially in this high range. Somewhat better ε values, around 0.85, were only measured on a slightly newer non-selective collector (8 years old).

It should be emphasised that the coatings of non-selective absorbers showed no, or little, efficiency losses as compared to new absorbers of the same type. In the system grouping (solar system degree of utilisation) any slight efficiency loss of the collectors has even less effect on the efficiency of the system, as can be demonstrated using simulation models.

Selective Absorber with Nickel-pigmented Aluminium Oxide Coating

Two different makes of collector were investigated, both with aluminium absorbers and selective coatings made of nickel-pigmented aluminium oxide (aluminium roll-bond and »Sunstrip« absorbers). The coatings were covered with numerous white spots at many places in both absorbers. These spots were corrosion products from aluminium hydroxide, which indicates that the absorber area must have frequently become moist (probably due to condensation water). Water from the moisture film penetrated the porous aluminium hydroxide in the selective coating. Thereby the water reached the aluminium of the absorber and caused slight spot corrosion and the formation of aluminium hydroxide. The latter, in turn, diffused through the pores in the absorber surface. This selective coating is known to be moisture sensitive.

Figure 5.28 shows two areas of an absorber (aluminium roll-bond) which have differing degrees of coating defects. These two areas were investigated for their absorption and emission behaviour. The results are shown in Figure 5.29.

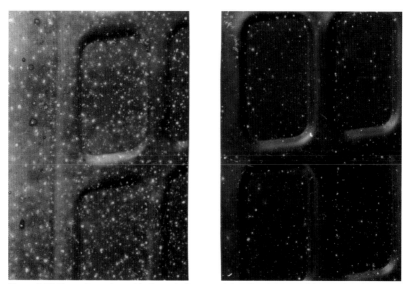

Figure 5.28 Strongly and weakly degraded areas of the aluminium roll-bond absorber with a selective coating of nickel-pigmented aluminium oxide

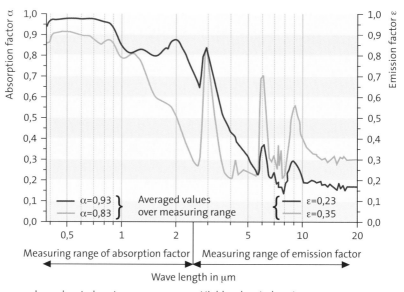

Figure 5.29 α and ε in strongly and weakly degraded area of absorber surface

The mean absorption coefficient (α) is 0.93 for the weakly degraded sample and 0.83 for the strongly degraded sample. Both samples showed emission peaks at 3 µm, 6 µm and 9 µm in the infrared range, however these were markedly less in the case of the weakly degraded sample at 6 µm and 9 µm. These peaks are typical of the aluminium hydroxide formation due to corrosion. The mean emission coefficient (ε) values were 0.23, with weak degradation, and 0.35 with strong degradation.

Despite the clearly demonstrated degradation of the absorber coating, the selective effect (higher absorption in short wave radiation range, low emission in long wave range) is still marked in these collectors, even if greatly weakened. Degree of efficiency characteristic curves and comparative calculations with other (relatively new) collectors show that the efficiency of the collectors has only deteriorated slightly due to the degradation of the selective coating. This only causes a reduction in yield of the solar installation of some 1–2% (relative) depending on specific load (temperature) in the solar grouping.

Due to the moisture sensitivity with the concomitant effects described above, this coating is hardly used today.

Selective Absorber with Black Chrome Coating with and without Nickel Sandwich Coating on Copper

Black chrome coatings are still used today. The base material for the coating is copper. (There were attempts in the past to apply black chrome onto aluminium absorbers; however this was not successful due to technical difficulties in production.)

The absorbers of the flat plate collector are protected against oxidation with a nickel layer in this coating process, otherwise the black chrome layer would peel off when the copper oxidised. In the case of vacuum tube collectors where no oxidation can take place in the tubes due to the lack of oxygen, the nickel base material can be dispensed with and the black chrome applied directly onto the copper. Since the emission properties are slightly affected by the nickel layer, black chrome coatings applied directly onto copper generally have better spectral values than when applied onto nickel.

The coatings investigated after approx. 6 years in operation gave an optically perfect impression. No aging indications could be seen.

The result of the investigations using measurements is shown for an absorber in Figure 5.30. The absorption and emission behaviour of the absorber reverse side (bare copper) is also shown in this Figure for comparison. The a value of just under 0.96 and the ε value of 0.11 are in the range to be expected in new condition, even after 6 years. It can therefore be assumed that there is hardly any deterioration due to aging. The low values for absorption and emission of the copper reverse side correspond to the new condition.

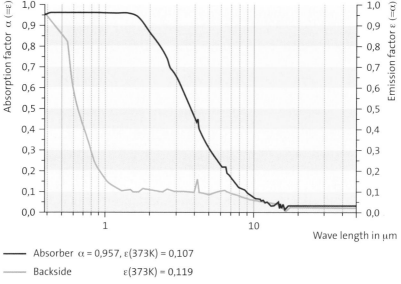

—— Absorber $\alpha = 0{,}957$, $\varepsilon(373K) = 0{,}107$

—— Backside $\varepsilon(373K) = 0{,}119$

Figure 5.30 α and ε of a 6-year old copper absorber with a coating of black chrome on nickel

Vacuum tube collectors which were investigated after 20 years in operation. These had copper absorbers and black chrome directly applied to the absorbers. The values for »α« were 0.92 to 0.93, those for »ε« was 0.05 to 0.07. The values for the new tubes were stated by the manufacturer as $\alpha = 0.90$ to 0.95 and $\varepsilon = 0.05$, so that the optical values were still in the »new« condition even after 20 years. In comparison to the »black chrome on nickel« coating of the flat plate collector mentioned above, the mean emission values were are, as expected, somewhat lower.

The excellent measurement values of the old black chrome coatings and the optical impression of the absorber are verification of the very good resistance of this coating.

Selective Steel Absorber with Cobalt Sulphide / Oxide Coating

A vacuum tube which had been in operation for 15 years and one which had been stored for the same period without having ever been used, were investigated. Both tubes had retained their vacuum. The absorber coating made a good optical impression. The measurement results confirmed the optical impression. The value for α was between 0.91 and 0.94 for both absorbers; ε was 0.04 to 0.07. The new values were stated by the manufacturer as $\alpha = 0.95$ and $\varepsilon = 0.05$. No degradation of the selective absorber properties had occured in the 15 years of use.

Nevertheless this coating is no longer used today.

Enamelled Selective Steel Absorber

The enamelled absorbers often gave a bad impression. The enamel coating had flaked off in some places and the steel was rusted at these points (see Figure 5.31). Rust points were also frequently found on the edges of the absorber. In addition, the colour of the absorbers appeared very different, some darker blue/green/red colour, some more pale yellow/red colour. Thus two absorbers (one dark and one pale) were investigated.

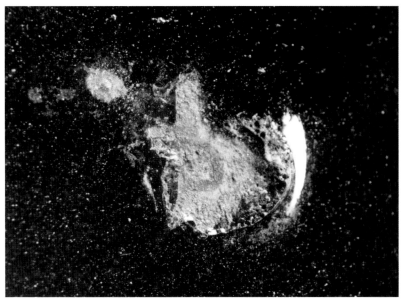

Figure 5.31 Absorber areas with destroyed enamel coating and slight rust deposits

The investigation results showed that »α« for both absorbers was approx. 0.91. The emittance however was scattered between 0.24 and 0.38 for the darker absorber and between 0.56 and 0.72 with the paler absorber.

Since the absorbers were subject to the same operating conditions, it may be assumed that the great differences in the selectivity of the two absorbers did not arise due to aging but are due to quality variation in production.

The absorber coatings used in the past have shown very good durability, with the exception of the enamel coating and with restrictions due to the moisture sensitivity of the nickel-pigmented aluminium hydroxide. The latter two products are today no longer on the market. The results of the investigations show that it is possible to manufacture absorber coatings with good optical properties and at the same time high stability.

5.4.3 **Current Absorber Coatings**

Of the coating materials mentioned in Chapter 5.4.2, the black chrome coating is mainly used today.

Black Nickel

In the coil coating process, copper coil is generally passed continuously through several baths with solvent and cleaning agents. Subsequently, nickel and/or chrome are applied electrolytically. In the bath process, complete absorbers are coated in several individual baths one after the other.

The electro-plated coatings have good selective properties; the production processes are tried and trusted in practice and long-term stable.

Since black chroming and nickeling include production steps which are hazardous to health, extensive workplace protection is essential.

The energy consumption for the production of black chrome layers is, according to various manufacturers, between 2.7 and 12.4 kWh/m^2.

Black Crystal

After the copper sheet has been cleaned, a nickel layer is in turn coated with special crystals (the composition is not stated) and subsequently covered with a sprayed on liquid glass. This is an electroplating process. The cleaning solutions and nickel baths are treated chemically and added to the effluent.

Protective measures are required for dealing with the alcohol vapour in the area where the liquid glass is sprayed on (alcohol solution).

There are conflicting statements by manufacturers and processors concerning energy consumption.

PVD (Physical Vapour Deposition)

An electron beam is directed onto a crucible containing coating material, all within a vacuum chamber containing the surface to be coated. The material vaporises and is deposited on the copper coil, whilst oxygen and nitrogen are introduced at low pressure into the evacuated chamber. The absorbers manufactured in this manner are on the market under the brand name »Tinox« or »Ecoselect«.

In the case of the Tinox coating, a quartz topcoat serves optically to adjust the refractive index between the layer and the air. The layer below this comprising titanium, nitrogen and oxygen, forms a robust transition to the copper. Thus it is possible, with this type of coating to create different colours of the absorber surface by adjusting the layer thicknesses. »Non-blue« absorber layers can thus also be produced; these have excellent selective properties.

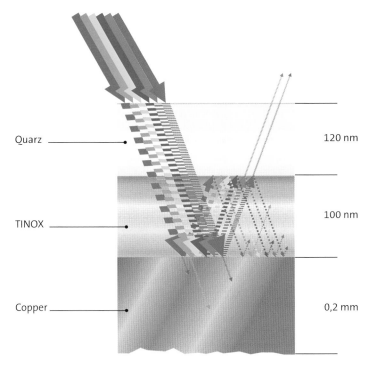

Quarz   120 nm

TINOX   100 nm

Copper   0,2 mm

Figure 5.32 Incident light and absorption on an interference coating

Sputtering

This takes place in a chamber filled with argon. For d.c. sputtering a glow charge is struck between an anode and the coating material connected as the cathode. Due to the field created, argon ions are accelerated towards the cathode, which is eroded due to the bombardment, i.e. it is »sputtered«. The ions released are deposited on the copper coil. Absorbers manufactured according to this process are on the market under the names Sunselect (Interpane) and Sunstrip (Teknotherm).

PECVD process

In addition to coating on the basis of the PVD process, a further layer is applied in CVD (Chemical Vapour Deposition). In the CVD process, a volatile chemical compound which contains components of the coating required, is placed in a reaction chamber with the absorber. The compound decomposes on the heated copper coil and leaves a layer of inorganic elements or compounds behind.

Characteristic Values of Current Absorber Layers

All selective absorber layers on offer today have, without exception, absorption coefficients of 0.95 or more in the solar spectrum. Non-selective coatings, such as solar paints, have absorption coefficients of 0.9 to 0.95.

Emissions coefficients ε of the selective absorbers available today are between 0.05 and 0.12; however the production tolerances of individual products vary considerably. Coatings which require a further layer as a substrate (e.g. black chrome on nickel) can achieve a minimal emission coefficients of approx. 0.11, very thin coatings, such as TiNOX or Interpane layers can achieve minimum emission coefficients of approx. 0.03. In practice, the values of the series are slightly above this optimum.

In contrast, the emission coefficients of solar paints (not selective) range from 0.85 to 0.95.

Firm	Product	α	ε	Coating	Process	Absorber	Available
Tekno Term	Sun Strip	0,95± 0,02	0,15± 0,02	Ni on oxidized Alumin.	electro-chemical	Alumin.	yes
MTI	Black Chrome	0,95± 0,02	0,12± 0,02	Black Chrome on Nickel	Coil process	Copper	yes
Batec	Batec	0,95± 0,02	0,12± 0,02	Black Chrome on Nickel	Coil process	Copper	yes
GIBO	GIBO	0,95± 0,02	0,12± 0,02	Black Chrome on Nickel	Coil process	Copper	yes
INCO Alloys	Maxorb	0,97± 0,02	0,11± 0,01	Black Nickel	glued foil	Alumin.	yes
Energie Solaire	Solar Absorber	0,94± 0,02	0,18± 0,04	Black Chrome on Nickel	Coil process	Stainless steel	yes
Thermafin	Black Crystal	≥0,95	≤0,1	Nickel	Coil process with crystallization	Copper	yes
Tinox	Tinox	0,95	0,05	Tinox	PVD	Copper	yes
Tinox	ecoselect	0,92	0,05	Tinox	PVD	Copper	yes
Interpane	Sun-select	0,95	0,05	Material mixture	Sputter	Copper	yes
Tekno Term	Sun Strip new	0,95	0,1	Nickel	Sputter	Alumin.	yes
Ikarus Solar	Absorber 2000	0,95	0,1	a-c:H/metall	PECVD	Copper	vague
Solel (Luz)	Solel	0,98	0,08	no report	no report	Copper	vague
Shiroki	Sydney-Absorber	0,96	0,03	no report	no report	Glass	yes
SCHOTT	no report	no report	no report	no report	Sputter	Glass	yes
div. provider		0,9± 0,02	0,2± 0,05	paint process	paint process	Alumin./ Copper	yes

Table 5.3 Characteristic values of absorber coatings currently on the market.

Current Selection Criteria and Artificial Aging

From experience with older solar installations and from the determination of the efficiency of older absorbers, the claim that the coatings in flat plate collectors are not durable enough can now be regarded as disproved; although this is still claimed by some participants in the market. In connection with the values stated for the absorption and emission, quality control in series production is to be regarded critically and questioned, there are significant differences. At this point, the user can only trust to the quality awareness of the collector supplier.

Testing Long-term Durability

The rapid technical advances mean the question of long-term durability and handling of coatings is posed again and again. Up to now there has not been any long-term experience in real operation of solar installations with these coatings.

In order to test the durability of selective coatings without long-term field trials, a test procedure was developed in co-operation with various research institutes within the framework of Task 10 of the IEA (International Energy Agency). This test procedure simulates ambient conditions, e.g. the effect of temperature, moisture etc., on the selective layers. Using comparisons with absorbers which aged in normal use, a test cycle was developed which permits the testing of new and old coatings for suitability for everyday use under real conditions. This so-called »Task 10 Test« confirmed, that the efficiency of coatings after 25 years in the collector was at least 95 % of the original efficiency. The many years of work on simulating external conditions means that the Task 10 Test Procedure offers the purchaser, now, a relative certainty of the long-term usefulness of the coating after successful testing. Task 10 Tests are carried out, amongst others, by the International Technikum Rapperswil (ITR), Switzerland, the Fraunhofer Institut (FhG-ISE) Germany and the Swedish National Testing and Research Institute. At present the ISO standard ISO/CD 12952 T2, is in preparation; this means that the Task 10 Test is to be converted to a standard. In cases of doubt, users can obtain corresponding test certificates from collector suppliers and, thereby, from absorber suppliers.

5.5 Collector Casings

5.5.1 Task and Function

For flat-plate collectors, the casing encloses the absorber and heat insulation of the collector, so protecting them from moisture and mechanical damage.

For vacuum tube collectors, the evacuated glass tubes form the casing for the absorber, and the vacuum provides the heat insulation.

5.5.2 **Collector Casings in the Past**

Early solar technology had, most collector frames made of profiled aluminium, however plastic or galvanised steel troughs as well as glass fibre reinforced plastic (GRP) profiled frames were also used.

No significant degradation has occurred on any casing made of profiled aluminium during the 15 years operation of the installations. The Glass fibre reinforced plastic frames also made a good impression.

In the case of galvanised steel troughs, the sheet was often rusted from the inside and outside (condensation in the collector) because the zinc layer had worn in some places. The collector was thus some-times unsightly, however there was no danger that the trough would rust through, since the rust was only on the surface (see Figure 5.33). However, the corrosion process proceeds much faster when the zinc layer has been worn off. It is perhaps doubtful whether all such zinc troughs would have withstood a further 10 years without substantial damage.

Figure 5.33 Corrosion on the outside of a galvanised steel trough collector casing (inside of trough similarly corroded)

In some cases, the sheet cover on the rear of the collectors was loose. Thus rain water was able to penetrate, so the insulation to be wet and the absorbers to become corroded.

In one collector type, the transparent front cover was pressed on to the frame with an aluminium rail running around the frame. The aluminium rails were screwed together at the corners by angle sections. The absorber itself was also attached in the frame with screws. In some collectors, the absorber attachment screws had loosened and had fallen between the absorber and the cover. The attachment screws of the angle sections were partly loosened (see Figure 5.34).

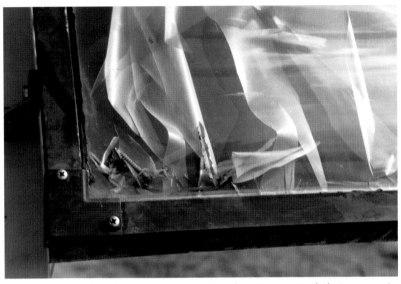

Figure 5.34 Partial view of a collector frame with angle sections to attach the transparent front cover (absorber attachment screw is loose in the collector; film is torn and split)

All the collector frame, damage observed was due to constructional weak points which have been eliminated to a great extent in today's collectors. Therefore it is unlikely that such defects will be repeated. The collector casing is thus regarded as less critical in the assessment of the service life of today's collectors, provided that high-quality materials are used. Galvanised steel troughs are only suitable, in our opinion, if an especially thick zinc layer is applied.

5.5.3 Current structural forms

Today, collector casings are mainly manufactured from aluminium.

If the rear and side walls are only formed by thin materials, e.g. insulation laminated with aluminium, then there is a danger that these walls may be damaged through to the insulation during transport or fitting. This hardly affects the function of the collector, provided that the insulation has closed pores and no rain water can penetrate into the casing. However, the visual impression made by laminated insulation damaged in this way is not good, e.g. if the reverse wall remains visible after collector fitting (in outdoor set-ups, on flat roofs, pergolas etc.).

In the case of some flat plate collectors for in-roof fitting, wooden frames are also used. In this structural form, wood protection is necessary to prevent the penetration of moisture and to maintain the moisture balance in the wood. The wood is generally completely covered with a frame.

The wooden frame should be separated to the interior space using an edge insulation of the absorber, to prevent excessive temperature loads in the case of collector stagnation.

5.6 **Reflectors**

5.6.1 **Task and Function**

Reflectors direct a portion of the radiation, which does not otherwise hit the absorber, onto the absorber by reflection. This ensures a higher radiation density on the absorber or direct sunlight on to parts of the absorber not otherwise irradiated.

Natural reflectors are, for instance:

- few white clouds in the sky
- water or areas with white gravel in front of the array

Artificial reflectors may be flat or also slightly curved for concentrating (depending on requirements). They are attached behind the absorber.

Since no rear insulation material is required for vacuum tube collectors, it is reasonable to have the radiation that passes unused between the tubes on the side of the absorber away from the sun (flat and round absorbers) away from the sun reflected into the glass tubes. This also applies to the CPC described in Chapter 5.2 .

5.6.2 **Experience with reflectors**

An array with vacuum tube collectors was installed in a solar house in Freiburg-Tiengen in Germany. These collectors have a reverse side aluminium reflector which is to direct radiation passing the tubes onto the absorber reverse side.

The most noticeable negative effects were aging of the reflector, with partial moss and lichen growth on the reflector and the reverse of the tubes. The system had Philips tube collectors. The reduction in efficiency of the system due to dirt accumulation was estimated at approx. 15%, relative to yields shortly after installation and allowing for approx. 15 years' operating time. The reduction in efficiency may be more for an individual collector tube. Since the vacuum tubes themselves (without reflector) did not show any aging in the laboratory tests, the logical consequence is that a decrease in efficiency would not have occurred without the reflectors. No reflector would have become dirty and the dirt accumulation on the backs of the tubes would not have had any effect, since the reverse side would not have been subjected to any (reflected) solar radiation. Therefore, the question arises of the suitability of such reflectors located outdoors. There is certainly a slightly higher efficiency with new reflectors, however this effectiveness decreases greatly in the course of time. Whether the additional cost for such reflectors is justified seems doubtful on the basis of the results of the investigation.

5.6.3 Requirements for reflectors

The reflector materials should be very smooth, with polished surfaces which repel dirt very well, and permanently corrosion-free, or free from the formation of rough anti-corrosion layers. Shiny aluminium surfaces do not, for example, comply with the latter condition.

White screens or pale gravel may have good reflective properties at the beginning, however in the course of time, they may loose much of their reflective power due to greying or moss or lichen-type growth.

When planning the use of collectors with reflectors, a decline in reflection and concomitant losses in performance should be recognised for reliable long-term yield forecasts.

5.7 Collector cover

5.7.1 Task and function

The transparent collector cover has several purposes:

- it protects the absorber and heat insulation in the collector casing from environmental effects

- it is part of the heat insulation because it, as with glass in a greenhouse, it permits the entry of sunlight and makes heat emission more difficult

- it should reflect as little radiation as possible from its surface and absorb as little light as possible into its interior so that almost all of the solar radiation hits the absorber

- it must have a long lifetime, be robust and withstand environmental effects (rain, hail, wind, UV radiation) and large temperature fluctuations

5.7.2 Covers in the past

Plastic covers were very common in the early stages of present solar technology; frequently in combination with a second, interior cover made of a film material. In some cases, cheap window glass (ferruginous, containing iron) was used for the glass covers; this has poorer transmission properties than the non-ferruginous glasses used today. Some makes of collectors had a double glass cover.

The double cover resulted from attempts to keep heat losses at the front as low as possible. However this was at the expense of the transparency to solar radiation. This construction principle with double cover was abandoned with the spread of improved selective layers.

The most frequently used plastic covers were acrylic glass domes (polymethylmethacrylate (PMMA)). Regardless of collector make, many acrylic domes had cracks at the attachment points to the collector frame.

These probably occurred due to embrittlement of the material after longer use, possible promoted by internal stress in the material caused by production and the great temperature changes in operation. With the exception of these edge areas, most domes made a relatively good impression despite frequent fine hairline cracks and fulfilled their function.

Ruptures outside the edge areas were only often observed in collectors from one manufacturer (Esser). This collector is a rare construction type typical of the enthusiasm for experiments at the beginnings of solar technology. However, after a few years this type showed defects to the acrylic dome and other damage (torn film, matt reflectors, defective seals between acrylic dome and frame, interior corrosion in the absorbers), so that most of these installations were switched off in the mid 80s. The manufacturer ceased production of these collectors after a short period.

All acrylic domes looked clear and transparent (c.f. transmission measurements on an acrylic dome of a different make of collector in Chapter 5.7.4). In collectors, the seal between the frame and dome had been squeezed out, probably due to the relatively high heat expansion of the plastic dome (around ten times more than glass) and the associated frequent movement of the dome around the area of the seal.

Only glass fibre reinforced plastic (GRP) covers from one manufacturer (ZinCo) were investigated. All the GRP covers inspected were very yellowed and opaque.

PVC (polyvinylchloride), PVF (polyvinylflouride) or polyester materials were used for the films. PVC and PVF films were without exception embrittled, fragile and frequently torn. PVC films were partly so friable that they crumbled when removed. Approx. 50% of the polyester films were torn in the collectors in all installations. Films still intact »burst« very easily on attempts to remove complete collectors for further investigations when the collector frame was bent by only a few mm during removal or transport. In one collector, the film tore during the collector test.

Fracturing of glass covers was only reported in isolated cases. The doubts frequently expressed on the durability of glass covers have not been confirmed. In addition, the fact that today's collectors are subject to much more stringent test criteria (e.g. reliability test) than those produced at that time must also be taken into consideration.

Experience in these investigations established that the mechanical durability of glass covers is considerably superior to that of plastic domes. Interior films as a second cover have not proved useful. We are also sceptical in the case of the few film materials used today whether they can fulfil the requirements for long collector service lives (over 20 years), particularly when the collectors are operated at high temperatures (frequent stagnation periods).

5.7.3 **Dirt accumulation on collector covers**

Exterior dirt accumulation on flat plate collectors

Regular cleaning of the cover was not carried out by any of the installation operators who were asked. In order to be able to estimate the effect of dirt accumulation on the performance, measurement of the conversion factor (η_0) was carried out on four collectors (two with acrylic domes, two with glass covers) before and after cleaning of the cover (see Table 5.4). Measurements from the Institute for Solar Technology Hameln-Emmertal, Germany (ISFH) for an installation on the roof of a heating and power station (Project »Nahwärme Göttingen«) are also included.

Location	Cover	Year in Opera-tion	η_0 [1] dirt accumu-lation (cleaned)	η_0-reduction due to dirt accumulation
Office building 10 m high outskirts of Bayreuth	Acrylic	16	0.737 (0.747)[2]	0.01[2]
Motorway kiosk rural area	Acrylic	15	0.680 (0.686)	0.006
Office building 55 m high city centre of Düsseldorf	Glass - clear	16	0.731 (0.736)[2]	0.005[2]
Office building 10 m high city centre of Regensburg	Glass - textured	8	0.712 (0.715)	0,003
Heating and power station (near rail station)	Glass - textured	2	0.665 (0.730)	0.065

[1] Reference: aperture area, wind speed 3 m/s
[2] Dirt could not be removed completely; η_0 in new condition and thus η_0 reduction due to dirt accumulation therefore probably greater

Table 5.4 Effect of dirt accumulation

Four collectors were installed at locations with common levels of air pollution and dust. In this case, the difference in the optical efficiency »η_0« before and after cleaning is between 0.003 and 0.01, i.e. after 8 to 16 years in operation without cleaning, the conversion factor only deteriorates by 0.3 to 1% (absolute). In the dimensioning of a solar installation as a pre-heating system, this represents a reduction in yield due to dirt accumulation of approx. 2 to 6 kWh/(m^2·a). Related to the annual yield of a pre-heating installation, the percentage reduction is approx. 0.5 to 1.5% (relative).

The acrylic and glass cover surfaces could not be cleaned completely. With the acrylic domes, persistent hazing remains; with the glass, the dirt was »burnt-on«. For these two collectors the actual »η_0« reduction due to dirt accumulation must therefore be somewhat higher than can be seen in Table 5.4.

The conversion factor for glass collector covers in the solar installation at the Göttingen heating and power station, which is installed near the main railway station, had in contrast already deteriorated by 6.5%

after 2 years (absolute) /25/. The cause of the dirt accumulation is probably road traffic and exhaust fumes from diesel shunting locomotives. The proportion from the gas fuelled heating and power station is probably low. In this case, the reduction in yield of approx. $30\,kWh/(m^2 \cdot a)$ would be considerable (reduced annual yield of solar installation by 7–10% (relative) depending on operating temperature). The array should be cleaned regularly at this emission-loaded location.

In total, the results confirm the procedure customary in practice: that natural dirt accumulation is generally rinsed away with rain and that manual cleaning can be dispensed with at locations with normal levels of air pollution. However, regular cleaning is recommended for locations with high levels of air pollution and dry climatic zones with high dust loads.

Manual cleaning should be carried out extremely carefully with acrylic covers since this »soft« material can easily be scratched by careless treatment; scratches can under certain circumstances reduce efficiency more than slight dirt accumulation.

Exterior dirt accumulation on vacuum tubes

The effect of dirt accumulation on four vacuum tube collectors was investigated within the framework of investigations on the solar house at Freiburg-Tiengen, Germany. The different types of tubes had been in use for nearly 19 years (15 years for the Philips) next to one another in the same solar installation, without ever having been cleaned. They were exposed to the same environmental effects in a rural area but were of differing constructions.

In the the Corning collectors, the heat transfer fluid flows directly through the absorber in the tube. Six tubes are connected in a collector module. The collector module was fitted so that the reverse side of the tubes lay directly over the inclined roof tiling. Three tubes of this type were investigated.

The Philips collector comprises 12 heat pipe vacuum tubes. The absorber in the tubes is selectively coated on both sides. There are polished aluminium reflectors underneath the vacuum tubes; these reflectors reflect the light which passes through the gaps between the tubes onto the reverse side of the absorber.

All the tubes had normal dirt accumulation on the front; both makes had moss growth on the reverse sides of the tubes. The rear reflectors used with one collector type (Philips) were dull with reduced reflectivity and also partly covered with moss. The dirt on the tubes could be washed off easily; the dirt on the reflectors however could not be removed completely. After cleaning, the tubes were clear and clean, the reflector remained somewhat »dull«.

In the case of the two collectors without reflectors (Corning), the cleaning of the tubes led to an improvement in the conversion factor of 0.008 i.e. approx. 1% relative (conversion factor after cleaning: approx. 0.77 – 0.78 referring to aperture area), this is within the range of flat plate collectors with normal dirt accumulation. Since the previously dirty and »mossed« reverse of the tubes did not have to be transparent to sunlight, this optical deficiency did not reduce the conversion factor, that is cleaning the rear side did not have any effect.

In the case of the collectors with reflectors (Philips), the difference in conversion factor before and after cleaning was considerable at 0.073 (i.e. more than 11% (relative)) (η_0 cleaned: approx. 0.65, referring to aperture area). Due to changes in the surface of the aluminium reflector and to moss growth, both the reflector function and the transmission through the rear side of the glass tube were affected. Therefore the optical effectiveness was greatly restricted. Since the reflector was still somewhat »dull« even after cleaning, then the conversion factor of the dirty collector modules in total had decreased by approx. 15–20%, as compared with the tubes when new. On the basis of this reduction in the conversion factors of the collectors, the system efficiency of this solar installation had deteriorated by approx. 15% (relative). This reduction was with rural air, at lower levels of air pollution than urban environments .

The bad experience with the Philips collector causes doubt as to whether reflectors outside the collector casing, and therefore exposed to the surroundings, can fulfil their function in the long-term (particularly due to the dirt accumulation on the back of the tubes).

Interior Dirt Accumulation on Flat Plate Collector Covers
Very many front covers of flat plate collectors, had deposits on the inside. This arose from condensation run off, perhaps related to gas evolution from the insulation and/or absorber coatings. A detailed treatment of the internal dirt accumulation would have required exhaustive analyses of composition and quantity of the deposits and collector component compounds. Such an investigation would have exceeded the scope of this project. It is known that the binders contained in rock wool insulation can evolve gas at higher temperatures, as can the propellant in polyurethane (PUR) insulating foams, particularly if the permissible operating temperature of the foam is exceeded. Condensation run-off tracks were frequently observed; these varied greatly in scope even with identical collectors within an installation. Probably the extent of condensation and ventilation varied between collectors due to production tolerances.

However some sample measurements of transmission with both uncleaned and cleaned insides were carried out. In the case of a glass cover (MAN collector) with visible high dirt accumulation and many condensation run-off traces on the inside, transmission improved due to cleaning from 0.793 to 0.797, i.e. only by 0.4% (absolute). In this case the inside dirt accumulation looked worse than it actually was.

Two samples were taken from a domed acrylic cover; in this case transmission increased due to the interior cleaning by 1.3 and 2.1% (absolute). The inside dirt accumulation was more critical than that on the outside.

The few measurements do not permit reliable interpretation of the cause of the varying degrees of interior dirt accumulation. If the transmission reduction is projected to the conversion factor, then the η_0 reduction due to inside dirt accumulation is approximately in the same range as from outside dirt accumulation (with »normal« air pollution). In some cases, the detrimental effects of interior accumulation were obviously worse than from exterior accumulation.

5.7.4 Aging of Transparency

Whether, and to what extent, optical transparency of collector covers has deteriorated could only be investigated if comparative values from new condition were available; this was not the case with any of the collector types. The investigations were therefore limited to a few random sample measurements. Some qualitative statements were subsequently formulated from the results of visual impressions.

The optical transparency of glass depends very greatly on the iron content. The lower the iron content is, the better the transmission. The collector covers made of white-glass achieve transmission values of up to 0.95. Normal window-glass was often markedly below 0.90. New acrylic covers were also around 0.90. These basic values provide an approximate way to analyse the older collectors investigated.

Table 5.5 lists the transmission coefficients of various older collector covers after 13 to 16 years in operation (measured after cleaning of both the cover inside and outside).

Collector manufacturer	Solar Diamant	BBC	MAN	Krupp Arbonia	Buderus	ZinCo
Material cover	White glass 1-fold	Window glass 1-fold	Window glass 1-fold	Window glass 2-fold	Acrylic	Glass fibre reinforced plastic
Years in operation	13	14	16	16	15	14
Transmission	0.92	0.87	0.80	0.71	0.84	0.45

Table 5.5 Transmission of collector covers after 13 to 16 years in operation

The transmission of the non-ferruginous white glass cover is still very high after 13 years, at 0.92. The window glasses of the 14 and 16 year old BBC and MAN collectors have considerably lower transmission values. As expected, the 16 year old double pane collector has the lowest value (0.71).

The acrylic dome listed in Table 5.6 still has a transmission value of 0.84 after 15 years and is thus between the two one-pane window glasses. This leads to the conclusion that acrylic domes, which at that time were used as the main alternative to window glass, hardly lag behind glass with regard to transparency, even after many years in operation. A further indication of the relatively good retention of transparency by acrylic domes, are the results of performance measurements on an old Viessmann collector in which the old dome had been replaced with a new one. The increase in performance due to the new dome was only minimal (increase in collector degree of efficiency of approx. 1 to 2% (absolute)). Comparative measurements of global irradiance underneath the old and new domes confirmed in transmission differences of this extent.

The glass fibre reinforced plastic (GRP) cover, of a 14-year old collector from ZinCo, is unsuitable as a collector cover. Transmission (τ) is effectively too low at a value of only 0.45.

GRP covers are rightly no longer used by any manufacturer.

Glass covers are preferable to acrylic glass, due to the better mechanical properties. Even in a comparison of the optical properties of acrylic with the white glasses used today, acrylic covers are not an alternative. Double transparent covers are not necessary today because of the modern use of selectively coated absorbers.

5.8 Heat Insulation and Seals

5.8.1 Task and Function

Thermal insulation is necessary in flat plate collectors to reduce heat losses. Generally the back wall and the sides of the collector casing are lined with these materials. As well as rock and glass wool, PUR foams and melamine resin are used. In rare cases, smaller manufacturers offer collectors with sheep's wool, flax or other »natural« insulation. The insulation materials must withstand the high stagnation temperatures of the collectors. In particular, the rear side insulation, on which the absorber mostly lies, must have high thermal stability. The insulation should not evolve gas, even at very high temperatures, otherwise inside deposition on the cover pane is to be expected.

The seals at the shaped impact points of the casing, at the glass cover and at the tube ducts are to prevent the penetration of rain water over the entire operating period. Above all, the seals at the tube ducts must withstand very high temperatures in the case of stagnation and also mechanical loading (movements of tubes due to temperature expansion).

5.8.2 Heat Insulation in the Past

In the collectors investigated, the insulation consisted almost exclusively of polyurethane (PUR) rigid expanded sheets or rock wool, sometimes also both materials in combination. Insulation was both without or with aluminium lamination (laminated on one or both sides). Rock wool is still used frequently today. PUR sheets (not in combination with other materials) are rare.

All rock wool insulation was undamaged and corresponded in appearance to nearly new condition, regardless of whether it was used in selective or non-selective collectors or whether aluminium lamination was present or not. The measurement of thermal conduction of rock wool insulation from a 16-year old collector resulted in a value of $\lambda_{10°C} = 0.034$ W/(m·K), which is within the range of new condition. The thermal conduction is stated as 0.032 W/(m·K) in a brochure from the manufacturer from the early 80s.

Figure 5.35 shows a cross-section through insulation from a selective flat plate collector after 15 years in operation. It consists of a 4.5 cm thick PUR rigid expanded sheet with an additional rock wool mat on the side towards the absorber (as shown in Figure 5.35). The thickness of the rock wool mat is approx. 4 cm when the absorber board is removed, compressed to 2 cm with the absorber plate on top. The rock wool is not laminated with an aluminium film, i.e. its upper side lies directly on the back of the absorber. There is a plate made of mineral fibre lamina at the edges of the collector to attach the insulation.

Figure 5.35 Rock wool insulation (top) and PUR rigid expanded mat (below) of a selective flat plate collector after 15 years in operation

Figure 5.36 Absorber-proximal surface of a PUR rigid expanded mat after 15 years in operation (heat transfer fluid flow ducts are shown)

While there was no change observable in the rock wool except, for some loose dirt residues, the PUR mat, which is pale coloured in a new condition, was discoloured brown on the surface at the absorber and was hardened at the top. Figure 5.36 shows this surface of the rigid expanded mat. The meander-shaped heat transfer fluid ducts of the absorber are shown also.

The areas with dark brown discolouration are at the middle of the collector and at the uppermost edge in the area of the collector outlet. There is less brown discolouration at the lower inlet area. The intensity of the discolouration thus follows the temperature development in the absorber. Even in this case with the insulation mat »protected« from the absorber by the rock wool mat, damage to the PUR foam has occurred. In other selective collectors in which the insulation mat was directly on the absorber back, the PUR foam was partly so crumbly that the aluminium lamination on the insulation plate no longer adhered.

In contrast, none of the PUR rigid expanded mats in non-selective collectors showed any discolouration – a clear indication of the low temperature load.

The question arises, referring to collector efficiency, of the extent to which the material destruction near the absorber has an effect on insulation properties. The cell structures of the PUR foam are partially destroyed due to material over-heating and to the escape of the gas within the insulation. This means that the heat conductance of the PUR mat increased, however it is still low in comparison to new rock wool (PUR foam manufacturers state heat conductance values of λ =

0.030 W/(m•K) for insulation mats without propellant). The laboratory tests carried out to to determine quantitatively how thermal conduction depends on temperature load, confirm that thermal conduction is still very low even after partial gas evolution of the propellant, but has deteriorated by approx. 20% (relative). (New condition: $\lambda_{10°C}$ = 0.020 W/(m•K); after one week in an oven at 150°C: $\lambda_{10°C}$ = 0.024 W/(m•K))

The continuing good insulating properties of PUR rigid expanded foams even after many years are confirmed by measurements on this material from two 14 and 13-year old collectors. The thermal conduction was $\lambda_{10°C}$ = 0.025 W/(m•K) for a non-discoloured insulation from a non-selective collector. It was 0.029 W/(m•K) from a selective collector in which the insulation mat lay on the back of the absorber and, similarly to the PUR mat in Figure 5.36, had considerable discolouration on the absorber side, however it was only slightly yellowed to the collector back. The thermal conduction has decreased considerably for both insulation mats (by 25% and 45%), however it is still relatively good and comparable with that of new rock wool.

Even if PUR rigid foam mats are not intended for use in selective collectors by insulation manufacturers due to their low temperature resistance the damage which occurred is not critical to the function of the collector. Such damage only has a slight effect on efficiency if the collector working temperature is not too high. We recommend that either (a) any PUR foam used is protected from contact with the hot absorbers by an intermediate layer of rock wool, or that (b) only rock wool is used, particularly in very efficient collectors used in large-scale installations which are frequently exposed to high stagnation temperatures.

The seals at the tube ducts are to be regarded more critically than the insulation. Figure 5.37 shows two of the seals, made of an undefined white elastomer, after approx. 15 years in operation with some stagnation periods. The seal from the collector outlet is on the left, from the collector inlet on the right. It is clear to see that the deformed and highly crumbled seal from the collector outlet could no longer fulfil its purpose.

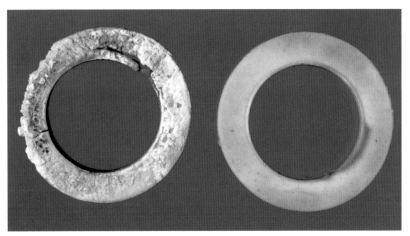

Figure 5.37 Seal between collector casing and collector tubes
Left: collector outlet; right: collector inlet

5.8.3 Current Experience with Heat Insulation Materials

The thickness of the back wall insulation is, in most cases, between 40 mm and 70 mm. Increasing the thickness of the insulation beyond this has only led to a slight improvement in the k value.

Under certain circumstance, greater effects can be achieved by using an edge insulation. Particularly with collectors with frames made of aluminium or stainless steel, the edge insulation can prevent a thermal bridge between the absorber and frame. This markedly improves the k value. Furthermore, even smaller thermal bridges to the tube ducts are to be avoided by using suitable insulation. Careful construction at these points, also in consideration of any vibration during transport, is generally more effective than further increases in insulation thicknesses.

Panels with deposits on the inside of the cover occur again and again, even with tried and trusted collector models. One cause of this is quality fluctuation in the insulation material or production defects, but also improper storage. The interaction with other materials in the collector, such as glass and absorber coatings should be tested for all materials before their use by the manufacturer. This testing should be carried out with every material before its use, since the high temperatures in the collector cause gas evolution in almost all materials.

Sheep´s wool, flax, hemp or similar natural materials are used in some collector models. These alternative insulations must be subject to very close testing due to the possible gas evolution from the material at high temperatures. Some of these materials have proved to be unsatisfactory in practice, this becomes noticeable due to condensation on the inside of the collector cover or to decomposition.

5.8.4 **Requirements for New Sealing Materials**

Materials based on ethylene-propylene-dien-monomer (EPDM) have proved themselves for the seal profiles used between the frame and the pane of glass. These materials have also been used satisfactorily in vehicle construction.

The adhesives used are mostly silicon-based. In this case, care should be taken, since many of the products on offer have completely different compositions despite having the same name. When using these materials, the interaction between them with regard to adhesive power, material softening and gas evolution must be tested as well as their long-term stability.

The seals in the tube ducts should be temperature resistant to the stagnation temperature (approx. 180°C) in order to guarantee permanent sealing against leaks. Some silicon-based materials are suitable for this purpose.

5.9 **Inspection and Testing Procedures for Collectors**

Between 1994 and 2000, the new European standards for thermal solar installations and collectors were devised by the Technical Committee 312 of the European Standards Organisation CEN (CEN TC 312, CEN: »Comité Européen de Normalisation«). These were based on the recognised ISO standards (ISO: International Organization for Standardization) existing at that time, as well as on national standards. The adoption of ISO standards in EN standards, and vice versa, is frequently carried out on the basis of an agreement between the standardisation institutions ISO and CEN.

Since 2001, the EN standards for solar collectors and solar installations have been in effect common throughout Europe. The corresponding national standards valid until then, were withdrawn in the course of 2001. For solar collectors, only EN 12975-1 /26/ has applied throughout Europe since mid 2001, and only EN 12975-2 /23/ since 2002. Both standards apply to fluid collectors without integrated storage tanks and without trackers.

EN 12975-1 describes the criteria for solar collectors to be fulfilled for verification of conformity with standards. On one hand it deals with the evaluation of test results, questions of safety as well as product documentation and identification. Furthermore, it gives information on conformity to standards, on materials and their resistance, on ecological factors and on repeat testing for constructional modification.

EN 12975-2 describes the testing procedure applicable for uncovered collectors (so-called swimming pool absorbers), and for flat plate or tube collectors with transparent covers. Section 5 describes the reliability tests. Section 6 explains the procedures to measure thermal efficiency including loss of pressure and capacity determination.

5.9.1 **Testing Collector Reliability**

So-called »type« testing mainly comprises the reliability testing, whereby clear criteria for passing the test are given. In addition, the performance measurement must be carried out. However, collectors usually pass this latter criteria without difficulty. Thus the reliability test is of central importance for a solar collector.

In 1995, the international standard ISO 9806-2 /27/ was published, including the description of the qualification test procedures. Several years of development work in the ISO standardisation committees and expert groups which participated, preceded this. ISO 9806-2 is the basis of the test procedures described in Section 5 of EN 12975-2. In addition there the EN standard includes the mechanical pressure and so-called loading tests.

The following tests and investigations are carried out within the framework of reliability testing:

- Stock receipt examination: inspection for damage, completeness and outward conformity with documentation.

- The documents (drawings, installation and operating instructions) are examined for completeness.

- Testing of the pressure resistance of the absorber with 1.5 times the maximum operating pressure before and after exposure phase.

- Exposure phase, during which the collector is exposed to weathering (uncooled) over at least 30 days' sun (over $4\,kWh/m^2$ per day) and at least 30 hours' sun (over $850\,W/m^2$). High-temperature testing is also carried out in this phase and the very important stagnation temperature is determined (see below).

- Internal and external shock loading, for which the hot collector is suddenly cooled with cold water from inside and from outside during the exposure phase.

- Testing of rain-proofing which during both outside exposure and in a separate rain test.

- Testing for frost-proofing. This can be omitted for collectors which are operated with an anti-freeze mixture as the heat transfer fluid. However, the test must be carried out for collectors that are emptied (drain back or drain down operation), as well as for inherently frost-proof collectors.

- Mechanical tests: these include a test for (a) sufficient strength of the glass attachment, (b) the frame holder with a suction load of $1,000\,N/m^2$, (c) the strength of frame, holder and glass to an overpressure of at least $1,000\,N/m^2$. Optionally there is the so-called impact resistance test, in which steel or iron spheres hit the collector with considerable impact.

- The tests are completed with the concluding inspection from out-side, as well as dismantling of the specimen during which confor-mity to drawings and any damage due to loading is investigated.

The test report concludes by stating if the specifications in EN 12975 have been observed.

The individual reliability tests generally lead to results which are either positive or negative for the specimen. The measurement of stagnation temperature is the exception in this case. It is stated as the highest temperature which can occur in the collector at an irradiance of $1,000\,W/m^2$, an ambient air temperature of 30°C and low wind speed. The stagnation temperature is decisive for the design of the materials in the collector, the connection technology and loading of the heat transfer fluid. The materials used must be designed accor-ding to their installation position so that they can permanently with-stand the temperatures to be expected at these points.

While the EN standard only states one climate classification (so-called moderate climate) with the reference conditions $1,000\,W/m^2$ irra-diance and 30°C air temperature; there are two further climate classi-fications in ISO 9806-2 which have markedly higher loading: i.e. the sunny climate with $1100\,W/m^2$ and 40°C air temperature and the very sunny climate with at least $1200\,W/m^2$ and 40°C. If, for example, the stagnation temperature of a flat plate collector is 200°C in the moderate climate classification, then in the sunny climate this would be 223°C and in the very sunny climate over 236°C.

5.9.2 Testing Collector Efficiency

Collector efficiency measurement methods have been in existence as national regulations since the mid 70s. An important and wide-spread procedure is the ASHRAE standard 93-77 /28/ developed in the USA which is still in use today in its principles. In this test, the collector degree of efficiency is determined completely under irradiation. An alternative procedure which determines the heat losses of a collector in a dark test was frequently in use in Europe until the mid 90s.

In 1994, the standard ISO 9806-1 /24/ was passed, with the description of performance measurement procedures for solar collectors with glass or acrylic covers. The test procedure described there is in turn based on performance measurement under irradiation. There are only slight differences in test methods and conditions between ISO and the EN standard, which has been applicable since 2002, with the exception of the quasi-dynamic test procedure first introduced in EN 12975-2 /26/.

The performance test procedure described in EN 12975-2 (Section 6) is presented briefly below. In the main, the following also applies to ISO 9806-1.

The standard-conform complete performance measurement includes determination of the degree of efficiency curve (with the parameters η_0, a_1 and a_2), the zero loss collector efficiency, as well as capacity and collector pressure loss. The characteristic values determined therefore describe the efficiency of a solar collector (see Chapter 5.1):

- The conversion factor η_0 (frequently also called zero loss coefficient) is the degree of efficiency when the mean collector fluid temperature equals the ambient air temperature.

- The heat loss coefficients a_1 and a_2: both coefficients together describe the heat losses of a solar collector. They can be summarised using the difference ΔT between collector and ambient temperature in an effective loss coefficient $a_{eff} = a_1 + a_2 \cdot \Delta T$.

- The incident angle modifier (θ): these values state the extent of change in degree of efficiency with sloped incident sunlight below the angle of q compared to vertical irradiance $(\theta = 0°)$. In the case of tube collectors, there is a further differentiation in which direction the angle deviation is (longitudinally or cross-wise to the collector).

- The thermal capacity of the collector C: this value describes the quantity of heat which must be input into a collector to heat it by 1 K.

- The collector reference area A: a complete set of characteristic values applies for one respective reference area which must be defined clearly (see Chapter 5.1.4. for area definition).

The evaluation of measurements of degree of efficiency according to EN is effected using the difference between the mean collector fluid temperature and ambient air temperature (ΔT). The characteristic values are to be interpreted accordingly. In tests according to ISO 9806, the difference between input temperature and ambient temperature is mostly used for this purpose. This means that a direct comparison between collector parameters is no longer possible.

In addition, the collector reference area must be taken into consideration: while ISO relates test results refer to the absorber of gross area, the aperture of absorber area is used in EN. Any comparison of collector characteristic values must begin with a check of whether reference area or reference temperature have been used similarly. If this is not the case then the characteristic values must be converted correspondingly.

The EN standard permits several test procedures. Firstly the stationary degree of efficiency determination, which is carried out either (a) in the laboratory under precisely specified solar simulators, or (b) in an outdoor test on a fixed test roof or a test area with solar tracking. Secondly, an alternative new non-stationary (quasi-dynamic) test procedure has been introduced.

The test conditions may also differ: the incident angle and the diffuse radiation proportion (in outdoor tests) may also affect the measurement data as can the spectrum (in the simulator test). It is also important whether water, as in many test locations, or a water/glycol mixture is used for the test.

To determine the degree of efficiency curve, the collector is installed in a test installation and the flow is set according to the manufacturer's instructions. The inlet temperature of the medium is maintained at a constant level. The main measurement values such as inlet and outlet temperatures, irradiance, ambient temperature and wind speed as well as flow rate are recorded and evaluated. To obtain performance data at different operating temperatures, the inlet temperature is gradually increased during the test. Thus a number of degree of efficiency measurement points are obtained. These permit determination of the generally parabolic degree of efficiency characteristic curve with the coefficients η_0, a_1 and a_2. It must be noted that according to ISO 9806-1, the results can also be stated in a linear degree of efficiency characteristic curve with the coefficients η_0 and a.

In measuring the incident angle modifier, the procedure is analogous. However in the determination of the degree of efficiency curve, the inlet temperature, but not the incident angle, is changed. In this case, the inlet temperature of the medium is kept constantly low and the incident angle is varied. The degree of efficiency ratio between inclined irradiance and vertical irradiance is determined.

5.10 Differing Performance Test Results

In addition to the possibly differing test conditions mentioned above, the measurements recorded include a measurement uncertainty, which is reflected in the characteristic values. Therefore deviations between the testing institutions are to be expected in the measurement results. The deviation in the conversion factor is typically ± 2%. This value is aimed at by recognised testing institutes in Germany.

The fact that measurement results may vary between test institutes must be taken into account in comparative interpretations. It is in principle possible to restrict the range of test conditions as well as to reduce measurement uncertainty, to minimise the above mentioned differences . However the equipment requirements, time required and thus costs increase significantly for a performance test.

5.11 **Use of Characteristic Values, Yield Calculations**

The set of performance characteristics presented above for comparison between various products, is simplified if the measure of performance is reduced to one single characteristic value. This may be a theoretical collector yield, which can be calculated using a yield simulation program.

Firstly the solar installation into which the collectors are to be integrated has to be defined. Then the installation parameters and the collector characteristic values are entered into the input mask of a simulation program. It is important that (a) the collector area type used and (b) the reference area for the collector characteristic values from the test report, are identical. In Europe, this is either the aperture or the absorber area (see Chapter 5.1.4); both sets of characteristic values are stated in the test report according to EN standard. According to ISO, the gross area may also be stated.

In some countries, the calculation of collector yield, or the computational verification of collector minimum yield, is included as a marketing argument or as a subsidy pre-condition. This has also led to confusion in the past:

- The yield values calculated differ according to installation type, location and alignment, collector area, heat requirements and details of installation design.
- The use of different simulation programs leads to different results. In addition, the result from a simulation program can only be good if the system has been simulated correctly by the operator. The more complex and free the simulation program is in system definition, the more experience the user generally needs. Two users can achieve results which differ greatly from one another even using the same simulation program for the same system.
- In Switzerland, so-called »gross heat yields« are calculated. In this case the model collector is operated at a constant inlet temperature of, for instance, 40 °C for one year. These values generally exceed the system yields stated above.
- In general, these are ideal values which have little to do with the actual operating conditions of a thermal solar installation. High area-related yield values are frequently calculated; the installation operator however cannot expect these in his installation. This, however, is difficult to pass on to the operator when the gross heat yield is stated in the installation data sheet.

Due to the variety of possible configurations, comparisons between products should always be carried out using the same simulation program with the same settings. In doing so, measurement uncertainty in the determination of the characteristic values must be considered and is must also be made clear that the yield which can actually be expected are very different (generally lower).

5.12 **Identification Issue**

The type testing comprising complete testing according to EN 12975-2 with confirmation of conformity to standard according to EN 12975-1 is the minimum a collector should fulfil. The various European countries have national certification programs based upon which identifications are issued; these identifications confirm conformity to standards. In Germany this is the »DIN Tested« symbol issued by DIN CERTCO (Berlin).

Work is currently in progress on a European certification program so that these national symbols are also recognised internationally. The result is then a so-called »Key Mark Label« which is issued in addition to the national symbol. A customer in Europe thus has the certainty that, regardless of manufacturing location and testing location, the quality minimum required by the type testing is observed.

Submission of a type test for solar collectors, or submission of a corresponding conformity symbol, is demanded in some national building laws and standardised contractual procedures.

The safety of pressurised equipment and components has been dealt with within the framework of the so-called European pressurised equipment guidelines since 1999. From 29th May 2002 this European guideline implemented in the respective national law will supersede all previous legal regulations. Up to now, the issue of CE symbols according to the pressurised equipment guideline was of no significance for solar collectors. This may change in the future. While individual collector modules may only fall into category I, due to their low pressure-volume product, and thus only require a manufacturer's declaration. Collector components frequently fall into category II and, in the case of large-scale systems (e.g. pressure-volume product greater than 200 bar•litre, which usually occurs above a collector area of 30 to 60 m^2), in category III. In this case, an institution accredited according to the pressurised equipment guideline must be involved in the conformity procedure. The CE symbol of verification, is affixed by the manufacturer.

In some countries, there are more extensive symbols, e.g. eco labels. These demand further minimum standards beyond the type testing with regard to environmental compatibility in production, operation and recycling or disposal. One well-known example is the »Blue Angel« symbol issued in Germany.

The variety of symbols means that consideration must be taken to properties of the product or the criteria for which the symbol has been awarded.

5.13 **Further Test Procedures on Collector Components**

Further standards have been developed in the ISO Technical Committee 180; these standards concern the reliability of collector components.

Absorber coatings are subject to an extensive procedure according to ISO 12952; this is mainly known as the Task X method. The procedure was developed within the framework of the International Energy Agency, Solar Heating and Cooling Programme, Working group – Materials in Collectors (Task X). The coatings have to fulfil performance criteria which describe the absorption and emission characteristics. The tests consist of long-term temperature loading, loading in moist atmosphere, with condensation formation on the absorber as well as exposure to corrosive atmosphere.

Aging tests for transparent collector covers under stagnation conditions are described in ISO 9495, the testing method for sealing materials is explained in ISO 9553.

5.14 **System Tests**

The European standards for system tests have been available since 2001. These are divided into EN 12976 /29/ for prefabricated installations (Factory Made Systems) and ENV 12977 /30/ for custom-built installations (Custom Built Systems). ENV means that this is a preliminary standard whose validity is initially restricted to 3 years.

Prefabricated installations are mass products with a trade name, which are considered as complete »ready to install« construction sets with a fixed installation method. Custom-built installations are either manufactured in individual production or selected from a range of components.

The question of which class to use is easy to answer if the installation is an integrated collector-storage tank system, a thermo siphon installation (EN 12976) or an individually designed, mostly, large-scale installation (ENV 12977). Small domestic water installations with forced circulation can frequently be tested according to both standards.

Part 1 of EN 12976 and of ENV 12977 stipulate requirements regarding durability, reliability and safety of solar installations. Part 2 describes the respective test procedures. Furthermore, ENV 12977-3 also stipulates test procedures for the thermal evaluation of hot water storage tanks. In addition to the testing of safety technology of solar installations, efficiency is also to be tested in particular.

In the case of prefabricated installations, there is a differentiation as to whether the installation has auxiliary heating or not. If so, the performance of the entire installation is tested according to the so-called CSTG procedure. If not, it is tested according to the so-called DST procedure. Both procedures produce long-term forecasts concerning performance.

The CSTG procedure (CSTG: Solar Collector and System Testing Group) is described in ISO 9459-2 (ISO 9459-2: Solar heating – Domestic water heating systems – Part 2: Outdoor test methods for system performance characterization and yearly performance prediction for solar only systems). The DST procedure (DST: Dynamic System Testing) is described in ISO DIS 9459-5 (ISO DIS 9459-5: Solar heating – Domestic water heating systems – Part 5: System performance characterization by means of whole-system tests and computer simulation).

For custom-built installations, the efficiency does not have to be measured. As an optional measurement procedure, the EN 12977-2 describes the so-called CTSS procedure (CTSS: Component Testing, System Simulation), here the component characteristic values are determined separately: for the collector according to EN 12975-2, for the storage tank according to EN 12977-3 and for the control system according to EN 12977-2. The behaviour of the entire installation is calculated with a simulation program using these characteristic values.

The additional heat requirement to cover the design heat specification is determined as an indicator of performance. A solar fraction is calculated for systems without auxiliary heating. The auxiliary energy requirement for pumps, control systems etc. is a further indicator of performance.

System performance tests have advantages over the above mentioned yield calculations from a purely collector test. Weak points which may reduce the actual yield are more likely to be discovered in this case. It remains to be seen what experience will be made with the system standards in the next few years. Standardisation does not remain at a standstill; always contributes to ongoing revision for the future.

Application of Test Procedures within the Framework of the Test Results Presented

The collector performance measurements, carried out within the framework of the research program »Solarthermie 2000« (sub-program 1) in Germany, were aimed at comparing the current performance of old collectors with reference to their original performance. Therefore efficiency tests were carried out based on the DIN V 4757-4 (1995) /31/ standard valid at the time of the project. The degree of efficiency curve was determined under irradiation in every case (some 800 to $1000\,W/m^2$), with fluid inlet temperatures of approx. 20 to approx. 90°C, and with simultaneous application of an ambient air speed of 3 m/s. The measurements were carried out either in the laboratory with a solar simulator or on an outdoor test facility with solar tracking. Determination of the incident angle modifier and thermal capacity was not performed.

The determination of the collector parameters η_0, a_1 and a_2 has not changed in essence between DIN V 4757-4 (1995) and the current EN standard. The parameters measured can therefore be interpreted as characteristic values determined according to the stationary methods from EN 12975-2. The reference area for the collector characteristics in this case is the aperture area.

6. Collector Assembly Types

Apart from considerations about orientation of a collector (azimuth and tilt angles), architectural and visual factors are most significant for the location of the solar array.

Apart from the obvious on-roof-assembly, the circumstances may favour a facade mounting, or partial roofing of a veranda, conservatory or atria or a free-standing rig on a garage or pergola etc.

Regardless of the type of assembly, particular attention is required for the materials used and the processing techniques. Components are exposed to the environment for a very long time (some 20 to 30 years) and thus need to be resistant against:

- temperature fluctuations within the expected limits; e.g. parts near the collector need to withstand higher temperatures
- rain, hail and snow
- UV-radiation
- pollutants and corrosives (such as salt in coastal regions)
- birdpecking

If galvanized components are used, the zinc layer has to be of a high grade and has to be protected from damage under all circumstances, because otherwise they might corrode excessively within 25 years. If only small components are needed for the attachment of the solar panels, corrosion-insensitive materials (such as stainless steel and aluminium) are preferable.

On-roof assemblies make sense only if the remaining lifespan of the roof-skin exceeds the working life of the collectors.

Flat-plate collectors, in their (liquid filled) operating condition weigh approximately $25\,kg/m^2$. Vacuum tube collectors are somewhat lighter. Mountings and supporting framework need to be able to absorb this additional load, as well as the potentially very large forces due to wind and snowfall. Note that the wind load on tubular collectors in an open framework is less than on the equivalent flat collectors.

Figure 6.1 This roof needs refurbishment prior to collector assembly

6.1 **On-Ground Assembly**

The free-standing rig directly on the ground or on top of a carport, pergola etc. offers a cost-efficient solution. The underlying surface is often still available for other usage (e.g. as a shelter). The danger of impairment (e.g. vandalism at freely accessible sites) needs to be considered.

Figure 6.2 Free-standing rig on the ground (Stiebel Eltron, Germany)

6.2 **Assembly on a Sloped Roof**

If collectors are mounted on a sloped roof, their orientation is naturally tied to the slope of the particular roof. However, the usual roof slopes of some 45° correspond well with the desired tilt of the panels in mid latitudes. Here, sun-facing roofs with slopes of between 20° and 50° provide minimal yield losses (less than 5%). Even if azimuth angle of such a roof deviates up to 45° from north/south, the solar yield diminishes only slightly. However in such cases, less inclined roofs perform somewhat better. Also, requirements for a particular use may affect the choice of a proper roof surface, e.g. for auxiliary solar heating, a relatively steep slope is needed, see Chapter 4.4. Furthermore and local climate phenomena (e.g. morning fog, smog etc.) may affect the choice of best orientation.

6.2.1 **On-Roof Assembly**

For an on-roof assembly (on a sloped roof), the framework for the solar panels is fixed above the roof support structure by brackets and rafter braces designed not to allow entry of rain. The collectors are then fixed to the framework, so a space of a few centimetres remains between the collectors and the roof. The roof skin itself is opened only temporarily as assembly necessitates. After the procedure is finished, the skin is closed completely, so entry of water is effectively impossible. Compared with other methods, the labour for this type of assembly is the least and thus available at low cost. In case of damage, the panels can be replaced easily. The collector weight acts as an additional load on the roof structure. Visually, the on-roof collector is often perceived as a foreign object.

Figure 6.3 On-roof installation of flat collectors (Solvis, Germany)

To be considered:

- never pierce bricks or seal with silicone (due to corrosion sensitivity)
- for attachments (e.g. rafter braces), bricks may be ground (with angle grinder) to prevent edges from sticking out
- airvent-bricks should be used for induction of pipes
- all penetrations of the lower roof skin have to be sealed carefully
- hooks and attachment rails need sufficient material strength and corrosion-resistance
- pipe connections require careful and complete insulation
- for installation on (fragile) slated roofs, seek advice of a professional roofer

6.2.2 Integration into the Sloped Roof

For in-roof installation (»Solar Roof«), the solar panels are directly mounted onto the roof shuttering or lathing, and in place of the conventional roof covering. Visually, the collector appears as an integral part of the roof. It is integrated and girded by a covering frame just like a dormer window. At the location, the tiles, or other covering, are removed or, in case of a new building, cancelled. Since the solar panels are usually less heavy than the regular roofing, there are no static load problems involved. The labour expense for this solution is considerably higher than for the on-roof installation, but has much better visual appearance. The necessity of assuring long-lasting waterproofness requires high grade framing. The possible replacement of damaged solar panels is somewhat more complicated than for the on-roof installation.

Figure 6.4 Roof-integrated collector (Roto Frank, Germany)

Usually, the in-roof installation requires a minimal slope of about 20°. Otherwise, the manufacturer might not guarantee aginst ingress of water. In such cases, an on-roof installation may be preferable. For large-scale systems, a complete roofing with »Solar Roof« modules is available. The modules can be pre-manufactured together with roof elements (e.g. rafters) for immediate assembly by crane. An in-roof assembly for vacuum tube collectors is not on offer yet.

Figure 6.5 Solar Roof for auxiliary heating at Neckarsulm (ITW, University of Stuttgart, Germany)

To be considered:

- delivered roofing systems need to be assessed with respect to material strength and to matching the roof tiles
- the roof tiles require a minimum overlap
- tiles have to be carefully fitted to the covering frame, with adapters if necessary
- if watertightness is questioned, test with a watering hose and claim from the manufacturer if necessary
- do not use silicone for sealing
- careful sealing of lower roof skin at cable- and pipe-ducts

6.3 Rigging on a Flat Roof

6.3.1 Prerequisites for Assembly on a Flat Roof

In the case of a flat-roof assembly, the optimum tilt angle for the solar collectors can be achieved by using a suitable framework. The minimal collector-row spacing in order to prevent overshadowing depends on the roof slope and local conditions (e.g. midwinter solar noon). The lowest elevation of lowest solar noon occurs on December 21 in the northern hemisphere and on June 21 in the southern hemisphere, and vice-versa for annual high solar noon.

On March 21 and September 21, the zenith angle is at its median any-where on earth. The apex of the sun's apparent path on this day reaches an angle α of:

$\alpha = 90° -$ latitude

In summer and winter, the zenith angle shifts by $+23.5°$ and $-23.5°$, respectively.

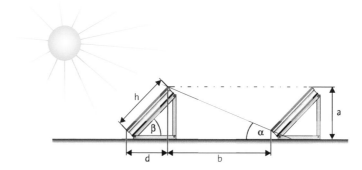

Figure 6.6 Minimal collector-row spacing for free-standing rig

For an array with collectors of height a, the row-to-row spacing b (see Figure 6.6) is equated as:

$b = a / \tan \alpha$

In order to just prevent an overshadowing at the lowest solar noon, the required spacing is calculated as follows:

$\alpha \ 90° - \text{latitude} - 23.5°$

e.g. for Rome, 42° n.l.

$b = a/\tan \alpha = a/\tan (90° - 42° - 23,5°) = a/0.45 = 2.2 \ a$

e.g. for Berlin, 52° n.l.

$b = a/\tan \alpha = a/\tan(90° - 52° - 23,5°) = a/0.258 = 3.87 \ a$

In Rome, the required row spacing would be 2.2 times the height of the panel. For Berlin, the according factor would be close to 4. Since the months of winter give a relatively minor contribution to the annual solar yield, a somewhat reduced spacing with some shadowing causes only a slight performance decrease.

When considering the available roof surface, one needs to take into account the required margin of 1.5 m at all roof edges. This is necessary for maintenance accessibility and safety against strong vortices and the danger of falling debris (in case of glass fracture) near the roof edges.

Depending on the local climate, provisions must be made for uninhibited slip-off of snow. Therefore it is recommended to leave sufficient space between the lowest edge of the collector panel and the roof. For accessibility during minor repairs, the gap should not be less than 30 cm in any case.

The necessary roof penetrations for pipes and attachments should be made with great care. To assure enduring lasting watertightness, the penetration points should be raised at least 8 cm above the possible water level by using sleeves or glued flanges. Furthermore, susceptible components should be insulated carefully to prevent of frost damage.

In addition to the static loads of the collector, the anticipated dynamic wind loads have to be accepted by the supporting framework. An expert stress analyst should perform the necessary assessments.

6.3.2 Flat Roof with Area Loads

On flat roofs with area loads, the collectors can be anchored with concrete slabs, ties or gravel-filled tubs, which are simply placed on the roof. To protect the roof surface, which nevertheless remains unpenetrated, these anchoring elements are placed onto high grade preservative mats.

A prerequisite for this cost-effective solution is an adequate load rating of the roof construction for the considerable additional loads. Gravel-topped roofs are best suited for this solution.

Figure 6.7 Free-standing rig with concrete weight

6.3.3 Flat Roof with low Distance Supports

This roof type has a closely fitted interior supporting framework. There-fore the solar collector framework could be supported within low distances. Constructions of steel or open web girder, simmilar to scaffolding, can be used. The solar collector framework should be designed as an assembly to fit the interior supporting structure, with the number of roof penetrations optimized for each particular case. The assembly can be supplied and fitted at relatively low cost. In the cases studied, the installation cost was approximately 75 Euro per m^2 of collector surface.

Figure 6.8 Supporting framework with open web girder for rigging of collector array at Otto-von-Guericke-University of Magdeburg, Germany

6.3.4 **Flat Roof with widely-spaced Supports**

Fitting solar asemblies on roofs with no intermediate supports often necessitate massive and expensive structures, that sometimes have to bridge the whole roof. In particular cases, the construction cost was up to 225 Euro per m^2 of collector surface.

Figure 6.9 Flat-roof rigging with massive steel supporting framework (Berlin-Lichtenberg, Germany)

A notable cost reduction can be achieved by using cross braces or open web girder, out of standard parts e.g. as used in scaffold constructions.

To be considered:

- assure watertightness by careful work and proper sealing
- when dimensioning the braces, one needs to account for dynamic loads due to wind and snowfall, in order to prevent the collector from shifting or even »taking off«
- apply adequate thermal insulation where necessary
- apply pre-manufactured duct elements and suited mountings for pipe- and cable-fittings
- in cases of doubt, employ a specialized roofer

A recent research program was dedicated to the development of »Subconstructions for Solar Installations«. Results are published in a design reference book for the rigging of solar Installations (currently available in German only). /32/

6.3.5 **Vacuum Tubes on a Flat Roof**

Theoretically, vacuum tubes need no subconstruction and can simply be laid horizontally onto concrete blocks (such as pavements slabs) which are put onto the roof, with preservative mats underneath. However, this solution cannot be recommended for regions with snowfall. Melting and re-freezing snow between the tubes can develop a remarkable destructive power, which may break the tubes themselves or the duct fittings. In principle, this type of assembly is suitable for collector tubes with direct throughflow. Heatpipe vacuum tube collectors always require a small tilt so they function correctly (see Chapter 5.2.3). In some tube designs, the absorbers are rotatable, such that they properly face the sun.

The savings in the supporting framework may well compensate for the increased cost of the vacuum tubes with respect to flat collectors.

Figure 6.10 Vacuum tubes on a slightly sloped roof (Solarpraxis Berlin, Germany)

6.4 **Facade-Mounted Collectors**

6.4.1 **Principal Considerations for Facade-Mounted Collectors**

Compared with a surface of optimal slope, a vertical surface in mid latitudes receives only about 70% of the irradiance. In equatorial regions, the proportion is much less. Therefore if visual considerations, or the lack of other available surfaces, require vertical fixing, then the solar yield is reduced accordingly. However if a vertical installation is used for auxiliary winter space heating, then summer surplus and the risk of stagnation are reduced. If the solar panels are arranged one above the other, the different static pressures, according to position, need to be accommodated.

Since facade-mounted collector panels are often arranged in alternation with windows or balconies, a relatively large expense for the pipe work may result.

6.4.2 Facade-Mounted Flat Collectors

Flat Collectors can be attached to the facade at various angles, thus serving, for instance, as sun shades or as auxiliary roofs. They can also be fully integrated into the facade. The matching stud-bolt-systems are available from various manufacturers. The facade-integrated collector panels can reduce, but not replace, the required facade thermal insulation. Moreover, they may substitute for decorative elements and thus reduce cost.

Figure 6.11 Flat collectors on the facade (Stiebel Eltron, Germany)

6.4.3 Facade-Mounted Vacuum Tubes

Vacuum tubes can also be attached to external components and vertical surfaces. Being relatively lightweight, some vacuum tube collectors may incorporate rotation order to face the sun; as such that they achieve notably better yields than the equivalent facade-mounted flat collectors. Since the tubes are to be placed in front of the facade itself, they have little effect on facade thermal insulation.

Figure 6.12 Facade-mounted vacuum tubes (Foto: DGS)

6.5 Assembly of Pre-Manufactured Thermosyphon Systems

A special situation exists when complete thermosyphon (or »gravity«) systems are installed. A typical pre-manufactured unit consists of one or more collector panels integrated with the storage tank horizontally mounted at the top. The weight of the complete unit is relatively large, because of the storage tank, at about 50 to 80 kg/m^2 of collector area.

6.5.1 Assembly on Superficially Loaded Flat Roofs

The most common and simplest assembly is on flat roofs. Thermosyphon systems are preferable in moderate climates that have short or no freezing periods. Accessible roof surfaces are ideally suited for this type of assembly. Here, they can be easily installed and connected to the conventional water supply, since the ordinary water reservoir is usually also situated on the roof. Due to the heavy weight of the system itself, additional attachments or weights for fixing to the roof are not needed. Obviously, the roof itself must have sufficient load bearing strength to take the additional loads.

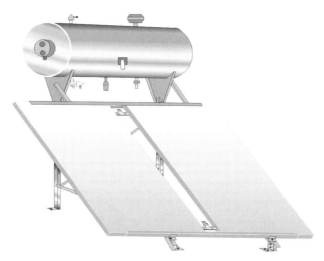

Figure 6.13 Pre manufactured thermosyphon system for installation on flat roofs /Intersolar, Greece/

6.5.2 **Assembly on Sloped Roofs**

The assembly of complete collector-storage combinations on sloped roofs (see Figure 6.13) requires a large additional carrying capacity of the roof truss. The attachment of the storage tank on top of the roof skin requires a reliable supporting structure which, at the same time must not impair the watertightness of the roof. Visually, this type of structure may be perceived as disturbing. However such installations are common in some countries, e.g. Australia.

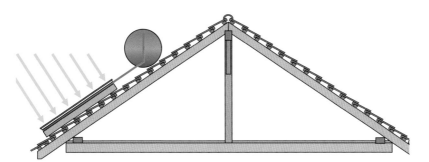

Figure 6.14 Thermosyphon system on a sloped roof, with storage tank outside

An alternative for an integrated, single unit, thermosyphon system is an arrangement of the collectors outside the roof, with the storage tank under the roof cover (see Figure 6.14). To maintain the thermo-syphon, it is essential that both the flow and return pipe lines lead upwards with respect to the collector. Thus, there must be sufficient room inside the rooftop and above the collector for the storage tank. For instance, this type of assembly is not usually possible in an attic-flat.

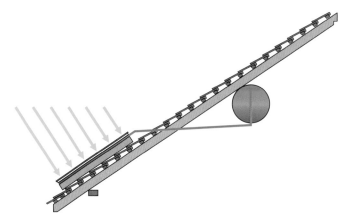

Figure 6.15 Thermosyphon system on a sloped roof, with storage tank inside

7. The Collector Loop

7.1 Principal Requirements on Components and Materials

7.1.1 Components of the Collector Loop

Basically, the collector loop consists of the following components (see also Figure 7.1):

- collectors
- pipelines among the individual collector panels and to the storage tank
- tube insulation
- air vent
- safety equipment (safety valves, expansion vessel)

Loops containing anti-freeze agent and/or a separate storage medium:

- heat exchanger
- heat transfer fluid in the collectors and pipes

Loops with forced circulation:

- pumps and valves

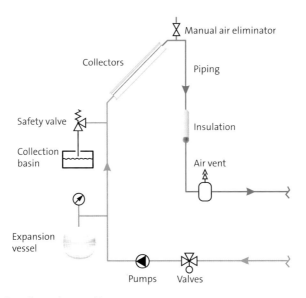

Figure 7.1 The collector loop and its components

The heat exchanger's primary side, which circulates the collector liquid, still belongs to the collector loop. Its secondary side, however, can be assigned to the solar storage loop or (if no separate storage unit is used) to the consumer loop. Since the heat exchanger in some cases (especially small installations) is integrated into the storage tank, the collector-loop interface is placed before the heat exchanger. In this latter position, the accessibility allows the installation of measurement devices (such as flow-meters, see Chapter 3.2). Therefore, heat exchangers are treated in a separate Chapter.

7.1.2 Governing Temperatures in the Collector Loop

All of the above components must be tuned to the governing temperatures and pressures in the collector field or collector loop. During stagnancy in strong insolation, high temperatures can cause critical problems. In systems with forced circulation, stagnancy occurs during controlled shutdown of the pump (e.g. for maintenance), controller or pump failure or safety shutdown due to imminent storage tank overheating. If solar radiation is intense during stagnancy, temperatures of 200°C in flat collectors and up to 300°C in vacuum tube collectors may be reached.

These peak temperatures usually occur in the collectors and nearby pipe connections only. The further the components are away from the collector array, the lower are the heat loads. However, in special cases (see Chapt. 7.1.4), high temperatures can occur in even remote parts of the system.

If the pump is restarted after a shutdown of this kind, temperatures inside the advance of the collector loop may peak to 160°C (directly at the collector outlet). It depends strongly on the actual collector, the storage temperatures and the geometry of the pipe system, how far such a »heat front« propagates further through the loop. The higher the temperatures are at collector and solar return pipe, and the higher the ratio of collector- to pipeline-weight, then the hotter the heat transfer fluid arrives at the storage tank. Also the warmer the preheated lower stratum of the storage tank, the less is the heat exchange with the incoming fluid from the collector. In the worst case, if the heat transfer fluid enters the heat exchanger at 150°C, then at the collector return, the temperature may be in excess of 120°C.

To prevent heat loads like this, the collector loop should be regulated so that post-stagnancy operation resumes only after the collectors have cooled down to a bearable temperature, such as 140°C. This necessitates a temperature sensor at the absorber and an adequate control system.

Yet, in low-flow systems with an external heat exchanger and even during regular operation, the collector loop may heat up to 120°C for some minutes. 120°C is significantly hotter than in conventional heating installations. The collector advance pipe (from collector to heat exchanger) is hottest, while temperatures in the collector return pipe usually stay below 100 °C. During the beginning of stagnation, high temperatures can even reach components in the advance pipe, as hot fluid passes into the expansion tank.

Figure 7.2 depicts the temperature conditions during normal operation, when the temperature in the solar buffer tank (which is filled with heating fluid, not potable water) has nearly reached its allowable maximum. The given temperatures apply to a low-flow installation with a rather low circulation of some 15 litres per hour and m^2 collector surface (see Chapter 7.3.2).

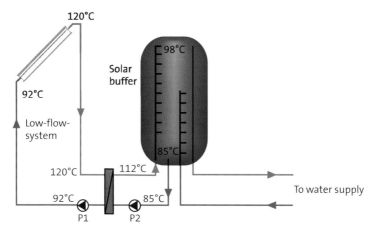

Figure 7.2 Governing temperatures during normal operation, with heat buffer almost fully charged

7.1.3 Governing Pressures in the Collector Loop

In order to keep the cost of a solar installation reasonable, one seeks to use components with a certified hyperbaric pressure tolerance of up to 1,000 kPa. Most collectors are designed for the same pressure (but sometimes for only 600 kPa). The pressure gradient between the individual components varies according their relative height: if the collectors are situated on the roof and the storage is in the basement, the interior pressure of the heat exchanger (primary side) and attached pipes is dramatically higher than at the collectors. The pressure gradient amounts to 10 kPa per 10 m water column (technically the geodetic altitude).

Under all circumstances, the collector must be prevented from an under-pressure (leading to suction of air into the loop). To assure this, while still providing safety against vaporization (see Chapter 7.4) and at the upper-limit temperatures mentioned in Chapter 7.1.2, the collector field is usually operated at hyperbaric over-pressure. Depending on the specific design of the installation (geodetic altitude) and the expansion vessel (see Chapter 7.7.3), hyperbaric pressure between almost zero and up to 300 kPa should be maintained.

In order to keep a low-flow installation (whose operating temperature at the collector may well reach 130–140°C) operable, high pressure is required. If the installation is alternatively shut down when reaching such high temperatures, the collector operating pressure can be adjusted to a significantly lower value.

Figure 7.3 depicts the pressure conditions of a typical installation with the storage unit (located in the basement) operating at either 600 or 1,000 kPa. The design of the expansion vessel (see details in Chapter 7.7) has not been considered for this hypothetical presentation.

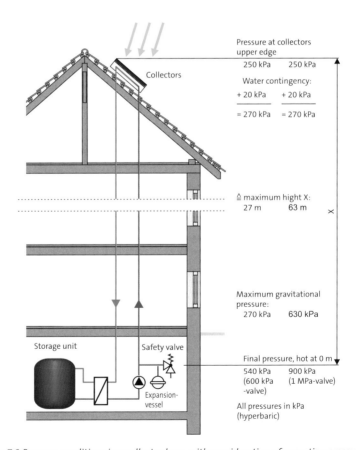

Figure 7.3 Pressure conditions in a collector loop, with consideration of operating pressure and structure height

7.1.4 **Vaporization in the Collector Loop**

Modern collectors have selective absorber coatings, so peak temperatures may occur during stagnancy. Consequently safety against vaporization of the heat transfer medium (usually a 50/50- or 60/40-mixture of water and anti-freeze agent) requires an operating pressure of 1,000 kPa and beyond. In such a case, however, other components located on a lower level would be exposed to even higher pressure, depending on the height of the water column (100 kPa per 10 m). Economically, a design of this kind would not be feasible.

Theoretically, a different fluid mixture (of higher vaporization temperature) could be used, but this possibility has to be considered with its technical, ecological and economical limits also (see Chapter 7.4)

If a solar installation is designed for a high solar fraction, this requires either a large and expensive storage unit, or frequent and extended periods of stagnancy. Thus only a high operating pressure provides safety against vaporization. For example, a 60/40-mixture of water/anti-freeze starts vaporizing at 160 °C, at a hyperbaric pressure of 500 kPa. The mixture remains liquid at lower temperatures or higher pressures. Yet, the whole collector loop will be exposed to high thermal stress for extended periods. So the liquid mixture may age at an accelerated rate, so the medium is altered chemically and so decays and changes its quality. On the other hand, if the medium vaporizes (e.g. at 140 °C), then only the relatively few molecules of the vapour phase bear the thermal stress of the overheating collector. This significantly reduces the thermal stress on the remaining liquid filling, since only a small fraction of the medium is exposed to the excessive temperature increase. Therefore, it is preferable for installations with extended periods of stagnancy to set at a relatively low operating pressure, thus allowing moderate vaporization. A reasonable setting would be 300 kPa for the operating (hot, yet vapour-free) collector, thus allowing vaporization at approximately 140 °C. Alternatively, one may choose a medium of increased heat resistance.

A disadvantage of frequent vaporizations is that some contents of the heat transfer medium (anti-corrosive additives or contaminations) may stick on the absorber's flow channels. If the collector loop is kept clean (e.g. with strainers or adaptions of the transfer medium), this problem is usually under control for the system use.

It is an advantage if the collector has only a small filling volume, such that, once vaporization occurs, the collector volume is completely evaporated as soon as possible.

The evaporation characteristic of the collector is determined by the particular design and the pipework. If the collector inlet is located at the lower end, the boiling (yet liquid) collector volume can be displaced into the return tube (if the gravity break does not prevent this). In such a case, only the amount of vapour required to fill the collector volume is produced. This could be considered as an »good-natured« characteristic of evaporation. For example, at 150 °C and 300 kPa, a volume of only 5 cm^3 of water suffices to evaporate a typical collector volume of 3 litres.

If both collector inlet and outlet are located at the upper edge, such as in vertically mounted direct-heat vacuum tubes, the liquid cannot escape. Then the collector volume evaporates completely, if the irradiation persists. The same applies if the collector panels are interconnected, such that a slug of water prevents the escape of the boiling medium. Hence, the medium leaves the collector as saturated vapour for a long period until it has boiled away. This generates a continuous supply of steam which is pushed into the feed lines, where it emits heat and condenses. Depending on the heat transport and the length of the pipes, the vapour zone may well extend into the heat exchanger, pumps, mountings valves etc. In particular, roof-mounted installations for domestic heating and those with short feed lines are endangered here.

On the other hand, for large-scale systems with a high solar fraction a »good natured« evaporation characteristic of collector and pipes is favourable. Nevertheless, this demand often contradicts the requirement for cost-effectivness in manufacture and assembly. As in many other areas, a compromise is needed.

In addition, large volumes of non-evaporised medium should be prevented from re-entering the collector from the advance pipe. This would cause an unnecessary and stressful heat transfer process (see Chapter 7.7). This problem applies in particular to interconnected solar arrays on facades or sloped roofs. In case of stagnation, large amounts of liquid out of connecting pipes will flow down into low-lying collectors and evaporate there.

7.1.5 Boiling Behaviour of Thermosyphon Systems

In thermosyphon systems, the storage vessel is heated by natural circulation (gravity). Circulation in the collector loop occurs only when the collector is significantly hotter than the storage. A limitation of the storage temperature is therefore not possible. If there is no heat demand by users, the storage temperature becomes nearly as high as the collector stagnancy temperature.

During high solar radiation and low consumption, the heat transfer fluid may boil in both the collector and the storage vessel (depending on pressure).

If collector loop and storage vessel are separated by a heat exchanger, the pressures of both may differ. If the collector loop pressure (e.g. 100 kPa) is lower than the storage pressure (e.g. 500 kPa, if connected to the potable water network), the heat transfer medium in the collector will start boiling at a lower temperature than the water in the storage vessel.

Since the collector is situated below the storage vessel, the collector liquid cannot be displaced by vapour, as is the case when the collector is above the tank.

If high solar radiation persists and the storage tank is not cooled, the heat transfer fluid in the collector will continue to evaporate. The large vapour volumes produced in the collector are difficult to catch in an expansion vessel. They exit the loop through the safety valve. It makes sense to place this safety valve at the highest point of the loop, i.e. higher than the highest point of the collector. The placement and design of the safety valve must comply with the safety standards of anti-scald protection for operating personnel.

Initially, the liquid loss (due to vaporization) is equalized by the reservoir in the expansion vessel, which must be refilled during regular maintenance.

Too small expansion vessels and long maintenance intervals, in combination with frequent and long periods of stagnancy, lead to large losses of heat transfer liquid and to insufficient liquid in the collector loop, especially after cooling down. The suction of air and a collapse of loop circulation may result, so the system becomes inoperative.

If the collector loop is operated at a higher pressure than in the storage vessel (so that the heat transfer fluid evaporates at a higher temperature), it is possible that the storage water starts boiling without collector evaporation. Thus, the solar heat is transformed into steam in the storage vessel when no hot water is consumed. Depending on the location of the safety valve, steam or water is squeezed out of the storage vessel. Here, too, the safety standards must be considered in order to protect the operating personnel from scalding.

Often, thermosyphon systems are equipped with simple, less efficient collectors, and the pipe and storage insulations are relatively thin. In these systems, the (high) heat losses are made up by solar energy, even when no hot water is drawn off. In these simple systems, evaporations and associated problems do not occur.

Highly efficient, selective absorbers with high stagnancy temperatures can not be recommended for thermosyphon systems, especially when frequent periods of high radiation and low heat consumption are to be expected.

7.2 **Collector Circuitry**

The Collector circuitry aims at a uniform flow through each individual collector panel. This would enable each collector to operate at optimal performance and prevent dead zones (useless or insignificant areas with negligible flow) in the collectors.

All types of circuitry, with their various pipe dimensions need to be assessed for their effect on the heat load and thus on the arrangement of the collectors in a field.

7.2.1 **Small Installations in Parallel Connection**

Theoretically, parallel connection provides each collector with identical flow. To achieve this, a minimal flow rating as established by the manufacturer must be met (to prevent dead zones and assure turbulent flow). The rating (depending on the design) lies in a typical range between 40 and 80 litres per hour and m^2 of collector surface.

Example:

an array of 4 collectors of 2.5 m^2 each, parallel-connected
total collector area:	$10\ m^2$
minimal flow rating (by manufacturer):	$40\ l/(h \cdot m^2)$
minimal flow per collector:	$2.5 \cdot 40 = 100\ l/h$
minimal total flow of array:	$4 \cdot 100 = 400\ l/h$

By parallel connection, a nominal flow (meeting the minimum requirement) is fed to the whole collector array in this way.

Due to the parallel arrangement of the connections, the typical pressure losses due to flow resistance of collectors and pipework are fairly small and do not add up. On the other hand, the total flow is extraordinarily high. The characteristic is similar to a heating network and allows the application of standard heating pumps (if they satisfy the increased temperature requirements).

Parallel Connection According to Tichelmann

In heating engineering, the application of a so-called Tichelmann-ring satisfies the requirement of uniform flow through heaters. When a Tichelmann-ring is applied to a collector array, all collectors are parallel-connected and the total length of the flow and return feed lines is made equal for each single collector. This supposedly results in identical pressure losses along each of the parallel connections. Yet, secondary singular resistances due to pipe surface roughness and unwanted flow obstructions (e.g. at soldered interfaces, forks and turnings) are not considered.

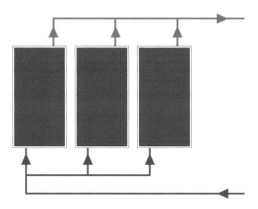

Figure 7.4 Example of a Tichelmann parallel connection

Figure 7.4 is example of a small array of 3 collectors. Even though the pipework is relatively expensive, a uniform flow is achieved only if:

- the individual collectors have the same resistance, which must be larger than the resistance of the pipes by a factor of at least 3

- the secondary resistances are negligible with respect to the resistances of collectors and pipework

For gravity systems, a parallel connection is necessary because of the low buoyancy due to density differences. Furthermore, a uniform flow can only be achieved with a Tichelmann-ring. There is a positive temperature gradient in the upwards direction, from inlet to outlet.

In the past, the Tichelmann-ring has been the standard scheme of circuitry, but recently it has become rather less popular.

Parallel Connection Alternatives to Tichelmann
For small solar arrays, manufacturers offer collectors which are interconnected in a parallel arrangement without external pipes. The collecting and distributing pipes are integrated into the collectors. Only the cumulative pipelines to the storage unit are put externally. This dramatically reduces the total expense for pipework. This method, however, is only suitable for a very limited number of collector panels (approximately 4). The collectors have either a meander or a »harp« shape, see Figures. The meander absorber consists of a single, wound heat transfer tube while the harp absorber has a large number of straight channels. The tubes have a diameter between 5 and 10 mm.

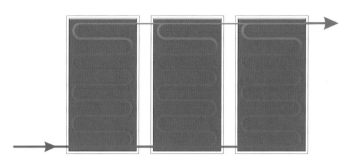

Figure 7.5 Directly linked meander absorbers in parallel connection (Viessmann)

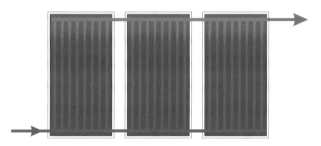

Figure 7.6 Directly linked harp absorbers in parallel connection

As in the Tichelmann-scheme, one aims at uniform flow through each collector, and the same prerequisites must be met to achieve this. The pressure loss in the absorber should be at least three times as large as in the total internal pipe, and secondary resistances should be negligible.

In an effort to allow a rather larger number of collectors to be connected, some manufacturers have significantly raised the dimensions of the cumulative tubes. This lowers the total pressure loss of the pipelines and helps meeting the requirements for uniform flow in the complete scheme.

In its basic characteristic regarding for pressure loss and temperature distribution) the arrangement is similar to the Tichelmann-ring, as explained above.

7.2.2 Small Installations in Serial Connection (Row)
In a serial connection, the same transfer medium flows through all collectors, one after another. Automatically, all collectors have thus the same flow (which is equal to the total flow). This type of arrangement, with its rather low nominal flow rate, is best suited for low-flow installations.

Example:

an array of 4 collectors of 2.5 m² each, serial-connected

total collector surface:	10 m²
minimal flow rating (by manufacturer):	40 l/(h•m²)
minimal flow per collector:	2.5•40 = 100 l/h
minimal total flow of array:	100 l/h

nominal field flow rate: total flow / collector surface = 10 l/(h•m²)

In the above example, the nominal field flow rate is rather small, even for a low-flow system (see Chapter 7.3.2). This leads to a very large temperature spread which has adverse effects on the overall efficiency. To achieve a better solar fraction, a somewhat increased flow (such as 15 l/(h•m²)) is recommended. On the other hand, a flow rate increase, greatly raises pressure losses and therefore has its ultimate limits.

For a serially connected circuitry, the nominal volumetric field flow rate is defined as the total flow divided by the total collector surface (see example).

Serial connections are characterized by a relatively low-flow rate and a high total pressure loss, since the losses of the individual collectors (lying in a row) are added up. Thus the characteristic of a serially con-nected array is entirely different from a regular heating network. It is quite difficult to find suitable pumps of good efficiency for these ope-rating conditions (i.e. large pumping head and low volumetric flow). A recent research project at the WILO company, subsidized by the Ger-man Ministry of Economics (BMWi) is dedicated to the development of pumps which fully satisfy these requirements.

For the purpose of keeping pressure losses within affordable limits, one should consider the application of harp absorbers.

Serial Connection of Large Panels

Figure 7.7 shows the basic arrangement of a serial connection for large harp-shaped collector panels (6−12 m² of absorber surface). The individual flow channels are exactly parallel. Again, the sum of the flow resistance of the collectors must be at least 3 times as large as the resistances of the interior collecting and distributing pipes.

Figure 7.7 Large collectors in serial connection

The total flow is circulated through the entire row of collectors, and pressure losses are cumulative. There is a positive temperature gradient from the lower left (inlet) to the upper right (outlet) corner. It should be assumed that the gradient is approximately constant for the whole array, so that each collector panel would contribute the same amount of heat.

Serial Connection of Small Panels

To satisfy the required ratio of collector to pipe resistance (larger than 3:1) when connecting small solar panels (i.e. larger than 3:1), only one half of the harp-shaped absorber runs parallel and is row-connected to the other half. This artificially increases the pressure loss in each collector (to an amount typical for large panels), so that the above condition is met. The principle is shown in Figure 7.8.

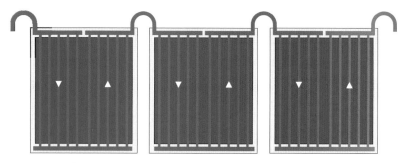

Figure 7.8 Serial connection of small absorber panels

7.2.3 Circuitry of Large Installations according to Tichelmann

In the past, the Tichelmann-ring was also applied to large collector arrays. This was done in an effort to avoid a serial connection which led to increased operating temperatures, if the nominal flow rate was not raised (which, in turn, increased the pressure loss). Depending on the particular design (e.g. steel cushion absorber, aluminium roll bond absorber), the desired nominal flow rates (per m^2 collector surface) used to be significantly lower than today. For collectors without selective coating that is immediately plausible, since such models lose efficiency at high temperatures.

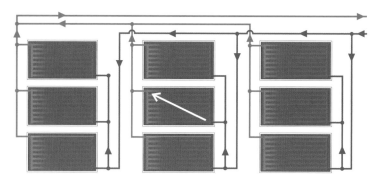

Figure 7.9 Circuitry of a large collector field according to Tichelmann

Figure 7.9 sketches a collector field consisting of 3 rows of 3 collectors each. The large amount of pipework is evident. Even though, a uniform flow is rarely achieved with this arrangement (see also Chapter 7.2.1), especially with vacuum tubes working with the heat-pipe principle (with very low pressure loss in the collector's interior heat exchanger) this goal has practically never been achieved. Some tubes had always a particular strong circulation while others were always close to stagnancy. This might be one of the reasons for the observed corrosive damages of tubes, as reported in Chapter 5.2.3.

7.2.4 Alternatives to Tichelmann for Circuitry of Large Installations

Since modern flat collectors are able to work efficiently at high temperatures and high-flow rates, they are well suited for parallel connection. Furthermore they can achieve a low-flow characteristic that may be an advantage for particular cases (see Chapter 7.3.2).

As already mentioned in 7.2.2, the number of collectors to be parallel-connected is limited. Therefore, one chooses a combination of serial and parallel connections for large installations, as shown in Figure 7.10.

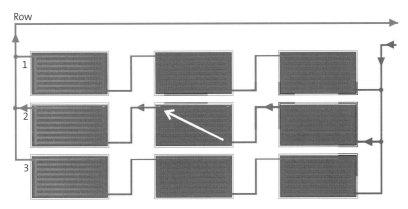

Figure 7.10 Collector field consisting of 3 parallel-connected sub arrays of 3 row-connected collectors each

The serial connection of the collectors within each sub array raises the pressure loss sufficiently to avoid the Tichelmann-ring for the parallel connected sub arrays. By a clever dimensioning of field partitions and collecting/distributing lines, one is able to meet the required ratio between collector and pipe resistances (at least 3:1).

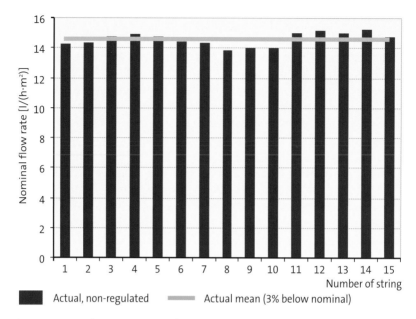

Figure 7.11 Exemplary presentation of nominal flow rates for the individual strings of a 600-m²-installation (each string consists of several serial-connected collectors; the strings are parallel-connected and operate at fully opened regulation valves). Source: project hydra, University of Dortmund / TGA, Germany

The sample presented in Figure 7.11 shows that a nearly uniform flow during full operation is achievable with this arrangement.

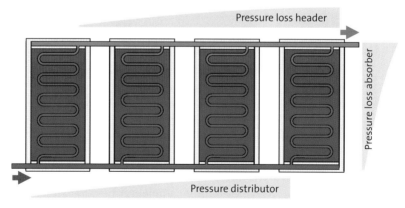

Figure 7.12 String and field circuitry and distribution of pressure loss

Note that the total pressure loss of the field must remain reasonable, otherwise the choice of an appropriate pump is difficult (see Chapter 7.8.3). Therefore, one should avoid the serial connection of too many collectors within a sub array. Furthermore, remember that the flow rates (and pressure losses) along the various collecting and distributing lines are not identical.

The following table gives a notion of recommended maximum pressure losses of the entire collector field (according to size)

Field size [m²]	Pressure loss (kPa)
50	30
200	60
500	80
1,000	100

Table 7.1 Recommended upper limits of pressure loss for various collector field sizes

If a collector field consists of several connected sub arrays, the arrangement of barriers (e.g. stop taps, capped valves, additional safety valves) is necessary, so a separate shutdown of individual sub arrays is possible for maintenance or repair.

7.3 Modes of Flow Operation for the Collector Loop

7.3.1 »Usual« Flow (High-Flow)

The »usual« mode of flow, referred to as high-flow, means that the nominal flow rate of the total field amounts to about 40 (sometimes up to 80) litres per hour per m² of collector surface. This mode is chosen if all collectors are parallel-connected, so the minimal flow as given by the manufacturer, is satisfied. This avoids »dead zones« which give only a negligible contribution to the collection of heat.

The volumetric flow of the entire field becomes relatively large at »regular« flow, which implies a grossly dimensioned pipework for the heat exchanger/storage unit.

At favourable solar radiation of 1,000 W/m² and an assumed collector efficiency of 60 %, the resulting heat power reaches 600 W/m². Considering regular flow and a heat capacity of a 60/40 mixture of water/anti-freeze of 3.7 kJ/(kg·K), one achieves a temperature spread of approximately 15 K:

ΔT = heat flux / (flow rate · heat capacity)

$$= \frac{600J / (s \cdot m^2)}{\frac{40kg}{3600\ s \cdot m^2} \cdot 3700J/ kg \cdot K} = 14.6\ K$$

The temperature difference between collector outlet and inlet is thus only a few Kelvin, which enables the entire system to work efficiently. In the past, the »regular« mode was quite popular for completely parallel-connected solar installations, typically running at a nominal flow rate of 25−40 litres per hour and collector-m².

7.3.2 **Low-Flow**

The low-flow mode is characterized by a nominal flow rate of 12–20 litre per hour and per collector-m^2. This mode requires that, at least partly, a serial connection is applied, so that each collector receives a minimum of flow.

Compared to the high-flow example above, the resulting temperature spread between outlet and inlet, at similar conditions, but with reduced flow rate, amounts to about 30–50 K:

ΔT = heat flux / (flow rate • heat capacity)

$$= \frac{600J/(s \bullet m^2)}{\dfrac{12....20kg}{3600\ s \bullet m^2} \bullet 3700J/\ kg \bullet K} = 29.2....48.6\ K$$

Due to the increased heat loss at significantly higher outlet temperatures, the solar yield is reduced. To keep this disadvantage of low-flow installations under control, the operating temperature at the heat exchanger has to be kept as low as possible. A suitable installation involves careful tuning of all components (e.g. generously dimensioned heat exchangers and well stratified storage units).

Low-flow operation is well suited to the instant generation of high temperatures for domestic auxiliary heating and for installations with stratified charging tanks. The aim is to reach sufficient high temperatures to avoid the use of primary heating systems, such as boilers or immersion heaters. The desire is to limit the intermittent operation of these devices (which increases the solar pre-heated water only by a small amount up to nominal temperature) and usually keeps them out of operation. This somewhat improves the contribution of solar energy (i.e. the solar fraction) to the total heat supply. In order to have such a system work properly, fine tuning of solar and boiler control is absolutely necessary.

The appeal of low-flow operation of larger installations lies in its savings in pipe network. The saving potential is remarkable, particularly when the entire solar field is partitioned into a number of parallel-connected sub arrays (and the Tichelmann-ring is avoided). The slight decrement in performance is then made up by the installation cost savings. Such a design is suitable for the majority of the larger installations.

7.3.3 »**Matched**« **Flow**

If an installation runs at »matched« flow, the volumetric flow of the entire collector field is adapted to the actual solar radiation by a controlled circulating pump. The aim is to achieve high storage temperatures, even at low irradiance, by throttling the flow rate and thus to reduce the engagement of primary, backup heaters. The effect of this control strategy strongly depends on the particular system. For small installations, designed only for potable-water preheating, the performance advantage is minimal, but the control system is more complex than for high- or low-flow. Thus the effects of this control strategy should be checked on each design (e.g. with simulation programs) prior to deciding on the installation of a matched-flow system.

7.4 Heat Transfer Fluids

7.4.1 Requirements on Heat Transfer Fluids

Heat transfer fluids within the collector loop must fulfil the following requirements:

- temperature invariance up to the maximum anticipated level during collector stagnancy
- anti-freeze protection, if the installation runs year-round and the local weather involves frost
- anti-corrosive protection, if mixed or corrosion prone materials are present in the collector
- no special requirements on the materials of the collector loop, so that cost-efficient components can be purchased (standard parts where possible)
- a high heat capacity and conductivity allowing efficient heat transportation from the collector
- non-toxicity and environment-friendliness
- low viscosity to disburden the circulation pump
- low cost and availability

A mixture of water and glycol proved to be a good compromise among the properties listed above. Over decades, such mixtures have shown their value for anti-freeze and anti-corrosive protection in cars. Their application for solar installations operating at reasonable thermal stresses thus found its popularity cause practical utilization possibilities. Only adaptions for the inhibition of corrosion were necessary.

Whereas ethylene-glycol was frequently used in the past, recently (in systems for heating potable water) more food-compatible propylene-glycol has been used.

In individual cases, highly temperature-invariant thermal oils (as used in thermal power plants) have been applied to domestic solar installations. Due to their high demands on pump, expansion vessel, valves and sealings, they have gradually disappeared from this market.

When using water-glycol mixtures as heat transfer medium, one should consider the following:

- For anti-freeze protection, it is sufficient in all but a few climatic zones, to use a glycol content of 40 % or less. This assures operation until 24° Celsius below zero. At even lower temperatures, a viscous slurry of ice develops, but this does not burst the pipework. A glycol content in excess of 50 % should be avoided, since it increases viscosity and lowers heat capacity.

- Furthermore, glycol has a notably more intensive creeping property than water. Therefore the sealing requirement for glycol-tightness is considerably mor difficult than assurance of watertightness. Therefore one should check most carefully for the smallest leaks in the collector loop.

- Glycol is not compatible with zinc. So pipes with internal zinc galvanising should not be used. Glycol can also attack some other materials (e.g. sealings). Therefore, only materials certified for use with water-glycol mixtures are suitable for the collector loop. However, most materials are non-critical in this respect.

- There is an upper limit to the allowable temperature envelope at about 150 – 160 °C (nevertheless, different manufacturer ratings are contradictory). A newly developed product is claimed to be always acceptable to such high temperatures.

For a safe operation, only water-glycol mixtures that are explicitly certified for solar installations should be used.

If a solar installation with pure water circulation (such as drain back systems) is run at a frost-prone location, the protection from frost damage demands that complete drainage is required. Due to the large energy consumption, continuous circulation for prevention of frost is not recommended.

Extended Requirements for Installations with High Thermal Stress
The optimization of collectors, particularly of the absorber coating, has led to significant raised temperatures during stagnancy in both flat and tubular collectors. Heat transfer fluids are thus exposed to increasing thermal stress. Furthermore, the over-sizing of collector surfaces (e.g. installations for auxiliary room heating) leads to more frequent and extended periods of high thermal stress during stagnancy.

Direct-heat vacuum tubes and flat collectors operating at peak temperatures of 220 °C and above need specifically tailored heat transfer fluids. Unsuitable fluids are chemically cracked at such high temperatures, i.e. they disintegrate into insoluble substances which may jam the collector loop. This kind of decay may produce corrosive acids.

7.4.2 **Long-term Assessment of Heat Transfer Fluids**

All of the 15 different installations assessed in this survey used water-glycol mixtures with anti-corrosive additives. All but a few of the purchased products could be identified, but in some cases a cocktail of different products were utilized, which made analysis of glycol content and the intactness of corrosive protection difficult. However the heat transfer fluids were in use for a period of 6–18 years. According to the operators, a complete refilling never occurred, but it is reasonable to assume that replenishments took place during maintenance. In some cases the very low content of anti-freeze agent (insufficient for frost protection) suggests that pure water was used to refill. Table 7.2 gives an overview of the results of the assessment.

System ID	Years of operation	Product name	Glycol-content mass-%	Freeze protection to:	Corrosive Protection Checked metal	Functionality
A	16	BASF Glyther-min 100	55	−30°C	Al 99,5 ST 37-2	not existent reduced
B	15	HOECHST Antifrogen L	35	−9°C	SF-Cu ST 37-2	existent still existent
C	16	unbe-kannt		−22°C	SF-Cu ST 37-2	not existent existent
D	17	BASF Glyther-min P44	42	−18°C	SF-Cu ST 37-2	existent existent
F	16	not known		−14°C	Al 99,5 SF-Cu ST 37-2	absent still existent reduced corrosive damage
G/H	8	not known		−40°C	SF-Cu ST-2	existent existent
I	6	BASF Glyther-min P44	17	−6°C	SF-Cu ST 37-2	existent existent
K	9	BASF Glyther-min P44	36	−16°C		existent existent
L	16	not known		−30°C	SF-Cu ST 37-2	absent existent
M	13	BASF Glyther-min P44	52	−32°C	SF-Cu ST 37-2	existent still existent
P	13	BASF Glyther-min 100	80	below −50°C	Al 99,5 ST 37-2	existent reduced
Q	16	BASF Glyther-min GP42 *due to leakage in absorbers liquid frequently refilled	60	−50°C*	SF-Cu ST 37-2	existent* reduced corrosive damage
R	16	BASF Glyther-min 100	70	below −50°C	Al 99,5 ST 37-2	absent reduced
Y	18	HOECHST Antifrogen mixture of L and N		−32°C	SF-Cu ST 37-2	existent existent
ρ	7	Schilling-chemie	47	−25°C	Al 99,5 SF-Cu ST 37-2	existent reduced existent

Table 7.2 Assessment of heat transfer liquid samples taken from old solar installations

The judgement about the integrity of anti-corrosive protection was based on electrochemical measurements (flow density potential characteristics) and the criteria that is formulated in the research paper »Inhibitors for Heat Transfer Fluids of Solar Installations« /33/.

In about 50% of the cases, the anti-corrosive property was still intact. In the remaining cases, however this property had significantly deteriorated.

Three samples (C, L, ρ) showed aggressive reactions against copper, but were otherwise intact. This is relatively unimportant, since copper is not particularly prone to corrosive stress (i.e. in the presence of transfer fluid with oxygen content). Cases C and L had copper pipes, yet they were fully intact in spite of the missing corrosive protection within the system.

In another three cases, such as A, F and R, the anti-corrosive protection of aluminium had diminished and was, in one case (F), completely absent. Considering that aluminium is very prone to corrosion and that the roll-bond absorbers used were made of aluminium, the failure of protection in these installations was critical.

Five samples (A, F, P, Q, R) showed diminished protective properties for steel, which is also crucial.

Thus, the three samples A, F and R showed total failure of corrosive protection (of aluminium and steel).

Installations F (heat pipe with aluminium-condensor and steel heat exchanger) and Q (flat-roof collector with steel absorber) showed extensive corrosion damage. In the latter case, the fluid sample probably showed a much better consistency than was typical for most of its service life, since extensive leakage required frequent refills.

Diminished or vanished corrosive protection does not immediately entail corrosive damage, since the collector loop is a closed system. A decisive factor is the permeation of oxygen or air into the loop. This is possible if leaks remain unfixed, if oxygen-containing water is frequently refilled, or if air elimination is incomplete. Therefore thin walled absorbers are particularly inclined to corrosive damage.

Check for anti-corrosive protection and for complete air elimination are important precautionary measures, particularly if the heat transfer fluid comes into contact with aluminium or steel. If the pressure drops and refills occur frequently, the integrity of the complete system (including the pipe connections underneath the insulation) should be checked. In case of low pressure, air may be sucked in.

In addition, the density, pH-value and alkali reserve of each fluid sample was examined. At a pH-value below 5, corrosion may occur even in the absence of oxygen. The anti-corrosive additives are usually tailored for protection against oxygen-based, but not acid-based, corrosion. The alkali reserve is a measure for the buffering ability of the heat transfer medium against age-induced acidification of Glycol.

In the examined cases, all pH-values were above 7.4, so the probability of acid-based corrosion was negligible. The measured alkali reserve (between 3 and 8) were satisfying, except in case of installation I, were a value of only 1.4 indicated the danger of acidification as a result.

7.4.3 Proper Application of Heat Transfer Fluids

The chemical and thermal characteristics of the heat transfer mixture should be adapted to be compliant with all materials of the collector loop and to match the thermal loads of the installation.

When initial operation takes place, the loop should be well flushed (for at least 10 minutes) to minimize high-temperature interaction of heat transfer fluid with the pipes. This should be included in the instructions for operation and filling. A good example for this is the manual by Roto Frank (see Fig. 7.35).

Apart from specific requirements, the final pressure in a collector field (in hot operating conditions, without vaporization) should not exceed 300 kPa (overpressure). Vaporization of the heat fluid usually starts at relatively low temperatures (130−150°C, depending on the glycol content). Since, in such cases, only a small fraction (the vapour phase) of the fluid is exposed to very excessive temperatures, the thermal load of the majority (the liquid phase) continues to be limited. A desirable property of the heat fluid would thus be to condensate and dissolve without residual deposits after vaporizing.

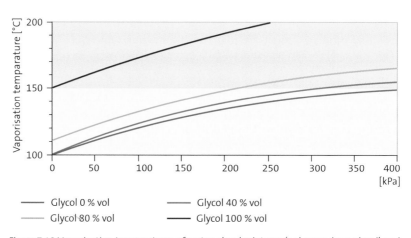

Figure 7.13 Vaporization temperatures of water-glycol mixtures (polypropylene-glycol) and dependence on pressure (Tycocor L, source: Tyforop Chemie GmbH, Germany)

At the same time, the cold (at around 15°C) operating pressure near the location of expansion vessels and safety valves (usually in the basement) should be some 80 to 150kPa above the pressure defined by the geodetic altitude (height of the water column) of the collector loop. This prevents under-pressure in the loop even when cooling down to −20°C or when releasing minor amounts of air through the air vent. Under-pressure could lead to »sniffing« of air.

The anti-corrosive effect of additives vanishes if components are not continuously wetted by the heat transfer medium, for example sucked air which accumulates in the upper regions of the loop during stagnancy. Especially if aluminium or steel are used for the collector loop, complete and enduring air elimination is necessary.

If heat fluid is lost due to leakage or partial bleeding during maintenance, pure-water refills are not allowed, since this dilutes and so impairs anti-freeze and anti corrosive protection. For refills, one should apply the same water/glycol mixture and brand as used for the initial filling of the installation. Only when the anti-freeze ability of the heat transfer fluid appears to be insufficient, undiluted glycol of the identical brand should be used for refill. Otherwise, heat capacity and pressure losses are degraded unnecessarily.

If the integrety of the heat transfer fluid is doubted, a sample can be taken and sent to the manufacturer, to assess its quality. The sample should be well mixed and is best taken from a short drainpipe while the circulating pump is running.

Installations with frequent stagnancy should be checked at least every two years, with respect to pH-value and anti-corrosive properties. Installations which always run under normal conditions need to be checked in this regard only every five years.

7.5 Pipework of the Collector Loop

7.5.1 Requirements of the Pipework

The operating temperatures and pressures (see Chapter 7.1), the flow mode (Chapter 7.3) and the heat transfer fluid clearly limit the choice of applicable pipe materials and connection techniques. The following requirements enable the system to work as needed:

- heat resistance up to 150 °C anywhere in the collector loop and up to stagnancy temperature near the collector
- compatibility with the heat transfer fluid (water/glycol-mix)
- material properties and laying techniques have to assure the unproblematic handling of thermal expansions within the temperature envelope (some −20 to 150 °C)
- stability of pipe connections under thermal and mechanical stress due to expansion (soft soldering is ruled out!)

At a temperature difference of 100 K, a 1 metre copper pipe (regardless of its cross section) elongates by approximately 1.7 mm (i.e. relative elongation of 0.17 %). Since seasonal or operational temperature differences in the collector loop may range up to 200 K, the resulting length changes of the pipe material must be taken into account.

7.5.2 **Long-term Survey of Collector Loop Pipework**

Interior Corrosion of Pipes

For the survey, small sections of the pipes were removed and checked for interior corrosion, heat transfer sediments and erosion. Samples were collected at eight installations, with ages of between 13 and 16 years. In the first three cases, tubular pieces were taken from each of the following three positions:

- collector advance (hot side)
- collector return (cold side)
- lowest point of collector loop

The pieces from flow and return were taken to compare with respect to thermal stress. The piece at the lowest point was taken to check for sedimentation which might considerably narrow the tube cross section. The investigation showed that all three pieces were in the same condition. Therefore, only one piece was taken from each of the other five sample installations.

The interior pipe surfaces in all eight cases showed no effects of corrosion or erosion. Only a uniform, thin cover was observed, without any effect on the system's function. The pipes were good for many further years of operation.

Figure 7.14 Interior surface of a steel tube from a collector loop pipework

In Figure 7.14, the condition of a steel pipe after 14 years of service is shown. The pipe is almost as good as new.

For interior corrosion, the condition of the pipes was not critical. The tubes were fully intact, even at installations where the lack of anti-corrosive agents in the heat transfer fluid had brought about excessive corrosion at the interior part of the absorber. An explanation for this might be that the pipework is practically always filled with heat transfer fluid and is rarely exposed to oxygen, while sucked-in air ascends to the highest point (usually in the collector).

Critical with respect to corrosion are those tubes, which run above the absorber and so the highest point of the system. If air enters the system and is not completely eliminated, it accumulates in these elevated locations (while displacing corrosion-inhibiting heat transfer fluid) during inoperative periods. This may pave the way for corrosion. That is why, adequate air elimination is essential for the prevention of corrosion, especially in elevated steel pipes.

Exterior Corrosion of Pipes

Externally, the examined steel pipes were in excellent condition, regardless of their belonging to a pipework in the open air or inside a building. Even when humidity had penetrated the pipe insulation, it was seen that the corrosion (rust) was rather harmless. In some cases, the slight attacks of corrosion were to the detriment of the outer appearance of the pipes, but operation would have remained unaltered, certainly for several years.

Figure 7.15 shows the condition of steel pipes (still with partial insulation). The screw connection at the T-piece (left) was hemp-sealed and showed no trace of leakage. The hemp seal was totally leak-proof for Glycol.

Figure 7.15 Exterior view of steel pipes from a collector loop pipework

Within the survey, all (except one) copper pipework was in excellent condition. In the exceptional case, the upper side of the copper pipe showed sediments of loose white powder. Analysis established that the powder consisted of lime and copper corrosion products. The corrosion was caused by humidity but was not critical.

The generally very positive image of the pipe's outer appearance was somewhat faded by a corroded nipple of a storage tank, although it did not directly belong to the collector loop. A galvanized steel cap had been screwed to the steel nipple. Contact corrosion (at the contact point of the noble and ignoble material) in the upper part of the cap caused wall breakthrough (see Figure 7.16).

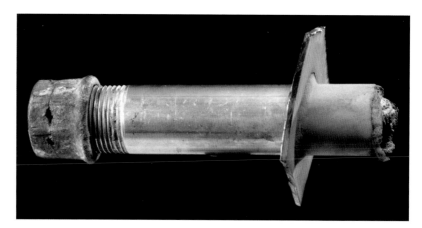

Figure 7.16 Corrosive damage at the connection of different metals (nipple and tank, see tank wall at the right, of stainless steel and cap of zinc galvanized steel); a plug of rust narrows the nipple entrance

All the examined pipework was in a good condition after up to 16 years of service. Slight corrosion of steel and copper pipes was cursory and did not necessitate replacements. In general corrosion of collector loop pipework was uncritical providing contact corrosion (contact of different metals) is avoided.

7.5.3 Proper Installation of Collector Loop Pipework

Tubes of copper, steel and stainless steel, as well as flexible tubes of corrugated stainless steel, are suitable for collector loop pipes. However the avoidance of contact corrosion is important.

Synthetic materials are not to be used, if they are not explicitly designated for pipework in solar installations. Currently they are not on offer for this particular purpose. The application of zinced galvanised steel tubes is not recommended, because of the chemical interactions between zinc and glycol.

Solder fittings and press fittings with special sealing elements and clamping ring screw joints are suitable for connection of copper tube segments. The same relates to some O-ring sealings, flat or conical sealings and a few additional connection techniques and materials. All materials must be resistant against heat, pressure and exposure to glycol. Manufacturer's ratings concerning the ranges and limits of operation should be implemented.

If copper tubes are used for collector loop pipes, the application of soft soldering is quite common. Recent assessments by manufacturers of soft solder showed that soft solder is well suited for flat collector installations. However, according to the German Industrial Standard, welded or hard-soldered connections are preferable. Negative, albeit rare, experiences support this recommendation. This particularly applies to those pieces near the collector which are exposed to very high temperatures and the resulting thermal expansion. Although precautionary measures should ease the forces due to expansion, this is not always achieved. For the collector loop, hard soldering is suggested as a safe solution. For installations with tubular collectors, hard soldering and welding are to be used exclusively.

Threads can be sealed with hemp. Due to the creeping property of glycol, teflon tape is only of limited use.

Solar installations and their pipes should not be attached to gas or water supply lines and should not serve as carrier or other pipework or loads. Noise protection may become an issue for the attachments of water or water-glycol pipes. For hot water pipework, thermal expansion has to be taken into account. All of the above comments should be borne in mind when choosing and arranging the pipelines.

7.6 Insulation of Collector Loop Pipework

7.6.1 Requirements for Insulation

In order to transport the collected heat as efficiently as possible from the collector to the storage unit, careful and unbroken insulation of the whole collector loop is necessary. The thickness of the insulation is usually chosen in accordance with the heating system's regulation. Typically, an insulation thickness equal to 100 % of the nominal tube width (interior diameter) is chosen. In individual cases, an insulation thickness of 200 % has been chosen, as opposed to 50 % at locations difficult to access. There is no binding standard for collector loops, but the heating system recommendation provides a solid foundation.

Line	Nominal width of pipe / fitting (outside diameter)	Minimum thicknes of insulation based on a thermal conductivity of $0,035 \, W \cdot m^{-1} \cdot K^{-1}$
1	up to 20 mm	20 mm
2	20 to 35 mm	30 mm
3	35 to 100 mm	according to width
4	more than 100 mm	100 mm
5	Pipes and fittings according to line 1 to 4 in cutting through of wall or ceiling or crossing or connecting points	$^{1}/_{2}$ of the standard of line 1 to 4

Table 7.3 Recommended insulation thickness according to the heating system regulation

The requirements on insulation materials differ for in- and outdoor pipelines. The following requirements are applicable in both cases:

• Insulation must endure the highest occurring temperatures (near collector: some 170 °C, distant from collector: at least 120 °C)

• Low heat conductivity

• Open-cellular materials are allowable if moistening is no issue

If the pipework is laid outdoors, additional requirements come together:

• Insulation must endure environmental impact (air pollution, UV-radiation) and exposure to animals (bird pecking, mice etc.); otherwise additional means of protection (shells) are necessary

• To prevent moistening, the insulation material should be sealed porosity. Even additional shells cannot prevent moisture from soaking in. Soaked insulation loses most of its effectiveness.

7.6.2 Long-term Survey of Pipe Insulations
The samples originated from installations aging between 13 and 16 years.

Insulation Materials
Mineral wool had been widely used for insulation at the examined solar installations (see Figures 7.19 to 21). Since the protective outer shells were unable to keep humidity out, most of the open-cellular materials were moist and had partly lost their insulating properties, at least until the moisture evaporated by heat from the pipes. This detrimental effect was avoided in cases where sealed-cellular insulation was used (see Figure 7.22).

If insulating materials were not protected against the environment, much of the insulation had (mostly through UV-radiation in connection with high temperatures) disintegrated into small crumbs. In many cases, excessive damage was attributed to birds and mice (material was ripped off for nest building, see Figure 7.17).

Figure 7.17 Damage due to bird-pecking on sheathed foam insulation

A pure wrap-around of adhesive tape was entirely unsuccessful since tapes eroded or became brittle by the time.

For indoor pipeles, in contrast, open-cellular insulations (such as mineral wool) are well suited. If mice infestation is no issue, foam materials can be used as an alternative solution.

Sheathing of Pipe Insulation

In total, five pipe-insulation sheathings of galvanized steel and one of aluminium were examined.

In three random samples, the exterior surfaces of the steel-sheet sheathings were in a good condition and the zinc layers were intact. In one case, the outer side of the sheathing had corroded heavily, but there were no holes yet (see Figure 7.18). The visual impression was very bad in that case, and excessive corrosive damage was only a question of time.

Figure 7.18 A collector field with heavily corroded zinc-plated sheathing

In another solar installation, corrosive damage had already occurred. Especially at spots where openings (for valves, nipples etc.) were cut into the sheathing, the attack of corrosion was expedited since the zinc layer was violated (see Figure 7.19). Accordingly, the sheathing showed advanced stages of rust at many spots. In four out of five examined installations, the interior corrosion of sheathing was heavier than outside (Figure 7.20). In all of these cases, the strong corrosion was caused by humidity, which entered through longitudinal or transverse lap joints or improperly sealed forks (tube branching, air eliminators, nipples etc., see Figure 7.19).

Figure 7.19 Corrosive damage of a zinced sheathing

Figure 7.20 Interior corrosion with wall-breakthrough of a galvanized zinc-plated sheathing

Only one of the five assessed installations was predominantly free of rust. This was the only case where all lap joints were sealed with aluminium foil and the sheet overlap at the joints was in accordance with the directives of the AGI worksheet Q 101 (Insulation works at steam originators) /34/. The sheathing was protected well, albeit not completely, against the entrance of moisture, which was shown by the intactness of the interior surface. However, the outer side had suffered severely, due to the depletion of the zinc layer, but was still intact.

As a tendency, it was observed that zinced sheathings suffer rather less from corrosion if they are sheltered (e.g. underneath the rear of flat-roof mounted collectors). Figure 7.21 documents this on the basis of two instances: The sheathing of the return pipe (cold side; upper half of the picture) was put in a sheltered position behind the collectors and shows only slight corrosion. In contrast, the flow pipe (hot side, lower half of picture) was unprotected and corroded heavily as it is shown.

Figure 7.21 Rust-free sheathing of sheltered pipe (upper half), as opposed to corroded, unsheltered pipe (lower half)

Another tendency observed was that sheathings of flow (hot) pipes appeared to be more corrosion-prone than return pipework.

Although only five installations have been studied in detail, the results are confirmed by several experiences with these installations. Apart from pipe insulation sheathings, corrosion of zinced components was frequently observed on galvanized clips, rigging struts, collector tubs and screws. Although these components, owing to their relatively thick walls, were not impaired functionally (apart from unremovable screw joints), the visual impression of the solar systems suffered from multiple patches of rust.

Galvanized components, if exposed to the open air, thus need a high grade zinc layer which must not be intentionally violated (e.g. by drilling additional holes or subsequent curtailing).

The exterior surface of the single aluminium-sheathing examined in detail, appeared faint, but was fully intact (see Figure 7.22). The appearance is identical to the usual atmospheric corrosion of aluminium. All of the old installations (examined in the scope of the other surveys) with aluminium sheathings showed a similar condition. And no corrosive damage was noticed.

Figure 7.22 Aluminium sheathing of sealed-cellular insulation

Although no special care was applied to the integrity of the lap joints of the aluminium sheathing, the interior surfaces showed a metallic shine, except at branchings, where white traces of corrosion products where visible.

In the case examined, a properly sealed-cellular insulation foam was used, which in addition was carefully wrapped into aluminium foil.

Some solar installations with indoor pipework had unnecessary (and expensive) sheathings made of galvanized steel or even aluminium. For indoor pipelines, the use of regular heat-resistant insulation foams is sufficient. Plastic sheathing should be fitted over mineral wool. When examined, all indoor insulation sheathings (both metal or plastics) were in a spotless condition.

Remarks on Zinc-galvanized Steel Sheets and Components

A zinc layer depletes over time and does not ensure an enduring protection against corrosion. The durability of a component is determined by the thickness and quality of a zinc layer, as well as by the concentration of air pollutants (which sets the rate of zinc depletion).

In the typical manufacturing process of zinc-plated steel sheets, the sheet is led through the molten zinc in a string-pass procedure. The thickness of the zinc layer is normally 15 to 25 µm. This type of sheet is very common, since it is inexpensive and easy to process in the construction site.

If components are zinced in a single-part submersing procedure, the zinc layer is relatively thick (80−150 µm). This technique is the most expensive for sheets. Due to the thickness of the layer, the sheets must be shaped before galvanization.

According to the literature /35/, the annual depletion rate of a zinc layer may lie between 1 and 14µm, depending on air pollution (see table 7.4)

Atmosphere	Reduction of thickness [µm/year]	
	Unprotected steel	Zinc layer
country site	4−60	1.3−2.5
town	30−70	1.9−5.2
industrial area	40−160	6.4−13.8
ocean site	60−170	2.2−2.2

Table 7.4 Progress of corrosion on steel and zinc layers

This means that the zinc layer (15−25 µm) for string-passed sheets may be depleted after only a few years. After another few years, the wall of the steel sheet (thickness 0.6 to 1mm) may break through. Thus, even under favourable environmental conditions (rural air), the desired long-term endurance of at least 25 years for solar systems can not be guaranteed.

According to the German Zincing Association (Deutsche Verzinkerei e.V., Düsseldorf), string-pass zinc-plated sheets are not suitable for outdoor applications. Instead, sheets subjected to a melt-submersing procedure with an aluminium-zinc alloy (e.g. Galvalume, 55 % AlZn or Galfan, 5 % Al) would offer sufficient durability. Additional protection is achieved with a plastic coating. Sheets of this kind have served many years as material for exterior construction (e.g. for industrial halls), and are preferred.

Apart from coated steel sheets as described above, one may use sheets of aluminium or stainless steel for outdoor protection of insulated pipework. When choosing the proper material, the purchase of standardized components is to be considered. According to our investigation, the following options are available:

- synthetic materials (for indoor application; outdoor application possible if resistant against weather, UV-radiation and bird-pecking)
- zinc-plated steel (zinc coat of 275 grams per m², giving a unilateral layer of some 19 µm)
- aluminium 99.5
- aluminium saltwater resistant
- stainless steel and aluminium-zinc as special merchandise

7.6.3 **Proper Choice and Installation of Insulating Materials**

The insulation of collector loop pipework must cope with temperatures more than 120 °C during normal operation and short-time peaks of some 150 °C (in cases of restart after stagnation).

For outdoor pipework, the insulation definitely needs additional protection against animal impact, weather and UV-radiation. Thus protection of the insulation material itself does not have to withstand the harshnesses of the open air exposure.

Since sheathings of outdoor-pipe insulations are not absolutely waterproof, the insulation materials must be sealed-cellular. The minimal requirements (temperature endurance up to 130 °C) are met by insulation foams (e.g. Armaflex HT or Aeroflex SSH). Considering the large peak temperatures that may occur during stagnancy, it is also recommended to have foam materials of suitably improved temperature resistance. However off-the-shelf foam materials that are used for regular heating systems (rated to 90 °C) are satisfactory.

The durability of outdoor sheathings strongly depends on the quality of the material. The lap joints should have sufficient overlap, facing opposite to the harsh weather side. Additional sealings along the lap joints are helpful. A remarkable improvement of durability can be achieved if the outdoor pipes are laid in a sheltered position.

Regarding long-term endurance (25 years and above) of metallic outdoor sheathings, only aluminium (and not galvanized steel) is recommended.

The higher material cost (compared to steel) is not significant, since labour makes up the greatest share of the assembly cost.

The outdoor application in coastal regions demands that aluminium has saltwater protection.

If extensive metal sheet work is needed for pipe sheathings in large-scale projects, the employment of special companies with bulk material and dedicated tools is recommended.

The availability of completely pre-manufactured pipework, tailored to the specific demands of solar installations (including insulation and sheathing and branchings, e.g. as used for district heating) is recommended. This would contribute to a significant improvement of cost efficiency, since a large part of the labour-intensiveness of the assembly could be saved. For small installations, initial steps have been taken into this direction. Pre-manufactured insulated copper pipes and electric cables (for temperature sensors) have recently entered the market (e.g. Osnasol and Twin Tube).

For indoor pipework, inexpensive mineral or glass wool (such as Rockwool or G+H Isover) or melamin resin are adequate, since moisture is not usually an issue. For outer protection, a thin sheathing of plastic is sufficient. Foams without sheathing can also be used if they fulfil the minimum requirements for temperature endurance.

In order to keep the heat loss of the collector loop pipes sufficiently low, an insulation thickness approximately equal to the interior tube diameter (details in table 7.3) is recommended.

7.7 Expansion Vessels

7.7.1 Purpose and Requirements

The purpose of an expansion vessel is to compensate volumetric fluctuations of the collector loop liquid due to thermal expansion. This is done to preserve the components from damage, which may otherwise result for uncontrolled expansion and resulting pressure increase inside the closed system.

It also prevents the escape (and loss) of heat transfer medium through the safety valves, and acts as a buffer, from which the liquid can drain back into the loop, when the heat transfer medium cools. Without expansion vessels, the frequent loss of fluid through the safety valves (during »hot«, high-pressure periods) would necessitate frequent refills and would lead to suction of air through the air vent (when the system cools down again). The presence of an »air cushion« in the collector loop leads to system shutdowns which may remain mostly unnoticed (until the next routine check) if the conventional heating systems automatically takes over the hot water supply. That is why the solar installation needs dedicated safety equipment which assures operation under all conditions (including temporary overheating).

In the European norm (EN 12976-1), protection against overheating is required for solar systems. According to this standard, the system has to be designed for safety, so that even continuous high solar radiation without heat consumption does not lead to conditions, that would require intervention by the user, in order to bring the system back to normal operation. Systems designed that way are also called »inherently secure«.

Two strategies are possible to satisfy this norm:

1. The installation is designed so that the safety valve does not respond during continuous heat input without heat consumption. To ensure this, even in case of large-scale evaporation (i.e. when the collector volume is completely filled with vapour), the expansion vessel must be sufficiently large. This is not only for the thermal expansion of the liquid filling of the loop, but also for the temporary storage of a complete collector volume filling (as well as a generous margin). The expansion vessel would then be much larger than in conventional heating systems.

2. The installation is designed so that the safety valve does respond during evaporation. The expansion vessel would be much smaller, but in order to prevent a malfunction of the installation during temporary evaporation, the controlled boil-off, condensation and recycling of the medium must be secured with off-loop containers and appliances. After the system has cooled down (owing to reduced radiation or increased consumption), the control system has to take care of the automatic refill of lost collector-loop liquid. Such an approach does not offer inherent security in a strict sense (the installation cannot resume regular operation if the automatic refilling system is out of order), and the increased expenditure for control (additional pressure and temperature sensors, pumps, maintenance) is not outweighed by the leaner expansion vessel. Therefore, this option does not offer an completely satisfactory solution.

Usually, the inherent security, of small or large installations, is achieved with sufficiently large expansion vessels. Since the size of the expansion vessels may be problematic for very large installations, the controlled boil-off and refill might be allowed if an on-going draw-off of heat during the hot periods is assured and if the control system can be inspected by the operators.

The dimension of the expansion vessel must suit the anticipated temperature and pressure regulations of the collector loop. The material must sustain the continuous exposure to glycol.

Apart from ensuring inherent security for the solar loop, the expansion vessel must prevent the »breathing« (air suction) of the collector loop. For this purpose, it is put under a pre-set pressurization so that (under consideration of geodetic pressure), at the highest point of the loop, a hyperbaric margin of some 50–100 kPa remains, in the worst-cases (e.g. »cold« condition).

7.7.2 Long-term Assessment of Expansion Vessels
In the examined six installations (from the ZIP research program, 13 to 16 years old), ordinary expansion vessels for heating systems (maximum temperature 120 °C) with rubber membranes (rated for 70 °C) were in use. Five vessels were located indoors.

The outer surfaces of the vessels were all in a good condition. In one case, the vessel was installed outdoors and had suffered from weather exposure, so that it had to be replaced after a few years. The outdoor installation of expansion vessels is rather uncommon, and ordinary vessels are not designed for such a requirement.

For the assessment of the interior surfaces, the vessels were cut open radially, while the membranes were removed. In five out of six vessels, traces of rust were observed on the gas side. Water vapour had diffused through the membrane and condensed on the cold inner face of the gas side, before being deposited at the bottom of the vessel. Since the gas sides were filled with air (and not pure nitrogen, as recommended), the condensation products were able to trigger slight attacks of corrosion in the presence of oxygen. Although newly purchased vessels are delivered with nitrogen filling, it is quite common to re-pressurize them with ordinary air. Otherwise, one would need to purchase specific nitrogen refill packages.

The interior surfaces of the heat-transfer sides of three vessels were completely undamaged. In these cases, the anti-corrosive additives of the heat fluids fulfilled their tasks. Another two vessels showed a light crust and one was heavily corroded at the wetted surface. In two of these cases, the heat fluid's anti-corrosive additives (for steel) had severely diminished.

Figure 7.23 shows the interior of a 13 year-old expansion vessel. The gas side is as good as new, and the heat fluid side shows only slight traces of rust. In Figure 7.24 the condition of another vessel (16 years old) is shown. Corrosion is light on the gas side and heavy on the heat fluid side.

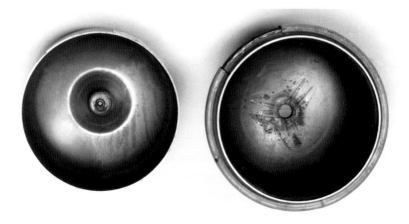

Figure 7.23 Interior view of a 13 year-old expansion vessel; left: gas side, right: heat-carrier side

Figure 7.24 An expansion vessel after 16 years of service; left: gas side, right: heat-carrier side

None of the observed corrosion prevented system operation. Replacements would not have been necessary.

All but one of the examined vessels had non-severe ferruginous deposits (»boiler deposits«) on the liquid side. They were probably swept in from the collector loop.

The membranes (black elastomer, 2−5 mm thick) gave a very good impression after cleaning (two of them were covered with ooze). Only one membrane had a rather rough surface.

The membranes were put to a material analysis which included a burst test. The results (in comparison to the material standard /49/) are shown in table 7.5.

System ID	Years of operation	Manufacturer, Article, content	Rubber material of membran [1]	Tensile strength [Mpa]	Elongation of tear [%]
A	16	not known	Ethylen-Propylen-Dien-Monomer (EPDM)	16.8	360
C	16	Ex-Solar, 25 l	Acrylnitril-Butadien (NBR)	18.8	382
L	16	Reflex, 50 l	Styrol-Butadien (SBR)	16.2	400
M	13	Flexcon Sol, 8 l	Styrol-Butadien (SBR)	14.6	490
P	13	OTTO Expansomat, 180 l	Styrol-Butadien (SBR)	12.4	280
Q	16	Flexcon Sol, 80 l	Styrol-Butadien and natural-Poly-isopren (SBR-NR/IR)	14.7	341
			nominal value:	>10.0	>450

[1] EPDM: Ethylen-Propylen-Dien-Monomer; SBR: Styrol-Butadien (stable up to 85 °C)   NBR: Acrylnitril-Butadien ; SBR-NR/IR: mixture of Styrol-Butadien- and natural-Polyisopren

Table 7.5 Results of burst analysis of expansion vessel membranes

The tearing pressure of all examined membranes were still very good. However, due to the long-term service, the elasticity had decreased as expected. Considering the age of 13 to 16 years, the membranes were in good condition. Replacements would not have been necessary.

It may be of interest here, that those membranes which were exposed to heat-transfer liquids with a very high glycol content (up to 80 %) were still functioning well. If and how a high gylcol content might contribute to the deterioration of the membrane material remains to be investigated in a statistical analysis.

The examinations of expansion vessels and membranes indicated these as non-critical components of the solar heating system. When applying this statement to newly built solar systems (possibly operating at higher temperatures), it is necessary to consider the following points:

- Due to the drastically over-dimensioned collector areas in the ZIP program, stagnation periods were certainly frequent, however, due to the relatively low collector efficiency, the resulting temperatures were mostly below 160 °C.

- The storage units were filled with potable water and were pre-set to a max. temperature of 70 °C. Because of »usual« high-flow operation, the storage was never heated above 100 °C during normal operation. At the location of the expansion vessel (solar return pipe) temperatures of 80 °C were usual.

7.7.3 **Proper Dimensioning of Membrane Expansion Vessels**

The following recommendations concern the »inherent security« criteria (see 7.7.1). This specifies that the safety valve should not respond when the highest possible operating temperature is reached in the system (otherwise fluid will get lost). The volume of the expansion vessel is dimensioned as follows:

First, the installation volume V_i is calculated, which includes the complete liquid filling of the collector loop (collector, pipework, heat exchanger and accessories).

The volume of copper pipes is listed in the table below according to their diameter.

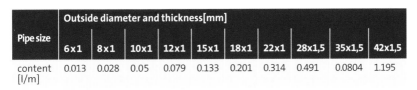

Pipe size	Outside diameter and thickness[mm]									
	6x1	8x1	10x1	12x1	15x1	18x1	22x1	28x1,5	35x1,5	42x1,5
content [l/m]	0.013	0.028	0.05	0.079	0.133	0.201	0.314	0.491	0.0804	1.195

Table 7.6 Volume of copper pipes with different diameter

The following symbols will be used (all pressures hyperbaric):

V_i	[l]	liquid collector loop volume (installation volume)
n	[1]	nominal expansion coefficient
V_e	[l]	liquid expansion volume
V_{wr}	[l]	water reservoir volume
V_v	[l]	anticipated vapour volume
V_{use}	[l]	usable volume of expansion vessel
P_f	[1]	pressure factor
V_n	[l]	nominal volume of expansion vessel
H_{geo}	[m]	geodetic altitude (height of water column above expansion vessel)
p_{geo}	[kPa]	geodetic pressure at expansion vessel
p_{cf}	[kPa]	pressurization at highest point of collector field
p_{gas}	[kPa]	gas pressurization of expansion vessel (adjusted in disconnected mode)
p_{wr}	[kPa]	pressure equivalent of water reservoir
$p_{initial}$	[kPa]	initial (filling) or (cold) operating pressure at expansion vessel
p_{final}	[kPa]	final or maximal pressure (hot, with evaporation but without safety valve response)
p_{SV}	[kPa]	nominal responding pressure of safety valve

p_m [kPa]   pressure margin between regular (hot) operation and safety valve response

When the collector loop is heating up, the liquid expands accordingly. The manufacturers of water-glycol mixtures (e.g. Reflex) offer details on the nonlinear expansion coefficients. Especially for large installations, the available tabulations should be consulted.

$$V_e = V_i \times \int_{T_{min}}^{T_{max}} \gamma(T)dT = V_i \times n(T_{max} - T_{min})$$

n: nominal expansion coefficient (tabulated)

For a basic, self-contained approach on preliminary dimensioning, it may be necessary to use a generic, linearized expansion coefficient γ_{lin}:

$$\gamma_{lin} \approx average \ of \ \gamma(T) \ between \ T_{min} \ and \ T_{max}$$

$$V_e \approx V_i \times \gamma_{lin} \times (T_{max} - T_{min}) = V_i \times n$$

It is reasonable to assume a worst-case temperature difference between cold filling (e.g. 10°C) and operation close to overheating (140 °C, averaged over the entire collector loop) of some 130 K. Linearisations of expansion coefficients for pure water and a 60/40 mixture of water/propylene-glycol (fitted to the above temperature range) are:

$$\gamma_{lin, water} \approx 0.00018/K$$

$$\gamma_{lin, 40\% glycol} \approx 0.00654/K$$

With an anticipated temperature difference of 130 K, the expansion volume of a 60/40 water/glycol mixture is calculated as following:

$$V_{e, 40\% glycol} \approx V_i \times 0.00654/K \times 130K = 0.085 \times V_i$$

In addition, the expansion vessel is filled with a water reservoir which is allowed to drain back into the loop to equalize volumetric losses (due to safety valve and air vent operation) as well as contraction at very low temperatures. To account for contraction, one may use the expansion coefficients above and assume another worst case between filling (at 20°C) and operation in coldest temperature (e.g. at −24°C) of approximately 44 K. This is a very safe estimate, since some pipes are located indoors and never get this cold. For the 60/40 mix of water/glycol, the necessary reservoir for contraction would be:

This is a generous contingency for contraction (some 3 % of the installation volume).

$$V_{wr} \approx V_i \times 0.00654/K \times 44K = 0.029 \times V_i$$

The reservoir should not serve for equalization of leakages, since liquid losses should simply not occur in a sealed, pressurized and inherently secure system. On the other hand, it is quite common that some of the water reservoir simply disappears due to air vent activity during initial operation. Therefore, the water reservoir volume should be at least 3 litres, even for small installations.

$$V_{wr} > 3l$$

The estimated vapour volume is the sum of the complete collector volume and a partial filling of the attached pipework. The collector volume is easily taken from manufacturer ratings, but the possible vapour volume in the pipework is much harder to determine. The reserve for expected vapour volumes of a solar installation has to be estimated case-by-case. Here, the experience and intuition of the designer is beneficial.

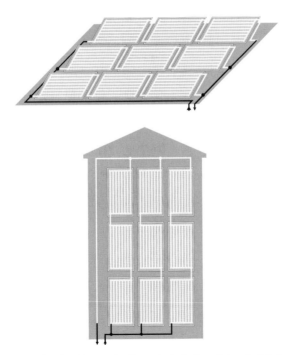

Figure 7.25 Flat-roof-(top) and vertical collector installations; tubes that lie in a potential vapour zone are hatched in light grey

Pipe volumes located at greater height than those of the collectors will likely be displaced by vapour produced in the overheating collectors. This problem applies in particular to widespread installations with non-horizontal surfaces (i.e. on facades or sloped roofs). If the overheating and evaporation process continues long enough, the heat-fluid column in the pipework below the collector may also gradually decompose to vapour. In the extreme case, the complete collector loop filling could boil off. If the expansion vessel is not designed for this case, the safety valve would have to respond to such an excessive volume (and pressure) increase. In order to keep the vaporization problem as small as possible, one would have to:

- minimise the collector filling volume and the interior pipe diameters (usually not realistic options)

- avoid pipework that are located higher than collectors (where possible)

- use system design strategies that allow for an »good natured« and fast evaporation process (see also Chapter 7.1.4).

The usable volume of the expansion vessel is equal to the sum of expansion, water reservoir and vapour volumes:

$$V_{use} = V_e + V_{wr} + V_v$$

The total volume of the expansion vessel must be significantly larger than the usable liquid volume, since it is pressurised with a gas-filled membrane (which is squeezed when liquid enters from the collector loop). The relation between usable and nominal volume of the expansion vessel is determined by a pressure factor:

$$V_n = P_f \times V_{use}$$

The pressure factor is the quotient of (actual) final pressure (p_{final} + ambient pressure) at the vessel, and the »operating pressure reserve« (the offset between final and initial pressures that defines the maximal contraction of the gas side):

$$P_f = \frac{p_{final} + 100kPa}{p_{final} - p_{gas}}$$

The geodetic altitude is the height offset between the expansion vessel and the highest point of the collector loop. The latter is usually defined by the upper edge of the collector or by the air vent. The geodetic pressure p_{geo} is equivalent to the gravity pressure (the head) of a water column of this height.

$$p_{geo} = H_{geo} \times 100kPa/10m$$

The desired overpressure p_{cf} of the collector field (at the highest point) is set for safety against suction of air into air eliminators or small leaks. A recommended value for small installations is 50 kPa; large installations usually have less.

The (hyperbaric) pressure of the gas side of the expansion vessel must be calibrated (when disconnected from the loop) to the sum of geodetic pressure and the desired overpressure of the collector field. Since the newly purchased vessel usually does not have the matching pressurisation, the adaptation is made during installation.

$$p_{gas} = p_{cf} + p_{geo}$$

The response pressure of the safety valve (p_{sv}) is a red-line danger limit that should never be reached during regular operation. Solar loop components are often certified for 1 MPa (or 10 »atmospheres«), while 600 kPa (0.6 MPa) is also quite common in small installations.

$$p_{sv} = 600kPa \ or \ 1MPa$$

A margin between red-line pressure and maximum operating pressure is necessary to safely prevent safety valve response during regular operation. The margin is set to 10 % of the safety valve pressure, but at least to 50 kPa.

$$p_m \geq 0.1 \times p_{sv} \qquad p_m > 50kPa$$

From this, one directly derives the final or (hot) operating pressure:

$$p_{final} = p_{sv} - p_m$$

With the volume of the water reservoir determined, one is able to compute the pressure equivalent of the reservoir. The cold initial operating pressure (pushing against the membrane from the liquid side of the expansion vessel) is set to a value that exceeds the original gas pressure by this equivalent. In this way, a carefully measured amount of liquid (reservoir) is swapped from the loop into the vessel, once the readily pressurised expansion vessel is in connection with the collector loop. The pressure equivalent of the water reservoir is the contribution of the reservoir to exhaustion of the free »operating pressure reserve«:

$$p_{wr} = (p_{final} - p_{gas}) \times V_{wr}/V_{use}$$

Especially in large-scale installations, the system planner must give the correct value of p_{wr} to the fitter for the correct initial setup.

The initial filling pressure of the solar installation is equal to the initial gas pressure in the expansion vessel, plus the equivalent of the water reservoir:

$$p_{initial} = p_{gas} + p_{wr} = p_{cf} + p_{geo} + p_{wr}$$

Example computation:

array with 100 m² collector area, volume (0.6 l/m²)	60 l
volume of pipe network and heat exchanger	150 l
installation volume $V_i = 60\ l + 150\ l =$	210 l
nominal expansion coefficient n = (40 % glycol, heated from 10 °C to 140 °C)	8.5 %
expansion volume $V_e = 8.5\% \cdot V_i =$	17.85 l
water reservoir set to minimum $V_{wr} =$	3 l
collector volume to be displaced by vapour	60 l
estimated vapour volume in pipes	4 l
vapour volume $V_v =$	64 l
usable volume of expansion vessel $V_{use} = V_e + V_{wr} + V_v =$	84.85 l
geodetic altitude (given) Hgeo =	20 m
geodetic pressure $p_{geo} = 20\ m \cdot 100\ kPa/10\ m =$	200 kPa
desired collector field pressurization $p_{cf} =$	50 kPa
initial gas-side pressure of expansion vessel $p_{gas} = p_{geo} + p_{cf} = 250\ kPa$	
response pressure of safety valve (given) $p_{sv} =$	600 kPa
pressure margin for safe operation $p_m = 10\% \cdot p_{sv} =$	60 kPa
final or maximal (hot) operating pressure $p_{final} = p_{sv} - p_m =$	540 kPa
free operating pressure reserve of vessel $= p_{final} - p_{gas} =$	290 kPa
pressure equivalent $p_{wr} = V_{wr}/V_{use} \cdot (p_{final} - p_{gas}) =$	10.25 kPa
pressure factor $P_f = (p_{final} + 100\ kPa)/(p_{final} - p_{gas}) = 640/290 = 2.207$	
required nominal volume of expansion vessel $V_n > P_f \cdot V_{use} =$	187.26 l
next available size of expansion vessel $V_n =$	200 l

After determining the required volume of the expansion vessel, one chooses the next available size of vessel from catalogues. One can also choose a combination a several smaller vessels to fulfil the requirements. If the required volume of the vessels happens to be slightly greater than a particular size (e.g. 205 l in the above example), one can choose a somewhat reduced collector field pressure, so that an even smaller vessel can be used. In principle, one could set the collector field pressurisation to zero, since a small overpressure (below 10 kPa) exists due to the presence of the water reservoir. However this slight reserve may reduce and even disappear (due to air elimination) during initial operation.

Since the size of the expansion vessel does not reach critical limits in small installations, and since the water reservoir is not very large in comparison with the other volumes (especially the vapour contribution), one can artificially increase the size of the water reservoir by lowering the gas-side pressure of the vessel to the geodetic pressure only ($p_{gas} = p_{geo}$). The liquid side would still be set to the usual value ($p_{initial} = p_{geo} + p_{cf} + p_{wr}$).

A problem concerning to the calculated exsample is the relatively high geodetic altitude. If the expansion vessel could be mounted further away from the storage unit and closer to the collector field, the initial operating pressure of the vessel could be considerably reduced. On the other hand, the thermal stress at such a location would be more critical and could easily damage the membrane, if there is no auxiliary reservoir (see Chapter 7.7.5).

The amount of vapour and the pressure factor are decisive for the dimensioning of the expansion vessel. The smaller the pressure difference between initial gas filling and final (hot) operation (the operating pressure reserve), the larger the pressure factor and thus the dimension of the vessel.

When determining the pressure conditions in the collector loop, one should take into consideration a few points, below:

- The larger the operating pressure, the larger the evaporation temperature of the heat medium. The heat transfer liquid must withstand these temperatures and pressures. During sustained evaporation, a continuous pressure increase (due to generated vapour) further increases evaporation temperature and pressure (up to the allowed limit).

- The more the pressure rating, the more the cost of the expansion vessel. On the other hand, a greater pressure rating may allow a much better usable volume fraction. Both factors need to be checked case-by-case.

- When using larger vessels with high pressure ratings, it may be of advantage to use an external pressure source. This variation may be more cost-efficient.

- Often, a combination of smaller vessels (even when considering increased labour expense during installation) is cheaper than a single, large vessel.

- To protect the vessel from excessive heat, it must be attached to the collector return pipe (»cold side«). In addition, a long, uninsulated connection with the collector loop could help reduce the high temperatures on the liquid side of the vessel. If these measures cannot safely protect against overheating, an auxiliary reservoir needs to integrated between loop and expansion vessel.

7.7.4 Proper Installation of Expansion Vessels

Since ordinary expansion vessels are rated only for 120 °C (membranes: 70 °C), entry of vapour must be prevented. The German qualification approval for solar collectors demands that the expansion vessels are installed so that the volume inside the pipework between collectors and vessel is at least 50 % of the usable expansion vessel volume. Otherwise, an auxiliary reservoir must be connected for protection of the expansion vessel (see section 7.7.5)

The vessel should be installed upstream to the pump (Figure 7.26). An arrangement behind the pump (especially when the pump overcomes a large pressure loss) should be avoided due to unfavourable pressure conditions.

It is certainly an advantage to position the vessel with the liquid side to the top and the gas reservoir to the lower side. Then, the heat stress of the membrane (at the bottom of the liquid) remains limited, due to the natural thermal stratification of the liquid. Furthermore, this naturaly prevents steam bubbles reaching the membrane.

To prevent the connection of collector and the vessel from being shut off involuntarily, it is preferable to place capped (rather than »conventional«) valves between collector field and expansion vessel.

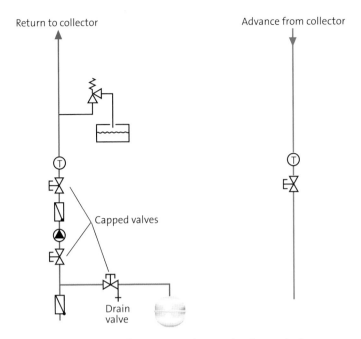

Return to collector   Advance from collector

Capped valves

Drain
valve

Figure 7.26 Possible placement of pump, expansion vessel and capped valves

7.7.5 **Application of Auxiliary Reservoirs**

Auxiliary reservoirs serve the purpose of protecting the expansion vessel membrane from excessive temperature. The auxiliary reservoirs are usually small buffer tanks installed (serially) between collector loop and expansion vessel.

Their dimensioning must secure a sufficient temperature decrease (between inlet and outlet) even under critical conditions (vaporization in the collector loop). There is no generally binding regulation for the size of the auxiliary reservoir, but supplementary guidelines do exist. For example, the qualification approval of the »Euro C18 collector« (source: Governmental Presidency of Darmstadt, Germany) states that: »The water content of the pipelines between collectors and expansion vessel must be at least 50% of the properly dimensioned water capacity of the expansion vessel.«

This can be interpreted as the combination of the volumes of connecting lines (apparently, the shortest connection between vessel and collector along the return line is meant) and the tank volume of the auxiliary reservoir should add up to the recommended minimum.

Example:

At given boundary conditions (Chapter 7.7.3), the usable volume of a 25 litre expansion vessel is 17.2 litres. The liquid filling volume of the flow and return pipes of the roof-mounted solar system add to five litres. The expansion vessel is situated at the collector return pipe. The pipes between vessel and collector field (along the return pipe) contains a volume of two litres only.

To achieve the desired total volume (50 % of 17.2 l = 8.6 l), an auxiliary reservoir of 8.6 l is required. If only the short return pipe is considered, a volume of 8.6 l−2 l = 6.6 l would be required.

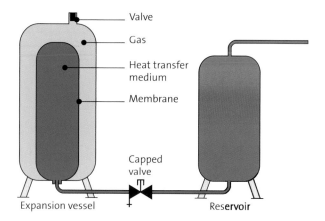

Valve

Gas

Heat transfer medium

Membrane

Capped valve

Expansion vessel   Reservoir

Figure 7.27 Installation of expansion vessel with auxiliary reservoir tank.

7.8 Circulating Pumps

7.8.1 Purpose and Requirements
The pump ensures the continuous circulation of the volume inside the closed loop. The collector circulating pump must be unaffected by the operating temperatures of the loop for many years. Due to the accordingly lower thermal stresses during operation (flow: 120 °C, return: 100 °C, see Chapter 7.1.2), the pump is installed in the collector return pipe. Even there, it must sustain short-time temperature peaks (return pipe: up to 130 °C) when (after standstill) hot medium out of the collector is pressed into the expansion vessel. Since these peak temperatures occur infrequently and last for only a few seconds (in a properly dimensioned system), an enquiry to the manufacturer can often lead to a generous evaluation of pump operation.

A statistically investigation of the extent and endurance of worst-case temperature peaks at solar loop and solar buffer is not available yet. Suitable experiments (actuation of the pump at unfavourable conditions) must be carried out manually and are time consuming. The layout of the collector loop also has a decisive role in the entire system. The lighter the weight (and thus heat capacity) of the collector loop pipes in relation to the weight of the absorbers, the less the temperature peaks will be reduced.

Apart from heat resistance, it is obviously necessary that the pump sustains continuous exposure to the heat transfer medium (water/glycol). This applies not only to the pure material compatibility, but also to the integrity of all sealings with respect to glycol.

In addition, the pump is required to:

- operate with good efficiency at the designated operating point
- be tough against fatigue, in spite of frequent switching cycles
- be inexpensive

7.8.2 Long-term Assessment of Circulating Pumps

The pumps of nine solar installations were examined (originating from the ZIP research program). Six of these installations were still operative, while the other three were put back into operation in the scope of the assessment (and only then, were their damages determined).

System ID	Years of operation	Manufacturer, article	Housing material	Impeller material	Functionality	Remarks
A	16	Grundfos/ UPS 50-120	cast iron	stainless steel[1]	electrical: no	
B	15	KSB/Etath. H 65-13/084	cast iron	cast iron	yes	
C	16	Wilo/RS 25-80	cast iron	plastics	yes	light deposit on impeller
O 1	16	Wilo/RS 25-1v	cast iron	plastics	electrical: no	light deposit on impeller
O 2	16	Wilo/RS 25/ 80	cast iron	plastics	yes	light deposit on impeller
β	16	Wilo/RS 30/ 80	cast iron	plastics	electrical: no	
P	13	Grundfos/ UPS 40-120	cast iron	stainless steel[1]	yes	
Q	16	Wilo/RS 30-1	cast iron	plastics	yes	impeller melted
R	16	Wilo/RS 30/ 80	cast iron	plastics	mechanical no	heavy deposit on impeller

[1] Stainless chrome nickel steel

Table 7.7 Overview of examined circulating pumps

First, the pumps were examined with for their electrical operation. Three pumps were discovered to be electrically inoperative; while one had a rotor rotor jammed with dirt, which prevented a trial run.

After this test, the pumps were disassembled and the condition of components was examined separately.

The casings were of cast iron. Six (out of nine) casings had a thin covering layer, but none showed corrosive damage.

Examination of the movable parts showed that all pumps except one were mechanically intact. The shaft of one pump was stuck to the bearing. The pump had stood still for two years. Deposits from the heat transfer liquid were found on the rotor, bearing and casing of this pump (Figure 7.28). The liquid entered through the seals of the shaft bearing. Components of three other pumps had traces of similar sediment. As these results suggest, the entrance of water/glycol into the casing is not an isolated case.

Figure 7.28 Two pump rotors with slight (left) and strong (right) sedimentation

Figure 7.29 Perfectly intact casing of a pump without sediments

The running wheels of eight (out of nine) pumps had no traces of degradation. Out of these, four had a thin covering layer.

The synthetic running wheel of one of the pumps had a molten edge due to the local overheating (Figure 7.30). The designation and temperature rating of the synthetic material could not be established properly, nor the conditions producing the damage. The pump was still operating, but probably with reduced capability.

Figure 7.30 Synthetic running wheel of a circulating pump with molten edge

The it-sealings (compressed asbestos fibre sheet) were still intact in all pumps. Yet, the O-rings of two pumps were slightly out of shape, which indicates that the material was affected by the thermal stresses.

7.8.3 Proper Application and Dimensioning

Pumps of solar installations working according to the low-flow principle, with external heat exchangers, are critical for thermal stress. Here, the recommended installation on the solar return pipe can still lead to operating temperatures above 90 °C (up to 100 °C) and temporary peaks of up to 120 °C under critical conditions. The thermal load of the pump and all its components is in this way significantly higher than in installations working on the high-flow principle. Eventually, this may necessitate the integration of a thermometer at the collector and a control algorithm that prevents a run-up before the temperature has fallen below 130 °C. This measure (which is not common in practice yet) would limit the return pipe temperature to 100 °C.

Due to its significantly higher viscosity, a glycol content above 50 % in the heat transfer medium may be problematic for the run-up arrangement itude of the pump. Such an »over-dosage« of glycol would also increase the flow resistance and lower the liquid's heat capacity.

The positioning of the pump must be according to instructions by the manufacturer (e.g. horizontal alignment of the shaft).

Accessories such as sliding valves or automatic air vents should not be located vertically above the pump since they might leak; the interior of the pump could be damaged (short circuit etc.) by leaking heat transfer fluid.

When the pump is newly installed and the collector loop is freshly filled, the pump can be protected from damage if the loop is heated (to dissolve oils etc.) and flushed carefully.

A particular problem of installations operating in low-flow mode is the large pumping head, combined with a low flow. Especially when collectors are row-connected (to keep the pipework expense low) in a small installation (with a small pump), the accumulative pressure loss burdens the pump to its limit. If then a dirt trap is refitted incorrectly or slightly contaminated, or a flow-meter is slightly stuck, or the planner has underdimensioned the pump, the loop circulation may break down. The pump would turn, but would not pump significant volume.

Figure 7.31 shows the characteristic field of a pump working in a loop with too great a pressure loss. As it is shown in the example, a pump was designed for temperatures up to 130°C and a flow of 1,200 l/h, which for a solar array of 100 m^2 gives a flow-rate of 12 l/(m^{2}h). A pumping head of some 8 metres was calculated necessary to overcome pressure losses. The choice of available pumps was very restricted by the specifications (temperature 130°C, flow 1,200 l/h, pumping head 8 m), while the cost of suitable inline pumps was prohibitive.

It turned out that the actual pipe network characteristic deviated significantly from the calculated curve (see both lines in the Figure 7.31). The flow-rate was 7,000 l/h instead of 12,000 l/h. Due to miscalculations by the planner (accessories and sensors in the pipe system had not been calculated), the characteristic curve of the network was much »steeper« than calculated. The pumping head needed to be increased by 1 metre.

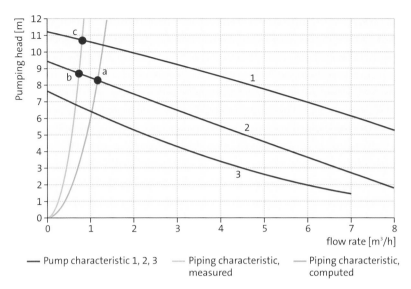

Figure 7.31 Pipe network characteristics (calculated and actual) and pump operating lines (three speed increments); theortetical (a, c) and actual (b) operating points

The theoretical pipe network characteristic in the Figure runs rather steeply and intersects with the pump's operating line (speed 2) at operating point a. Although the calculated pumping head was only marginally overstepped (by 0.5 m or 6 %), the volumetric flow (intersection with actual grid line) decreased dramatically (to 700 l/h or 60 %) at the actual operating point b. At this reduced flow, the whole collector loop would get hotter and operate less efficiently. With a pipe characteristic of this steepness, a higher pump speed does not solve the problem. A shift to »high gear« (speed 1, operating point c) raises the pumping head significantly (by 2 m), but the flow increases only marginally and falls short of the designated value.

In the above sample, one would wish to have a pump whose characteristic runs much steeper and intersects with the axes at (0 m³/h; 15 m) and (2.5 m³/h; 0 m). A standard pump with these properties is not yet available.

At the same time, the pump works in a region of poor efficiency. Since a good pump efficiency is more important (pumping work/electrical power), one would prefer to operate pumps at high speed with mediocre flows (such as the median section of pump curve 1). Regular heating pumps of the considered size (200−500 W_{el}) reach an efficiency of 25−35 %, but drop to 10 % near the edges of the pump curve. Pump efficiency (but not necessarily solar yield) also drops if one switches to a lower speed.

The pump in the example would operate at a poor efficiency of only about 10 to 15 %. It is hoped that pump manufacturers keep working on efficiency improvements (up to and beyond 50 %) and particularly recognize the requirements to develop pumps that are tailored to the conditions (such as described above) of collector loops. A positive step in this direction has been taken by the German Wilo company. Two pumps were developed and optimized for solar loops. New pump hydraulics and actuation (electronically controlled actuation with permanent magnets) nearly doubled the efficiency.

From the statements above, it can be concluded that the ratio of pressure loss (pumping head) to flow rate of a collector loop must not be too high. Although a serial connection of multiple solar panels is preferred in low-flow systems, their number must be kept small (until better pumps are available). Likewise, the pressure loss of the pipework system and heat exchanger must be considered. A scheduled cleansing of dirt traps and filters, as well as continuous air elimination, prevents the increase of pressure losses during operation. The achievement of uniform flow through derating (with choking valves) of sub-arrays of the collector field should be avoided. Careful dimensioning of the pipework and an adapted combination of parallel and serial collector connections can often substitute regulating valves.

7.9 Accessories

7.9.1 Requirements

As in many applications of housing technology, the solar collector loop is equipped with thermometers, manometers, strainers, stop-, nonreturn- and regulating valves. The accessories include monitoring devices and equipment for operational safety and maintenance. The devices must comply with the following specifications:

- certified for operation up to 130 °C (and in the collector advance, peaks up to 150 °C) or highest occurring temperature (at the location of the device)

- compatibility with materials of other components and with heat transfer fluid (water/glycol)

- certified for operating pressure range of collector field (up to response pressure of safety valve)

- reasonable cost

The display of the flow-meter (attached to regulating valve) should be calibrated to the heat transfer medium, or opportunities of rescaling should exist.

Due to the high operating temperatures, flow-meters should not consist of synthetic materials. Regulating valves with glass displays of flow are best, they can be fitted without flow meters.

7.9.2 **Long-term Assessment of Collector Loop Accessories**

In a random survey, specimens of several accessories were taken from six solar installations (approximately 15 years old) and put to further examination.

Pipe fittings consisted of red bronze and were all in a good condition. Some of the samples were covered with a thin green layer (deposits from the heat transfer medium). Operation of the parts was completely unimpaired.

O-ring seals (black elastomere) of stop valves were still intact and undamaged. Nevertheless, seals of this kind tend to become leaky with time. Under the imposed operating conditions, ball valves are better suited than o-ring sealed stop valves.

Some screw connections had become leaky when sealed with Teflon tape. Hemp seals are better for assurance of long-term protection against glycol at high temperatures.

In some cases, the collectors were connected by fibre-reinforced rubber hoses. Due to continuous thermal stress, these had become stiff, crumbly and rutted and proved to be utilized only for limited use. During many years of support service for solar installations, the experience was made that clamped hose connections (a common practice in the past) are weak points of the loop, particularly for glycol integrity. Nowadays, hose connections are almost never used, since available alternatives (screw or interlock connections) are operationally safe and easy to assemble.

When actuated valves are used, experience shows that magnetically operated valves are unsuitable. Even when properly actuated, they usually demand a minimal (dynamic) flow pressure of some 30 kPa to allow a flow. In a loop that is already heavily burdened with pressure losses, this is not acceptable and useful. Actuated valves with servo motors are the preferred solution.

7.10 **Air Elimination**

7.10.1 **Purpose and Requirements**

When a heating system or collector loop is filled with liquid, the heat transfer medium displaces the air that was initially present in the system. However, small bubbles of air are carried away with the flowing liquid and gradually vents off again. Another small fraction of air dissolves in the liquid, until it is gradually released at higher temperatures.

Air always accumulates at the highest point of the closed system. In a casual arrangement of heaters or pipework, the air may form

»bubbles« at local high-spots (where no ascending connection exists to the highest point).

When air bubbles are present in a closed flow system, they are noticeable by acoustic noise (burbling and rumbling). Larger amounts of air can lead to a break down of the circulation. Then, the increasingly hot collector liquid does not reach the heat exchanger, in spite of continuous pumping activity. This problem frequently occurred in poorly maintained solar systems.

If air accumulates in the pump and is not eliminated or carried away with the flow, the bearings of the (usually water-cooled) pump may run hot and eventually be damaged.

The presence of air in a gravity brake causes a characteristic flapping noise which is often attributed to the pump. If an air bubble forms in front of a gravity brake, it can block the opening of the brake during pump run up. This may cause pump overheating and bearing damage.

The conclusion is that, air must be kept outside (and heat transfer liquid kept inside) the collector loop as much as possible, and small amounts of air, if present, must be carefully and safely eliminated.

Air elimination can be split into two categories:

(1) Air elimination during initial filling (when large volumes of air are displaced by the incoming liquid) and (2) sustained elimination of small air bubbles during regular operation.

During the filling procedure, all air eliminators (at locations where the formation of air bubbles is suspected) must be opened (not necessarily in a pressurized filling procedure), so that the air can be released without inhibition. Automatic air eliminators (permeable for gases, but not liquids) fulfil this task without further regulation. Automatic air eliminators are very sensitive and require rather slow filling. A manually operated air eliminator must be closed when liquid starts to pour out from its opening. A cyclic filling procedure is also possible with manual eliminators: in several stages, liquid is guided into the system (under pressure, with eliminators closed) before the eliminators are opened to squeeze the air out.

During regular operation, the formation of air bubbles (which are thus kept separate from the liquid) is allowed at designated locations. After long intervals (during initial operation more often, later only every few months), this air is released by manual opening of the air eliminators. The integration of automatic air eliminators at these collecting points is more convenient, but not suitable for spots that may accumulate vapour (which would simply steam off) during »hot« periods.

If the system is carefully regulated, properly dimensioned and always slightly pressurised, the suction of air into the loop should not be an issue. However, the situation is quite different if small leaks remain unnoticed and an underpressure develops at the highest point of the collector field. This phenomenon was frequently observed in older solar installations.

Air eliminators located at the highest points of the system must sustain temperatures close to the peak temperatures (up to 200 °C) at the collector (since hot vapour is certain to reach them). Eliminators with stainless steel floaters are excellent for heat resistance, but they cannot be closed manually and for this reason are unsuitable. At the remaining spots of the collector loop, fitted air eliminators should be certified for at least 130 °C.

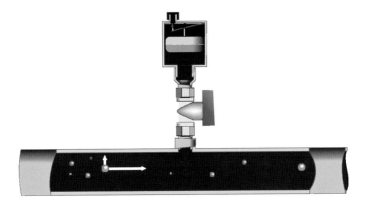

Figure 7.32 Lockable automatic air eliminator without pacification area

In order to assure the proper functioning of the eliminator, without leaks or contamination, the following remarks should be considered:

Automatic air eliminators must be locked off during pressurisation tests, refills or pressure adjustments. Usually, 3/8" ball valves are integrated for this purpose.

To prevent dirt particles from being swept into the automatic air eliminator while (re-)filling, the filling should take place very slowly.

Figure 7.33 Manual and (lockable) automatic air eliminators with pacification area

During operation, automatic eliminators near the collectors must be locked off to prevent unintentional loss of vaporised heat transfer medium during collector stagnation. They are therefore not particularly useful at these locations. Automatic air eliminators should rather be used in automatically degassed pumps or in connection with absorptive degassers or cyclone eliminators.

Figure 7.34 Cyclone eliminator (may not be used at steam-prone locations!)

Full-metal, manually operated eliminators with air pots are a good alternative for steam-prone locations. In the simplest case, the air pots are small containers leading upwards from the pipe. The manual eliminator is attached to the top of the pot, or both components are delivered in a pre-manufactured unit. The air pots must be well insulated in order to reduce heat losses.

Some solar systems function without eliminators near the collectors and rely completely on a centralised air eliminator at the solar station. Pressurised degassing is achieved within the simultaneous filling and flushing procedure. To get this procedure to work, the water-jet effect of the flow must be sufficiently strong to carry air bubbles away. This is hard to achieve in parallel-connected arrays.

For this purpose, two bfd-valves (ball valves for filling and draining) are integrated (both are separated by an additional stop valve) into the collector return pipe. First, the stop valve between the two bfd-valves is closed, next a strong external pump is attached to the return side and squeezes water into the collector loop. Through the other bfd-valve air (and later, a water-air mixture) is let out. The pump remains active until all air bubbles are flushed out of the loop (requiring at least for 10 minutes). If the outlet hose is submerged slightly, the presence of air bubbles is easily checked. Thereafter, the bfd-valves are closed, the pump is shut off and the inlet hose is attached to a tank with sufficient anti-freeze agent. Then the pump is restarted and the bfd-valves are reopened (the inlet valve first, to prevent air suction). Now, anti freeze agent is pressed into the system, where it displaces water. When traces of anti-freeze agent (easily identifiable by colour and constitution) exit the outlet hose, the exit bfd-valve is closed immediately. So the pump builds up the necessary system pressure. Then the inlet bfd-valve is closed, the pump is shut off and the stop valve (between the bfd's) is reopened. Finally, a sample of the liquid should be taken to check the concentration of anti-freeze agent. The filling/flushing procedure is illustrated in full detail (with only few words) in the filling and operating manual of the Roto Frank company.

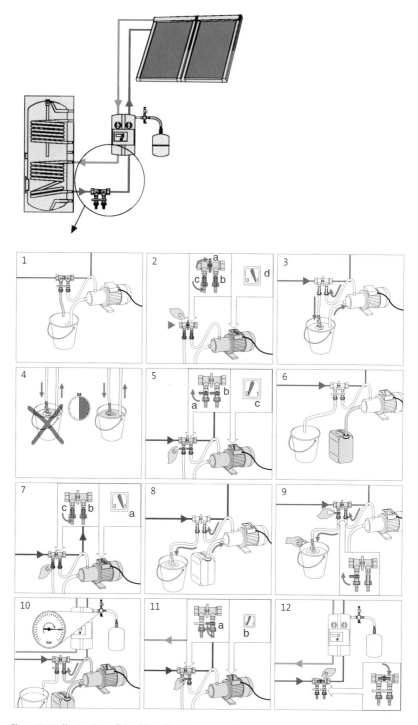

Figure 7.35 Illustration of the filling/flushing procedure in a manual by Roto Frank

It is strongly recommended to take a sample of the fluid afterwards, to check for the proper concentration of glycol.

The same procedure (without flushing) is applied when the installation refilled.

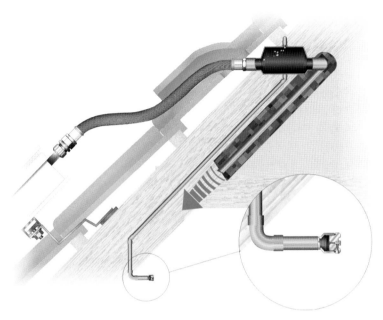

Figure 7.36 Central air eliminator

If the highest point of the collector loop is situated at a difficultly accessible location on the roof (e.g. near the roof top), an air accumulator can be integrated, as shown in Figure 7.36. A thin tube from the accumulator leads downwards to an accessible position below, with a manually operated air eliminator. Remember, that this connecting tube fills with liquid after opening the eliminator for the first time. During the following opening cycles, the liquid column present in the connecting tube needs to be squeezed out before air can escape. Therefore, it would be good to know the volume of this liquid column, in order to prevent large losses of liquid (if no air is present).

So-called air separators are principally similar to air pots. The guidance of the liquid flow is optimised for the separation of air. Since air separators are to be operated frequently, it is desirable to have easy access to them (e.g. in the basement of the building).

In order for an air separator to work at a relatively low point of the system (where air bubbles would never move themselves), the flow velocity must be sufficiently large to carry the air downwards. The velocity (due to buoyancy) of air bubbles in water is approximately

0.25 m/s. A significantly larger flow velocity (say, 0.4 m/s) everywhere in the collector loop would assure that the air bubbles reach the separator. In order to satisfy this condition, the diameter of the pipes must not be too large, and the flow rate not too small. It was frequently observed that, especially in small installations (e.g. with 5 m^2 of collectors), the fitter had chosen a pipe diameter that matched the interfaces of the delivered pumps, valves and accessories but not the requirement of a minimal flow velocity.

It is also important to note the necessity of careful air elimination to prevent corrosion, since corrosive attacks occur a lot faster in the presence of air oxygen. The presence of air appears less critical when relatively corrosion inert materials are used (copper or sufficiently thick steel). However, corrosive products could contaminate the heat transfer fluid and could deposit during evaporation. This could lead to a local blockage at the pipe's interior cross section.

Another factor is the accelerated ageing of anti-freeze agents in presence of air. In an extreme case, the pH-value of the liquid could fall significantly below 7 due to acid corrosion products. This, in turn would cause in increased corrosion, especially at soldering seams in the collector. If the pH-value of the heat transfer liquid is below 7, a complete replacement of the liquid is recommended.

7.11 Safety Equipment

7.11.1 Requirements

Safety standards for thermal solar installations are reported in the European Industrial Norm EN 12975, EN 12976 and ISO 9806 which have already been referred to in Chapter 5.

Safety equipment is needed for the assurance of operational safety and the prevention of damage to the installation, as well as for the operator. In order to fulfil its purpose, the equipment needs to be dimensioned, chosen and installed carefully.

There are reported cases of personal injury, when hot steam (during stagnancy) was collected in a completely unsuitable vessel. Therefore, all the safety equipment of a solar installation must be properly adapted to the specific operating conditions (pressures, temperatures and periods of stagnancy). Especially in the case of large installations, this is the task of the planners, since they are the only people with complete information about the expected operating conditions. The on-site fitter would most likely be overtaxed with this.

7.11.2 **Security Concepts**

When a larger collector field is separated into several sub arrays (e.g. to do maintenance work at one sub array without necessarily shutting down the entire system), each sub array needs to have its own safety valve. It must be impossible to shut off any of the safety valves with respect to the collector loop. The safety valves must be certified for the highest temperatures that may occur at the collector. They should have connections into a single recapturing vessel or, if they are too far apart, into several nearby vessels. The blow-off lines should be safe against corrosion (e.g. copper). The recapturing vessel should be highly heat resistant and weather-proof. Galvanised steel, due to possible interaction with the heat transfer fluid, is not suitable for the vessel. The cross section of the safety valve and of the outlet nozzle must be in accordance with the regulations, and the safe discharge and collection of steam (without danger for operating personnel) must be assured.

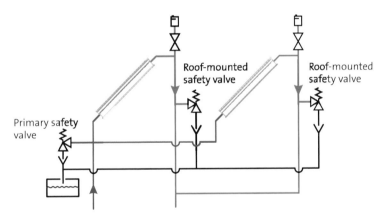

Figure 7.37 Detail of safety-valve liquid discharge and recapture

It would be of obvious advantage to keep the on-roof safety valves out of the vapour zone, since otherwise the blown-off steam would be much harder to recapture.

The safety vessels must be large enough to safely blow off the steam-equivalent of the maximum heating power of the installation. The following valves according to the corresponding collector arrays are recommended:

Valve size (inlet diameter) [mm]	Collector area [m²]
15 mm	50
20 mm	100
25 mm	200
32 mm	350
40 mm	600

Table 7.8 Safety valve sizes (inlet diameter) according to collector area

Installations with inherent security (sufficiently large expansion vessel to absorb the vapour volume) can use somewhat smaller safety valves, certified for liquid blow-off only.

The main safety valve must be certified for at least 120 °C. The response pressure must be below or equal to the maximally bearable pressure of the weakest component of the loop. The locking pressure must be at least 90 % of the response pressure.

The regulations for the classification and identification should be obeyed.

The monitoring of the installation can be optimised if the response pressures of main and local are calibrated so that the main safety valve responds to a significantly lower pressure (and thus responds first). If main and local valves are vertically separated by more than 10 metres, this is not necessary, since it is then certain that the main valve responds first (to the higher water-column pressure).

The blow-off line guides the (condensed) heat transfer liquid to a recapturing vessel. It is important for safety and maintenance, to have a single vessel that should be large enough for a complete collector loop volume. The blow off-line and recapturing vessel must prevent danger to people. A manual refilling by a manually operated pump should be possible.

Example:

A large installation (collector area: 100 m²) with a collector filling volume of 60 l is separated into two sub-arrays (30 l each). Two safety valves 15 mm (at collector fields, certified for 225 °C), four ball valves (for shut off) and one main safety valve 20 mm (in the basement, certified for 120 °C) are used. All safety valves are set to response pressure of 600 kPa. Due to the higher water column (some 10 m), it is certain that the main safety valve will respond first.

7.11.3 **Long-term Experience with Safety Equipment**

The examined installations (from the ZIP research program, 13–16 years old) had somewhat less efficient collectors and used a heat transfer liquid with high glycol content (up to 80%). The intention was to prevent evaporation during stagnation completely, and in most of the cases the expansion vessels were dimensioned accordingly small.

Due to deficiencies that occurred during the assembly, small leaks were very common, with the result that the necessary pressure to inhibit evaporation could not be maintained. Blow-offs therefore occurred frequently, especially since most of the installations were overdimensioned (for collector and thus, heat input) and were often stagnant.

In combination with low-grade recapturing vessels (designers had not expected an extensive blow-off), this resulted in a potential danger for operating personnel.

For safety, experience shows that it is essential to design for vapour characteristics with properly dimensioned pressure vessels and safety components. To disregard the possibility of vaporization can not be recommended.

The response arrangement of the examined safety valves was straightforward, so long as, their frequent response was not a difficulty.

In some cases, it was attempted to avoid stagnation and evaporation by using auxiliary means of heat discharge, such as circulating the hot liquid through an arrangement of radiators or basins for emergency cooling. All these measures proved to be working, but only at highly increased cost and with the addition of components which are themselves corrosion-prone.

A similar concept of emergency cooling is the so-called »emergency cooling safeguard« recommended for those solar installations which may produce very large and difficultly controllable volumes of vapour during stagnation. The preferred concept for an installation would be to prevent stagnation altogether by a »lean« dimensioning (relatively small collector area). However, this is difficult to achieve during the hot months of summer, if high solar radiation occurs when there is a low use of thermal power. In such cases, an emergency cooling system would be useful. For example, a swimming pool as auxiliary load for emergency cooling would be a reasonable effective solution.

Example:

An emergency cooling system with thermal safeguard (such as in use with solid fuel boilers) was fitted to a 50 m^2-installation with tubular collectors. When a temperature of 95 °C is exceeded in the collector loop, a valve opens and the medium is cooled with freshwater through a heat exchanger. The heat exchanger is (according to its operating characteristic) dimensioned for $300\,W/m^2_{\text{collector}}$. The incoming freshwater line was set to the minimal flow rate of 8 l/min, and a fitted to a flow-meter for monitoring. The freshwater outlet is, according to regulations, safe against scalding. When this particular system was put into operation, it was observed that the safeguard valve responded properly, but did not close afterwards. Therefore much freshwater and solar heat were dissipated.

Take care, that additions to the system, installed to eliminate weaknesses, do not themselves become new weaknesses.

8. **Solar Storage Unit**

The dimensioning of solar storage tanks has been considered in detail Chapter 4. This Chapter considers other important aspects of storage.

8.1 **Function and Requirements**

Storage units serve the purpose of a »battery« that separates the heat input of solar radiation from the user's energy consumption. Since the temporal pattern of energy input usually does not match that of energy consumption, this separation is necessary in all but a few solar-thermal systems. The time period of storage varies between a few hours, days or (in case of seasonal storage), months and strongly depends on the consumption side of the system (e.g. swimming pool, potable water or room heating) and the desired solar fraction.

The goal is to store the available solar energy as completely as possible during periods of low power demand and later supply this energy as efficiently as possible when needed.

Requirements on the solar storage unit:

- high heat capacity of the storage medium
- good heat efficiency (small tank surface and good insulation)
- a thermally well stratified structure of the tank filling
- a desired life cycle of 25 years (or more) for the complete system
- low cost and good availability
- tank and storage medium must be compatible with the environment and hygiene (e.g. potable water)
- the system must withstand the expected range of pressures and temperatures

Due to its good heat capacity, environmental-friendliness and availability, ordinary water is the commonly chosen storage medium. It is possible for domestic water systems to use potable water directly as the storage medium, or, if an auxiliary solar buffer and heat exchanger is used (see Chapter 3), non potable »heating water«.

Alternative systems (latent-heat concepts and chemical storage) have entered experimental development and will not be described further at this point. Non of the surveyed systems used storage media other than water.

8.2 **Types of Construction**

8.2.1 **Potable Water Storage**
Potable water storage tanks must comply with high standards of hygiene. This problem is explained in detail in Chapter 3.3. Furthermore, the tank must withstand corrosion in the presence of oxygen (contained in the potable water).

Zinc galvanised Storage Tanks
Zinc galvanised storage tanks are quite common. However such tanks for potable water are not compatible with copper pipework, since a galvanic voltage would build up between both metals, causing degeneration of the zinc layer and corrosion. The use of copper installation in the water flow behind galvanised pipes and storage is less damaging.

Enamel-Coated Tanks
Enamel coatings are very commonly used for the protection of storage tanks from interior corrosion. Enamel, a kind of glass, is burnt into the steel container. Since small faults in the material are unavoidable, enamel contains small particles of magnesium or other anodic materials as cathodic protection against corrosion. Enamel storage tanks can be easily and cheaply manufactured.

However, the material must be protected from impacts during transport, otherwise the enamel coat could suffer damage.

Plastic-Coated Tanks
This type of anti-corrosion protection includes coatings of duro-, thermo- and rubber-plastics. These coatings are considerably cheaper than enamel, but their long term endurance is questionable.

In particular, thermoplastics are certified for 85 °C only and should not be exposed to a temperature gradient increment of more than 10 K at the coated wall. This makes thermoplastics unsuitable for combo-storage units and those with internal collector-loop heat exchangers.

Stainless Steel Tanks
Stainless steels are relatively inert to corrosion, due to their high content of nickel and chromium. Common brands of stainless steel are »Nirosta«, »V2A« (steel of grade 1.4301 and 1.4541) and »V4A« (grade 1.4571). However, welded connections of stainless steel may corrode at high concentrations of chlorine. If the allowable maximum concentrations of chlorine is considered (V2A: 50 mg/l, V4A: 125 mg/l), stainless steel is a very durable material. It is more expensive than plastic- or enamel-coated materials.

8.2.2 **Solar Buffer Tanks**

Buffer tanks are used in large solar systems for potable water heating or auxiliary room heating (see Chapter 3.3 and 3.4). Since these systems require relatively large storage volumes, the storage medium is separated from the potable water for hygiene reasons.

If the storage tanks and its attached pipework form a closed loop (i.e. no additional oxygen is entering the loop), the requirements for anti-corrosive protection can be somewhat relaxed. The pressure load of the buffer tank is also much lighter than on a potable water tank. Both these factors contribute to the low cost of a buffer tank.

Lightly Pressurized Buffer Tanks

In a closed system with slight over-pressurization, buffer tanks made of ordinary steel are commonly used (e.g. St 37). These can be used without particular care for corrosion, since the system is filled only once with water and the overpressure inhibits the entrance of oxygen. The water used for the first filling should be carefully decalcified and filtered to prevent sedimentations on pumps, valves etc.

»Combi« Storage Units

Figure 8.1 Combi storage unit »Swiss Solartank« of the Jenni company, Switzerland

»Combi« units combine a potable water tank (stainless or coated steel) with an integrated buffer. In this way, the potable water reservoir can be kept small, even with large volumes of heating water (in the buffer). The heat in the buffer is transmitted through the wall of the vessel. An additional heat exchanger is not needed.

Open-System Buffers

Due to their good resistance against corrosion, plastic materials are well suited for the buffer storage tanks of unpressurised, open-loop systems. In this type of system, an open expansion vessel (without membrane) is used.

No safety valve is needed. However, the allowable temperatures of the materials used must be considered. In systems with pump circulation, this can be safeguarded with an integrated safety temperature limiter (but not one of those models that have to be unlocked manually). An arrangement of this kind is not possible in thermosyphon systems (without pump), so plastic materials cannot be recommended for this particular application (unless the »natural« operating temperatures stay sufficiently low).

Seasonal Storage

Seasonal storage units absorb large amounts of heat during summer, in order to release them when needed during the heating periods of winter. This requires very large storage volumes of 10 to more than 100 m^3 for a single house or several 1,000 m^3 for a local heating network (see also Chapter 4).

Storage tanks of steel, sizied up to several tens of cubic metres can be integrated into buildings or be buried underground /22/. Recently, tanks of fibre-enforced plastics have been used for the same purpose.

Large tanks for local heating networks can be incorporated into terrestrial basin storage, terrestrial probe storage and aquifer storage tanks (detailed information available in literatures /17/ and /18/).

8.3 Storage Tank Insulation

The heat losses of conventional storage tanks are very significant. In order to keep heat losses of solar storage units within reasonable limits, special requirements must be met for insulation:

- a small surface to volume ratio of the tank
- closely attached insulation
- complete insulation of the tank, including upper and lower sides
- insulation of all pipe connections and fitted accessories
- pipework guided into the storage tank or below the insulation
- avoidance of in-tube circulation (heat losses caused by convection within the pipe)

Example:

A properly designed storage unit with a volume of 300 litres and a set temperature of 45°C has heat losses of approximately 1.5 kWh per day. A conventional storage unit of the same capacity may lose 2.5 kWh per day, which is equivalent to the yield of more than one square metre of collector surface.

For insulation, common materials are used (see also Chapter 7.6). The use of PVC is not recommended.

The quality of the storage unit with for heat heat losses should be checked.

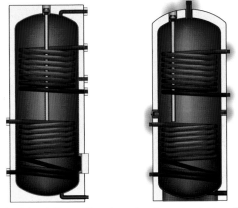

Figure 8.2 Storage tank insulation with and good and poor insulation of outlets

8.4 Charging and Discharging of the Storage Unit

8.4.1 Charging

When a storage tank is charged, (i.e. hot water enters the tank), it is very important that the thermal stratification (i.e. cold water at the bottom, hot water at the top) remains as undisturbed as possible. Indeed, it is desirable to actively encourage stratification during the charging process. In order to achieve this, one needs a relatively lean and tall tank (even though this is not optimal with respect to heat losses).

Stratification in beneficial, so the draw-off temperature from the top of the tank is a maximum and so the heat exchange processes are as efficient as possible. Without stratification, draw-off temperatures will be less, and back-up heating will switch on more frequently. See below.

The varying solar radiation during day (at constant volumetric through-flow) leads to temperature fluctuations in the solar flow pipe. Therefore, stratification is unlikely without special provisions for the charging process.

Likewise, it is necessary that the discharging process (i.e. draw-off from the storage tank) does not disturb the stratification.

Unstratified Buffer Tanks with Unregulated Pumps

In storage systems without provisions for stratified charging, the hot-water line is attached to the upper part of the tank (see Figure 8.3). The cold sides are located near the lower end. If solar radiation on the collector fluctuates, so does the hot-water inlet temperature. Although the incoming water will eventually find its appropriate thermal stratum in the tank, there is considerable (and undesirable) vertical motion and heat exchange (and reduced temperature due to the mixing) involved.

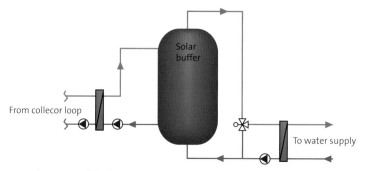

Figure 8.3 Charging and discharging of a buffer tank without special provisions for stratification

Only the cold thermal layer at the bottom of the tank remains relatively undisturbed. Even this is true only if the water returning from the discharge heat exchanger is sufficiently cold. Otherwise (e.g. if there are several users with varying temperatures in the returning flow) a stratification device must be connected to the heat exchanger of the discharging side to maintain the desired (top-to-bottom) temperature gradient of the storage tank.

A disturbance of the tank's stratification results in the following:

• the highest water temperature (delivered from the collector loop) is not kept at the top of the storage tank and is thus not available for user draw-off

- the mixing zone with mediocre temperatures is extended
- the efficiency of the storage is reduced: an after-heater (e.g. boiler) must contribute more heating energy to satisfy the hot-water demand although the collector might supply sufficient energy

An extended mixing zone is a disadvantage because the desired high temperatures (available for draw-off) are not achieved and so a conventional back-up heater has to make up for the difference between the reduced temperature of hot water inlet (from the solar loop) and the hot water outlet (to the user). Scientificfally, if stratification is disturbed, no energy is lost, but the quality of the supplied energy (exergy) is reduced (and entropy is increased with the disorder of mixing).

However, if a boiler is needed for after-heating, the overall efficiency of the system is slightly reduced, even with a perfectly stratified tank, since most of the time only a fraction of the capacity of this boiler is used. This entails a slight decrease of the solar fraction.

Particularly problematic are heating systems or networks relying on solar energy, because they need a relatively high solar operating temperature (the solar flow must be at least a little higher than the temperature in the heating return pipe). Installations for domestic water heating are less critical in this context since the incoming (cold domestic) water can always be expected to be cold enough.

Any mixing in the upper part of the tank usually causes only a very small increase of temperature at the bottom, and thus in the collector loop, and so reduces the efficiency only marginally.

In contrast, any mixing at the bottom of the tank, due to the incoming warm (or hot) water from the discharging heat exchanger, is more critical. The lower part of the tank gets warmer than necessary and the temperature in the solar return is raised, such that efficiency and the amount of usable solar energy are both reduced.

The necessity of stratified charging for a good efficiency is stressed; it is especially important in systems with variable or fluctuating temperature levels.

As well as in case of ordinary heating systems, simulation programs (without consideration enforced stratification) are only of limited utilisation.

In small and closely dimensioned solar installations (with small storage tanks) for domestic water heating, the provision of stratified charging does not give a great advantage. Here, stratified charging makes sense only if no other measure (such as installation of a regulated pump) provide for good efficiency (i.e. sufficiently low temperature at the bottom).

Stratified Buffer Tanks with Regulated Pumps (Matched-Flow Systems)

An installation, such as shown in Figure 8.3, can be fitted with a regulated pump. The speed of the pump is reduced always when solar radiation is reduced or when the temperature off-set between solar flow and return has fallen short of a specified value (e.g. 4K). In this way, the solar-loop liquid takes a longer time for one circulation and so has more time to heat up in the collector, and the influx of insufficiently heated liquid into the buffer is prevented.

However, the operating range of pumps for matched-flow systems is limited. The limit is reached during periods of low radiation and if the temperature difference between top and bottom is at its maximum.

Buffer Tanks with Externally Actuated Injectors

In order to support the build up of thermal stratification, several injectors can be integrated. An example with two injectors actuated by switching valves is shown in Figure 8.4. If the incoming heating water is warmer than at the measurement point (between both injectors), the upper valve opens. Vice versa, the lower injector is switched open if the incoming water is colder than at the measurement location. Instead of the switching valve, one could also attach independently actuated pumps (one for each injector).

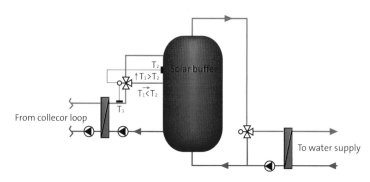

Figure 8.4 Stratified charging with two injectors

The more the number of separate injectors are integrated into the tank, the expense the expense for regulation/control and the more the system is fallible. A large number of injectors, heat exchangers, pumps, electrically operated valves and other gadgets may well contribute to a slight efficiency increase but the ratio of cost and benefit should always be considered. Also, the more the number of components, the greater the likelihood of faults

Buffer Tanks with Internal Stratification Appliances

Internal stratification appliances allow the self-acting build up of thermal layers inside the tank.

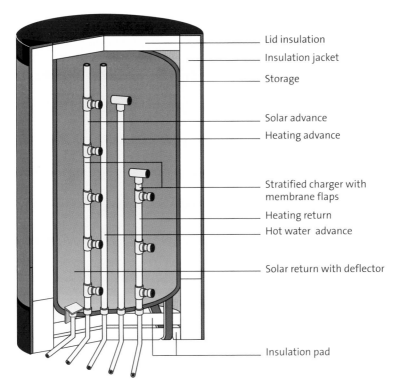

	Lid insulation
	Insulation jacket
	Storage
	Solar advance
	Heating advance
	Stratified charger with membrane flaps
	Heating return
	Hot water advance
	Solar return with deflector
	Insulation pad

Figure 8.5 Stratified-charging tank »Stratos« , SOLVIS, Germany

In the »Stratos« tank (see Figure 8.5) of the German SOLVIS Company, the incoming hot water is guided through plastic tubes (so-called »charging lances« of polyethylene) with a number of vertically spread membrane flaps. If the incoming water is hotter than the surrounding heat transfer liquid, it also has a lower density and pressure, so that the membrane flaps stays closed. If the temperatures in and around the tube are equal, the flap opens and the water is released directly into the appropriate thermal layer. This greatly assists in the build up of good thermal stratification.

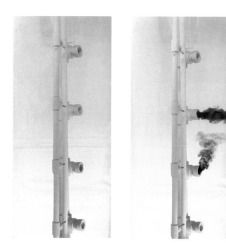

*Figure 8.6 The functioning of stratified injection with a »charging lance« by SOLVIS ,
Germany (inflowing water coloured)*

The volumetric flow of charging units working on this principle is limited. If the pressure of the flowing liquid becomes too high, the »wrong« flaps tend to open as well, such that the stratification effect is lost. A decrease in efficiency would result.

The through-flow of a single charging lance is limited to 1,000 l/h, when approximately 70 % of the water is deposited at the correct layer. At a through-flow of 700 l/h, the injection occurs to nearly 100 % at the correct thermal stratum. Therefore, a number of (parallel-connected) charging lances are needed for larger installations. A parallel arrangement of several tanks (with one charging lance each) cannot be recommended because this would severe the uniformity of charging and discharging (see also Chapter 8.4.1).

Reality showed that the application of charging lances was beneficial for the the rapid production of high temperatures, especially in medium-sized installations with high solar fraction. A marginal improvement of the solar yield has also been observed if the system was fitted with a carefully tuned control system (for discharge and after-heating).

In solar installations with a small solar fraction, the stratification appliances would incur a cost increase of some 15–20 %, which is justified, considering the long-term savings in fuel consumption of back-up heating.

8.4.2 **Discharging**

The discharging of potable water tanks occurs automatically, by simply drawing off the hot water. On the other hand, if solar buffer tanks are used for heat storage, there is an additional heat exchanger that separates the storage tank from the potable water. This calls for a special discharge regulation (more details in Chapter 10.3).

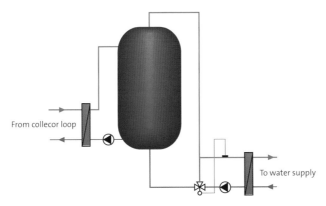

From collecor loop

To water supply

Figure 8.7 Principle of buffer discharging (conventional system / auxiliary heating not shown)

The buffer is discharged by a so-called discharge-circulation pump. While the water of the tank can be fairly hot (up to 95 °C), the temperature at the discharging heat exchanger should not exceed 65 °C, to prevent calcification on the potable water side of the heat exchanger. In order to achieve this, one needs a thermostatic three-way-valve with temperature limitation regulation that mixes the waters from the hot and cold lines. The mixing would not be necessary if the drinking water is already sufficiently decalcified.

8.4.3 **Integration of Circulation Lines**

The hot-water circulation line (at the buffer tank) is usually only a few degrees of difference (e.g. 5 K) colder than the hot tap exit temperature (e.g. 55 °C) of the after-heater. The returning line to the solar array should not become this hot, because it would decrease the thermal efficiency. Therefore, the returning circulation (from the potable water tank) is guided to the solar system only if it is at least a little colder than the (bottom) temperature of the solar buffer.

For closely dimensioned installations, this does not make much sense, since there the above condition is met only infrequently. The cost of the installation would increase unnecessarily, without any benefit in solar yield. However, with installations dimensioned for relatively high solar fraction, the active embedding of the hot water circulation into the solar system is meaningful or even necessary (to prevent periods of stagnancy during summer being too long).

Partial cover of circulation losses, (e.g. because of the need to avoid stagnation) can be realised by entering the circulation return into the solar storage, This necessarily implies a disturbance of the thermal stratification. Therefore, the volume circulated should be kept as small as possible. Consider the German guideline requiring a minimum of 55 °C in the circulation return for protection against germs, it is necessary to have a well tuned and fully insulated circulation network.

Figure 8.8 shows how the the circulation return enters either the buffer or the potable water reservoir (depending on temperature) for a small installation.

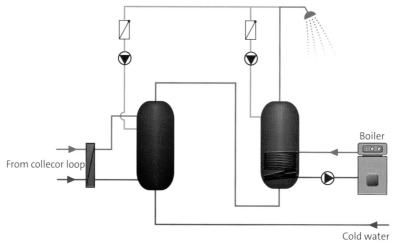

Figure 8.8 Pipe network for circulation return into a solar buffer and/or potable water reservoir

Usually, a circulation pump is actuated by a differential control. When the temperature at the solar storage section is higher than the circulation return, then the flow is injected into the middle of the (lower) solar part of the tank. In the opposite case, the return flow is switched to the middle (above the solar section) of the tank. Instead of two pumps, one can also use one pump and a switching valve.

Always avoid hot water being fed to the bottom of the tank's solar part or to the bottom of the solar buffer. Otherwise, the low-temperature stratum at the bottom will be disturbed, which in turn leads to drastic losses of thermal efficiency of the entire system.

A simpler version of bivalent storage is described as follows:

One sets the nominal temperature for the conventional hot water relatively low, so the temperature maximum that is to be achieved by solar heating is several degrees Kelvin more. Whenever the temperature of the solar-heated water exceeds this nominal value (to be achieved by conventional heating), circulation losses are automatically covered by solar energy and no auxiliary heating is required.

In small installations for domestic water heating that are not subject to the recommendations for legionella or other germ protection, the nominal temperature of the hot water could be set to 50 °C, while the solar water temperature is limited to between 60 and 65 °C (not hotter due to the danger of lime sedimentation). If the nominal temperature of the standby storage unit is 60 °C, there would be little margin for the temperature of the solar-heated water.

Only for water with low lime content should higher storage maximum temperatures than 65 °C be allowed. Temperature limitation by mixing with cold water serves two purposes: (a) anti-scald protection, and (b) reduction of thermal losses due to circulation. The cold water mixing procedure alone is insufficient, since it is activated only during periods of hot water draw-off. The circulation, however, may be active also at times when no hot water is drawn off.

Large buffer storage systems need controlled integration of the circulation into the buffer storage tank or into its outlet. If auxiliary heating is operating into the buffer or its outlet, no specific measures are necessary to cover circulation looses with solar energy.

8.5 Partition of the Solar Storage Volume / Circuitry of Solar Storage Units

The storage volume should be accommodated in a single, thin, standing vessel. If the integration or connection of a large storage vessel is not possible in the building, the alternatives of an on-site welded structure (e.g. in a basement) or a free-standing arrangement outdoors are worth consideration. A specially constructed large-volume store may not cost more in total than an assembly of smaller tanks, in spite of possibly more expense on its hardware components. This is despite the costs of on-site welding or increased insulation and waterproofing for outside placement.

Horizontal storage tanks are, due to the poor thermal stratification, not well suited for low-flow systems, unless the volume is partitioned into approximately three row-connected vessels with enforced stratification and, if necessary, non-return valves in the connecting lines.

Nevertheless an assembly of interconnected small storage volumes may usually be used. Not more than four are recommended. The question is then, whether to connect these tanks in series or parallel.

Figure 8.9 is a considerably simplified diagram of both types of circuitry and of the positioning of sensors for regulating charge and discharge. Note that non-return valves are not shown. The Tichelmann pipework (recommended for parallel connection) has been omitted for the sake of simplicity. However, his type of thermal circuitry does not safely solve the problem of non-uniform through-flow unless further measures are taken, as described below.

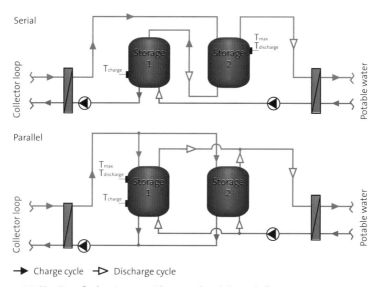

→ Charge cycle   ⇾ Discharge cycle

Figure 8.9 Circuitry of solar storage with unregulated through-flow,
top: charge and discharge row connected, bottom: parallel charge and discharge

The storage control sensors for charging (T_{charge}) must be installed at the lowest and coldest part of the volume. Sensors for discharging ($T_{discharge}$) and for the temperature limiter (T_{max}) must be installed in the hottest part at the top. It is important that the sensors for charging and discharging are placed at the appropriate storage outlet, which in turn should be as close to the bottom and top of the tank as possible.

Both types of circuitry (parallel or serial connection) have advantages and disadvantages (as listed in table 8.1). The decision between them depends on the particular case. Table 8.1 is valid only for unregulated charging and discharging flow, that is when charging and discharging is not regulated by an automatic flow-volume control.

Theoretically, the greatest disadvantage of an unregulated serial connection is the temperature divergence of the individual storage tanks, especially during charging. Rapid establishment of new thermal stratification over the complete liquid volume is not possible due to the separation of the individual tanks. This characteristic is usually not a difficulty for ordinary potable water systems. Only when (in comparison to the daily draw-off) the tanks are dimensioned very generously (e.g. for space heating), when high temperatures should be maintained and when draw-off varies strongly, is the characteristic disturbing. The energy efficiency of the system (if the solar system is not over-dimensioned) decreases only insignificantly, since no significant energy is being lost. The only adverse aspect is that the quality of supply, the exergy, but only exergy, decreases. In addition, with »regularly« sized tanks (60 – 70 % of the daily hot water draw-off) a complete discharge and orderly restratification is achieved within a single day without strong solar radiation. This is similar in larger storage tanks, but the time increment for restratification is longer. The positions of the control sensors are unequivocally determined by the directions of the charging and discharging flows.

Multi-exit charging lances (see Figure 8.6) are not suitable for large installations with series connected tanks, since the volumetric flows for charging and discharging are very large. Thus one would have to install bundles of charging lances, which in turn leads to unjustifiably high cost. On the other hand, they would not be a great advantage, since the serial connection of the tanks leads to a specific, although not optimal, stratification.

With parallel connection, each single tank receives only part of the charging and discharging flow. This type of arrangement is better suited for charging lances.

Practical experiences with parallel connections (as in Figure 8.9, bottom) confirm that the charging and discharging flows to and from the individual tanks are often not uniform, regardless of whether or not the pipes are laid according to Tichelmann (equal lengths of all flow and return pipes). This leads to different temperatures inside the storage tanks (see also Chapter 8.6.1). This causes major difficulties, especially for the charging and discharging control and for temperature limitation (see also Chapter 10.3).

	Charging:parallel /discharging: parallel	Charging : serial / discharging: serial
Advantages	Charging and discharging flows are spread over a number of parallel storage vessels; low-flow in each individual storage vessel; good formation and stability of thermal stratification. Well suited for the application of charging lances due to the low throughflow of each tank	The complete charging and discharging flow passes through each storage vessel; high throughflow and mixing in each individual vessel; disturbance of thermal stratification. Still reasonable thermal strucutre under normal operating conditions. The charging and discharging flows are precisely equal for each vessel; pipework is not critical. Clearly defined coldest and hottest storage vessel under most operating regimes; easy placement of temperature sensors for charging and discharging control.
Disadvantages	Uniform throughflow through all storage vessels is difficult to achieve, since flow rate depends on pressure losses in the flow and return pipe connections; extremely careful pipework according to Tichelmann is necessary, but often insufficient. Due to difficulties in the achievement of uniform flows, critical with respect to placement of temperature sensor for charging and discharging control as well as for the temperature limiter; it is possible that all switching signals are given too early or too late.	Throughflow through all storage vessels may be too high for application of charging lances; within limits solvable (at high cost) by using bundles of charging lances for each of the vessels. The temperature levels of the tanks may shift if the temperature difference between coldest spot of the »cold« vessel and hottest point of the »hot« vessel becomes very large. Automatic reformation of a new thermal stratification between separated vessels is only possible if each tank has sufficient throughflow.

Tabelle 8.1 Advantages and disdvantages of unregulated parallel or serial storage throughflow

Sometimes, systems with regulated charging and discharging flow are installed in an effort to establish definite thermal stratification within the individual storage tanks, so that optimal temperature conditions are created for the collector field, as well as for the energy supply to the user.

It would exceed the scope of this book to describe the the seemingly countless number of technical solutions. Some of these may be recommended when one wishes to achieve a specific minimum storage temperature in a particular tank. Most of these varieties are not needed for pure domestic water heating.

8.6 **Results of Inspections**

8.6.1 **Problems with Parallel Connection of Storage Tanks**

Figure 8.10 shows the temperature curves for two parallel-connected tanks of four cubic metres each. The installation belongs to the »Solar-thermie 2000« research program. The position of control sensors for the charging and discharging control are in accordance with Figure 8.9 (bottom). The tanks were fitted with charging lances. The temperatures at the bottom and top of both tanks are displayed for times between 06.00h and 19.00h. The relevant control sensors (C) are placed in tank 1. Since the measurement and control sensors are placed at the same height inside the tank, the temperature curves for measurement and control are identical.

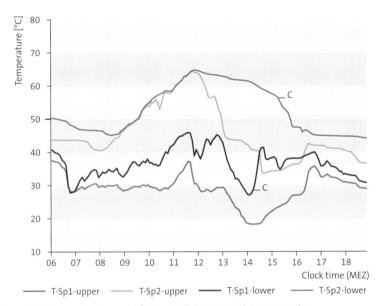

Figure 8.10 Temperature curves of two parallel-connected storage tanks

Within the course of a day, both tanks are charged and discharged, often simultaneously. It appears clearly that the bottom temperatures of both tanks differ during the whole day. Only between 06.30h and 07.00h, when both tanks cooled down (to about 28°C) due to peak hot water consumption (and lack of solar radiation) in the early morning, both temperatures became nearly identical. During the rest of the day, the bottom temperatures drift strongly apart. At 14.30h, the diffe-rence amounts to 20K.

In the upper range, the temperatures are nearly equal only until 12.00h when the tanks are charged and the draw-off is low. Regardless of the amount of inflowing hot water, the two sensors at the top of both tanks measure the temperature of the inflowing water; however, the speed at which the hot stratum shifts downwards is different. After some time, the tanks have noticeably different volumes of the hot water. During the draw-off peak at noon, the temperature in tank 2 drops rapidly, while the temperature drop is much less dramatic in tank 1. Additional measurements in the attached pipes established that the volumetric flow rates of both tanks were quite different. Surprisingly, the tank with the longer pipe connection had a better (i.e. larger) through-flow. The differences in the through-flow of both tanks offer only a partial explanation for the different temperatures. Another problem is found in the discharge control (see Ch. 10.3).

A uniform through-flow of parallel-connected storage tanks with unregulated charging and discharging flow, is only possible if identical flow resistances are built into all charging and discharging pipes. Without such equal impedances, small differences in flow resistance of pipes or lances (e.g. due to surface roughness, flow redirections, contaminations or flaps) lead to dramatic variations of the flow rate. The additional flow resistances must be large enough, so that the resistances due to small disturbances become negligible. This in turn results in the demand for a somewhat more powerful pump for the charging and discharging cycle.

The temporarily very strong temperature drop in storage vessel 2, suggests that the upper flaps of the charging lances were not properly closed, so that relatively cold water was injected into the hot thermal stratum. The volumetric flow of the lances (one in each tank) was approximately two cubic metres per hour, which is twice as high as the recommended maximum (see Chapter 8.4).

The temperature curves in Figure 8.10 that are valid for the control are marked with a »C«.

It is quite obvious that such strong differing temperatures can lead to malfunctions in the control of this system (e.g. too early or too late switching of the pump, depending in which of the storage tanks the sensor is located).

The storage system of the installation was modified. Flow resistances were built into the pipes, and the single charging lances were replaced by bundles. Time will show if, after these changes, satisfactory results will be achieved for the uniformity of through-flow and the thermal stratification. Results are available on the Internet at: www.zfs-energietechnik.de during 2003 and afterwards.

8.6.2 Evaluation of the Storage Conditions in Old Installations
Only nine operators (from 114 installations that participated in the ZIP program) reported corrosive damages of their storage units. In two cases, it was proved that enamelled tanks corroded because the sacrificial anodes were depleted and had not been replaced. Sacrificial anodes consist of magnesium and should be placed into potable-water filled, enamel-coated steel tanks.

The inspection and possible replacement of a sacrificial anode must occur during the annual maintenance program for enamelled tanks. If these inspection intervals are to be avoided, one has to use externally powered electrical anodes whose function, also, has to be checked.

In one other case, the installation corroded due to improper material choice. The complete tank, including all feeding nozzles and the internal spiral heat exchanger coil were made of stainless steel. After 16 years of operation, the interior surfaces of the tank and the outer surfaces of the heat exchanger were in a spotless condition, except for a thin layer of »external« rust (from elsewhere in the loop) that was easily removable. A welded socket of stainless steel was closed with a cap of zinc galvanized steel. This cap had suffered from contact corrosion between the electrochemically less noble steel and the more noble stainless steel. A wall break-through had occurred from the water side of the cap.

Contact corrosion between metals of different electrochemical potential should be prevented by the proper choice of materials.

Three tanks made of stainless steel (built in 1980 and belonging to the same installation) had leaks along the weld seams. This was due to manufacturing defects (which have meanwhile been fixed) in that particular type of tank.

The above examples for tank corrosion are not solar-specific. The same corrosion could have occurred in any storage tank for potable water. Causes of corrosion are poor maintenance, defective assembly or (rarely) manufacturing defects. Compared to the experience with regular space heating systems, solar storage components are not crucial.

8.7 Check of Manufacturer Ratings

8.7.1 Performance Ratings

Often, the manufacturers of combined storage units working on the flow-heater principle (with integrated tubular heat exchanger) had made inaccurate statements concerning the performance of their products. Most often, the errors resulted from the assumption of a too large boiler performance or too high temperature levels within the whole vessel. For example, one cannot assume a hot water temperature higher than 60 °C for a combined solar storage unit with a thermostatic mixing valve (service water mixer), since this is the maximum acceptable temperature for the hot water draw-off. The service water mixer is usually set to this value, therefore temperatures higher than 60 °C cannot be offered, cause mixing with cold water.

When determining the performance ratings for combined solar storage vessels, one may not assume a continuous heating of the solar section, since (depending on the dimensioning of collector field and storage size) the solar part remains cold during periods of very low solar radiation. This may lead to comfort deficits which may cause complaints against the manufacturer.

If there are uncertainties concerning the suitability of specific components for the given task, one should ask for written confirmation from the manufacturer prior to purchase.

8.7.2 Dimensions and Weights

Especially when new models become available, it is quite common that the manufacturers give inaccurate statements for the size and weight of their newly built storage tanks. Especially when the space for the integration of tanks is very limited, one should ask the manufacturer for binding statements.

Some suppliers give obviously false statements on the thickness of the insulation. In one case, for example, delivered insulations were only 80 mm thick, instead of 100 mm.

Errors of this kind lead to unnecessary expense and increase heat losses of the storage unit unnecessarily, and are thus completely unacceptable. Circumstances may allow a claim for compensation by the supplier. Planners and fitters should, in case of repeated complaints, purchase from a different supplier.

9. Heat Exchangers

9.1 Function and Requirements

»Heat Exchanger« is a somewhat imprecise, but, in practice, commonly used term for a heat transfer or heat exchange device.

Heat exchangers are used to transfer heat between different heat transfer substances, whilst keeping them separate from each other, (e.g. heat conduction between water/anti-freeze mixtures in the collector loop and potable water or water from the buffer tank tank in the demand side).

They must fulfil the following requirements:

• chemically inert with respect to the heat transfer media used

• compatibility with other materials in the connected loops

• unaffected by temperatures within the range to be experienced

• good heat transfer and conduction properties

• small temperature difference across the exchanger walls

• small pressure loss

Based on the above requirements, stainless steel or copper are the commonly chosen materials.

9.2 Construction Types

9.2.1 Internal Heat Exchangers

In most solar-thermal installations for domestic use, one utilizes storage units with internal heat exchangers, and filled with potable water. These internal heat exchangers are made of copper (smooth tube or corded tube), smooth stainless steel tube or steel tubes with anti-corrosive coating (e.g. enamel). The hot fluid is forced to pass through the tubes, the outer fluid is moved by gravity circulation.

Jacketed (also called mantel) storage units are often used in thermo-syphon systems. The storage tank is surrounded by a cylindrical jacket. The heat transfer liquid from the solar loop is guided into the space between jacket and storage, and the heat is exchanged through the outer surface of the storage unit. Both the storage unit and the jacket are often made of low-grade steel, while the interior of the tank (if in contact with potable water) is either enamelled or zinc-plated (galvanized).

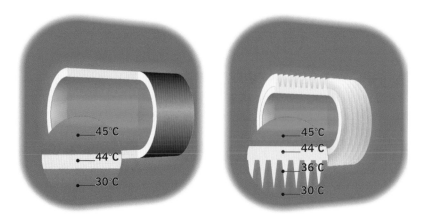

Figure 9.1 Temperature regimes of smooth- or corded-tube heat exchangers

In smooth-tube heat exchangers, the heat transfer is through highly conductive tubular surfaces. The surfaces of the tubes are quite small, so a considerable tube length is required.

In corded-tube heat exchangers, the available surface (per metre tube length) for heat transfer is greatly enlarged by undulations on the surface. However, there is a significant temperature gradient towards the edges of the cords, so the heat transfer does not improve directly as the increase in surface area (in contrast to smooth-tube exchangers).

A one square metre surface of smooth-tube heat exchanger therefore performs somewhat better than a one squaremetre of corded-tube heat exchanger.

Larger collector fields need appropriately sized heat exchangers. If multiple solar storage units are charged and discharged independently, a heat exchanger sized for the full conductive performance is needed in each tank. Therefore, using internal heat exchangers would be rather expensive. As with most large installations, it is usually better to use external heat exchangers with an independent charge and discharge strategy.

9.2.2 External Heat Exchangers
In external heat exchangers, the both heat transfer fluids are forced in reverse flow over the metallic surfaces that separate them.

The are two common types, (a) cane bundle, and (b) plate heat exchangers.

Cane-bundle heat exchangers (see Fig. 9.2) have a small pressure loss, due to their relative large cross sections for flow, and are less prone to contamination. They are made of stainless steel, copper or steel tubes.

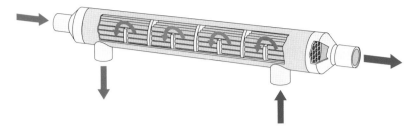

Figure 9.2 Structure of a cane bundle heat exchanger

A relevant and common application, for example, is the solar heating of swimming pools. In order to prevent corrosive damage, soldered plate heat exchangers should not be used with the chlorinated pool water.

Plate heat exchangers are either screwed or soldered.

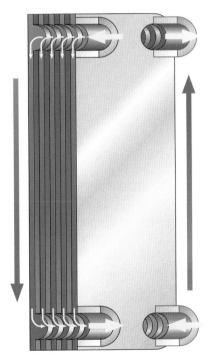

Figure 9.3 Cut view of a plate heat exchanger

The embossed sheets of a plate heat exchanger are either soldered to-gether, or fitted with gasket seals and bolted together. Usually, soldered units are available only in selected sizes. Especially in the lower range of performance, they are cheaper than the bolted types. For the solar installations described in this book, plate heat exchangers working on the cross flow principle are mostly used.

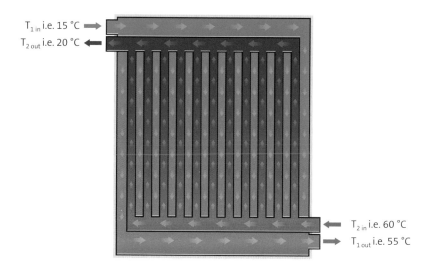

$T_{1\,in}$ i.e. 15 °C

$T_{2\,out}$ i.e. 20 °C

$T_{2\,in}$ i.e. 60 °C

$T_{1\,out}$ i.e. 55 °C

Figure 9.4 Temperature regime in a cross flow heat exchanger

Making use of the various simulation programs from manufacturers of heat exchangers simplifies the calculation of the relevant design parameters. They exchangers differ in plate geometry, type of through-flow and design principle. Thus, one particular heat exchanger should not be replaced by another model, even of the same manufacturer, without recalculation.

9.3 Design Recommendations

9.3.1 Internal Heat Exchangers

For the design of storage tanks with integrated heat exchangers having a logarithmic mean temperature difference of 10K (the average temperature difference between both heat transfer fluids), the follo-wing rules of thumb apply:

Smooth-tube heat exchanger:
approx. $0.2\,m^2$ heat exchanger surface per m^2 collector area

Corded-tube heat exchanger:
approx. $0.3-0.4\,m^2$ heat exchanger surface per m^2 collector area

If a lower temperature difference across the interface is desired, the heat transfer surface must be increased. The indicated, relative large value of 10K is acceptable for small installations only. For instance, when the storage tank is filled with potable water and a single heat exchanger is placed between the potable water storage and the col-lector loop.

9.3.2 **External Heat Exchangers**

It is not feasible here to describe all aspects of heat exchanger design. Detailed information on the dimensioning of charging and discharging heat exchangers of large solar installations can be found in the literature.

Every heat exchanger necessitates a temperature difference across the interface, the collector loop should operate at as a low temperature as possible for greatest solar yield. Since this temperature difference represents an unwanted loss, heat exchangers must be dimensioned large enough for least temperature difference and, therefore least loss.

The best design of the charging heat exchanger (between collector loop and solar buffer) is not difficult to achieve, since the pumps give a fixed volumetric flow on both primary and secondary sides.

At a relative strong solar radiation of some $800\,W/m^2$ on the solar collectors at standard operating conditions (mediocre collector temperature), a net heat flux of $500\,W/m^2$ is generated and must be removed by the heat transfer fluid. In a solar installation with $100\,m^2$, this amounts to $50\,kW$. In a low-flow design with $15\,l/(h\cdot m^2)$, the temperature difference (water-glycol mixture) between collector outlet and inlet is approx. $35\,K$. On the secondary side (buffer storage-water) the temperature difference would be $30\,K$.

The temperature of a collector loop, while passing through two heat exchangers (in the buffer storage system) should not be lowered too much on the way to the consumer. At the same time, the temperature at the collector inlet should be kept close to the cold water temperature. The averaged temperature-increase required for heat transmission at the exchanger thus should remain as low as possible, as explained previously. A temperature increase of about $5\,K$ is recommended. This value has proved to be a good compromise for large solar installations, with regard to cost effectiveness and technical demands.

If realistic operating points are set for installations of this kind, adequate temperatures are reached for the heat exchanger (see table 9.1). Note however, that other operating conditions may apply, due to changes in solar radiation. In any case, the inlet temperature change on the collector side of the heat exchanger is inversely proportional to the change of the volumetric flow. Likewise for the outlet temperature on the secondary side. The composition of heat transfer fluid (glycol type and content) in the collector loop also influences the systems temperature structure.

	Low-Flow		Standard Flow	
	Primary side	**Secondary side**	**Primary side**	**Secondary side**
Through flow	12 resp. 15 l/(h·m²) Glycol: 40% Water: 60%	12 resp. 15 l/(h·m²) Water	35 resp. 45 l(h·m²) Glycol: 40% Water: 60%	35 resp. 45 l/(h·m²) Water
Specific power collector array	approx. 500 W/m²			
Mean logarith-mic tempera-ture difference	$\Delta\vartheta$ approx. 5 K			
Mean specific power	ca. 100 W/K/m²$_C$ (C = Collector surface)			
Inlet temperature	75 approx. 67 °C	Target: 30 °C	58 resp. 56 °C	Target: 40 °C
Outlet temperature	33 °C	68 resp. 60 °C	44 °C	52 resp. 50 °C
Pressure loss	max. 100 KPa			

Table 9.1 Characteristic design parameters for a heat exchanger between solar loop and storage charging loop (approximated to integral values of °C)

With these design parameters, an averaged specific transfer power of some 100 W/K per m² collector area is required. This value applies to low and high-flow modes of operation.

With identical heat transfer surfaces, exchangers with different interior circuitry are available. So, for example, the pressure loss with equally sized area and throughflow can be varied by the properly chosen type of exchanger (one- or two-way). Heat exchangers with a large pressure loss and two- or multi-way circuitry usually have better heat transmission than one-way exchangers, – due to the longer piping and the higher flow speed. Only careful re-calculation by the manufac-turer, or use of the simulation software from the manufacturer, safe-guards that the pressure-loss limit (e.g. 10 kPa) is not exceeded.

The dimensioning of the discharge heat exchanger, is necessary for all systems with a solar pre-heater or buffer storage tank, connected to the hot water network as described in Chapter 3. In this case, both sides of the heat exchanger are filled with water. When the system operates at design load, the logarithmic temperature difference should not exceed 5 K. In /2/, detailed data are given for discharging heat exchangers.

The design of a direct-heat discharge heat exchanger (see Chapter 3) is quite complicated due to the varying throughflow (between zero and full load at unknown amounts). Figure 9.5 is intended to give an approximate representation of the fluctuations within a very small time frame, when different averaging periods are used. Under no circumstances is it feasible to design the heat exchanger for the hour-based average flow rate. The temporal resolution must be in the region of a few seconds.

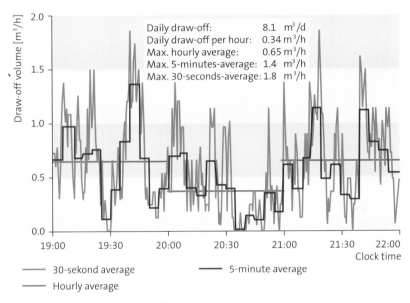

Figure 9.5 Dynamics of the draw-off volume at various temporal resolutions

Figure 9.5 is taken from the publication /2/. The values shown apply to a very large residential building with daily hot water consumption above $15\,m^2$. Note that the daily peak in hot water use in relation to the average, is especially distinctive for smaller residential buildings.

10. Control of the Solar Installation

10.1 Purpose and Requirements

Control of a solar installation aims to regulate the energy flux between collector, storage unit and consumer. The components of a control system are:

- Charging control for the optimal transmission of solar radiation into heat and its transfer into the solar storage unit

- Discharging control (if discharge does not occur automatically by draw -off) to guarantee optimal heat discharge from the storage tank to the consumer.

In small installations with bivalent potable water storage (i.e. with a solar and a conventional component, unified in a single vessel) the discharging control is not necessary.

The control of a solar system must meet the following principal requirements:

- For optimal collector optimal efficiency, the solar loop temperatures should be kept at a minimum.

- The solar control should not spoil the operation of the linked conventional system (and vice versa).

- Characteristic system features (e.g. the inclusion of pre-heat stages) must be taken into account.

- For a simple system configuration, which is recommended, avoid unnecessarily complicated controls.

- The costs of the investment, maintenance and electric auxiliary power (for control, pumps and regulated valves) should remain within justifiable limits.

- The control manual must include clear details of all components and their operation, together with a description and circuit diagram of the control system itself. This should be adequate for a competent person to make all necessary adjustments, without having to contact the manufacturers for technical support.

- The switching temperatures, temperature intervals for hysteresis and the time delays, should all be adjustable to fine tune the system without additional cost .

- Sensors should be integrated into the system so accurate values are always delivered to the control logic.

- The precision of the control components, e.g. sensors and electronics should be sufficient to prevent switching errors at the pre-set threshold values.

- A functional check of the system should be possible independently of the control system itself.

Control systems are often available with many extra functions and gimmicks, e.g. after-heater regulation, switching of the hot water circulating pump, protection against collector freezing or overheating, heating power measurements, data transmission and logging. Avoid undue complication which in itself may produce faults.

10.2 Principal Methods for Solar Charge Control and Storage

The charging control consists of two parts: (a) the collector loop regulation, and (b) the heat exchange control into the storage unit. The collector loop regulation can be similar for small and large installations although there are some differences in the heat supply to the storage unit, since the heat exchangers may be internal or external. Under certain circumstances (see below), both parts of the control can be nearly identical.

10.2.1 Charging Control of a Storage Unit with Internal Heat Exchanger

Figure 10.1 shows the scheme of a collector loop with a heat exchanger integrated into the storage tank. It does not matter if the tank is filled with potable water or if it is a buffer tank filled with non-potable water. Also, it is not relevant wheather an auxiliary-heater is integrated into the storage or kept separate. The integration points for the control sensors are indicated as below:

E: sensor for the measurement of solar radiation onto the collector plane

T_c: sensor in the collector to measure the temperature of the heat transfer fluid

T_{ac}: temperature in the collector flow pipe, prior to the entrance of the heat exchanger

T_{sl}: temperature in the lower part of the storage unit

T_{su}: temperature in the upper part of the storage unit

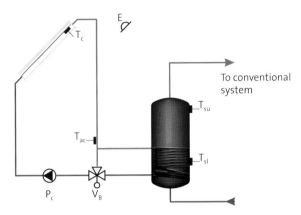

Figure 10.1 Collector loop with integral heat exchanger and marked position for control sensors.

Control Only by Temperature Differential

The collector circulating pump (P_c) switches on when the temperature difference between collector (T_c) and the lower part of storage tank (T_{sl}) is greater than a specified value. It switches off again, when the temperature difference has fallen below the appropriate specified switching value. The adjustment of a properly set minimum running time of the pump is recommended, so the collector loop can stabilize.

Typical values are:

Temperature difference for switching on:	approx. 6–10 K
Temperature difference for switching off:	approx. 3–4 K
Minimal running time of the pump:	approx. 3–5 min

If there is no bypass (with the regulated valve v_B) as marked in Figure 10.1, the switch-on of the collector circulating pump starts simultaneously with the heat transport from the collector into the storage unit. The control of collector circulation and heat transport is identical.

During warm summer nights and with a cold storage tank (especially with potable water storage with temperatures as low as 15 °C), even with no sunshine, the temperature differences may cause the pump to be switched on. Then, the pump switches off only when the temperature difference has fallen below the specified value and after the minimal running time has been exceeded. This procedure does not waste any previously stored solar heat energy, indeed there is some heat gain into the stor. but some electricity is used for the pump. Any slight gain is probably trivial compared with the annoyance of pumps switching and needless use of electricity.

If there is a long pipe between collectors and storage (especially outdoors or in unheated rooms), this simple type of control may lead to faulty functioning because the system may quickly switch off after a short period of operation because cold water from the pipe is pushed into the collector. The collector temperature drops much more than if warm water from the storage tank had entered, so pumping is switched off. This happens if it is not possible to set a minimum run time for the pump or when this time is set too short.

During such short or intermittent operational periods, heat from the warm store is transferred into the cold collector loop (collector return pipe), only to be lost after the rapid switch off. This process may repeat several times before the whole loop operation becomes stabilized.

This stop and go process can be prevented by extending the minimum run time of the pump.

Another method of preventing intermittent operation of the collector circulation pump is to have a bypass, as depicted in Figure 10.1. The bypass is activated by a 3-way valve V_B that is controlled by the temperature difference between collector flow pipe T_{ac} (just before the heat exchanger) and the storage temperature T_{su} (near bottom). Initially the valve is set for the fluid to circulate only in the collector loop pipework, and not through the heat exchanger. When the temperature, T_{ac}, of the circulating fluid is more than T_{su}, the valve switches for fluid to enter the heat exchanger.

The valve switches back to bypass when the temperature difference becomes too low (slightly below the switch-off threshold of collector circulation pump).

Here again unwanted and annoying switch-on during warm summer nights may occur. Fitting a time clock (which prevents switching between, say, 19:00 h and 7:00 h) prevents such thermostatic switching.

A single temperature sensor mounted inside one of several parallel collectors, only senses a representative temperature if all the collectors have equal through-flow. If the sensor is placed inside a collector where the volumetric flow is somewhat higher or lower than the others, the signal would lead to a premature or delayed shut down.

The temperature sensor can also be used to prevent premature switch-on after a period of stagnation due to vaporization of the heat transfer fluid (see also Chapter 7.1.2).

The temperature sensor T_{su} serves as a temperature limiter. If its value in a buffer storage system exceeds about 90°C ,or about 60°C in a potable water system, the system shuts down and stagnates. In a potable water system with decalcified water, up to 90°C are acceptable in the storage tank. More details on this topic are given in Chapter 8.4.3.

It is never acceptable to open the bypass after the temperature limit is reached and during pump operation. Otherwise, the whole collector loop (not only the collectors) might heat up excessively. So, during vaporization inside the collectors, the pump might continue to pump the liquid volume into the collector until a large proportion of the collector loop volume evaporated.

Control by Irradiation and Temperature Difference

When the collector-circulating pump is regulated by the solar irradiation, a radiation meter (aligned with the orientation of the collectors) is used instead of a temperature sensor. When the irradiation exceeds a specified value (e.g. $150-200 \, W/m^2$), the collector-circulating pump is switched on.

If such a control has only a specified radiation threshold, it does not take the temperature in the lower part of the storage unit into account and so the pump might switch on too early. Therefore, the bypass of the heat exchanger must be definitely activated, until sufficient temperature difference, $T_{ac}-T_{sl}$ of about 5 K, has occurred. If the bypass remains inactive, the pump switches off when the minimum operation time of the pump has run out or the irradiation has fallen below the specified minimum (e.g. $120-170 \, W/m^2$). However, if the bypass is closed and the solar heat is transmitted to the heat exchanger, the signal from the radiation meter will be deactivated. Then, the shutdown of the circulating pump is triggered only when the deactivation threshold is reached. That is when the temperature difference $T_{ac}-T_{sl}$ becomes small enough (2-3 K, typically).

The deactivation of the switch-off signal from the radiation meter prevents a premature system shutdown when a dark cloud passes by or when, during late afternoon in weak insolation, there is still usable residual heat in the collectors. A fixed threshold regulation is not very suitable for installations with strongly fluctuating storage temperatures (e.g. installations for auxiliary space heating). The fixed threshold value (adapted to a minimum storage temperature) leads to unnecessarily long periods of pump operation when, e.g. during days of high radiation and low consumption, the water in the storage unit gets very hot. For systems of this kind, an automated control depending on irradiation, combined with a temperature differential control control is a better solution. This should be adapted to the actual temperature in the lower part of the storage tank. To get such a system to work properly, the characteristic response of the control system (i.e. the dependence of the switch-on threshold on the storage temperature) must be well calibrated to the features of the particular solar system. So-called self-learning controls with adaptive bypass characteristics take this into account. Regularly dimensioned systems for potable water heating (with a somewhat predictable daily draw-off) do not need such a sophisticated control.

Photovoltaic cells are suitable as radiation meters. An uncertainty of ±10 % in the measurement is acceptable. It is more important to have an adjustable set point or to have a digital input for the threshold values, so the adjustments can be checked and adjusted at will. Off-the-shelf photo diodes (as used for twilight switches for streetlights) are not suited for this task. Within periodical maintenance procedures, the cleanliness of the photo meter should be checked, since contamination (e.g. bird excrements) reduces the signal. The radiation meter must be installed at a position that is never shaded. When a malfunction of the control system is suspected, one should check the radiation sensor first.

In this kind of charging control, there is no need for a temperature sensor inside the collector. However, there should be such a sensor in systems which are prone to stagnation (see also Chapter 7.1.2).

10.2.2 Charging Control with External Heat Exchanger

Figure 10.2 shows a solar system with an external heat exchanger (not including the attached conventional system). The recommended integration points for the probes are included. These are labelled according to the nomenclature in section 10.2.1.

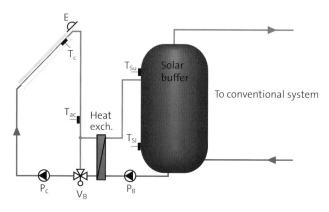

Figure 10.2 Collector loop with externally charging heat exchanger

The control of a system with external heat exchanger always consists of a collector loop regulation and a heat delivery control. In contrast to systems with an internal heat exchanger, both controls cannot be identical, since a second, independent pump P_B is needed (i.e. the pump belonging to the buffer charging loop).

The collector loop control is practically identical with the variety of controls with internal heat exchangers (see 10.2.1). The buffer charging $T_{ac} - T_{sl}$, has become sufficiently large (e.g. 5−7 K).

A secondary precondition here is that the circulating pump is already in operation. Otherwise, T_{ac} (probably measured inside a very warm furnace room) may be inaccurate since the room temperature may well be higher than the lowest storage temperature. In this case, the charging pump would switch on and continue to run (even when the collector circulating pump is shut down), because the temperature T_{ac} does not influence its operation.

The charging pump switches off when $T_{ac} - T_{sl}$ has fallen to less than 3 K.

The bypass shown in Figure 10.2 would not have bring the collector loop to a stable temperature before the heat delivery control is switched on. The run-up of the heat delivery control can be influenced by a separate pump control P_B. So long as the charging pump does not run, the collector liquid still flows through the heat exchanger while the secondary side of the exchanger remains stagnant. Only when there is a stable temperature regime at the heat exchanger inlet, does the charging pump starts working.

The primary task of the bypass is to protect the water-filled secondary side of the heat exchanger from freezing. During a cold winter night, the heat transfer liquid inside outdoor tubes can withstand temperatures down to $-20°C$. However, if the morning sun heats the collectors, they do warm up while liquid in the outdoor tubes remains cold. When the collector loop switches on, a very cold flow of liquid is pushed into the heat exchanger. If the indoor part of the piping is very short (e.g. directly underneath the roof), the liquid flow heats the tube only slightly (perhaps to some $-15°C$). If this cold liquid enters the heat exchanger, the water on the secondary side would freeze immediately, so the heat exchanger may rupture. Defects of this kind have occurred in practice. That is why, the bypass is opened always when $T_{ac} < 4°C$ and is closed when T_{ac} has risen significantly high.

When reaching the maximum allowable storage temperature T_{su}, both pumps must be switched off. The whole collector loop could heat up excessively if only the charging pump is switched off.

10.2.3 Charging Control Optimised for High Temperature or Target Temperature

In all the control and system variations described above, one can influence the storage temperature within certain limits. This is done by using a flow controlled pump to vary the volumetric flow; this is called »matched-flow«. In installations with an external heat exchanger, both pumps must be regulated accordingly.

To reach a specified minimum temperature, the collector loop should start to circulate slowly, until the lowest intended operational temperature is reached. Afterwards, the volumetric flow is increased gradually, so there is no or only a slight temperature increase.

This concept is advantageous especially when high temperature is needed (e.g. for solar space heating or for process heat as e.g. for solar cooling). This concept is also advantageous to minimise auxiliary energy. However, if one wants to optimise the solar yield, it is necessary to work with a finely tuned and regulated auxiliary heating system.

The need for a high temperature inside the collector has the result that heat losses increase and the solar yield from the collector is reduced. Nevertheless, it is more sensible to produce less energy at a usable temperature, rather than to have more energy at an unusable low temperature.

In installations for pure domestic water heating, or in combined installations with low solar fraction, this concept has little advantage while it increases the likelihood of faults.

10.2.4 Multi-Level Charging

In Chapter 8.4.1, the storage concepts for stratified charging were explained in detail. The information given below is only a summary for the sake of completeness here. There are three basic principles for stratified charging:

- Active stratification is arranged with valves and pumps. These guide the hot fluid into the heat exchangers or feeding nozzles placed at different levels inside the storage tank, so producing thermal layers (see Figures 8.4 and 10.3).

- serial connection of multiple storage units with controlled charging of one of the tanks

- passive stratification, produced by the density difference principle (e.g. with charging lances, see Figure 8.5)

For active stratification, no more than two or three feeding levels are recommended, so the additional expense for control and piping remains justifiable. This is because the increase of system efficiency is not in proportion to complexity.

The same is true for serial connection of storage tanks, if these are charged individually or one by one, depending on the thermal structure. No more than two or three storage units or groups are recommended.

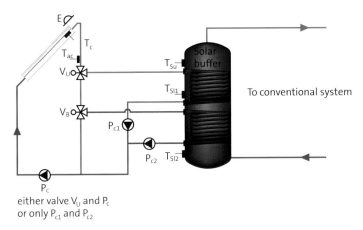

Figure 10.3 Charging of a storage tank with multiple feeding levels and internal heat exchanger

If active stratification with several temperature levels is desired, sophisticated control is required. Such a system would be advantageous due to faster heating of the specified level. When the collector tempe-ratur is falling, the cycle switched to a lower (and colder) stratum of the tank. In this case the temperature T_{sl} determines the temperature in the collector return pipe. If T_{sl} remains very low, temperatures at the collector flow never become high enough to change back to a warmer thermal layer.

Either, (a) one needs to switch the charging cycle off (e.g. every half hour) for a few minutes so the collector loop runs idle and stabilizes at a higher temperature or, (b) one needs a relation between the solar radiation (measured by a radiation meter, E) or collector temperature (T_c), and the storage temperature (T_{su}). Then, the necessary switching processes can be done independently of the particular thermal struc-ture in the charging cycle.

An additional advantage is that these external control measures can be checked separately, so malfunctioning components can be easily identified and replaced.

In internally stratified systems, it is important to take the manufac-turer's recommendations for the maximum through flow into account. Otherwise it is almost certain that the stratification is lost by mixing. If the charging lances are overburdened, the warm water mayreach the bottom of the tank, where it destroys the low-temperature layer of the tank.

A poorly operating charging system is worse than no stratified charging!

It is almost impossible to control the function of an internally strati-fied charging system without excessive utilisation of measurement devices (e.g. temperature sensors at multiple levels inside the tank). Maintenance and repairs are expensive and require the whole storage system to be emptied.

Within the scope of the research program »Solarthermie−2000«, many stratified charging systems were installed in Germany. It may be quite revealing to assess these installations (especially the ones with movable parts) after 10 or 20 years of operation.

10.3 Principal Opportunities of Discharge Control for Solar Storage

The storage units of solar installations that are filled with potable water (nowadays mostly for domestic use) are discharged automati-cally when hot water is drawn off and cold water flows back into the lower part of the tank. A more sophisticated control is only necessary when an active integration of the circulation is desired (e.g. switching the circulation return between the point of injection into conventional storage to solar storage). This way, also a fraction of the conventional energy demand is covered by the solar energy supply. More details are given in Chapter 8.4.3.

In buffer storage systems, where the solar heat energy is not stored by potable water, but is transmitted to the domestic water through an external heat exchanger, a discharging control is needed. The control must be well tuned to the characteristic features of both the solar- and the conventional domestic hot water system. If the discharging heat exchanger is integrated into the solar buffer tank, such a sophi-sticated control is not needed. Thus, the following paragraphs will be dedicated to systems with external discharge and, consequently more complicated controls.

10.3.1 Domestic Hot Water Systems

Buffer Discharge in a Solar Pre-Heat Vessel

The discharge of buffer storage into a potable water filled pre-heat vessel (see Figure 10.4) is relatively simple to control.

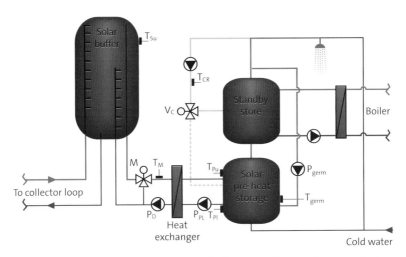

Figure 10.4 Discharge control of a system with buffer, external heat exchanger and solar pre-heat vessel with integrated hot water circulation.

The size of the solar pre-heat vessel is chosen as approximately 15 % by volume of the solar buffer (in regularly dimensioned systems) or about 10 % of the daily hot water consumption (independently of the system dimensioning).

When the temperature difference between the upper part of the buffer tank and the lower part of the pre-heat vessel ($T_{su} - T_{pl}$) becomes larger than the pre-set value (e.g. 6 K), then both the buffer discharging pump and the charging pump of the pre-heater are always switched on simultaneously. When the difference has fallen down to 3 K, the pumps are stopped. Through the operation of the pumps on both sides of the heat exchanger, the flow conditions are fixed, even when the flow volume on the domestic hot side is slightly influenced by the hot water draw-off. The design of heat exchangers for this particular application does not involve extraordinary requirements other than in the design of conventional heat exchangers. The requirements are:

At the pumped volumetric flow, the regular (not maximum) temperature spread at the bufferside (e.g. inlet 20°C, outlet 50°C) and a cold water temperature is approx. 15°C, the mean logarithmic temperature difference at the heat exchanger is supposed to be about 5 K. The pressure drop should not be higher than 10 kPa. Any peculiarities of the local potable water supply must be accounted for (e.g. pressure drop, flow resistance, draw-off peaks etc.). Details on the design of heat exchangers are found in /11/.

The power of the two pumps should be chosen so the volume flows on both sides of the exchanger are approximately equal. In this case cooling the buffer water and heating the domestic water are optimal. In large dwelling complexes, without particularly strong peaks in the daily draw-off, the hourly flow volume should be 20 – 30 % of the daily hot water consumption (to be measured is the amount flowing through both pre-heat vessel and stand-by store at 60°C, calculated in cubic metres per day, not the hot water outlet at 40°C!)

Example:

Daily consumption: 7 cubic metres per day

Volumetric flow of pumps: 1.5 – 2 cubic metres per hour

During periods of low water consumption, the lower part of the pre-heat vessel and the return from the heat exchanger to the buffer may get relatively hot. Therefore, a stratified injection of the return into the buffer is advantageous. Alternatively, function in the control system is included that limits the temperature for which the lower part of the pre-heat vessel is to be charged (e.g. 35°C at T_{pl}). However, this function would increase the switching intervals of the pumps.

When the cold potable water is not sufficiently pre-decalcified, a temperatur limiter is required on the buffer side of the heat exchanger, mixing with cold water.

The mixer (M) and the temperature sensor T_M are acting as a limiter to the buffer flow entering the heat exchanger, e.g. to 65°C, in order to prevent lime sedimentation. When the supplied potable water has very high lime content, a water softening system is recommended for the whole potable water supply (including the conventional system).

The pre-heat vessel, after being filled with potable water, is subject to regulations to prevent germ reproduction. The pre-heat stage should therefore be regularly be heated up to 60°C (e.g. once a day) for disinfection. The simplest way to achieve this is by creating a connection between the exit of the conventional system and the lower part of the pre-heat vessel.

It is recommended to have a separate feeding nozzle for this purpose, rather than coupling to the existing cold water inlet. In the latter case, the hot-water coming from the conventional storage would be directly mixed with the cold water that flows back during draw-off. Therefore it would be difficult to achieve the recommended 60 °C at the interior of the pre-heat vessel. If a separate nozzle is chosen, it is more likely that 60 °C is obtained. Through the pump, 60 °C hot water is transported from the outlet of the stand by storage into the pre-heat vessel (given that the conventional storage is kept at 60 °C, as recommended; otherwise this method would be useless).

Certainly, it is also possible to heat the pre-heat vessel directly by a conventional auxiliary-heating system. This would be done by integrating the pre-heat vessel into the auxiliary-heating return by a switching valve.

If the thermal disinfection of the solar pre-heat vessel has to occur once a day, the question of the best time arises. A procedure that starts between 2 to 3 pm has proved the best. At this time, the pre-heat stage is usually hot, so less conventional energy is needed to reach the 60 °C demanded. In addition, the draw-off at this time is relatively low, so the heating is less disturbed by inflowing cold water. During the hours of peak consumption in the late afternoon or early evening, the pre-heat vessel cools down, so the discharge of the solar buffer is largely unhampered.

The »German Recommendation for the Prevention of Germ Proliferation« (DVGW W 551) states that the complete pre-heat storage system has to be heated to 60 °C once a day. This requirement is rather impractical, since even during the period of disinfection there is some draw-off, and the lower part of the vessel would never reach 60 °C. Meeting the regulation would be possible only with a bypass for the incoming cold water around the pre-heat vessel, thus preventing cold water from entering the vessel during disinfection. As a compromise, the appropriate temperature sensor T_{germ} (not the disinfection inlet itself!) is placed at approximately a quarter of the tank height above the bottom of the vessel. The sensor T_{pl} is placed too low and should not be used.

Under no circumstances should the circulating return be used for thermal disinfection by guiding it to the pre-heat vessel with a switching valve. Since the circulating return is always a few degrees colder than the storage outlet (which is usually not more than 60 °C), the pre-heating tank would never get hot enough.

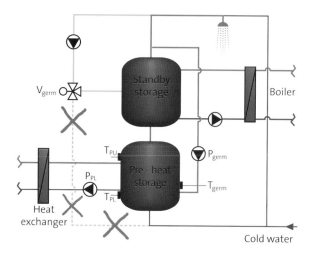

Figure 10.5 Wrong: use of the circulating return for thermal disinfection

The process of disinfection by conventional heat is not needed if the pre-heat vessel reaches the required temperature or 60°C by solar heat alone.

For this purpose, an »intelligent« control is needed, which stores the achieved temperature of T_{germ} (at least those above 60°C) and resets the memory every night, when the conventional disinfection is over.

The integration of the circulation can be done with a switching valve (V_C in Figure 10.4). The inlet into the solar pre-heat vessel must not be in the lower part, which would be heated by conventional energy and thus partially block the heat transfer into the solar buffer. A better point for the inlet would be at two thirds of the height of the vessel.

The circulating return may be guided into the pre-heat vessel only when the temperature T_{CR} is approximately 3 K lower than in the upper part of the vessel. If the return temperature comes close to the pre-heat storage temperature (approximately 1 K or slightly above, depending on the precision of measurement), the valve must be switched back, so the conventional storage is fed.

Buffer Discharging in a Bivalent Pre-Heat and Stand-by Storage Vessel

Principally, both the solar pre-heat vessel and conventional stand-by vessel can be combined into a single unit. However, special requirements for embedding this unit into the solar and conventional system occur, as described in Chapter 3.4.2.

The control of the buffer discharge is done as for systems with distinct pre-heat storage (see above). The positions of the temperature sensors in the pre-heat section correspond with those presented earlier for the separated storage. The same applies to tube connections.

Buffer Discharging without Solar Pre-Heat Vessel (Flow Heater Principle)

The simplest way of connecting the solar and conventional systems is to omit the potable water filled pre-heat vessel. In this case, the inflowing cold water (during hot water draw-off) is initially guided directly to the discharging heat exchanger of the buffer storage. Figure 10.6 shows the arrangement. This is a particularly cost-effective solution, since the pre-heat storage and the thermal disinfection-circuitry are avoided.

Another advantage of this principle is that the potable water side of the discharging heat exchanger receives cold water at the lowest possible temperature level, while higher mixing temperatures would occur in a pre-heat vessel.

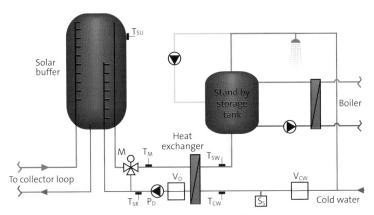

Figure 10.6 Buffer discharging without solar pre-heat vessel

The control of the buffer discharging pump (P_D) must fulfil three conditions for the entire system:

- The pump should be operated so the temperature in the upper part of the solar buffer is a few degrees (e.g. about 6K) more than the inflowing cold water.

- The pump should operate only when hot water is drawn off as consumption from the potable side of the exchanger .

- The pump must not pump more volume than is drawn-off from the potable waterside; in this case the return temperature to the buffer cools down as low as possible and the collector return is at a low temperature. It would be optimal if the flow volumes on both sides of the exchanger are always equal.

The minimum temperature difference between solar buffer and inflo-wing cold water is monitored by the temperature difference control. A simple temperature switch (which puts the pump into operation at a specific temperature) is not recommended, since the actual cold water temperature changes seasonally as well as with the draw-off volume (especially when the supply lines are very long).

The volume-flow can be measured by flow switches. These switches, however, eventually become unreliable. Monitoring the temperature (T_{cw}) inside the cold water line that leads to the heat exchanger, has been used for flow measurement. A temperature drop indikates water flowing. However, the following conditions must be taken into account:

- The »stagnant« water inside the cold water line (measured at T_{cw}) must be significantly warmer than the freshly inflowing cold water. This is often not the case in unheated basements during summer, when the cold water temperature is higher. Even when there is a solar pre-heat stage (e.g. waste heat recovery), this principle might not properly work.

- When there is a continuous draw-off, the temperature gradient diminishes, and another signal is needed to trigger the pump's switch-off when the draw-off is finished.

Analysis of the controls with draw-off recognition, used in the »Solarthermie 2000« research program, showed that they were un-successful.

A third opportunity for measurement is a flow meter in the cold water feeding line (V_{cw} in Figure 10.6) with an electrical output signal. These devices are fairly reliable, but their accuracy should be checked every few years.

The volume flow equality in the heat exchanger (both sides) can be checked only when volume-flow signals are monitored on both sides with flow meters V_{cw} und V_D. If the two flows differ, the discharging pump must be regulated accordingly. The flow detection mentioned above is automatically included in this type of control. A control system of this type is not available on the market yet, but a prototype is being developed in Germany.

In some control systems that work on the flow detection principle and according to temperature-drop measurement in the cold water line, volumetric flow equality may possibly be achieved by setting a lower temperature limit to the solar hot-water temperature (T_{sw}). This could be e.g. a fixed amount below the buffer temperature (T_{su}). However, this method does not take into account the more important require-ment for good solar buffer cooling, so that a low return temperature can be achieved in the solar loop. Furthermore, it is required that the mean logarithmic temperature difference has to be pre-set and must thus be known by the installer. Even when the value is known for a particular system, the actual properties may vary from manufacturer ratings.

Example:

A control is set up so the difference between T_{sw} and T_{su} is 5 K.

At the designed flow volume and temperature, the heat exchanger has a mean logarithmic temperature difference of 10 K.

However, for this, the discharging flow volume would become very large, in order to reach even a temperature difference of 5 K between both sides. The return temperature to the solar buffer would then be 20 K higher than the cold water temperature. The large discharging flow volume would not be sufficiently cooled by the cold water volume.

A control of the above kind is a good example of how conventional control strategies, i.e. efficient heating of cold water, are easily transfused to solar installations without consideration of the special requirements of solar technology, e.g. the need for low collector return temperature. In this case, one should at least place a limit to the temperature difference between buffer and cold water or regulate the pump-speed with regard to a specific temperature difference.

Nevertheless, the problem of calibrating the efficient control of the heat exchanger persists. This can not be done in advance by the manufacturer, because the individual system details are not known. Moreover, the installation technician knows the system components but usually not the functioning of the system in its entirety. Thus it depends on the the the operational manager to report the actual deviation of designs and operational conditions of the system.

For optimal buffer discharge, experience shows that, it is not recommended to use discharging controls that work with temperatures, temperature gradients and temperature differences alone. The results of the programme »Solarthermie 2000« confirm this, see Figure 10.7.

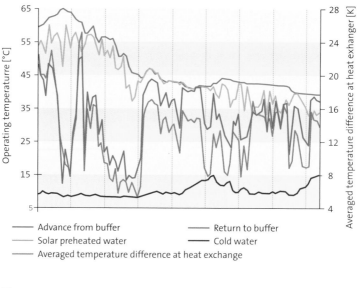

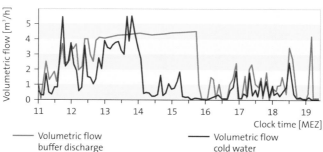

Figure 10.7 Temperature regime at discharge heat exchanger using a control based on temperature difference $T_{su} - T_{sw}$ for regulation of the discharging pump

In an off-the-shelf control available today, the pulses of the flow meter in the cold water feed line are used to regulate the discharging pump. Each pulse of the flow meter causes the pump to run for a set time interval between 0.5 and 1.5 seconds. If a new pulse comes within this time frame, the pump keeps working uninterrupted. If no pulse follows, the pump stops until it receives another pulse. In this way, equal volumetric flow is reached within an average of a few seconds.

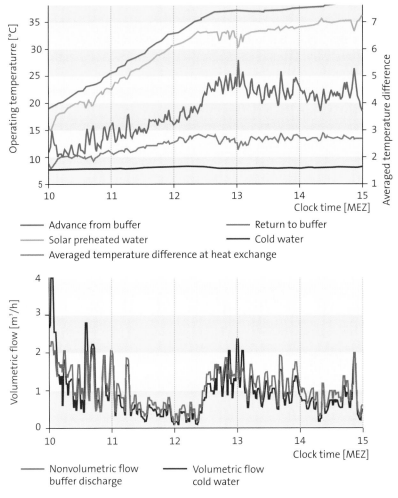

Figure 10.8 Temperature regime in a discharging heat exchanger using a control with volumetric flow measurement in the cold water line.

According to manufacturers' ratings, the pump switch operations are adjusted to the zero-crossing of the voltage. This is so switch operations do not produce electrical surges as pump motor starts. Also there is control so at short switching intervals, the pump comes to a complete rest, in spite of the inertia of the water in the tube. Since there may be a few thousand switching operations of the pump each day, the long-term fatigue behaviour of the pumps should be investigated within the »Solarthermie 2000« programme.

The duty cycle of the pump could be improved if the flow volume transmitter functions at a higher pulse frequency (e.g. one pulse per 0.01 litre). Large transmitters, with a so-called »reed-contact«, are designed for controls with a pulse frequency of 0.5 to 2 cycles per second (cps) (e.g. at 1 pulse per litre and a rated flow of 3,600 litres per hour:

1 cps; at 1,800 litres per hour: 0.5 cps). Volumetric flow meters with inductive pick-off (e.g. »Namur« principle) have scales that reach between a maximum 50 and 100 pulse per second. They are useful for pulse code modulation with pump on/off periods as low as 10 ms. Due to the inertia of the moving water column, the pump should keep turning during short intervals of shutdown from electric supply. However at very low flow the pump may stop.

An important requirement for the pulse flow meter is, that with an oscillating water column, which may occur in almost any potable water system, there are no erroneous pulses. Volume pulse transmitters with high resolution and rapid pulses are very sensitive to oscillations of the water column, since only a small turn of the measurement wheel leads to a pulse.

Another significant difficulty is that the actual characteristic curve of the discharging cycle is not known. Thus it is hard to determine when the pump has to work at full load and how the switching intervals are to be chosen with regard to the pulses of the flow meter. The total pressure loss of the cycle is fairly small, so small deviations with respect to the design have a large relative impact. In practice, another flow meter would have to be installed into the buffer discharging cycle for proper control calibration. Then a control with two flow meters would make more sense, as described above.

Due to the system inertia and capacitance, it is unrealistic to have control based on temperature measurements at all inlets and exits of the heat exchanger.

Another problem with the coupling of the solar system to the conventional hot water system is the dimensioning of the discharging heat exchanger (see 9.3.2). The dynamic range of the hot water draw-off can vary between zero and a few cubic metres per hour. It is difficult to find a heat exchanger that works well at low-flow (with turbulent flow) and still has an acceptable pressure loss at high-flow. The hot-water supply may collapse due to the high pressure loss at a high-flow rate.

Due to the unavailability of proper controls for this type of coupling, this type of control is currently not advisable for systems with a larger flow rate than three cubic metres per hour. However, within the research of the German »Solarthermie Programme«, new developments for adequate solutions for those problems might be found.

10.3.2 **Space-Heating Systems**

The application of solar installations for both potable water heating and for augmenting space heating are so varied and numerous that a complete specification of all varieties of buffer discharging systems is not possible within the scope of this book. However, a few introductory remarks can be made.

Similar to the buffer charging, the discharging will be considered from the point of view of exergy, i.e. for the quality and intrinsic value of the heat. This means that the buffer water should be taken from that stratum (thermal layer) where the temperature is close to, or a little more than, the hot water demand temperature required for the consumer. In this way, the largest available temperature in the upper layer remains relatively undisturbed, for possible use at a later time.

The return pipe from the domestic hot-water storage (if kept separately and not integrated into the buffer) and the space heating network should be guided back into the buffer through separate stratification devices. The combination of both pipelines, i.e. domestic water heating and space heating, would produce an unnecessarily warm temperature in the cold water return and therefore reduce the thermal efficiency.

The return into the buffer has to be so arranged as to keep the lower part of the buffer tank cold, even when the return temperatures from the heat exchanger are temporarily higher than the cold water supply. method for the feed to encourage stratification is of a secondary importance (see Chapter 8.4.1)

10.4 **Long-term Survey of Old Systems**

In the survey, the controls of solar installations often presented difficulty. Thus they are included within the most critical components of a solar system. One prerequisite for effective and orderly operation of a solar system, is the comprehensibility of the controls by the operating personnel so malfunctions can be identified. Many installations were so complicated and poorly documented that the actual cause of malfunctions remained a mystery. They could only be reported bluntly as »control deficiencies«. In other cases, one assumed the system to be functioning while there were major errors in the control functions (e.g. wrongly placed or defective control sensors, valves that opened when they were supposed to be closed, poor tuning). Usually, the operating personnel were unable to find the fundamental errors, since eventually the water heated somehow.

In addition, the controls were usually old and not standardized as nowadays. Often the controls were purpose-built for the individual solar installations. This often led to »black box« controls with v set-up parameters (e.g. unlabeled potentiometers).

Since electronic control equipment becomes obsolete quickly, attempted repair over the 15 year operation was very uncommon, as complete replacements were preferred, even when minor malfunctions occurred. Thus, actual ageing, i.e. lack of measurement precision due to wear, could not be evaluated in the survey. In any case, any possible results would not have been valid for present state-of-the-art technology.

Experiences of the control systems of old installation, once again confirmed the necessity for precise technical description and documentation of control components. Unfortunately, it was to be noticed that even nowadays the manufacturers of solar installations do not describe their products with sufficient precision in detail. Sometimes the manuals failed to elucidate the proper functioning, so essential pieces of information had to be obtained directly from the manufacturer.

Further investigations revealed that it is easiest to understand and operate control systems when the entire system control, and thus the control functions themselves, were kept as simple as possible. Out of the evaluated installations, there were 10 with DDC (direct digital controls). In only two of these cases were the operators able to comprehend the control strategy, since they were experienced in building-plant technology. In the other cases, neither the installation technicians nor the operators would have been able to calibrate the systems to the actual operating conditions when these deviated from the originally designed specifications.

Finally we would like to identify the problems that occurred during operation of systems with discharging controls based purely on temperature-differences, regarding the, in practice uncontrolled, parallel arrangement of buffer vessels. The results, shown in Figure 10.9, apply to a system with two parallel-connected buffers and a discharging control, without pre-heat vessel (see Figure 10.6). The discharging pump was regulated so the temperature of the solar-heated cold water was 5 K below the temperature in the upper part of one of the two buffer vessels (see also 10.3.1).

The lower part of Figure 10.9 shows the volumetric draw-off flow and the discharge flow. It is easy to see that until approximately 12.30 h, the control fulfilled its task with moderate success. However, between 12.30 h and 16.00 h, the pump operated at full load, although it was supposed to operate at reduced power. The reason is quite simple: from 12.00 h, the temperature in the upper part of buffer 2 decreased, while that in buffer 1 remained larger (see upper part of Figure 10.9).

Since the control sensor was placed in buffer 1, the pump was commanded to operate until the cold water was 5 K colder than the measured buffer temperature. However, since the temperature in buffer 2 reduced much more rapidly than in buffer 1, the cold water entering the heat exchanger (a mixture from both buffer 1 and 2) remained below the destination temperature for the cold water (5 K less than the upper temperature in buffer 1) untill about 16.00 h. Although the pump ran at full speed, even during low draw-off, the reduced mixing temperature at the entrance of the buffer side of the heat exchanger prevented the target temperature being reached on side of the conventional system. The high discharge flow rate, combined with almost no hot-water consumption raised the return temperature into the buffer significantly. The lower parts of the buffer tanks heated up accordingly and unequally, since the two buffers were not discharged with identical volumetric flows.

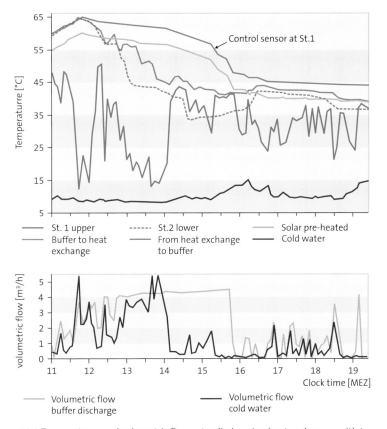

Figure 10.9 Temperatures and volumetric flows at a discharging heat exchanger with two uncontrolled parallel-connected solar buffers

Apart from the fact that in this system the collector loop (charging cycle) switched on too late (due to the temperature in buffer 1, where the charge control sensor was placed, being higher than in buffer 2), the discharge circulation tended to start operating too early (since the discharge control sensor in the upper part of buffer 1 became warmer than in buffer 2). Apart from the inherent insufficiencies of the control system itself, the different temperatures in buffer 1 and 2, led to aggravated disorders in the operation of the discharging pump and to unnecessarily high storage temperatures in the lower parts of the buffers.

10.5 Recommendations for Realisation

10.5.1 Solar Control and Process Control Techniques

The market offers a large variety of powerful control components suited to the requirements of solar installations. However, there is no optimal solution available yet for a discharging control according to the flow heater principle. Development efforts in this direction are under way. A good starting point is for a discharging pump that is controlled by draw-off volume pulses. Discharging controls that work with temperature sensors alone are still not satisfactory with regard to this working principle.

Depending on installation size, the cost of controls is between several hundred and one thousand Euro. In most cases, the cost for the proper monitoring of the solar system is included with this. Important features of the control are:

- simple operation and good documentation of the control functions
- compliance with local standards (e.g. CE certificate and electro-magnetic compatibility)
- illuminated mimic-board display for visualization of temperatures at collector, storage unit and collector advance and return Further options may include the status of pumps and valves and a timer for the service hours of the pump.
- operational checks (the debate on the necessity of operational checks is not yet finished)

Reasonable options:

A meaningful option would be a calorimeter (to measure heat quantities) in the collector loop (which is suitable only in connection with other measurements such as radiation in the collector plane, hot-water draw-off quantity etc.).

The application of process control techniques (DDC) often leads to greater system cost and problems in their accommodation, so their application for the control of solar installations rarely pays off. Only when process control technology is already present in a building and competent operating personnel are available, is it useful to integrate the controls of solar installation into the overall process control system. It is a prerequisite that the programmer of the process control technique fully understands the peculiarities of solar technology, because otherwise incorrect programming occurs, as happened in the surveyed installations.

10.5.2 Sensor Elements

Designation KTY

These are electrical resistance sensors whose resistance becomes larger with increase in temperature. The widely used sensor has semiconductor elements with PTC-attitude (positive temperature coefficient).

KTYs can usually endure operating temperatures up to 150 °C. Within the scale of measurement relevant for solar installations, their absolute precision is ±1.5 K. This means that the absolute error of a temperature difference measurement may (in the worst case) be 3 K (if the single errors of both sensors have opposite algebraic sign). Therefore, this type of sensor is not well suited for applications where small temperature differences are essential. They are sufficient for temperature limiters, when the precision of the switching temperature is not very important. The sensor is connected to the control system through a twin, double insulated, cable. In some digital controls, electrical noise disturbances occur when the cables pass near other live cables.

KTY-sensors can be damaged or made defective by high temperatures during continuous stagnation of the solar system. They are not suitable for temperature measurements in vacuum tube collectors without temperature limitation.

Designations Pt 100, Pt 500, Pt 1000

These are metal wire resistance sensors. In their Pt (Platinum) version, they also have a PTC-attitude. The sensor elements are made of platinum wires and are operable at temperature regimes between −200 °C and 850 °C. The number stated behind the »Pt« stands for the resistance coefficient at 0 °C.

Distinctions are made according to operational temperature and precision, between quality types A and B. Quality A is made for very precise measurements by the combination of so-called paired sensors. Two paired sensors are gauged together and are very precise with regard to heat quantity measurements, since both sensors have a very similar response over the whole measurement spectrum. For the control of solar installation, it is sufficient to use quality B mostly, whose precision is ±(0.3 + 0.005•T) K within the relevant temperature scale (T: measured temperature in Kelvin).

The high endurance of platinum elements against heat makes them suitable for collectors with very high temperatures at stagnation (e.g. evacuated collectors).

For control purposes, the sensor elements are usually connected with a twin cable. High precision measurements are done with four-way cables, so errors due to cable resistance.

Sensor Enclosure and Connection Cables

The sensor enclosures must protectthe sensory element from damage and severe weather, so they must be able to withstand high temperatures, corrosion and water ingress. Proper materials are tin-plated brass or high grade steel. In order to seal the enclosure against humidity, one uses electrical contact sockets of synthetic material that are roller-burnished or press-compacted with the cable. The quality of these seals is essential for the continuing integrity of the sensor. If humidity enters an enclosure through imperfect seals or if the enclosed sensor is damaged by high temperatures (e.g. of the collector), then defective temperature signals or short-circuits of the sensor may be experienced.

The connection cables of the sensors are usually insulated with PVC (often called oil flex cable) or silicone. In the upper temperature range, PTFE-cables may also be used, since PVC-cables may be damaged by high temperatures. This is true for both, the inner core of cables and the outer insulation, where faults may cause malfunction in either location. Due to the environmental questionability of PVC (due to its containing chlorine atoms and consequent waste incineration difficulties), this material should only be used where it is not specifically forbidden. The safest and most enduring option is silicone cable, with Teflon protection. These cables operate safely up to 230 °C.

Protective tubes of weatherproof synthetic material, or metal for outdoor applications, are used to prevent damage to cables and collector sensors by bird pecking or UV-radiation.

The use of unsuitable sensors may disturb or stop the operation of the solar system. The additional cost for high-quality sensors, with suitable enclosures and cables, is small in comparison to the fixing cost when serious malfunctions occur. Rejection of high-quality sensors is thus not justified.

Sensors in Submersible Enclosures / Contact Sensors

Sensors inserted into storage tanks and pipes may, or may not, have enclosures. The response time of a temperature sensor placed directly in the fluid or fixed to a surface is much quicker than if placed in an enclosure, due to the relatively very large thermal mass of any enclosure. However, the definite advantage of a sensor within a submersible or inserted enclosure, is the ease of replacement of a defective sensor without completely draining the pipe or tank.

The submerged sensor (without enclosure) measures the temperature of the medium in the tank or pipe directly. This is the most precise measurement if the sensor is installed correctly, i.e. when the medium flows against the sensor or when the sensor protrudes the medium. If sensors are placed in submersible enclosures, they should be be covered and located with heat conductive paste, so there is good heat transmission between enclosure and sensor.

The enclosures (or the jacket of the sensor itself, if used without socket enclosure) must be made of corrosion-resistant material (e.g. brass or high grade steel).

In solar technology, one often uses so-called contact sensors on surfaces in order to determine the temperature of a heat transfer liquid in pipes or storage tanks. The measurement accuracy depends on how well the shape of the sensor fits the contact area, whether heat conductive paste has been used, whether the sensor is securely fixed in contact with the surface (e.g. with a metallic strap retainer) and whether the sensor is thermally well insulated against other influences, e.g. the outside environment.

Only when all the above conditions are reached, is it possible to achieve a precise temperature measurement of liquid inside pipes and tanks. If the flow in a pipe is laminar, a sensor sensor fixed to the pipe surface measures flow temperature near the wall only and not the representative temperature of the entire cross section. A properly installed contact sensor gives sufficient accuracy for the measurement of a single temperature (say to ± 0.5°C). However, using the difference of readings of two such independent sensors (thereby with a total error of +/- 1.0°C) is not recommended for the measurement of small temperature differences (say 3°C) that are used as switching values for control purposes. In this case submerged and paired sensors must be used.

10.5.3 **Positioning of Sensors**

Errors often occur during the installation of sensors, so specific warning is needed to prevent them.

If a control sensor measures actual operating conditions, it must be placed in a position where the relevant operating conditions are always present.

Figure 10.10 shows the example of a switching valve which is controlled by a temperature difference. The correct and several false positions for the temperature sensor T1 are shown in the scheme. The only correct position for measuring the inlet temperature (T1) is before the switching valve, which position is independent of the switching action of the valve.

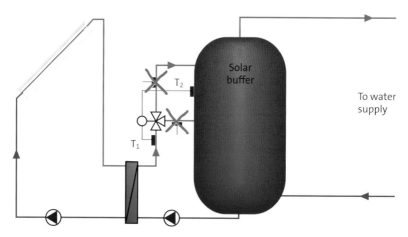

Figure 10.10 Correct and false positions for control sensor T1 (for measurement of temperature difference between T1 and T2 in order to control the valve switching position)

As seen in Figure 10.11, the temperature sensor for the collector field should always be in thermal contact with the hottest part of the collector field, which is normally at the output flow junction of the last collector in a string. When a parallel collector field heats up, all collectors should have approximately the same temperature. Once the circulating pump is put into operation, the collector flow may become up to 35 K hotter than the collector return. If the temperature sensor were placed at the collector return, the pump would start operation at approximately the same time, since, during stagnation the return pipes also gets hot. However, once the pump is running, cold storage water would reach the sensor and the circulation would quickly cease. In the worst case, when the storage temperature is relatively high, the intermittent operation of pump may lead to partial evaporation, at the »hot end« of the collector field, even during the start-up phase of the solar loop circulation.

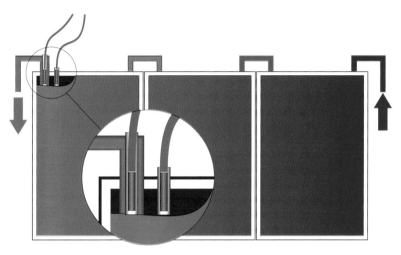

Figure 10.11 Position of the temperature sensor in the collector field

Whenever possible, the collector sensor element should be positioned in the middle of the flow pipe, as representative of the whole cross section of the fluid flow. Since this measurement is needed in practically any type of solar-thermal installation, it would be reasonable to expect the collector manufacturers to produce so-called »control collectors« already having the proper control sensor built into the upper collecting channel (header or flow advance outlet). Poorly located contact sensors may well produce an error of ±10 K at very high absorber temperatures, since they are often inadvertently in contact with colder air, they do not measure the temperature of the heat transfer liquid itself.

Cylindrically shaped temperature sensors against surfaces of collecting tubes or flat absorbers have only a very small contact area and thus give uncertain values. Sensors pushed into the collector outlet through a T-piece only measure the relevant temperature correctly if they reach far enough into the inner collecting tube and if the T-piece is well insulated. Relatively short sensors, combined with an uninsinuated T-piece (see Figure 10.12) give temperature values that are much too low, which leads to delayed switch-on of the collector circulating pump, especially in cold weather.

Figure 10.12 Poor installation of a short sensor into an un insinuated T-piece at an collector outlet

11. Characteristic Parameters of Various Types of Solar Systems

This Chapter is a summary of the operational experience and measured characteristics parameters for the range of solar installations described in section 3.2 and also referred to in section 3.4 to 3.6. Most of the findings were obtained from a monitoring and research program in Germany. Nevertheless, the results are universally valid, especially for medium to large sized installations.

Precise system behaviour, however, depends strongly on the actual operational conditions of the specific solar installation. Despite knowing the outline detail of a system, one has to consider the deviations of actual operational conditions.

We need to consider the operational arrangements as well as the long-term endurance, shortcomings and defects of the system components. Firstly, however, you are recommended to recall the detailed descriptions of the components in the previous Chapters. The relevant quantities referred to in the following sections (specific load, degree of utilisation, solar fraction, system performance figure, cost of usable solar heat etc.) are defined in Chapter 3.2.

11.1 Dependence of System Parameters on Location, Design and Components

The degree of utilisation and solar fraction are influenced by:

- the location of the system (average temperatures and solar radiation)
- the local weather conditions (and their seasonal shifts)
- the orientation of the collector field (tilt and azimuth angles)
- the quality of system components (collectors, storage unit etc.)
- the design (size of components in relation to annual and weekly hot water consumption)
- the actual operating conditions during the relevant year of operation (amount and variations of hot water draw-off, temperature of collector return)

11.1.1 Location of the System

The annually available amount of solar energy at a specific location varies between approximately 800 and 2300 kWh per square metre (see also Figure 11.1). For instance, in general for identical solar systems, those located, in a Mediterranean region have significantly larger solar fractions than those in Northern Europe.

Table 11.1 gives the values of solar fraction, degree of utilisation and solar yield for identical systems (and identical hot water consumption) at various locations. The values were computed with the simulation program T*SOL /36/. The numbers are valid for an installation with a collector area of six square metres and a daily hot water draw-off of 200 litres at 45 °C. The design is tailored for mid latitude locations. At locations with more insolation (i.e. received solar radiation), the collector area would be over-dimensioned for the nominated hot water consumption. Therefore, the listing is not to be understood as a design recommendation, but rather as an example to illustrate the correlation between solar fraction and degree of utilisation within various solar regimes.

Location	Solar Fraction in %	Degree of Utilisation %	Solar Yield kWh (collector loop)
Christchurch, New Zealand	39	30	1,414
Auckland, New Zealand	51	33	1,840
Hamburg, Germany	56	32	2,129
Johannesburg, South Africa	62	33	2,323
Berlin, Germany	60	34	2,352
Frankfurt, Germany	64	34	2,495
Freiburg, Germany	68	33	2,716
Athens, Greece	86	35	3,590
Madrid, Spain	89	33	3,760
Almeria, Spain	96	34	4,200
Tamanraset, Algeria	99.9	31.7	4,590

Table 11.1 Solar fraction, degree of utilisation and solar yield of a six-square-metre installation with a daily hot water usage of 200 l/d (45 °C) at various locations (simulation with T*SOL)

Depending on the local insoation, the solar fraction may vary between 40 to 100 %. However, as the storage temperatures increases with increasing solar fraction, so too the thermal losses increase. Nevertheless, the largest solar yield of the examples is more than three times that of the smallest.

The degree of utilisation, on the other hand, is less dependent on the location, with values between 30 to 35 %. Initially, it rises slightly with increasing solar radiation. When radiation becomes very high, it falls again, since the available solar power exceeds the demand, so frequent and extended periods of stagnation occur.

However, the seeming disadvantages and detriments of various locations and, climate conditions, are not particularly harmful. A well-optimised system dimensioning, a proper choice of components and the application of highly efficient products can make up for the difficulties. No region is excluded from being able to use solar energy.

11.1.2 Seasonal Differences of Local Weather
Past records show that the annual deviations of solar radiation and ambient temperatures at a specific location usually remain well below 10 % of the respective long-term averages. Therefore solar yield, system efficiency and solar fraction may be expected to vary from the average by +/-10 % in any particular year because of the weather conditions. Excessive deviations from »average« annual weather condition occur rarely. If weather conditions do change, perhaps due to Climate Change, then the deviation from calculated annual yield may be larger than +/-10 %. In order to prevent disappointment, the designer should investigate possible weather variation before sizing the solar components. This is especially the case when a specific system yield has been guaranteed, as checked by measurement later.

11.1.3 Orientation of the Collector Field
The orientation of a collector field is determined by the tilt angle from the horizontal plane and the azimuth angle (point of the compass). Both angels affect the insolation onto the collectors, and therefore the solar yield, degree of utilisation and solar fraction. These performance parameters are also affected by the particular loads and demand characteristics. For example, making a steeper collector tilt angle can improve the annual solar yield of a system for auxiliary space heating, while less inclined collectors are advantageous for swimming pool heating. In addition, there is a correlation between the optimal tilt angle and the azimuth. In general, the further the field faces away from north/south orientation, the flatter the tilt angle should be.

The optimal tilt angle also depends on the latitude. In Figure 11.1, this interdependence is shown for a domestic hot water system located at approximately latitude 50° north. For such installations on an annual basis , the orientation is southward with an optimal fixed tilt angle of 30° from the horizontal. However, at south-eastern or south-western orientation and with fixed tilt angles between 10 and 45°, the annual solar yield diminishes by only 5% or less. Even those systems with due eastern or western orientation deliver usable yields (approximately 15% less than optimal) when their tilt angle is relatively flat (30° or less).

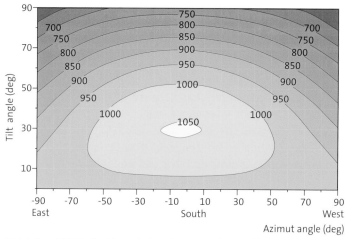

Figure 11.1 Solar yield (% of optimum) of a solar system for potable hot water, in dependence on the orientation of the collector field (located at latitude 50° north)

However, the interdependence shown in Table 11.1 depends strongly on the system dimensioning, the required minimum temperature level and the quality of the system components. The diagram is thus only useful for an initial estimate. For the design of large installations on flat roofs, when any orientation and tilt angles may be obtained simulation software should be used. This is because, the additional cost for a more expensive framework can be set against benefit of additional solar yield. A valid solution can be found by simulation only if the precise local weather (e.g. including morning fog, etc.) has been taken into account.

Solar systems only lose a small fraction of their optimal yield if they are not facing due south (in the northern hemisphere), as long as the tilt angle is set accordingly (see Figure 11.1). Deviations of 45° of the azimuth are entirely acceptable. During operation, an installation that faces east or west differs mostly in the time of day at which certain temperatures are reached, as compared with collectors facing due south. Since this might lead to disagreements between designer and operator, these factors should be recognised before a contract is signed.

11.1.4 **Quality of System Components**

The quality and suitability of the components do certainly influence the efficiency of the entire system. Yet this does not mean, that a system made up of 10 % more efficient components gives an overall increase in efficiency of 10 %. For instance, it is more likely that a high-quality system goes into stagnation as the critical temperatures are reached earlier. Therefore the theoretical advantage of higher quality only becomes realistic if the high-quality system is reduced in size so having the same solar fraction as the »weak« or ordinary system (see Table 11.2). This is particularly true when the »weak« system is already generously dimensioned, the exception being if the storage volume, and thus the heat storage capacity, is increased significantly. Nevertheless, certain quality standards should be met whatever the circumstances, for instance:

- The collector should have a large η_0 (see Chapter 5.1), so a large proportion of the solar radiation is transformed into heat. Heat losses should be kept minimal (low a-values and large η at the relevant temperature differences).

- The insulation of pipes and storage tank should be carried out thoroughly and should have large thermal resistance. It does not make sense to use high-quality (and expensive) collectors only to dissipate the produced heat in the rest of the system.

- The stratification of the storage unit must be adapted for consumer demand. If a minimum temperature is requested by the user (e.g. return temperatures of space heating networks), it is not useful to store heat at a lower temperature so it cannot be used. Here, the solar storage unit must be able to supply energy at a larger than minimum temperature.

The larger the solar fraction of a planned solar installation, the stronger the influence on solar yield of the chosen components (such as collector type, kind of stratification in the storage tank) and the more important is correct dimensioning. Although simple collectors and storage units are sufficient for domestic water heating systems, other installations require more specific attention. For instance for auxiliary space heating systems, one can achieve better yields per collector area with vacuum-tube collectors and stratified charging tanks if all components are well tuned and dimensioned (see below).

Table 11.2 shows how various collector parameters influence the performance of a large solar potable water heating system. For the computations, all components were kept constant, only the collector quality was changed (as indicated in the table). This is the usual way of analysis, although it is not always applicable if better performance leads to frequent stagnation.

FP: Flat plate collector VT: Vacuum tube collector	Conversion factor η_0 [%]	Heat loss coefficient a_1 [W/(m²·K)]	Specific load: 70 l/(d·m²)		Specific load: 40 l/(d·m²)		Specific load: 25 l/(d·m²)	
			Solar yield [kWh/(m²·a)]	System degree of utilisation [%]	Solar yield [kWh/(m²·a)]	System degree of utilisation [%]	Solar yield [kWh/(m²·a)]	System degree of utilisation [%]
FP moderate	76	4.0	517	43.9	423	35.9	331	28.1
FP a_1 very good	76	2.6	567	48.1	462	39.2	356	30.3
FP η_0 very good	84	4.0	571	48.5	457	38.8	352	29.9
FP medium	80	3.3	569	48.3	459	39.0	354	30.1
FP very good	84	2.6	624	53.0	490	41.7	372	31.6
VT without reflector	84	1.3	726	61.7	558	47.4	409	34.8

Table 11.2 Yield of large potable water heating systems with various collector types and three different degrees of utilisation (values refer to one square metre of collector area; $a_2 = 0.015\,W/(m^2 \cdot K^2)$ for all flat collectors; $a_2 = 0.01\,W/(m^2 \cdot K^2)$ for tubular collector)

Compared with a system havinng medium collector quality and lean dimensioning, systems with poor collector quality may obtain approx. 9 % less yield, systems with high quality flat plate collectors may obtain 10 % higher yield and systems with vacuum tube collectors may obtain approx. 28 % higher yield.

If the same systems operated at a low specific load (e.g. only 25 litres per day per square metre), so they become grossly over-dimensioned, a large energy surplus is generated by all the systems and the relative performance differences decrease. The »poor« system produces 6 % less usable energy, the high-quality system 5 % more and the vacuum tube collector 15 % more. The advantage of the high-efficient system is lost if no adaptation is made to store the energy surplus or reduce the system size.

Table 11.2 indicates that it is not sensible to use more sophisticated collectors in systems with low specific load in order to raise the solar yield. The entire system, especially the storage capacity and heat exchangers, must be adapted. The other and often preferable solution is to reduce the system size in accord with the better collector performance. Eventually, this does not necessarily lead to additional useful energy gains but either to cost reductions or to only marginally more expensive systems due to the more efficient and long lasting components.

It can also be seen that a good collector parameter does not guarantee good system efficiency. Benefit of a good η_0 can well be lost by a poor a_1-value, or vice versa. In a good collector, both parameters should be of similar quality.

If the suitable components and system size are chosen properly for a given solar fraction, the following results should occur when comparing flat and tubular collectors:

Solar fraction	Area vacuum tube	Area flat plate collector	Quotient area vacuum tube/ flat plat collector
25%	58 m^2	80 m^2	0.725
50%	113 m^2	200 m^2	0.655

Table 11.3 Collector field areas of flat plate (Solvis, selective) and vacuum-tube (Thermomax) collectors for achievement of specified solar fraction in large solar systems for potable water heating (8,000 litres per day)

Table 11.3 shows that for the achievement of identical solar fractions of 25%, the tubular collector has only (58/80) 73% as large the flat collector (with equally large storage capacity!). At a solar fraction of 50 %, the ratio would be even smaller (113/200 = 66 %).

Due to the different efficiencies of components (especially collectors), larger differences in the degree of system utilisation may result with different weather conditions. However, disadvantages of a location can be overcome by careful choice of components.

The practical effect of differing components and their dimensioning can be determined only by computational simulation, if all parameters are precisely known, or by measurement. EU-standards will require component tests and standardized system performance ratings that are more reliable than the tests required previously.

11.1.5 System Design

Depending on the desired dimensioning (specific load) or solar fraction of a solar system, the degree of utilisation may vary greatly. Small systems for domestic water heating, or systems for auxiliary space heating, are often designed for a high solar fraction, while a low degree of utilisation and a relatively high cost of usable solar heat are accepted. Large installations are usually designed for a reduced solar heat cost and so have a low solar fraction, combined with a high degree of utilisation.

It is generally valid that:

The larger the solar fraction, the smaller the degree of utilisation and the larger the relative cost of the solar heat. This is the common design strategy for small domestic systems.

The smaller the solar fraction is, the larger the degree of utilisation and the smaller is the cost of the solar heat. This is the common design strategy for medium-sized or large-scale solar systems for commercial use.

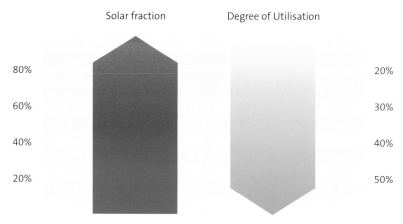

Figure 11.2 Solar fraction and degree of utilisation act against each other

The design of small domestic systems aims, to achieve either a solar fraction of nearly 100% during the hot months of summer or support of space heating during the transitional periods. Here, the main objective is to save fossil fuel (oil, coal and gas). Economic profitability is however not usually the motive. The decision to install a domestic solar system is frequently made out of considerations for environmental reasons and for independence from conventional energy supplies and for prestige. The relatively low yield per square metre of collector area or the higher price per unit of solar energy is of secondary importance.

Specific aspects of a particular solar design have a much larger effect on the system performance than than many other features, such as the geographic location, the local weather conditions within a specific year, the orientation of the collectors or the utilisation of less or more efficient components. Thus, an appropriate system design makes it relatively easy to build solar systems even at disadvantaged location and to create a supply of solar heat at relatively low cost.

11.1.6 Changes of Energy Demand
If energy demand is estimated too high during the planning of a solar system, there can be repercussions on the system efficiency (i.e. annual degree of utilisation) and on the cost of the solar heat. This has been observed very often when the estimated energy demand was later compared with the actual measured values. If, for example, the actual energy consumption was only two thirds of the estimated value (often the consumption is even lower), the degree of utilisation is reduced by approximately 15−25% (depending on the design). The more gene-

rously a system was dimensioned, the larger was the reductionin efficiency. Such a reduction causes the solar heat cost to increase rapidly, by approximately 18−33%. Similar consequences may result if systems are not designed to match summer conditions or with systems with low-consumption periods or when measurements are made during the »wrong« season and are not re-calculated for low-consumption period (see Chapter 4). In this context, buildings with extremely low energy usage during summer (e.g. student hostels or schools, sport halls) are particularly critical.

To achieve good system efficiency, it is essential to undertake a careful survey of the actual energy demand before a solar system is planned. In case of doubt, it is preferable to design the system somewhat leaner, rather than dimensioning it too large (see also Chapter 4).

The annual energy demand may may be expected to vary, due to changes in the conventional hot water system (e.g. introduction of water-saving devices), variations in the number of occupants or changes in the attitude of the users, e.g. water-saving.

If, for example, the consumption of a domestic medium-sized hot water system is 30% less than planned, the annual degree of utilisation may decrease by at least 15%, and the per unit solar heat cost may rise by almost 20%. Usually, such reductions of 30% or more in the energy demand occur only when energy efficiency improvements are taken after, rather than before, installation of the solar system.

Therefore before designing a solar system, one should consider if there are other, economically preferable solutions for the reduction of energy demand and for enhancement of the efficiency of conventional energy supply (e.g. by installing a new boiler with better efficiency at low specific load). If such »conventional« alternatives are found, they should be put into practice first. Afterwards, the solar system can be adapted to the reduced energy demand. This prevents the solar installation being over-dimensioned with respect to the actual energy demand and consequently being unnecessarily idle.

11.2 Characteristic Parameters of recently Built Solar Thermal Systems

The parameters used in the following sections (specific load, degree of utilisation, solar fraction and cost of usable solar heat) are defined in Chapter 3.2.

11.2.1 Domestic Hot Water Systems

The majority of the approximately 450,000 solar installations in Germany are domestic hot water systems. The typical collector area of these installations lies between 4 and 10 square metres, and the storage volumes are between 300 and 500 litres. Usually, bivalent storage units are used, the lower two thirds of them serve as solar storage vessel, and the upper third is conventionally heated if necessary.

In contrast to large installations from the »Solarthermie 2000« program (see Chapter 11.2.2), these systems are usually installed without any additional measurement system (except controls). Therefore, operational results of these systems are rarely available. This is because, for instance, a heat flow meter for hot water costs about 300 Euro, which would be more than 5% of the entire cost of a $5\,m^2$ solar system. For detailed measurements, at least two such meters and a device for the measurement of solar radiation are needed (although in some cases it is sufficient to have one heat flow meter and a water consumption meter for the hot water draw-off).

Since most systems have bivalent storage, i.e. auxiliary heating, if a malfunction of the solar system occures, the water will continue to be heated by the conventional system and the faults may remain unnoticed.

Without simple instrumentation and the regular interest of the user, an operational check is difficult and unlikely to happen. However, information about the temperature of the solar section of the tank (not just in the upper, conventionally heated section) helps to determine if the system is functioning during sunny days. However, such scant information is insufficient for knowing if the calculated amount of solar energy is being transferred to the tank.

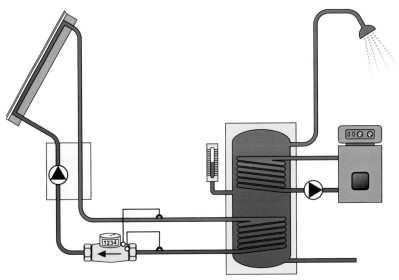

Figure 11.3 Solar system with thermometer in the solar part of the bivalent storage tank and calorimeter in the collector loop

If a heat flow meter has been installed, it is usually placed in the collector loop. These devices are imprecise unless they are not properly calibrated for the specific water-glycol mixture of the heat transfer fluid. In addition, the solar radiation on the collector plane has to be measured to obtain even an approximately accurate value for the degree of utilisation of the collector field (not of the entire system!). Obviously the collector field is usually not horizontal, so elementary published solar radiation oriented makes it difficult to use. Without knowledge of the actual energy consumption, or the amount of consumed conventional energy, and thus being unable to calculate the solar fraction, it is not possible to quantify the system performance. If computational data (e.g. from a simulation program) for the expected solar yield are available for the particular system in annual, or better monthly, intervals, a comparison can be made to the measured values. If the measured values are fairly close to the calculated values, it is at least possible to exclude malfunctions of the solar system. If there are large differences, there may be several reasons:

- The weather within the relevant measurement period is not equal to the long-term average. If the actual weather was rather »untypical« (e.g. an unexpectedly rainy summer), it is advisable to continue the observational period.

- The actual hot water consumption differs greatly from the planned hot water demand. This can be a temporary difference (e.g. during holiday periods) or it may be due to an entirely wrong estimation. Without additional measurements, only subjective assessments are possible.

- There is a disturbance or malfunction in the system.

Thus, a malfunction of the system may not be the reason for solar yield being lower than its »nominal value«. There may be one or more possible explanations. In such cases, it is recommended to continue detailed observations until the real cause can be identified. It is not possible to derive the solar fraction from readings of the heat flow meter only. A rough estimate of the solar fraction is possible during summer (when no space heating is used) if the fuel consumption of the conventional system is recorded and the (summer period) degree of utilisation (or efficiency) of the boiler system is known. If electric heating elements (immersion heaters) are used, one can monitor the consumption of electric energy separately. Note that low-cost »hour meters« connected to the mains electricity at a load give details of the time the device has been activated; the energy consumed equals the load power multiplied by the time.

The solar fraction (of the total energy use for water heating, including circulation and storage losses) in the period of observation, is the ratio of usable solar energy to the sum of consumed solar energy and auxiliary heat (e.g. total fuel consumption multiplied by the boiler efficiency). In which case:

Solar fraction = usable solar energy /
(usable solar energy + consumed fuel • boiler efficiency)

The value given by this equation is, however, likely to be likely to be only a very approximate estimate, because:

- Oil level displays or measurement sticks at or in oil tanks do not give an accurate measure of fuel consumption.

- The energy supply from the collector loop is not measured precisely enough. The solar heat from the collector is not equal to the used solar energy (due to storage losses).

- Boiler efficiency during partial-load operation in summer is usually not known. Depending on the design, it is usually up to 10 % less than the optimal efficiency during full-load operation.

Annual Degree of Utilisation and Annual Solar Fraction

The annual degrees of utilisation and solar fractions of small solar systems vary widely. In contrast to large systems, these are designed for high solar fractions, which make sense since the cost of a somewhat larger collector area is only marginal on the cost of other components, e.g. for piping and control system. As a function of increasing size, per square metre of collector area and within certain limits, system cost decreases more rapidly than solar yield.

In systems where a conventional boiler is used for auxiliary heating, a high solar fraction, e.g. an annual mean of 50 to 60%, is chosen so the boiler is completely out of operation during summer. This is sensible, because older boilers tend to have very poor efficiency when operating for domestic hot water only.

The spread of the results is shown in Table 11.4. For the same standard solar system (5 m^2 flat collector, 4.9 m^2 absorber area, 300 l bivalent storage volume, lower 2/3 solar part, upper 1/3 conventional part), various hot water draw-off rates (temperature: 45 °C) were set and the characteristic parameters of the system were calculated. The results were obtained with the T*SOL simulation program /36/, for the location of Frankfurt, southern orientation and 45° tilt angle.

Number of person consumption per person	3 low	3 moderate	3 high	4 high	5 high	6 high
Litre/day for stated person (45/60°C) [1]	70/47	120/122	180/122	250/169	300/203	360/243
Specific load [l/(d·m$^2_{coll}$) (45/60°C)] [1]	14/10	24/16	36/24	50/34	60/41	72/49
Utilisation coll. loop [%]	20	26	33	38	41	43
Annual yield / m^2 coll. [kWh/(m^2·a)] [2]	247	322	399	466	498	524
Solar fraction [%]	83	74	66	59	54	49

[1] Reference temperature = target temp. in stand-by storage
[2] Yield measured in collector loop, usable heat approx. 5−10% lower

Table 11.4 Collector-loop degrees of utilisation and solar fractions for a standard 5 m^2 solar system with various draw-off scenarios

The overall degree of utilisation, including storage losses, is approximately 5 to 10% less than the indicated value for the collector loop alone (depending on storage temperature and system dimensioning).

A dimensioning of 1.5 m^2 of collector area per person is very common for small solar domestic systems in Germany. If for a 3-person household, a system with two collectors (2.5 m^2 each) is installed, the solar yield may be only 270 kWh/(m^2·a) if the users consume hot water sparingly and have a sense of environmental care. This does not mean that the solar system operates »poorly« or is dimensioned »wrongly«.

The installation of only one 2.5 m² collector would not reduce the installed cost significantly. Thus, in spite of probably frequent periods of stagnation of the »over-dimensioned« system, the decision for two collectors instead of one is justifiable. However it is important to check the financial aspects of a solar installation, especially when the funds are short and other means of energy savings are possible.

The calculations were performed for the site of Frankfurt/Main, since this location with 1,078 kWh/(m²·a) represents the average insolation for Germany. Site insolation in Germany can vary between 10 % more and 15 % less than this average.

In regions with more insolation, the specific load can be increased by 30 to 50 %. In general, indicated inverse proportionality between solar fraction and degree of utilisation is universally valid.

The spread of results is further increased by the choice of collector qualities, i.e. collector orientations, storage systems, pipe lengths and the effect if the collector panels become shaded.

Cost of Investment

In small installations, the majority of the cost is determined by components that are independent of system size (e.g. control and sensor equipment) or that do not scale linearly with the collector field size (e.g. valves, pumps, pipework, storage tanks). Therefore, the curve of the specific cost, i.e. per unit collector area, decreases rapidly with increasing system size. This encourages a generous dimensioning of the collector area, since the marginal cost of an additional collector is small.

European market prices for installed flat plate collector systems, with about 4 to 5 m² collector area, are between approximately 800 and 1,300 Euro per m². This includes the storage vessel, assembly, installation and sales tax. The cost also depends on the quality of the components and on the on-site conditions (installation as a house is built, or refit to an old building). Furthermore, there are national and local price differences, as well as special offers and packaged deals. Under favourable conditions, the cost can be reduced to 800 Euro per m² in new buildings, e.g. if the cost reduction for not having a conventional storage unit can be credited.

Vacuum tube collector systems with approximately 4–5 m² are offered for 1,000–2,000 Euro per m² gross collector area, including sales tax. Especially when dealing with vacuum tube collectors, one has to consider the area definitions given in section 5.1.4.

Cost of Usable Solar Heat

The cost of the delivered solar heat can be equated from the annual solar yield (recorded from the heat flow meter minus about 5 to 10 % for storage losses, depending on the storage temperature and storage quality) and the annual total cost (cost of investment, operation and maintenance).

Since the spread of both the solar yield and the installation cost are very large, the actual solar heat cost has even more scatter.

If the calculation is based on an interest rate of 6 % per year and a service life of 20 years, the annuity loan is approximately equal to 8.72 % of the investment.

With investment costs (as mentioned above) between 800 and 1,300 Euro per m^2, the annual cost of a $5 m^2$-system is between 348 and 566 Euro.

According to Table 11.4, the annual yield of a $5 m^2$-solar system located in Germany lies between 1,240 and 2,620 kWh.

The benefit of the solar system can be evaluated by computing the theoretical cost of saved fossil fuel. If, for this purpose, one assumes an oil price of 40 Euro-cents per litre (or 5.5 Euro-cents per kWh), the solar installation can (depending on the number of users, consumption level and location) save fuels costs between 70 and 145 Euro annually.

This example makes it clear that, even under favourable conditions, abated heating oil costs do not cover the cost of investment for the solar system. This is still true if the system is situated at locations with higher solar radiation and has 30 % better solar yield.

Any maintenance cost has not yet been included in the above computation. A detailed computation with regional energy prices and yield parameters is omitted at this point, but it can be performed as the example above.

In the worst case, if one assumes (a) the maximum system cost (566 Euro p.a., plus 85 Euro for maintenance and electrical pumping power) and (b) minimum solar yield (1,050 kWh p.a.) then the maximum heat cost is 0.62 Euro per kWh. Assuming an optimistic scenario with minimum system cost (348 Euro p.a. with no maintenance cost) and maximum yield (2500 kWh p.a.), the solar heat cost is 13 Euro-cents per kWh. If one subtracts the cost of saved fossil fuel (5.5 Euro-cents per kWh), the additional costs of usable solar heat is 7.5 Euro-cents per kWh.

It is important to realise that no external cost has been included for the adverse environmental impact of using fossil fuels, e.g. pollution and climate change. Estimates of such external costs are significant, perhaps doubling the »real« price of fossil fuels. There is also the challenge of costing user satisfaction of harnessing solar energy.

Figure 11.4 shows the whole spread of possible heat cost for the consumption and solar yield scenarios from Table 11.4. Since there is a tendency towards over-dimensioning in the majority of small installations due to over-estimations of the hot water demand, the focal point of realistic solar heat cost lies in the range of low specific loads, at 25 to 30 Euro-cents per kWh.

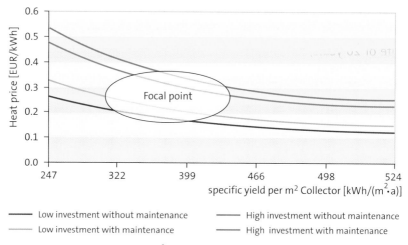

Figure 11.4 Solar heat price of a 5 m²-installation for a span of investment costs, as dependent on specific annual yield

Even if the heat cost and economic effectiveness are not the first priorities for small installations, the calculation shows that such systems (with approximately 5−10 m² collector area) can compete with conventional systems (fossil fuels) at only very high specific loads, low system prices (but durable components) and at favourable locations. In such cases, the solar heat cost is still approximately twice as high as the price for conventionally generated heat energy (oil or gas). Note especially that by comparison to the cost of electricity, solar heat is already competitive.

Solar thermal heat is, in its competitiveness with conventional energy supplies, much more justifiable than photovoltaic electricity generation.

11.2.2 Medium-Size and Large-Scale Solar Installations for Potable Water Heating

This section summarises the primary conclusions of the analysis of the potable water heating systems of the »Solarthermie 2000« research program. All such systems were at least one year in operation and were fully analysed. The results are also valid for medium-size solar systems with some caveats regarding the degree of utilisation and the slightly increased heat cost.

Annual Degree of Utilisation and Annual Solar Fraction

Figure 11.6 shows the achieved annual degrees of utilisation and solar fractions of the draw-off energy consumption (see definitions in Chapter 3.2) and the computed »optimal« and »realistic« trend lines. Each point in the diagram represents an observational period of one complete year of operation. For those installations that were observed for two years, two points were included in the diagram. Also included were (without trend line) measurements originating from those solar systems of the ZIP-program that participated in part 1 of »Solarthermie 2000« and were subjected to additional measurements in 1995/1996.

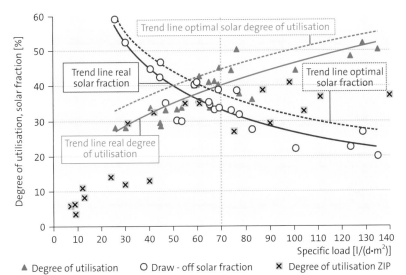

Figure 11.5 Annual degrees of utilisation and annual solar fractions in dependence on specific load of installations of »Solarthermie 2000« program and of old ZIP-installations after 15 years of operation

In accordance with the guidelines, the installations of the program »Solarthermie 2000« (part 2) were designed for specific loads of at least 70 litres (at 60 °C) per day and square metre collector. The fact that many of these systems still operated at significantly lower loads has to do with changes in the number of inhabitants and with additional water-saving measures that occurred after the solar systems were installed. Only in rare cases, was the actual water consumption during the observational periods more than documented during the preliminary consumption measurements. Most of the cases of high specific load had occurred because of limitations of available roof surface.

The trend curves show the typical progression of the degree of utilisation (rising with increasing load) and of the solar fraction (falling with increasing load). The actual trends are well below the »optimal« ones.

This is because most systems have small defects and do not operate perfectly. These defects include:

- imperfect buffer discharging due to non-optimised discharging control
- lower volume flow through collector array than planned
- lower performance of heat exchanger than originally given
- incomplete pipe insulation
- non-uniform charging and discharging of parallel-connected storage vessels

Nevertheless, most of the systems reached at least 90% of the manufacturer-rated performance (see Chapter 11.4).

The degrees of utilisation of ZIP-installations (built around 1980, service life approx. 15 years) were around 5 to 10% below those of newly built »Solarthermie 2000« part 2 installations. In most cases, this was due to the less efficient collectors that were built around 1980, but also due to decrease of collector performance over time (see Chapter 5). In some cases, moisture had entered the pipe insulation (see Chapter 7.6). It was observed also that many of the old ZIP-installations were grossly over-dimensioned, since the water consumption was largely overestimated (without preliminary measurements!), partially due to obsolete norms. In addition, these installations were incorrectly designed for an average solar radiation and not for the radiation during a typical sunny summer day. Both of these reasons led to specific loads of only 15 litres per day per square metre, or less.

In spite of the described shortcomings, the old ZIP-installations were still intact after 15 years of service and operated satisfactorily given the circumstances.

For optimised, newly built systems, situated in zones of moderate climate (such as Germany), the values of annual degree of utilisation and solar fraction given in Table 11.5 are applicable. These are normalised by reference to the specific load. These values are valid for collectors in mid northern latitudes, facing approximately south (±30°), with tilt angles between 30 and 45°. »Poor« sites are those areas with low annual solar insolation (e.g. 950 kWh/m²·a). »Good« sites have a higher insolation (e.g. 1,200 kWh/m²·a).

Specific load [l/(d·m²$_{coll}$)] (related to: 60°C)	30	45	70	100	140
Degree of utilisation medium location [%]	32	39	45	50	55
Annual yield per m² collector bad/good location [kWh/(m²·a)]	315/390	385/475	445/550	495/615	540/675
Solar fraction medium location [%]	55	46	38	32	27

Table 11.5 Annual degree of utilisation, specific yield and solar draw-off fraction of optimised large solar installations for potable water heating, per unit specific load (system components of mediocre quality)

The solar fraction in Table 11.5 is the total contribution of solar heat to the overall energy used for heating of hot water. These installations were, due to lean dimensioning, not designed to cover circulation losses nor technically equipped, with a circulation return, for this purpose. Therefore the choice of the solar draw-off fraction as the characteristic parameter is justifiable.

To compute the overall solar fraction (related to the total amount of energy used for water heating),), it is necessary to know the storage and circulation losses and the total amount of auxiliary heat, fed into the hot water system.

Usually, the storage losses are below 5%, but measurements of circulation losses gave sometimes rather startling results. In newer buildings with good insulation standards, when thorough insulation of the water pipe network can be assumed, approximately 30% of the total energy consumption for hot water supply is needed to cover circulation losses. In other words: circulation losses were approximately 40% as large as the energy demand for heating the hot water consumed. This is almost 900 kWh per dwelling per year. According to our measurements, this is approximately the lower limit that is applicable for domestic buildings that are well insulated in accordance with modern standards.

In other buildings, the measured circulation losses were approximately 60% of the total energy consumption of the hot water supply. Here, the circulation losses were actually greater than the energy demand for the heating of the drawn-off water. These values were rather typical for buildings with large piping networks (e.g. student dorms, youth hostels, hospitals and old peoples homes).

The overall solar fraction is computed by multiplication of the draw-off solar fraction with the ratio of energy used for the heating of consumed water, divided by the total energy consumption of the entire hot water system. This calculated solar faction is about 70% in favourable conditions and about 40% in systems with high circulation losses.

With a residential building that is insulated in accordance with the German Insulation Regulation of 1995, about 75–80% of the total energy is for space heating and about 20–25% for hot water heating. Out of the 20–25% for hot water, the solar system supplies approximately one quarter (i.e. this is the overall solar fraction for hot water, assuming low circulation losses). This means that solar energy covers about 5–6% of the total heating energy demand of a building (space and hot water heating) if the solar system operates at a designed specific load of 70 litres per day per square metre collector area.

Investment Cost

Figure 11.6 shows the distribution of investment costs (including planning fees and sales tax) on the various components of those installations in the »Solarthermie 2000« (part 2) programme. The costs of the individual systems were averaged as weighted according to the area of the collector fields. The averaged specific system cost, including planning and sales tax, was 655 Euro/m². Without planning and sales tax, the specific cost was nearly 500 Euro/m². The specific cost of the individual systems varied between 400 and 900 Euro/m². Without consideration of planning and tax, the spread was between 300 and 700 Euro/m².

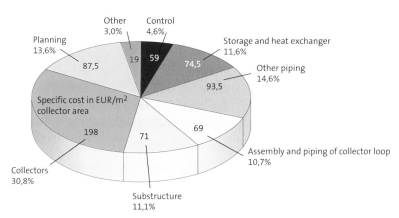

Typical system cost: with planning inclusive Vat.: 642 EUR/m²
without planning inclusive Vat.: 477,5 EUR/m²

Figure 11.6 Distribution of the averaged specific system cost of solar systems built within the »Solarthermie 2000« (part 2) programme; (control includes: electronics, sensors, pumps and regulated valves)

The values in Figure 11.6 are the averaged bid costs, since the costs of many systems were not finally settled. In special cases, e.g. when existing storage tanks were used, the costs were corrected as if regular systems had been built. In some of the finally settled cases, cost increases were taken into account due to unforeseen difficulties that occurred. These re-settlements were often related to the framework and to indoor pipework. The additional costs, however, amounted to only a few percent of the total bid cost; averaged over all systems, this cost increase was only 3−4 %. Since cost-increase difficulties may also arise in the future, it is reasonable to allow a margin of at least 3 % for such possibilities with respect to the values given in Figure 11.6.

The collectors are only about one third of the total system cost. This means that, even if one was able to reduce the collector cost by 30 % (due to rationalization), the total system price would fall by only 10 %. If one aims at larger cost reductions, the cost reduction potential of many other components has to be exploited as well.

At approximately 14 %, the design cost, for design and installation supervision, contributed the third largest fraction. If all designers had charged the maximum fee according to the German Fee Regulation for Engineers, the latter fraction would have been 15 %. Some engineers, however, settled for a somewhat lower fee. Within the »Solarthermie 2000« program, the supervising institutes carried out extensive preparatory work. Therefore, the design costs of the individual solar systems set at only 85 % of the standard cost. Under regular conditions, the design fees would have made up nearly 17 % of the total cost. A percentage this high confirms the importance of having better standardization of components and structures, in order to achieve lower design costs.

The cost fraction for the framework 11 % is relatively high because most of the systems were tendered for assembly on flat roofs, so requiring expensive rig structures. Therefore, considerable cost saving potential remains, especially for flat-roof frameworks. A research effort undertaken in Germany dealt with systematic structural analysis of buildings and with the development of cost-optimised support structures. The results are summarized in the book »Tragkonstruktionen für Solaranlagen« /32/.

Cost-saving developments can also be expected for outdoor pipework. This is especially so for the large labour expense for the protection of pipe insulation against physical damage and environmental impact.

Little cost-saving potential exists for indoor pipework, storage tanks and heat exchangers; these are already standardized components that are serial-produced and used in conventional heating systems.

Figure 11.7 shows the spread of the specific costs that were displayed in Figure 11.6. For the collectors, the percentile variations around the average are fairly small. However those for the framework are rather large. If the collectors are integrated into sloping roofs, the cost for the attachment of the collectors is very small and additional savings can be made for the amount regular roof tiling of new buildings. The mounting above existing tiled sloped roofs is also inexpensive (10−35 Euro/m^2). For flat roof installations, however, the cost varies strongly, between 50 and more than 200 Euro/m², depending on the carrying capacity of the roof, and thus on the complexity of the required framework.

The costs of other factors vary differently. The expense for »other pipework«, mainly between collector field on the roof and storage in the basement, strongly depends on the distances involved, e.g. building height. The variation in the cost for control is due to choice between simple controls or direct digital controls (DDC). However DDC are not always needed.

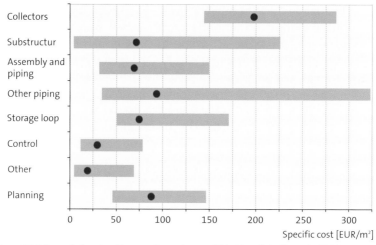

Figure 11.7 Spread of costs of large solar systems within the »Solarthermie 2000« programme. Average values are marked with a dark dot.

Figure 11.8, shows how the specific cost (Euro/m²) of solar systems of the »Solarthermie 2000« depends on system size (m² collector area). This distinguishes between (a) in-roof and on-roof assemblies on sloped roofs, and, (b) riggings on flat roofs. In spite of the wide spread due to peculiarities of the installation conditions and varying costs (especially regional variations of labour cost), a fundamental trend could be identified that specific system cost decreases with increasing system size. This is because some costs (e.g. control, storage and pipework between roof and basement) scale less than linearly with system size, so giving »economies of large scale«.

While the »smaller« of the nominally large-scale systems (about 100 m² collector area) have a specific cost (including planning and tax) of some 630−750 Euro/m², the cost decrease towards 500−600 Euro/m² for systems with 500 m² collector area. For larger systems built in Germany, the minimum cost would be around 400 Euro/m². This value was achieved at the largest evaluated system with a size of 1,600 m². The cost advantage for systems mounted on sloped roofs, as compared with flat roofs, amounts to approximately 50−100 Euro/m². This trend does not appear clearly in Figure 11.8, since few sloped-roof systems were installed within the »Solarthermie 2000« (part 2) programme.

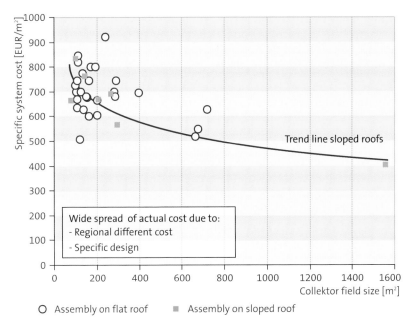

Figure 11.8 Dependence of specific system cost on system size

The trend line for the specific system cost in Figure 11.8 correlates closely with the specific cost curve shown in Figure 4.5 of section 4.3.5. However, some of the built systems lie above the trend shown in Figure 4.5, because there were special circumstances, e.g expensive framework, long pipework and high regional labour cost.

Cost of Usable Solar Heat
Computational Scheme for Determination of the Solar Heat Price
The cost of usable solar heat for systems of the »Solarthermie 2000« programme was determined with a simplified scheme based on only four parameters namely:

- The system investment cost (including planning and sales tax).
- The service life of the complete system (in part 1 of »Solarthermie 2000« it was established that an operational life of 20 years can be expected).
- an interest rate for the invested capital of 6 %
- the annual yield of usable solar heat

From the interest rate and service life expectancy, an annuity of 8.72 % was estimated from data at the time. The cost of usable solar heat is calculated as follows:

Cost of usable solar heat = (relative annuity • investment cost)/annual solar yield

For the sake of simplicity, it was assumed that all system components have the same life expectancy. In other computational schemes, one distinguishes between the life expectancies of different components, e.g. control: 15 years; pipework: 25 years. The differences between the final results are neglible. Also, it is doubtful if such discrimination is meaningful, since replacement of expensive items would probably not take place if many other remaining components had short residual lifetime. In other words, who would install an entirely new collector field, just because the pipes may last a few more years?

The simplified computation scheme does not account for:

• Maintenance cost: in large systems, taken as 1 to 2 % of the investment cost per year, (or considered as an added charge on a capital repayment loan, e.g. if the capital repayment is at 8.72 %/a, then the total with same maintenance expenditure is between 9.72 and 10.72 %/a); such maintenance would increase the solar heat cost by about 2 Euro-cent/kWh, e.g. from 12 to 14 Euro-cent/kWh)

• Cost of electrical auxiliary power (e.g. at a system performance figure of 50 and a price of 13 Euro-cent/kWh for electrical power, this would increase the solar heat cost by 0. 26 Euro-cent/kWh)

• Cost of saved conventional energy, e.g. at an oil price of 40 Euro-cent per litre or 4 Euro-cent/kWh and an assumed boiler degree of utilisation of 80 % for large systems, abated fuel costs would be 5 Euro-cents/kWh of solar heat heat (not including external cost reductions from the elimination of pollution etc)

The maintenance cost per kWh of solar heat is considered here as related to the fixed investment cost, however, per kWh delivered, it also depends on system efficiency. The operational cost includes auxiliary electrical power, and so depends on the system structure and on electricity prices at the time. Savings also depend on energy prices at the time, i.e. as the cost of the saved fuel. Therefore, one cannot derive universally valid costs, either by location or by future time. The only known fact is that there is never a charge for solar irradiation.

For the above example, one would calculate the overall solar heat cost as:

Investment cost of capital sum:	70,000 Euro
Interest rate of capital (annuity rate):	8.72%
absolute cost of annuity on capital sum:	6,104 Euro /year
Usable annual solar yield:	50,000 kWh/year

(Simplified) usable
solar heat price: (6104/50000)   12 Euro-cent/kWh

Maintenance cost   2 Euro-cent/kWh

Cost of auxiliary power
(system performance figure: 50)   0. 26 Euro-cent/kWh

Total cost of usable solar heat   14.2 Euro-cent/kWh

Reduction of fuel cost taken as oil price: 40 Euro-cent/l,
boiler efficiency 80%)   0.05 Euro/kWh

Additional price of
usable solar heat (14.2 – 5 Euro-cent)   9.2 Euro-cent/kWh

Thus, the additional cost with respect to the simple computational model (12 Euro-cent/kWh) would amount to (12−9.3=) 2.7 Euro-cent/kWh or 23 % of the (simplified) solar heat cost for an efficient system. This discount is, as mentioned, strongly dependent on the system configuration, degree of utilisation, actual maintenance cost and the type of saved conventional fuel.

Therefore, the simplified definition of the solar heat cost is based only on the annuity of the investment and the annual solar yield. This value is representative and comparable for all solar systems.

We emphasize however that the lifetime worth of a solar installation depends considerably on future energy prices and the value placed on abating pollution.

Achieved Cost of Usable Solar Heat

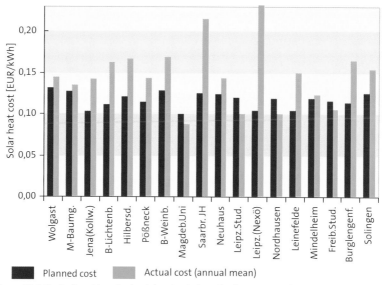

Figure 11.9 Cost of usable solar heat (see text above!) of systems within the »Solarthermie 2000«, part 2 programme (comparison of planned and actual cost, averaged over the evaluated years of operation)

Figure 11.9 shows, the costs of usable solar heat, both as calculated and as based on final settlements during the evaluation periods. These periods covered at least one full year of operation, and in some cases two or three years. The values include the design and constructional supervision fees and taxes. In order to compare heat costs, the life expectancy of older systems, originally designed for 15 years of operation, was corrected to 20 years. The differences between planned and actual costs are caused by:

- Higher investment cost due to unexpected additional labour expenses.

- Reduced system performance within permissible lower deviation (-10%) of guaranteed solar results.

- Changed system efficiency due to unexpected variation in hot water consumption.

- Changed weather conditions during actual evaluation period, in comparison with »statistical« weather used in design.

In four installations, the actual achieved cost was less than the estimated planned cost. In another four cases, the actual cost was less than 20% higher than planned. In six cases however, the final specific cost coefficient was more than 40% greater than planned, due to significantly less hot water consumption than expected. However only one of the latter cases, Leipzig-Nexö, failed to achieve the guaranteed solar result by a margin as much as about 40%. When evaluating the worth of guaranteed system performance, the actual operating conditions must be regarded (e.g. reduced water consumption, solar insolation). Therefore, almost all solar systems fulfilled the guarantee, in spite of sometimes having significantly overestimated energy yields (see also 11.4). But at the system »Leipzig-Nexö« culpable constructional faults had occurred.

After the programme evaluations, some of the systems were optimised (e.g. by adjusting or better switching control, volume flow). Therefore it is reasonable to expect improved solar cost evaluations in the future. However, if hot water consumption is less than planned for the size of installation, optimisation does not improve matters; the only option is to increase the demand, e.g. by connecting additional users to the hot water network.

With such intensive measuring techniques, it is possible to evaluate the effects of optimisations and compare performance before and after. This allows important conclusions to be deduced concerning the effectiveness of specific measures and simple modifications to the system, because local conditions (e.g. weather) and user behaviour (e.g. consumption) remain largely unchanged.

11.2.3 Combined Systems for both Potable Water Heating and Space Heating with Low Solar Fraction

In addition to the task of potable water heating, a growing number of small domestic solar systems are being utilised for auxiliary space heating.

Due the availability of solar energy (most in summer) and space heating demand (most in winter) being out of phase and not synchronised, in combined systems it is not possible to achieve as large solar fraction as for potable water heating unless there is seasonal storage.

The main contribution to space heating can occur by raising the »cold« return temperatures of the space heating system, during transitional periods (e.g. by solar pre-heating).

As with hot water demand, consumption for space heating may vary widely, depending on the type and design of the building, as well as on the local weather conditions. In the moderate climatic zone of middle Europe, space heating demand varies between $30 \, kWh/(m^2 \cdot a)$ (low-energy building) and $200 \, kWh/(m^2 \cdot a)$ (average for old buildings). Even within the same category of buildings, the heating energy demand varies widely (within a factor of two) and strongly depends on user attitude. Dimensioning is difficult, because the return temperatures from the space heating system (which are critical for the achievable solar yield) are usually unknown. Principal, the building should be first brought into line with the actual valid heat demand standards. Also, it should be equipped with a space heating system having a lower temperature. Thus systems with large-surface hot-water radiators, or under-floor or in-wall heating are an advantage for solar heating. Low return temperatures can actually be achieved by hydraulic balance of each single heat load cycle.

For the dimensioning, $1\,m^2$ collector area per $10\,m^2$ living area is assumed typically, in addition to the collector area needed for potable water heating. If the roof supporting the collectors has a small slope (slope less than 45°, in middle Europe), the summer heat surplus of these systems is large and causes frequent periods of stagnation. This automatically leads to low specific yields, which are also typical for »over-dimensioned« potable water heating systems with high solar fraction.

For a typical family house with $100\,m^2$ living area (and a ratio of surface area to volume of $0.8\,m^2/m^3$), the yields and solar fractions were calculated for three different insulation standards. The solar system was assumed to have a collector area of $15\,m^2$, and the buffer storage tank (with stratified charging system) was dimensioned for $1,000\,l$. The chosen location is Frankfurt/Main, as representative for Germany; the orientation is southwards and the tilt angle 45°. The daily hot water consumption at 45°C was set to $200\,l/d$. This gives an annual demand of $3,000\,kWh$ for water heating. In all three instances, the existence of a low-temperature heating system (flow: 50°C, return: 30°C) was assumed. The low ambient temperature set point for starting space heating was adapted to the building type.

Standard	Low energy building	Insulation standard 95	Insulation standard 84
Specific energy demand space head [kWh/(m²·a)]	30	86	160
Energy space heating [kWh/ a]	3,000	8,600	16,000
Energy hot water [kWh/a]	3,000	3,000	3,000
Total energy demand [kWh/a]	6,000	11,600	19,000
Degree of utilisation [%]	17	20	24
Solar yield [kWh/(m²·a)]	212	249	291
Solar fraction hot water [%]	69	66	63
Solar fraction space heating [%]	33	19	14
Total solar fraction [%]	52	32	22

Table 11.6 Solar yields and solar fractions of a 15 m² installation for potable water heating and auxiliary space heating for various insulation standards (living unit: 100 m², buffer storage: 1,000 l, location: Frankfurt/M, Germany)

The calculated results of Table 11.6 show that solar systems for auxiliary space heating can, if they are dimensioned for solar fractions below 20 %, achieve solar yields that are nearly as good large-scale systems for potable water heating (see Table 11.4). Since the specific heat cost decreases with increasing system size, part of the additional cost for the connection between the solar and space heating system is compensated. The resulting solar heat cost lies somewhat below the »worst case« of Chapter 11.2.1. To cover 50 % of the total energy demand of both water and space heating for the »low energy houses« in the sample, 2.5 m² of collector area is needed per kW of space heating demand. For such a large solar fraction, the degree of utilisation (i.e. the efficiency) of the system sinks below 20%. To increase the solar fraction further, much larger storage, especially seasonal storage is needed.

From Table 11.6, it can also be derived that the degree of utilisation and the specific yield of the system can be larger if the heating period is longer or if the building is insufficiently insulated. This is only true if the temperatures of the heating flow and return are calculated as equal within the individual buildings.

11.2.4 Combined Systems for Potable Water Heating and Space Heating with High Solar Fraction

If very large seasonal storage tanks are used, it is possible to achieve very high solar fractions for both potable water and space heating through-out the year. It is necessary, of course, to charge the tanks with a high proportion of the annual space heating demand during summer, to be a reserve for winter heating. The required storage volumes for a one family house may range up to $50\,m^3$.

If only 50% of the total annual heat demand of a low energy house (3,000 kWh, according to Table 11.6) is stored and has a working tem-perature spread of 60 K, then $21\,m^3$ of storage volume is reqired. Simi-larly, $61\,m^3$ are needed to cover an annual space heating demand of 8,600 kWh (second example in Table 11.6). This shows that it is very important to have high standards for insulation of space heating systems with high a solar fraction. The storage tanks are usually arranged in the building so heat losses remain beneficial in the heating season. However, it is obviously important to prevent storage losses during summer heatind the building unnecessarily. This requires special addi-tional measures.

The Swiss company Jenni Energietechnik AG has collected extensive long-term experience with the assembly and dimensioning of solar in-stallations for auxiliary space heating with seasonal storage.

For example, at Kloten in Switzerland with global radiation $1,123\,kWh/(m^2 \cdot a)$, the following reference values are given for dimen-sioning /22/:

Heating power (at −10 °C)	Annual energy for hot water + space heating	Collector area tilt angle 45° orienta-tion south	Storage volume	Collector yield	Total solar fraction	Degree of utilisation*
2.5 kW	8,053 kWh	20 m²	10 m³	5,672 kWh	70%	ca. 23%
2.5 kW	8,053 kWh	20 m²	20 m³	6,475 kWh	80%	ca. 26%
2.5 kW	8,053 kWh	40 m²	20 m³	7,454 kWh	92%	ca. 15%
5 kW	12,713 kWh	20 m²	20 m³	7,416 kWh	58%	ca. 30%
5 kW	12,713 kWh	40 m²	20 m³	9,548 kWh	75%	ca. 19%
5 kW	12,713 kWh	40 m²	50 m³	11,472 kWh	90%	ca. 23%
5 kW	12,713 kWh	80 m²	50 m³	12,709 kWh	100%	ca. 12%

* The degree of utilisation is estimated here, because it was not stated.

Table 11.7 Solar fractions and yields for two different buildings and different collector areas and storage sizes

From Table 11.7 it is evident that large storage volumes considerable improve the degree of utilisation, because the summer heat surplus is exploited better. While there is usually sufficient space for the collector assembly, the placement of the huge storage vessels inside the building is difficult. In practice, such seasonal storage is possible only in new buildings, when it is possible to construct the building around the tank. In such buildings however, the extra cost for the construction around required space of the tank is substantial. In order to cover the remaining 20 % of an existing system with 80% solar fraction, significant larger collector area and storage volume is needed. In which case, the degree of utilisation of the solar system would reduce to 15%. Therefore, such ambitious goals are seldom attempted using solar heat alone. In most of these buildings, wood stoves or boiler cover the remaining energy demand, so using renewable energy.

The total cost for a system with $20 \, m^2$ collector area and $10 \, m^3$ storage (upper line in Table 11.7) is approximately 37,500 Euro. A system with 100 % solar fraction (bottom line in Table 11.7) would cost about 75,000 Euro.

The following examples show that the solar fractions mentioned above can actually be achieved in practice. Unfortunately, complete data sets, of collector yields, heating energy demand etc, are not available.

Building	Rüsch	Schnider	Scheuzger
Location	Sevelen, St. Gallen, CH	Leuk, Wallis, CH	Staffelbach, Argau, CH
Type	Apartment house (8 Flat)	Single family house	Double family house
Collector area	$110 \, m^2$	$32 \, m^2$	$52 \, m^2$
Storage	$25.3 \, m^3$	$19 \, m^3$	$17 \, m^3$
Heating power (at -10 °C)	20 kW	5 kW	8.5 kW
Solar fraction	70%	90%	90%
Remarks			Additional $29 \, m^2$ transparent heat insulation at facade and ventilation with heat recuperation

Table 11.8 Swiss examples of solar systems for potable water heating and auxiliary space heating with high solar fraction

Figure 11.10 Low energy house of the Scheuzger family in Staffelbach, Switzerland, with 52 m² collector area and 29 m² transparent insulation. The solar fraction amounts to 90 % (photo: Jenni Energietechnik AG)

11.2.5 Installations Connected to District Heating Networks

Solar thermal installations that feed energy into a conventional two-line district-heating network are usually dimensioned within the following limits:

- Supply of heat consumption on a sunny summer day (i.e. consumption of hot water, including circulation losses and losses of the heating network; approximately 50 l storage volume per m² of collector area).

- Supply of 50 % of the annual heat consumption of the entire network, including all end users (i.e. hot water and space heating; seasonal storage with approximately 1.5 m³ per m² of collector area).

Various designs could meet these conditions, and even those for larger supply. In fact, there are no technical limits, only financial.

Installations tuned for Summer Energy Consumption

Installations that are only designed for summer energy consumption have a solar fraction of about 33 %. (Provided a heating network return temperature of 45 to 50 °C). This is a lower solar fraction than in domestic water heating systems, since solar energy is fed in only when the solar buffer is hotter than the heating return. Usually the return temperature from district heating networks is 45 to 50 °C, whereas it is 15–20 °C for domestic water heating.

The degree of utilisation strongly depends on the return temperature of the heating network. It is possible in principal to connect a solar system to a heating network with 60 °C return temperature during summer, but this is not economically feasible, due to the resulting very low degree of utilisation. Optimal conditions for integration are given when the return temperature of the heating network is below 40 °C (also during summer, when there is hot water consumption, but no need for space heating).

Despite the solar system being designed to cover only the energy demand for hot water and network losses during a sunny day in summer, in practice the solar system is integrated into the heating network so the solar energy is distributed to all end users of the entire network, covering hot water, space heating and network losses. Therefore the solar fraction should be related to the total heat demand.

The solar fraction of systems designed for summer demand is about 7–10 % of the annual total heat demand of the entire network. It strongly depends on the actual space heating demand, and thus on the quality of insulation of the houses. The lower value applies to buildings with a space heating demand of some 90 kWh per m^2 living unit per year. The higher value is valid for buildings that use approximately 30 % less energy, i.e. 60 kWh/($m^2 \cdot$a).

With collector areas greater than 1,000 m^2, the specific system cost of these network integrated solar installations is relatively low (400–500 Euro/m^2 collector). However, the solar heat price does not decrease in proportion to the increase in area as might be expected. This is due to the poorer efficiency of the systems that are integrated into the network. Thus, a solar heat price can be achieved approximately 0.10 Euro/kWh or slightly less (see also Chapter 11.2.2). Pure potable water systems with 500 m^2 collector area supply solar heat equally cheap, while systems of only 100 m^2 achieve a solar heat price of 0.13 Euro/kWh.

Installations with High Solar Fraction and Seasonal Storage

If a high solar fraction of 50 % or more is to be achieved within the total heat demand of a district heating network, very large collector area of several 1,000 m^2 is needed. If, in addition, a summer heat surplus is to be avoided, this energy must be stored until Autumn or even Winter. This would require a very large storage volume of about 1,000 cubic metres, or the same water equivalent of other storage media, such as soil or gravel.

Such very large storage requirement raises the cost of the entire system dramatically. The specific cost of these systems with 3,000–6,000 m^2 collector area and a water storage capacity of some 4500–1,2000 m^3 is at least 620 to 800 Euro per m^2 collector area, including design and taxation /37/.

Because of the large storage vessels and the long period of heat storage, the storage losses are proportionately large. Furthermore, only that energy available above the temperature of the network return temperature is usable. Both these facts have a detrimental effect on the degree of utilisation of the system, which is between 25 and 28%, at a solar fraction of 50%.

Since the specific costs are large and the degrees of utilisation small, the solar heat cost is relatively large. Including design and tax, the cost ranges between 0.18 and almost 0.30 Euro/kWh for large systems, and between 0.27 and 0.50 Euro/kWh for small systems /37/. These values, however, are valid only if the system is able to operate optimally. If the network return-temperatures are more than planned, as was often the case, the efficiency reduces and the heat cost increases.

For improvement of seasonal storages, especially with respect to cost reduction, the specific system cost and the heat cost can be expected to reduce. Figure 11.11 shows the cost curve for large seasonal storage systems.

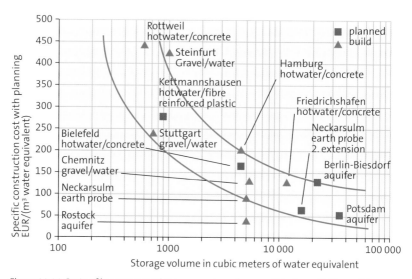

Figure 11.11 Costs of large seasonal storage systems (source: V. Lottner; D. Mangold: Status of Seasonal Thermal Energy Storage in Germany, 2000 /38/)

11.3 Aging and Performance Changes of Old Solar Installations within the ZIP- Programme

Within the scope of a German research effort, 19 old solar systems were included in a short-term measurement programme. The main aim of the measurement was to determine if the system performance had degraded through the years of operation. For this purpose, the actual measurements were compared with old data. During the supervision by the ZfS Institute, the performance of many of these systems was improved by alterations /39/, so they did not represent the original condition. Therefore, the new measurements in these cases were compared with test results obtained after the alterations, so the data comparison gives information on the improved systems.

11.3.1 Reasons for Efficiency Changes

Some of the systems, built between 1980 and 1985, were included in the measurement programme in 1996. Some of them showed significantly reduced degrees of utilisation. The reason could be traced to maintenance and installation faults, but were not related to the design principles. The following system faults were found:

Valves that were supposed to switch automatically from parallel to serial connection between the sub arrays (depending on the temperature difference) were exposed to the open weather and had corroded severely, so they had become inoperative. Thus, the sub arrays had non-uniform and non-optimal volume flow. Such »gadgets« are nowadays, and were in the past, unusual. This kind of error is not expected to happen again. The valves were removed and the collector circuitry was successfully repaired.

In general, an excessive number of filters had been built into the collector loop, and moreover had been poorly maintained. Deposits on these filters lead to severely reduced collector field through-flow, with flow reductions up to 80%, and drastically decreased efficiency. The surplus filters were removed, and the remaining ones cleaned. Afterwards, the through-flow was normal again.

If filters are built into a solar system, they must be satisfactorily maintained and cleaned. The deposit in the filters increases the pressure loss significantly and reduce the through-flow and the efficiency of the collector field.

Moist and permeable heat insulation was noticed frequently, because galvanised sheathing on the outdoor pipework was poorly sealed or corroded. This lead to very significantly increased heat losses at these parts of the pipework.

Incorrectly adjusted and defective controls, and defective control sensors were frequently observed. The defective parts were replaced. The controls were readjusted, with the switching points of the controls having been re-calibrated by submersing the sensors in water baths of accu-rately known temperature. In some cases, these re-calibrations showed large discrepancies between the marked scales on the poten-tiometer labels and the actual re-calibrated switching points. The extreme instance was a control that switched at a temperature difference of 11 K, although the scale indicated 6 K.

Some of the collectors showed strong signs of degradation that was attributed to the design and not a consequence of poor maintenance.

In many cases, the second (inner) cover of foil material was ruptured or had disintegrated. Nevertheless, in such cases the decrease in effi-ciency of the collectors, when operating at average temperatures, was small. Although the thermal losses (a-values) had somewhat increased, the missing foil had led to an increased η_0, so the efficiency loss was most effective at higher temperatures. These old solar systems were filled with potable water, so the storage temperature was limited to 65 °C; it was therefore rare that temperatures occured in excess of 70 °C during normal operation. Up to such temperatures, the lack of the second, inner, cover had little effect. Foil materials such as these are rarely used these days, so damage of this kind is not to be expec-ted anymore.

Some collector covers of fibre-enforced plastic had turned yellow. The transmission coefficients η_0 of these collectors was very poor indeed, approximately 0.4. Yet, the original transmission of these covers had not been very much better. Nevertheless, the degradation had lead to a significant decrease of system efficiency. Nowadays, fibre-enforced plastics are not used anymore to cover collectors. Some steel absorber plates had corroded inside the collector. This occurred in installations where air had entered the system, and where the air elimination was incomplete. Firstly the inhibitors against steel became depleted, and then corrosive occurred. Steel absorbers are not common anymore.

11.3.2 Changes of Characteristic Parameters
Naturally, the degree of utilisation of solar systems had altered when the inner covering foil had ruptured or when the plastic cover had be-come less transparent for solar light.

In the case of ruptured foil, the system efficiency had suffered a relative decrease of 5 to 10 % within 15 years, depending on the operating temperature of the collector field and on the number of defective col-lectors.

Strong degradation of the plastic covers reduce the annual degree of system utilisationby about 20 %.

In systems without these defects in the collector field, almost no decrease of performance was observed after 10 to 15 years of operation, apart from the maintenance and installation errors described earlier. The decreases were within the range of measurement accuracy that is of 3% or less.

If no principal defects were found, e.g. collector degradation or moist insulation, the solar systems not lost efficiency after 15 years. Therefore even first generation solar systems proved durable, so long they had not been constructed with unsuitable and out-of-date materials.

11.3.3 Peculiarities of Installations with Vacuum Tubes

In one case, a flat collector array had been replaced by vacuum tube collectors without reflectors. Subsequently, after years of operation, the tubes appeared to be still fully operational. The system efficiency had apparently not changed over time. In other vacuum tube systems from the same manufacturer, there had been difficulties due to the loss of vacuum and corroded tubes. Overall, the experience of this type of collector has been contradictory.

In another system, located at Freiburg-Tiengen in Germany, two collector fields had been equipped with two different types of vacuum tube collectors. One field consisted of direct-heat tubes made by Corning, the other field of vacuum tubes with heat-pipes and reflectors by Philips.

In the Corning-Field, 6% of the tubes had lost their vacuum after 20 years of operation. In addition, the sheathing of the distributing and collecting pipes (made of zinc-plated sheets) was heavily corroded and the heat insulation allowed moisture penetration. These deficiencies had decreased the overall efficiency of the system by 15 %. A large proportion of the decreased efficiency can be attributed to the defective tubes, since they are effectively uninsulated without vacuum. At high temperatures, these tubes became cooling elements rather than collectors!

The vacuum tubes of the Philips-array were all intact. Nevertheless, the efficiency of this field had decreased by 20−23% after 15 years of operation. The reason for this decrease was found in the design of the collector modules. They were equipped with aluminium-reflectors behind the tubes, which had become dirty. There was a mossy crust of dust on the reflectors, and at less contaminated spots the metal appeared blurred and rough. The overall optical characteristics of the reflectors had deteriorated. In addition, the back of the tubes themselves were covered in dirt similarly to that on the reflectors. Having reflectors, the rear of the tubes should have been transparent. Therefore, the contamination had decreased the efficiency significantly. Although tubes of the Corning-collectors showed similar signs of contamination on their rear side, this had no influence on the efficiency since the design had no reflectors at the backside.

The large decrease in the degree of utilisation of the Philips collectors was not due to the diminishing efficiency of the pipes themselves, as was established by investigations of individual tubes. The fault was that the rear reflectors were exposed to the environment. Without the external reflector design, the efficiency decrease would probably have been close to zero.

The example of the Philips collector field shows clearly that exposed reflectors are a weak point that, after long periods of operation, can lead to efficiency losses of nearly 20%. Certainly, aluminium, which develops a rough covering layer with time, was not the proper reflector material, but it is doubtful if other materials would have remained highly reflective, unless regularly cleaned.

Also it is important to keep the rear of the associated tubes clean. In total, with the large number of tubes used, such cleaning presents a large effort. Therefore, vacuum tubes of this type with external reflectors are not recommended.

11.4 Guaranteed Solar Results

In order to safeguard the calculated yields of a solar system, it is possible to offer the operator a guaranteed for the minimum yield. The basis for such a guarantee agreement should be a partnership between manufacturer, designer, fitter and operator. In practice, such a partnership has its legal limitations. Therefore, the general conditions of the agreement must be clearly defined. The operator must be prepared to cover the cost of monitoring of the system during the guaranteed period.

It is important for the operator to contract only with those persons or companies that were specifically involved in the execution of labour or the delivery of ordered items. The operator cannot be expected to deal with the manufacturer regarding the guarantee if the latter was not the direct contractor.

In the »Solarthermie 2000« programme, the fitter acted as contractor and had to guarantee a minimum system performance. The advantage was that the operator, had only one contact person regarding disagreements. However, the fitter could reinsure the system performance with the designer using a further contract. Consequently, the formation of a »guarantee community« is not ruled out.

The background for this kind of guarantee arrangement (defined in 1992 within »Solarthermie 2000«) was the realisation that the evaluation of a solar system should not only include the bid price, but also:

- the yield of the solar system
- the quality of the system design and components (in order to guarantee the yield over a long service life)
- the competence of the supplier
- the distance of the supplier from to the location of the solar system (important for maintenance and repairs)

The fact that the system yield should be included in the evaluation of the tenders, requires that the rated yield is actually guaranteed by the bidder. A theoretical, non-binding yield statement is arbitrary and useless, since the operator would not have redress if the expected yield is not achieved. A yield guarantee, on the other hand, forces bidders to give a realistic performance estimate and obliges them to carry out remedial work if the rated performance is not achieved.

In the programme »Solarthermie 2000«, solar heat costs were calculated from the bid prices and associated interest rates, (see also section 11.2 »Cost of Usable Solar Heat«).

In the consequent ranking of the bidders, the other criteria, mentioned above, were included, so that contracts were not necessarily placed with the lowest bidder.

Ranking tendered bids in accordance with the solar heat price and guaranteed solar yield has the following advantages:

- The bidders strive for a low system cost and yet for a high yield. If they estimate the guaranteed yield conservatively, to avoid guarantee problems, they might overestimate solar heat price. If yield is overestimated, the calculated solar heat price is too low. Consequently, bidders know they would be forced to carry out remedial work or to give discounts.

- Having a pure guarantee of the solar yield without computation of the solar heat cost, as done in an expired EU-program, is entirely useless, since the bidder is encouraged to grossly underestimate the solar yield. An evaluation after submitting the bid price is also meaningless, since weak and cheap components are likely to be used, which leads to poor system efficiency.

Because »Solarthermie 2000« was a research and demonstration project, the bids were not only evaluated from the financial point of view. In some cases, e.g. when a new collector model or a different system concept was offered, the offer chosen was not the cheapest.

In order to have equal preconditions for the calculation of solar results, all boundary conditions have to be fixed. These are: the energy demand (i.e. based on the hot water consumption), the intensity of solar radiation, the outdoor temperature and the local assembly conditions (collector orientation and tilt).

For the »Solarthermie 2000« program, data sets for radiation and outdoor temperatures were taken from the T*SOL simulation software. Of course, bidders may use different data sets, but then they themselves must supply the simulation program and weather datasets. The hot water consumption, based on preparatory measurements, was recalculated into values for 30-minute intervals, with the help of a table. These values, in combination with weekly and annual profiles, were compatible with the simulation program. In this way, the computations of all bidders become comparable, since they were based on identical operating conditions (at least with respect to local weather), and were independent of the particular simulation software.

The guaranteed solar yield of the system, i.e. the amount of solar energy delivered for beneficial heat, is given as an annual total. In addition, the annual degree of utilisation is computed from the annual solar yield and the annual amount of insolation on the collector plane. If the calculated yield or degree of utilisation is not reached, remedial work or penalties are due. A lower deviation of 10% is tolerated, in order to cover any uncertainty and imprecision of measurement and simulation.

Using these criteria, a guarantee declaration has to be attached to the tendered index of specifications. This declaration has to be signed by the bidder when a bid is placed. The yield ratings are evaluated after the bid has been placed. If they appear grossly overestimated, the bidder is notified. If the bidder affirms the apparently over-optimistic claims, it can be agreed that part of the system price is held back until the installation has proved its performance in reality.

In order to be able to check the solar yield within the course of one year of operation, a minimum of measurement equipment has to be installed /2/. However with recent research methods, a short-term measurement program of 8 weeks, is used, so there is no longer term interference between sensors and the pipwork system. Analysis of this short period allows a reasonable estimation of the annual solar yield. Given that such a performance test would cost about 7,500 to 10,000 Euro, it remains to be considered if a minimum set of sensor equipment should be built into the system from the very beginning. The cost for the measurement equipment would not be higher than the range given above, even though the processing of the results may be difficult. Fixed, built-in, measurement equipment possesses the advantage that one is able to monitor the system performance continuously or at short notice, and not only once. Moreover, it is conceivable that devices will be developed, that perform the guaranteed-result-computations directly from continuous measurements. In principal, such an instrumented system only needs to have a simulation program running in the background.

One principal problem is that the actually measured solar yield has to be compared with the theoretical value based on predicted boundary conditions. A comparison of the measured value with the guaranteed annual yield is not sufficient, since the actual boundary conditions of radiation, outdoor temperature and water consumption may not be equal to the earlier estimated values. It is not the fault of the bidder if during actual operation the hot water consumption is lower than pre-calculated, so the actual solar yield falls short of the originally specified and guaranteed yield. On the other hand, poor performance of a solar system should not be absolved by the coincidence that there was dis-proportionately more insolation during the period of measurement.

In the »Solarthermie 2000« program, a technique was developed to eliminate deviations between calculated and actual radiation, ambient temperature and hot water consumption. This makes it possible to determine any deviation from the guaranteed solar yield. At the same time, yield over- or underestimations of the bidder are corrected. The principal calculation technique is explained as follows.

- Since the bidder and the system supervisor may use different simulation programs, there may be slight deviations between their resulting statements. Differences in the results are also possible if the same software is used, since each programmer may define the system somewhat differently. As a first step, the bidder-guaranteed yield is compared with the result of the simulation executed by the system supervisor. Then a »correction factor« is determined from the ratio of bidder-stated and the re-calculated yields. This factor is used to correct all further calculations back to the bidder level.

- In a second step, the calculation is re-executed with the real weather and water-consumption data collected during the immediate period usually a year. The result is weighted by the correction factor of step one.

- As a third step, the measured system yield is divided by the backwards-corrected simulation result that was obtained with the real data (step two). If the correction factor is larger than 0.9 (90%), the guarantee has been fulfilled.

The three steps above are executed with the amount of usable solar heat and with the degree of utilisation, since all simulation programs create small errors when converting between radiation in the horizontal plane and sloped or tilted planes. For the fulfilment of the guarantee, it is sufficient if one of the two resultant correction factors is larger than 0.9 (90%).

The technique has proved useful for the evaluation of bids, as well as for the result itself. So far, all bidders have accepted this technique and considered it to be correct, since recalculations are performed very carefully and since the technique is reproducible. The bidders may have the scheme for re-calculation if they want this.

Figure 11.12 shows the results of the guaranteed-result-calculation technique for »Solarthermie 2000«, part 2. Charted are the quotients between actually achieved and realistically computed yields during the measurement periods. From this Figure, one can see if the system operates within the expected boundaries, even when the actual operating conditions have changed with respect to the plan, or if aggravating system errors are present.

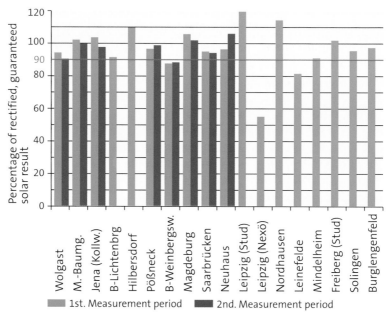

Figure 11.12 Ratio of real, rectified program guaranteed solar yield of installations belonging to »Solarthermie 2000«, part 2

Only three systems (»Berlin-Weinbergsweg«, »Leinefelde« and »Leipzig-Nexö«) have failed to achieve the guaranteed yield (minimum: 90 %). The system located in Berlin failed the goal value very closely. It can be expected that the guarantee will be fulfilled after additional optimisation. The system in Leinefelde needs another 10 % to fulfil the 90 %-guarantee. Here, it is also likely that optimisations will lead to a satisfactory result.

The system at »Leipzig-Nexö«, however, failed grossly. It is the only system of those shown in Figure 11.12, in which the conventional heating took place directly at the outlet of the solar buffer. This type of coupling of the solar system to the conventional installation, without modern safeguards, allowed heat from the latter to enter the solar buffer. This significantly interfered with the operational conditions for the solar system. Since early experimental results with a second installation of this kind also lead to unsatisfactory results, it was assumed that the fault lies in the coupling method, which was delivered as a »black box«. Currently, there are negotiations under way for system optimisation.

It is gratifying that 8 out of 18 systems (almost 50 %) achieved a better performance regarding actual operating conditions than was guaranteed.

Apart from the guarantee scheme described above, there are similar efforts within the scope of the GSR-project /40/ and under the DGS-certificate /41/.

11.5 Solar Contracting

An alternative to the previously described model is the so-called »Solar Contracting« for large solar systems or a number of small systems in newly built settlements. Within the scope of solar contracting, an external operator builds the solar systems (usually in combination with conventional heating systems) and operates them for an agreed period of time. In this model, the consumer pays the operator for the energy used, whether or not the heat results from the solar or from the conventional system. The operator has the responsibility for monitoring and operation of the solar system. Potential operators are head associations or heating system companies.

According to this principle, small solar systems in one-family houses are built and operated by energy supply companies in Denmark.

More details on solar contracting may be found in the literature /58/

12. **Appendix**

Literature

/1/   F. A. Peuser, R. Croy, J. Schumacher, R. Weiß:
      »Langzeiterfahrungen mit thermischen Solaranlagen«
      Eigenveröffentlichung der ZfS GmbH, 1997;

/2/   F. A. Peuser, R. Croy, U. Rehrmann, H. P. Wirth:
      »Solare Trinkwassererwärmung mit Großanlagen – Praktische
      Erfahrungen« ; Hrsg. Fachinformationszentrum Karlsruhe,
      Gesellschaft für wissenschaftlich-technische Informationen mbH

/3/   G. Stryi-Hipp; Der Europäische Solarthermie-Markt;
      In: 5. internationales Symposium für thermische und
      fotovoltaische Sonnenenergienutzung; 6.-9. Sept. 2000,
      Gleisdorf, Österreich; Tagungsband; p. 16-24

/4/   Werner Weiß, AEE INTEC (Arbeitsgemeinschaft erneuerbare
      Energie, Institut für nachhaltige Technologie),
      A-8200 Gleisdorf, www.aee.at

/5/   REfocus Magazine, March 2001, p 30-32

/6/   ENEL: Analisi della Campagna promozionale per la
      difusionne degli: Scaldacqu solari "Aqua Calda del Sole",
      ENEL, Catania, 1986

/7/   B. Nocke: Thermische Sonnenenergienutzung in Italien,
      Hochschule für Technik, Wirtschaft und Sozialwesen,
      Zittau/Görlitz; 1993

/8/   Instituto para la Diversificación y Ahorro de la Energía;
      Eficiencia Energética y Energías Renovables; Abril, 2001

/9/   Solar Energy Association of Sweden- SEAS; Sun in Action II

/10/ Chinas´s New and Renewable Energy Situation;
Energie Verwertungsagentur

/11/ OPET-India: www.teriin.org

/12/ World Solar Commision, World Solar Programme;
1996-2005-Africa; UNESCO interim report 1999

/13/ Department of Energy; Photovoltaics; Energy for the new
millennium; Washington D.C. 2000

/14/ Deutscher Fachverband Solarenergie (DFS); /3/, European Solar
Industrie Federation (ESIF), European Commission, /9/,
and others

/15/ DVGW Arbeitsblatt W551, W552 »Trinkwassererwärmungs-
und Leitungsanlagen – Technische Maßnahmen zur
Verringerung des Legionellenwachstums« 1993, 1996

/16/ C. Schwenk, M. Mack; Auslegung und Bewertung solargestützter
Trinkwasserbereitungsanlagen für Mehrfamilienhäuser
In: 7. Symposium Thermische Solarenergie 1997; Tagungsband;
Hrsg. Ostbayerisches Technologie Transfer Institut e.V. (OTTI);
Regensburg, Germany 1997; p. 372-376

/17/ M. Brenner, D. Mangold, E. Hahne; Solare Nahwärme –
Ein Leitfaden für die Praxis; Hrsg. Fachinformationszentrum
Karlsruhe, Gesellschaft für wissenschaftlich-technische
Informationen mbH; TÜV Verlag GmbH, Köln, Germany 1998;
ISBN 3-8249-0470-5

/18/ R. Kübler, N. Fisch; Wärmespeicher; Hrsg. Fachinformations-
zentrum Karlsruhe, Gesellschaft für wissenschaftlich-technische
Informationen mbH; TÜV Verlag GmbH, Köln, Germany 1998;
ISBN 3-8249-0442-X

/19/ M. Mack, C. Schwenk, S. Köhler; Kollektoranlagen im Geschoss-
wohnungsbau – eine Zwischenbilanz; In: 11. Internationales
Sonnenforum; Deutschlands Weg in eine solare Zukunft;
Köln 26.-30. Juni 1998; Tagungsband; Hrsg. Deutsche
Gesellschaft für Sonnenenergie e. V. (DGS); München, Germany
1998; p. 45-52

/20/ C. Fink, G. Purkarthofer, A. Müller; Thermische Solaranlagen
in Mehrfamilienhäusern – Erfahrungen aus Österreich;
In: 9. Symposium Thermische Solarenergie 1999; Tagungsband
Hrsg. Ostbayerisches Technologie Transfer Institut e.V. (OTTI);
Regensburg, Germany 1999; p. 131-138

/21/ Heizen mit der Sonne; Hrsg. Arbeitsgemeinschaft Erneuerbare
Energien; A-8200 Gleisdorf, Austria; or: Ökobuchverlag,
Staufen bei Freiburg, Germany

/22/ J. Jenni; Sonnenenergieanlagen mit hohem solarem
Deckungsgrad für Warmwasser und Heizung;
Hrsg. Jenni Energietechnik AG;
2. überarb. u. erw. Aufl. Oberburg (CH)1996;

/23/ prEN 12975-2:2000; Thermal Solar Systems and Components –
Collectors – Part 2: Test Methods; CEN, Brussels, Belgium

/24/ ISO 9806-1:1994; Test Methods for Solar Collectors – Part 1:
Thermal Performance of Glazed Liquid Heating Collectors
including Pressure Drop; ISO, Geneva, Switzerland

/25/ R. Tepe, K. Vanoli, R. Pfluger; Einbindung von Sonnenenergie in
die Wärmeversorgung der Stadtwerke Göttingen AG –
Koordination und wissenschaftlich-technisches Begleit-
proramm; Abschlussbericht des Instituts für Solarenergieforschung GmbH (ISFH), Hameln-Emmerthal zum Forschungs-
vorhaben des BMBF Nr. 0328876D, Nov. 1996

/26/ EN 12975-1:2000; Thermal Solar Systems and Components –
Collectors – Part 1: General Requirements; CEN,
Brussels, Belgium

/27/ ISO 9806-2:1995; Test Methods for Solar Collectors – Part 2:
Qualification Test Procedures; ISO, Geneva, Switzerland
ISO 9806-3:1995; Test Methods for Solar Collectors – Part 3:
Thermal Performance of Unglazed Liquid Heating Collectors
(Sensible Heat Transfer only) including Pressure Drop; ISO,
Geneva, Switzerland

/28/ ASHRAE 93-77:1977; ASHRAE-Standard: Methods to
Determine the Thermal Performance of Solar Collectors;
American Society of Heating, Refrigerating and
Air Conditioning Engineers, New York (for this Norm there
are new Updates available)

/29/ EN 12976-1:2000; Thermal Solar Systems and Components –
Factory Made Systems – Part 1: General Requirements; CEN,
Brussels, Belgium

EN 12976-2:2000; Thermal Solar Systems and Components –
Factory Made Systems – Part 2: Test Methods; CEN,
Brussels, Belgium

/30/ ENV 12977-1:2001; Thermal Solar Systems and Components –
Custom Built Systems – Part 1: General Requirements; CEN,
Brussels, Belgium

ENV 12977-2:2001; Thermal Solar Systems and Components –
Custom Built Systems – Part 2: Test Methods; CEN,
Brussels, Belgium

ENV 12977-3:2001; Thermal Solar Systems and Components –
Custom Built Systems – Part 2: Performance Characterization
of Stores for Solar Heating Systems; CEN, Brussels, Belgium

/31/ DIN V 4757-4:1995; Solarthemische Anlagen – Teil 4:
Sonnenkollektoren. Bestimmung von Wirkungsgrad,
Wärmekapazität und Druckabfall; Beuth Verlag, Berlin, Germany

/32/ Hrsg. Solarpraxis; Tragkonstruktionen für Solaranlagen,
Planungshandbuch zur Aufständerung von Solarkollektoren
Berlin, Germany, Juli 2001; ISBN 3-934595-11-1

/33/ W. Stichel; Inhibitoren für Wärmeträger in Solaranlagen;
Schlussbericht zum BAM-Vorhaben Nr. 1346 (im Auftrag der
ZfS); Bundesanstalt für Materialforschung und –prüfung (BAM);
Berlin 1994

/34 /   Dämmarbeiten an Dampferzeugern; AGI Arbeitsblatt Q 101;
        Arge Industriebau; Köln, Germany, 1978

/35/   Merkblatt: Feuerverzinken + Beschichten = Duplex-System;
        Beratungsstelle für Stahlverwendung und der Beratung
        Feuerverzinken; Institut für angewandtes Feuerverzinke GmbH;
        Düsseldorf, Germany

/36/   T*SOL (CD-ROM Version 4.0); Programm for dimensioning and
        simulation of solar thermal systems; Dr.-Ing. G. Valentin;
        Berlin, Germany; 2000; www.valentin.de

/37/   Solar unterstützte Nahwärme; BINE-Projektinfo 8/00;
        Hrsg. Fachinformationszentrum Karlsruhe;
        Eggenstein-Leopoldshafen, Germany 2000; ISSN 0937-8367

/38/   V. Lottner, D. Mangold; Status of Seasonal Thermal Energy
        Storage in Germany; In: Proceedings 8th International
        Conference on Thermal Energy Storage; Terrastock 2000;
        Stuttgart, Germany 2000; S. 53-60; ISBN 3-9805274-1-7

/39/   F. A. Peuser, R. Croy; Erfahrungen mit Solaranlagen zur
        Warmwasserbereitung; ZfS Rationelle Energietechnik GmbH;
        Hilden, Germany 2. Aufl. 1994;

/40/   U. Luboschik, P. Schalajda; Garantierte Wärmelieferung aus
        Solaranlagen – Eine Auswertung der Ergebnisse einiger
        Anlagen nach zwei Jahren; In: 7. Symposium Thermische
        Solarenergie 1997; Tagungsband; Hrsg. Ostbayerisches
        Technologie Transfer Institut e.V. (OTTI), Regensburg,
        Germany 1997; S. 246-250

/41/   Gütesiegel der DGS für große Solarwämeanlagen – Anreiz für
        die Wohnungswirtschaft; Hrsg. Deutsche Gesellschaft für
        Sonnenenergie e. V., München, Germany;
        SONNENENERGIE 4/2000

/42/   Hrsg. Berliner Energieagentur; Solares Contracting;
        Internationales Symposium, Berlin, Germany 4.12.2000;
        Tagungsband

We thank the following firms an institutions for the provision of photos:

DGS LV Berlin Brandenburg e.V.
Seestr. 64
D-13347 Berlin, Germany

www.dgs-berlin.de

INTERSOLAR S.A.
Dimosthenous Str. 267
GR-17674 Kallithea, Athens, Greece
www.intersolar.gr

Jenni Energietechnik AG
Lochbachstraße 22
CH-3414 Oberburg, Switzerland
www.jenni.ch

Roto Frank AG
Stuttgarter Str. 145-149
D-70771 Leinfelden-Echterdingen, Germany
www.roto-bauelemente.de

SOLVIS GmbH & Co KG
Grotian-Steinweg-Straße 12

D-38122 Braunschweig, Germany
www.solvis-solar.de

Stiebel Eltron GmbH & Co. KG
Dr. Stiebel Straße
D-87601 Holzminden, Germany
www.stiebel-eltron.de

ThermoLUX Solar GmbH
Unterwangerstraße 3
D-87439 Kempten, Germany
www.thermolux.de

Viessmann Werke GmbH & Co
Viessmannstraße 1
D-35107 Allendorf, Germany
www.viessmann.de

Adresses of Institutes, Companies and Organisations

Australia

Center for Sustainable Energy Systems
Department of Engineering
Australian National University
Canberra, ACT 0200

National Solar Architecture Research Unit (SOLARCH)
School of Architecture
Faculty of the Built Environment
The University of New South Wales
Sydney NSW 2052, Australia
Tel.: +61-2-3854868, Fax:++61-2-6624324

Austria

ARGE Erneuerbare Energie
Gartenstr. 5
A-8200 Gleisdorf
Tel.: ++43-3112-5886-17; Fax: 0043-3112-5886-18

Österreichisches Forschungs- u. Prüfinstitut, Arsenal GmbH
Faradaygasse 3
A-1030 Wien
Tel.: 0043-1-79747282; Fax: 0043-1-79747595

EUROSOLAR Austria
Wien-Arsenal Sonnenhaus, Objekt 219 C
Faradaygasse 3
A-1030 Wien
Tel. +43-(0)1-799 28 88, Fax. +43-(0)1-799 28 89
e-mail: info@eurosolar.at

Zentrum für Bauen und Umwelt
Donau-Universität Krems
Dr. Karl Dorrek-Strasse 30
A-3500 Krems
Tel. ++43-2732-893-2654; Fax: ++43-2732-893-4650
e-mail: kellner@donau-uni.ac.at

Belgium

International Solar Energy Society (ISES)
66 Rue du Centry
B-1390 Grez-Doiceau

Canada

International Solar Energy Society (ISES) Canada
SESCI Nat.Office, 7 Robertson Rd.
#26029 Nepean, ONT K2H 9R6
Fax:+1 613 596 1067

Germany

Bundesverband Solarenergie e.V. (BSE)
Elisabethstraße 34
D-80796 München
Tel.: 089-27813424; Fax.: 089-27312891
e-mail: info@bse.solarindustrie.com; Internet: www.bse.solarindustrie.com

Deutscher Fachverband Solarenergie e.V. (DFS)
Bertoldstraße 45
D-79089 Freiburg
Tel.: 0761-296209-0; Fax: 0761-296209-9
e-mail: info@dfs.solarfirmen.de; Internet: www.dfs.solarfirmen.de

Deutsche Gesellschaft für Sonnenenergie e.V. (DGS)
Augustenstraße 79,
D-80333 München
Tel.: 089-524071; Fax: 089-521668
e-mail: info@dgs-solar.org; Internet: www.dgs-solar.org

EUROSOLAR e.V.
Kaiser-Friedrich-Straße 11
D-53113 Bonn
Tel.: 0228-362373; Fax.: 0228-361279
e-mail: inter_office@eurosolar.org; Internet: www.eurosolar.org

Forschungszentrum Jülich GmbH
Projektträger Biologie, Energie, Umwelt (BEO) des BMWi
Wallstr. 17-22
D- 10179 Berlin
Tel.: 030-20199427; Fax: 030-20199470
e-mail: beo.beo41@fz-juelich.de; Internet: www.fz-juelich.de/beo/beo.htm

Fraunhofer Institut für Solare Energiesysteme (FhG-ISE)
Oltmannstr. 5
D-79100 Freiburg
Tel.: 0761-4588-0; Fax: 0761-4588-100
e-mail: Info@ise.fhg.de; Internet: www.ise.fhg.de

Informationsdienst BINE

Mechenstraße 57
D-53129 Bonn
Tel.: +49-228-92379-0; Fax.: 0228-92379-29
e-mail: bine@fiz-karlsruhe.de;
Internet: bine.fiz-karlsruhe.de (without »www«!)

Institut für solare Energieversorgungstechnik an der Gesamthochschule Kassel e.V.

Königstor 59
D-34119 Kassel
Tel.: +49-561-7294-0; Fax: +49-561-7294-100
e-mail: mbox@iset.uni-kassel.de; Internet: www.iset.uni-kassel.de

Institut für Solarenergieforschung GmbH (ISFH)

Am Ohrberg 1
D-31860 Hameln/Emmertal
Tel.: +49-5151-999-0; Fax: +49-5151-999-400
e-mail: public@isfh.de; Internet: www.isfh.de

International Solar Energy Society (ISES)

Villa Tannheim
Wiesentalstraáe 50
D-79115 Freiburg

Universität Stuttgart, Institut für Thermodynamik und Wärmetechnik (ITW)

Pfaffenwaldring 6
D-70550 Stuttgart
Tel.: +49-711-6853279; Fax: +49-711-6853242
e-mail: pm@itw.uni-stuttgart.de; Internet: www.itw.uni-stuttgart.de

Solarpraxis AG

Torstraße 177
10115 Berlin
Tel.: +49-30-726 296-300; Fax:+49-30-726 296-309
e-mail: info@solarpraxis.de; Internet: www.solarpraxis.de

Unternehmensvereinigung SolarWirtschaft e.V. (UVS)

Torstraße 177
D-10115 Berlin
Tel.: +49-30-44009-123; Fax: +49-30-44009124
e-mail: uvs@solarinfo.de; Internet: www.solarinfo.de/uvs

ZFS, Rationelle Energietechnik GmbH

Verbindungsstr. 19
40723 Hilden
Tel. : +49-2103-2444-0; Fax: +49-2103-2444-40
e-mail: zfs.energie@t-online.de; Internet: www.zfs-energietechnik.de

Zentralverband der SHK
Rathausallee 6
D- 53757 St. Augustin
Tel.: +49-2241-29056; Fax: +49-2241-21131
e-mail: info@zentralverband_shk.de;
Internet: www.zentralverband_shk.de

Bundesministerium für Wirtschaft und Technologie (BMWI)
Scharnhorststraße 46
D-10115 Berlin
Tel.: +49-30-2014-9; Fax.: +49-30-2014-7010
e-mail: poststelle@bmwi.bund400.de; Internet: www.bmwi.de

Greece

Eurosolar Greece
Laboratory of Plasma Chemie, Dep. of Chemical Engineering
University of Patras
P.O. Box 1407, GR-26500 Patras, Greece
Te.-Fax: +30-61993361
e-mail: dim@armodios.chemeng.upatras.gr

Great Britain

AMSET Centre
Bridgford House, Horninghold
Leicestershire LE16 8DH, UK
Tel.:+44-1858 555 204, Fax: +44-1858 555 504
e-mail: amset@compuserve.com

CREST - The Centre for Renewable Energy System Technology
Loughborough University
Loughborough, Leicestershire LE11 3TU, UK
Tel.:+44-1509 223466, Fax: +44- 1509 610031

Energy Research Unit
Building R63
Rutherford Appleton Laboratory
Chilton, DIDCOT, Oxon UK OX11 0QX
Tel.:+44-1235 44 6740, Fax:+44-1235 44 6863

International Solar Energy Society (ISES) UK
192 Franklin Rd
Birmingham B30 2HE
Tel.:+44-21 459 4826, Fax:+44-21 459 8206
e-mail: uk-ises@tfc-bham.demon.co.uk

Netherlands

International Solar Energy Society (ISES) Netherlands
PO Box 1
1755 ZG Petten
Fax:+31 2246 3214

Organisatie vorr Duurzame Energie (ODE)
postbus 750
3500 AT-Utrecht
Tel.:+31-30-769224

Spain

ALMERIA - plataforma Solar de Almeria
Aptdo. 22
04200-Tabernas
Espana
fon: +34 950 3879 00

European Forum for Renewable Energy Sources (EUFORES)
c/o FCC, Marques de la Ensenada 14, 3°, Oficina 25
E-28004 Madrid
Tel.: +34-1-3195904/08, Fax: +34-1-3198258
e-mail: 70630.1437@compuserve.com

Switzerland

Association des professionnels romands de l'energie solaire (PROMES)
Case postale 6
CH-2013 Colombier
Tel.: +41-32 843 49 88; Fax: +41-32 843 49 85
e-mail: secretariat@promes.ch

International Solar Energy Society (ISES) Schweiz
Sektion Schweiz
Postfach
8050 Zürich

SPF Solartechnik Prüfung Forschung Hochschule Rapperswil HSR
IPR Internationales Technikum Rapperswil
Oberseestr. 10
CH-8640 Rapperswil
Tel.: +41-552224621; Fax: +41-552106131
spf@solarenergy.ch; www.solarenergy.ch

Schweizerische Vereinigung für Sonnenenergie (SSES)

Societe suisse pour l'energie solaire
Socitea svizzera per l'energia solaire
Belpstrasse 69
Postfach
CH-3000 Bern 14
Tel.:+41-31 371 80 00, Fax:+41-31 371 80 00

Sonnenenergie Fachverband Schweiz (SOFAS)

Gubelstrasse 59
8050 Zürich
Tel.:+41-1 311 90 40, Fax:+41-1 312 05 40

United States of America

American Solar Energy Society (ASES)

International Solar Energy Society (ISES) USA
2400 Central Avenue, Suite G-1
Boulder Colorade 80301
Tel.:+1(303)443-3130, Fax:+1(303)443-3212

Center for Renewable Energy and Sustainable Technology (CREST)

SEREF
777N. Capitol St,N.E., Suite 805
Washingston, D.C. 20002
Tel.:+1-202-289-5370, fax:+1-202-289-5354

National Renewable Energy Laboratory (NREL)

1617 Cole Blvd.
Golden, CO 80401
Solar Energy Industries Association
122 C Street, N.W., 4th Floor
Washington, DC 20001-2109 U.S.A.
Tel.: +1-202-383-2600, Fax: +1-202-383-2670
e-mail: 71263,377@compuserve.com

Solar Energy Laboratory

University of Wisconsin Madison
1303 Engineering Research Building
1500 Johnson Drive
Madison, WI 53706-1687
Tel.:+1-608-263-1586

Others

Interactive consulting service:
www.solarfoerderung.de
www.solarserver.de

Index

Eco Living – Sustainable Heating

sunselect

The high selective absorber coating

The highly selective absorbing band **sunselect** from Interpane is forcing your colleagues to think again. The optically attractive **sunselect** absorber complies with the highest architectural standards. The colour homogeneity means that it becomes an interesting design object when integrated for example into facades.

Interpane's industrial vacuum coating process achieves a consistent, controlled quality and the highest reliability in further processing.

The absorbing band in widths of up to 1,200 mm has demonstrated its long-term and temperature resistance in ageing tests (Task X).

The high functionality, aesthetics and ecologically sound manufacturing process of **sunselect** are your advantages in competition. Safeguard your future with **sunselect** absorbing tape.

Ask for further information.

INTERPANE
Solar Beschichtungsgesellschaft

Interpane Solar Beschichtungs GmbH & Co · Sohnreystraße 21 · D-37697 Lauenförde
Phone +49 52 73 8 09-264 · Fax +49 52 73 8 09-238 · E-Mail: gerhard.stamm@solar.interpane.net
www.interpane.net

CD ROM slide set for the "Solar Thermal Systems" book

The slide set CD contains 200 all colour graphics, illustrations and tables from the "Solar Thermal Systems" book, adapted as high-quality presentation slides.

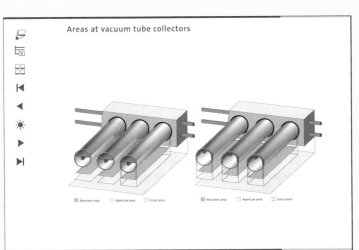

Icon	Function
	Full-screen mode on / off
	Bookmarks show / hide
	Thumbnails show / hide
	Previous chapter
	Previous slide
	Go to
	Next slide
	Next chapter

More than two decades of accumulated specialised knowledge is presented in a graphic and easy-to-use form.

- high quality presentation slides
- presentation slides can be individually printed
- highly suitable for digital projector presentation
- easy to use
- clear structure corresponds to the book
- suitable for both Windows and Mac OS
- accumulated knowledge of twenty years' experience

We will be pleased to create a set of slides in your firm's layout on request.

Yes, I hereby order:

_____ **CD ROM slide set "Solar Thermal Systems"**
€ 149,– (incl. VAT 7 % plus shipping and handling)

....
name/company

....
address

....
city, zip-code

....
e-mail

....
date, signature

Solarpraxis AG
Torstrasse 177
10115 Berlin
Germany

fax: + 49 | 30 | 72 62 96 309

e-mail: info@solarpraxis.de
Web: www.solarpraxis.de

we create the balance of
solar thermal & photovoltaic systems

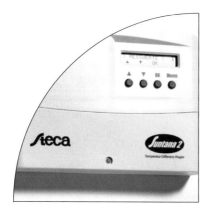

solar thermal controllers & components for hot water and heating systems from

1 output 2 inputs —up to→ 16 outputs 23 inputs

solar charge controllers & components for photovoltaic systems from

3 ampere —up to→ 140 ampere

High Technology Electronics
Solar Electronics
Battery Charging Systems
Cable Technology

Steca GmbH
Mammostraße 1
87700 Memmingen
Germany
www.stecasolar.com

Our expert recommends TYFO for your solar installation!

TYFOROP CHEMIE GmbH
Hellbrookstr. 5a · 22305 Hamburg · Tel. 040/61 21 69 · Fax: 040/61 52 99 · www.tyfo.de

Solar fluids for all thermal solar installations.

- High-quality anti-freezing and anti-corrosion fluids
  for flat-plate and vacuum-tube-systems
- Corrosion resistant – protection against deposition
- Environmentally compatible, non-toxic, biodegradable
- Supplied as concentrate or ready mixed
- Proven in thousands of installations

Brine for heat pump systems

Your heat transfer medium specialist since 1975.

Count on us ...

Solartechnology + Design = Solarpraxis AG

Benefit from our comprehensive expertise in solar technology.

The best technical and marketing expertise, a well-adjusted team of engineers, graphic designers and marketing experts guarantee top efficiency and optimum results.

- Technical support
- Marketing consulting
- Training
- Events

- Technical documentation
- Corporate design
- Advertising
- Catalogues
- Specialist literature
- CD ROM presentations

 www.solarpraxis.de